ROUTLEDGE LIBRARY EDITIONS: URBAN HISTORY

D1628315

Volume 2

SEMI-DETACHED LONDON

SEMI-DETACHED LONDON
Suburban Development, Life and Transport, 1900–39

ALAN A. JACKSON

Routledge
Taylor & Francis Group

LONDON AND NEW YORK

First published in 1973 by George Allen and Unwin Ltd,

This edition first published in 2018
by Routledge
2 Park Square, Milton Park, Abingdon, Oxon OX14 4RN

and by Routledge
711 Third Avenue, New York, NY 10017

Routledge is an imprint of the Taylor & Francis Group, an informa business

© 1973, George Allen and Unwin Ltd

British Library Cataloguing in Publication Data
A catalogue record for this book is available from the British Library

ISBN: 978-0-8153-5316-4 (Set)
ISBN: 978-1-351-13718-8 (Set) (ebk)
ISBN: 978-0-8153-8669-8 (Volume 2) (hbk)
ISBN: 978-0-8153-8671-1 (Volume 2) (pbk)
ISBN: 978-1-351-17514-2 (Volume 2) (ebk)

Publisher's Note
The publisher has gone to great lengths to ensure the quality of this reprint but points out that some imperfections in the original copies may be apparent.

Disclaimer
The publisher has made every effort to trace copyright holders and would welcome correspondence from those they have been unable to trace.

SEMI-DETACHED LONDON

Suburban Development, Life and Transport, 1900-39

BY

ALAN A. JACKSON

London

GEORGE ALLEN & UNWIN LTD

RUSKIN HOUSE   MUSEUM STREET

ISBN 0 04 902003 X

Printed in Great Britain
in 11 point Plantin type
by W & J Mackay Limited, Chatham

Contents

Illustrations

see captions for sources and acknowledgements

Maps

Graphs

'. . . the huge peaceful wilderness of outer London . . . sleeping the deep, deep sleep of England.'

George Orwell, *Homage to Catalonia*, 1938

Author's Preface

London's outward growth was impressive enough in the closing years of Victoria's reign, but the most important phase, in terms of land covered, came in the following forty years, which were marked by the unprecedented boom of the late twenties and early thirties. This book attempts a preliminary exploration of that great final period of unplanned suburban expansion. It was begun in order to answer questions arising from historical studies of the capital's transport systems and also to satisfy a certain curiosity about a long familiar environment. Written with the ordinary reader in mind rather than the academic, it contains little new analysis but does endeavour to make some explanations and to pay regard to the agents of change, notably the development of public transport facilities, which allowed suburban spread on a new scale. There is of course no room in one book to offer even a cursory survey of every part of the great sprawl which is outer London, but there are four district studies which, together with the chapter on the LCC estates, may serve as a microcosm.

Little is claimed for the work except perhaps that it breaks some new ground. The emerging school of urban historians, born of the great expansion in university education, will no doubt be digging this soil much deeper before long. It would be pleasant to think that what they find here might guide and stimulate such work. At least I hope to have demonstrated the wealth of interest that lies behind the seemingly featureless façade of what hack writers are still inclined to call the 'soulless suburbs'.

Many have helped during the research and preparation that has occupied much of the leisure time of the past twelve years. I am especially grateful to my friends H. V. Borley, Librarian of the Railway Club, Dr Edwin Course, of Southampton University, George Gundry, and G. T. Moody for reading the drafts and offering many helpful comments and suggestions. My thanks for courteous assistance and guidance go to the staffs of the British Museum Newspaper Library, the Greater London Council Library, the London University Library, the British Transport Historical Records Department, and the public libraries at Epsom, Hendon, Ilford, Sutton, Westminster and Wimbledon. M. A. Furnell and

V. H. Bone, Managing Director and Director of Homefinders (1915) Ltd, very kindly answered questions and looked through the final typescript. I am also much indebted to Mr Lees of Richard Costain Ltd, Robert Gillham of Davis Contractors Ltd, J. L. Wilkes and S. W. G. Dear of the Ideal Building Corporation Ltd, K. G. Jerrard and F. Saxton of John Laing and Son Ltd, and P. R. Jones of G. T. Crouch Investments Ltd, who provided recollections or material about the pre-1940 activities of these firms or their antecedents. On specific points, my thanks to John C. Gillham for information about London bus services and loan of a splendid collection of route maps; to B. N. Nunns for contributions on Sidcup and New Ideal Homesteads; to A. J. Kennet, for recollections of London suburban life in the thirties; to B. J. Prigmore and D. D. F. Adams, observant pre-1940 residents of Edgware, for assistance with chapter 14; to F. Sainsbury, Assistant Librarian of New Ham, for information about Edwardian Ilford; to Dr Vivian D. Lipman, for material on Jewish migration into the suburbs; to Alderman T. W. Lewis, for recollections of Stoneleigh in the thirties; to P. H. Denney, secretary of the Stoneleigh Residents' Association for loan of the pre-war file of *The Resident*; to the housing departments of the Greater London Council and of the London boroughs of Croydon and Greenwich, for housing statistics; and to the Deputy Keeper of Records, Corporation of London, for information about the Ilford estate.

Among the many newspapers and periodicals consulted, I would particularly acknowledge the usefulness of contemporary record and comment in the *Evening News*, the *Estates Gazette*, the *Golders Green Gazette*, the *Edgware Gazette*, the *Hendon and Finchley Times* (later *Hendon Times and Borough Guardian*), the *Homefinder and Small Property Guide*, the *Ilford Guardian*, the *Ilford Recorder* and the *Sutton, Cheam, and Ewell Times*.

And to all those in London's widespread suburbs who may have noticed a stranger taking an undue interest in their house or their road at some time in the past twelve years, my thanks for your kindly tolerance of what must have seemed like burglarious preparations.

Ashtead,
April 1972   ALAN A. JACKSON

Note

Those readers who are unfamiliar with London's geography will find it helpful to have at hand a street atlas showing the whole of the outer area, preferably with local authority boundaries as they existed before the formation of the Greater London Council in 1965. Any edition of Bartholomew's *Reference Atlas of Greater London* between 1940 and 1963 will meet the purpose admirably.

Although no rigid boundary is observed for the 'London' treated in this book, the term 'Greater London' can be taken throughout the text to mean the area covered by the Metropolitan Police District (i.e. roughly a 15-mile radius from Charing Cross) rather than the somewhat smaller territory now governed by the Greater London Council.

All amounts of money are shown in £ s d. Decimal currency equivalents obtained from conversion tables are of course totally misleading until adjustment is made for the steep decline in purchasing power since the 1930s.

Abbreviations

ARP   Air Raid Precautions
BTHR   British Transport Historical Records
CT   *Cheam Times*
DE   *Daily Express*
District   Metropolitan District Railway
DM   *Daily Mail*
ECET   *Epsom Courier and Ewell Times*
EG   *Estates Gazette*
EN   *Evening News*
General   London General Omnibus Company
GCR   Great Central Railway
GER   Great Eastern Railway
GGG   *Golders Green Gazette*
GLC   Greater London Council
GNR   Great Northern Railway
GWR   Great Western Railway
HC   House of Commons
HF   Homefinder
HFT   *Hendon and Finchley Times*
HTBG   *Hendon Times and Borough Guardian*
IG   *Ilford Guardian*
IR   *Ilford Recorder*
LBSCR   London Brighton and South Coast Railway
LCC   London County Council
LGOC   London General Omnibus Company
LMSR   London Midland and Scottish Railway

LNER   London and North Eastern Railway
LNWR   London and North Western Railway
LPTB   London Passenger Transport Board
LUT   London United Tramways
MET   Metropolitan Electric Tramways
Metropolitan   Metropolitan Railway
MRCE   Metropolitan Railway Country Estates Ltd
NHBRC   National Housebuilders' Registration Council
RCGDIP   Royal Commission on the Geographical Distribution of the Industrial Population
RDC   Rural District Council
RCLG   Royal Commission on London Government, 1921–3
RCLT   Royal Commission on London Traffic
RLTB   Reports of London Traffic Branch, Board of Trade
RM   *Railway Magazine*
SCET   *Sutton, Cheam and Ewell Times*
SECR   South Eastern and Chatham Railway
Southern   Southern Railway
SRA   Stoneleigh Residents' Association
SR   Southern Railway

Chapter 1

THE FERTILE
GROUND

Railway Suburbs

At the close of Victoria's reign the continuously built-up area of
London extended only insignificantly beyond a circle drawn eight
miles from Charing Cross and within that there was still much open
land. Outside, for a further five to fifteen miles, the settlement
pattern often showed distinct signs of metropolitan influence.

Although it owed something to early road services, this outer ring
was largely a product of the steam railways which in the last forty
years of the century had made it possible for those who could afford
the time and cost of daily travel to work in town and live in pleasant
rural surroundings. Yet the pattern of this dispersal was not always
related in a straightforward way to the provision of railway facilities, for there were other factors at work, notably the attitudes of
landowners and local authorities towards building development.
Thus the opening of railways through areas seemingly ripe for
suburban growth could sometimes bring disappointment to Victorian promoters, as along the South Eastern Railway's Hayes
branch and the Bexleyheath Railway.

On the map, middle-class suburbs such as Surbiton, Ealing,
and Sidcup seemed to snuggle closely against their lifelines. Most
of the houses would be within easy walking distance of the station,
but the larger villas of the 'carriage folk' were a little farther away,
perhaps on higher ground. Near the station would be cottages of
the serving classes and a row or two of shops with accommodation
above for their owners. Modest in population and entirely bourge-
ois in general character, these suburbs were laid out in fairly spacious fashion, with tree-lined roads and gardens of generous size.
Privacy and seclusion were at a premium; the fine villas of the First
Class season-ticket holders were hidden in elaborate nests of ever-
green trees and shrubs, approached by sinuous gravel drives which
not only dried quickly after rain, but provided convenient warning of

visitors. Many of these places were to be found south of the Thames where there were a larger number of existing communities to act as foci for suburban development, most of them well served by the dense network of the four southern railway companies, for whom short distance passenger traffic constituted an important item of revenue.

Woods and fields were never very far away, and *urbs* mixed most harmoniously with *rus*. It was pleasant indeed to dwell in such places as Surbiton and Chislehurst, where the air was sweet and filled with birdsong, where the daytime quiet of tree-shaded roads was disturbed only by the occasional tradesman's cart or modest carriage bearing a cosseted matron to 'calls'.

A little lower down the social scale was the still relatively small group of middle managers, supervisors and better-paid clerks. These sometimes settled in the less expensive parts of the middle-class suburbs, but as they grew in number the closing decades of the nineteenth century saw the formation of new districts in which they predominated. Such people were well catered for by the Great Northern Railway, whose low-fare services from Kings Cross and Moorgate, complemented by the North London Railway's trains out of Broad Street, offered a means of escape from their earlier 'walking' settlements in Hackney, Islington and Holloway. Although smaller, and closer together, their houses, in such places as Bowes Park, Palmers Green, Wood Green, Hornsey, Crouch End and New Southgate, offered more attractive and more sanitary alternatives to the older, inner area property, together with the opportunity, always eagerly grasped by this group, of improving social status.

Finally there was another, very different type of railway suburb, less attractive, less salubrious, quite lacking in any suggestion of *rus in urbe*. Tottenham, Edmonton, Walthamstow, Leyton and the southern parts of Wood Green, where artisans and clerks lived almost alongside the middle strata of the urban working class, had developed rapidly after 1870. Here most of the houses were in long terraces, standardised and depressingly dull to the eye, with back gardens distinctly minimal and front gardens merely nominal. Built to conform to the basic standards of the 1875 Public Health Act, they were crammed in tight at up to forty an acre. Trees were not much in evidence within the grid-iron street pattern, where houses stood 'rank behind rank like soldiers at a military review'. An oppressive greyness pervaded the arid, unrelieved vistas of stock bricks and slates.

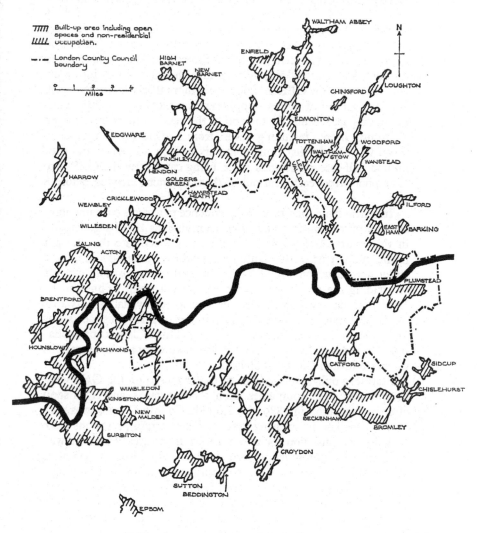

I London 1901: extent of the built-up area

This very distinct zoning of the upper and middle working class in the north-east (and to a smaller extent in the south-east) arose almost entirely from railway influences. In 1864, as an alternative to rehousing those displaced by the construction of its new City terminus and approach tracks, the Great Eastern Railway had accepted an obligation to run a train each morning and back again in the evening between Liverpool Street and Walthamstow and Edmonton at a fare of only 2d return. Although these trains barely paid their way, the GER in time ran far more than the Act required, and over greater distances, supplementing them with a large number of half-fare trains. By the end of the century there were fifteen 2d return trains, including seven from Enfield (21½ miles daily travel for 2d). At that time, some six million 2d return and four million half-fare passengers were being carried by the GER into Liverpool Street each year, all of them on trains arriving before 8 a.m.

It is clear from the Company's evidence to various parliamentary and official committees and royal commissions that its generosity in this matter arose from a concern to concentrate the cheaper traffic in one part of their suburban territory, thus discouraging a wider spread which would have damaged other districts capable of yielding the much more lucrative normal traffic. Thus on the Loughton line, workmen's tickets were not available outwards beyond Leytonstone and a higher number of First Class seats was provided on the trains at the expense of Third Class accommodation. On the main line, workmen's tickets were not issued at stations further out than Chadwell Heath.

Statutory obligations similar to that imposed on the GER were accepted by other companies from 1860 onwards, and from soon after its formation in 1889, the London County Council was particularly vigilant in ensuring that workmen's train provisions were included in legislation for new railways in its area. Some railway companies even provided workmen's fares voluntarily. A year after the 1882 Select Committee on Artisans' and Labourers' Dwellings, a Cheap Trains Act placed a general obligation on all companies in return for remission of Passenger Duty. A new era seemed about to dawn, but the 1883 Act proved ineffective because the Board of Trade took action only when complaints were received, and a legal ruling was obtained that the companies could not be forced to run cheap trains against their financial interest.

No other company was as liberal as the GER in the matter of

cheap trains, and apart from the GNR and the Metropolitan District, no others ran half-fare trains. It was only in GER territory that there developed to any pronounced extent distinctive suburbs inhabited almost entirely by the poorer white collars and the better-off manual workers.[1]

Those who travelled for 2d or 4d a day in an atmosphere of cheap shag and unwashed bodies were not the denizens of Shoreditch displaced by railway construction, but skilled workmen, shop and warehouse workers, and minor clerks who had made a voluntary move further out. In the central districts, where administrative and commercial expansion was forcing out residential accommodation, the overcrowding was becoming increasingly severe as the century drew to a close, with rents and land values responding accordingly. In 1892 it was estimated that if the law regarding overcrowding were to be rigidly enforced, some half a million people living in inner London would be displaced.[2] The limited facilities for cheap transport to the very few areas with low-rent housing were over-taxed, and it was clear that the railway companies had no enthusiasm for extending them any further. This was at a time when, to serve the burgeoning administrative and commercial activities of London, the ranks of the white-collar and distributive workers were steadily growing, intensifying the demand for modest homes within reasonable travelling distance of the centre. A precondition of the more extensive and dispersed suburban growth that in 1900 seemed so desirable was a widespread system of cheap and efficient local transport.

The agents for this expansion of settlement around London, the electric train and tramcar, and the motor omnibus, were standing in the wings.

A Surfeit of Transport

The development of London's public transport, especially on the roads, in the first fifteen years of the century was impressive, and in view of its importance to suburban growth both immediately before 1914 and after World War I, it is useful to look at this in some detail.

[1] A careful examination of the reasons for the uneven and generally unenthusiastic response of the railway companies is made by J. R. Kellett in his *Impact of Railways on Victorian Cities* (Routledge, 1969).
[2] R. M. Beachcroft, chairman of the public health and housing committee of the LCC, Joint Committee on Electric and Cable Railways (Metropolis), 1892, Q.1657.

Apart from a few mechanical oddities, London's road transport was entirely horsedrawn at the opening of the century. The buses and trams that traversed the main roads in the built-up area had played at least as important a role in the outward growth of the city as the steam railways, but their influence faded beyond six miles from the centre. With their inherently low speeds and the necessity for changing or resting the horses, it took about an hour to get that far, and an hour each way was the more or less tolerable limit for the daily traveller.

Except in the West End, where they had been successfully repulsed by property interests, the horse-tramways were found on most of the main radial routes and also provided many important cross connections. Their ordinary fares were generally lower than those of the buses, which started later in the morning, making no effort to attract workmen's traffic. Electric traction, which was greatly to extend the speed and range of street tramways, had been a practical proposition since the end of the 1880s, but new tramway construction by private companies had been effectively, if not deliberately discouraged by parliament. Whether promoters used the 1870 Tramways Act or private bill, they were obliged to obtain consents from frontagers and from the local and road authorities, and these tended to exact tribute by insisting that all sorts of often quite irrelevant improvements be carried out at the tramway company's expense. Existing companies, operating under the 1870 Act, and therefore facing the possibility of early compulsory purchase at scrap values by the local authorities, were naturally reluctant to make the heavy investment involved in electrification and extension, the more so as many of the local authorities would insist on the costly conduit system of current collection. Those local authorities which possessed powers of compulsory purchase awaited the time when they could use them; whilst the weaker authorities in the tramless outer areas were usually reluctant, for financial and social reasons, to promote their own tramway schemes. In his evidence to the Royal Commission on London Traffic, Stephen Sellon suggested that the compulsory purchase provisions of the 1870 Act had delayed the electrification of London's tramways by at least ten years and inhibited extensions to newly developed suburban areas.[1] The light railway procedure, which avoided some of the difficulties mentioned, but introduced others, was not available until after 1896.

[1] RCLT Vol. III, Appendix 38.

London's first electric tramways were promoted in the face of many difficulties by the London United Tramways Company, led by their forceful managing director and engineer, James Clifton Robinson.[1] Legislative powers were obtained in 1898, and within the following decade an extensive system was laid out in the west and south-west suburbs. It might have been even larger, reaching well into Surrey and the Thames Valley, but after the first few lines had been opened, the demands for wayleaves and road and bridge improvements in return for consents became both heavier and more outrageous, forcing the abandonment of several important proposals. After inaugurating its first lines, from Shepherds Bush tube railway terminus and Hammersmith to Kew Bridge and Acton on 4 April 1901, the LUT went on to build tramways to Hounslow (1901) and Uxbridge (1904), then through Twickenham, Hampton and Teddington until Kingston-on-Thames and Surbiton were penetrated in 1906. Local routes were constructed in Kingston, and the Surrey town linked with the LCC boundary at Merton and Summerstown via New Malden, Raynes Park and Wimbledon, in 1907. Most of these lines were entirely new; only a small part, in the Hammersmith area, was converted from horse-tramways.

Between 1904 and 1911 another large private company, the Metropolitan Electric Tramways, established electric services along the main roads outwards through north London, operating largely over tracks constructed under the 1896 Light Railways Act and leased from the Middlesex and Hertfordshire County Councils. At several points the MET terminated in almost open country; the electric cars were at Edgware in 1904 (going on to Canons Park in 1907), Edmonton in 1905 (extended to Ponders End in 1907 and finally Waltham Cross in 1908), Whetstone in 1905 (on to Barnet, 1907), Wood Green in 1904 (Palmers Green, 1907, Winchmore Hill, 1908, Enfield, 1909), and Stonebridge Park in 1906 (on to Wembley in 1908 and finally Sudbury in 1910). These long radial routes were linked by lines from Tottenham to Wood Green (1904), from Wood Green to North Finchley (1906-9), from North Finchley through Golders Green to Cricklewood (1909-10), from Cricklewood through Willesden Green to Craven Park (1906-7) and from Harlesden to Acton, on the LUT Uxbridge line, in 1909. Contact with the London County Council's tramways was established at

---

[1] For details see RCLT Vol. II Q.24776-25014 and Vol. III Appendix 82. For an excellent account of Robinson's career and his London tramway enterprise, see Geoffrey Wilson, *London United Tramways* (Allen & Unwin, 1971).

Scrubs Lane, Harlesden, at Highgate, at Manor House, Finsbury Park, and at Stamford Hill.

In east London the electric tramways were constructed and operated by the local authorities. Services were started along the main streets of East Ham in 1901–3, Ilford in 1903, Barking in 1903–7, West Ham in 1904–12, Walthamstow in 1904–5 and Leyton in 1906, some of them over existing horse-tram routes. Municipal ownership was also favoured in the south-east, where the local councils of Erith, Dartford and Bexley opened lines in 1903–6. In the far south, Croydon Corporation's electric system, replacing a much smaller network of horse lines, opened from the LCC boundary at Norbury to rural Purley, with branches eastwards to Thornton Heath, Selhurst and Anerley, and Addiscombe, in 1901–6. In the latter year, the electric cars of the third private operator, the South Metropolitan Electric Tramways and Lighting Company, linked Croydon with the LCC border at Tooting, and with Sutton, A proposed line from Tooting Junction to Sutton and Belmont got no further than Mitcham. This company also opened at the same time lines in Penge which extended the Croydon Corporation's Anerley branch to Crystal Palace High Level and Penge High Street.

In the County of London, the well-planned and efficiently operated system of the LCC employed the aesthetically neat but more expensive underground conduit system of current supply on most lines, and ran in part over horse-tramway routes which the Council had acquired. The first line, between Westminster Bridge and Tooting, was opened on 15 May 1903, serving the LCC's new cottage estate at the outer terminus. After this, the electric services gradually spread out all over north and south London, new lines being opened every year up to 1915, followed by some much more limited construction in 1921–32.[1] Although local political bickering and insularity frequently caused long delays, connections were eventually established between the LCC lines and most of the outer London tramway systems, usually with through services to the inner termini worked jointly with the outer area undertaking.[2] Such was the growth of the electric tramway systems that shortly before

[1] The development of the LCC system is too complicated even to sketch here, but a list of the opening dates of the major routes in the new suburban areas will be found in Appendix 2. For further detail see The London County Council Tramways Handbook (Smeeton, 1970).

[2] The first services were established in East London, as far as Ilford and Epping Forest, in 1910, and a through working to Barking, over three separate systems, was achieved in December 1912. Through running between the MET and LCC

1914 it had become possible, by making several changes of car, to travel by tram from Uxbridge in Middlesex to Horns Cross in West Kent, and from Waltham Cross and Barnet in Hertfordshire to Purley in Surrey.

Mechanically worked buses first appeared on London streets in 1899, but the early progress of this mode of transport was hampered by high operating and maintenance costs, also by an unreliability which contrasted sharply with the rugged efficiency of the electric tramcar. In 1905 there were 241 mechanically propelled buses licensed in the Metropolitan Police District; the total jumped sharply to 783 in the following year and reached 3,522 in 1913. With its solid, treadless tyres, unbraked front wheels, chain drive, noisy running, acetylene lighting and frequent breakdowns, the early mechanical bus was by no means a popular vehicle. It was utterly disliked by the road authorities, who were put to great expense by its punishment of the soft-surface horse roads. (In contrast to the tramway operators, who were obliged by the 1870 Act to maintain their tracks and margins, bus companies had no responsibilities for repairing roads.) At first there was much competition between the various bus firms, but the situation began to stabilise around 1908 when the long-established London General Omnibus Company absorbed two important rivals, the London Motor Omnibus Company (Vanguard) and the London Road Car Company (Union Jack), a move which added 611 motor vehicles to the General's existing fleet of 288.[1] Many of these early mechanical buses were attracted to the Edgware Road between Marble Arch and Cricklewood, a major radial route denied tramway service by the accident of having a county boundary down its centre.

The breakthrough for the motorbus in London came in October 1910 when the General produced the first of its efficient and reliable 'B' types, a thirty-horsepower vehicle which was to see the last of the horsebuses off the streets and would form the backbone of the fleet for the next decade or more. Effective at last, the bus now virtually sterilised suburban tramway construction in London, as it spawned a complicated network of routes reaching well beyond the main built-up area. Although a small number of operators had been busy at the rural fringe for several years, the General's guide

systems started in the same year, as far as Enfield. Cooperation was slower south of the river, and LCC cars were not seen on the Croydon system until February 1926.

[1] O. J. Morris, *Fares Please* (Ian Allan, 1953).

for 1910 showed only nineteen motorbus routes, with outer termini unambitiously sited [Appendix 3]. Absorption of the General into the Underground group of companies, combined with the arrival of the 'B' changed all this very quickly. In the four years up to 1914, regular and frequent daily services were opened up with great dash, the tentacles stretching as far out as Watford, Romford, and South Croydon. In addition a number of services were inaugurated from outer stations of the Underground, with through fares to and from central London stations.

Apart from providing direct and convenient, if slow, service into areas poorly served by the railways, the electric tram and the motorbus nurtured outward growth of the existing railway suburbs by enlarging the catchment areas of the stations. They also fostered new settlement along the cross links which they established between radial routes. We shall examine the relationship between road transport and suburban growth later in the book.

In this decade of transport expansion and improvement, the main line railway companies were not inactive. New lines and stations were opened in the suburban area, some existing lines were electrified, and services were strengthened. With the build-up of road transport facilities already described, some loss of inner area traffic was inevitable, and from around 1907 the railways began to cultivate middle-class suburban traffic in the 12- to 30-mile zone, where they were safe from intrusion. Publicity was stepped up. In April 1907 it was reported that the LSWR wanted more people to live at Epsom, only twenty-five minutes from Waterloo; that the Great Western was promoting the delights of residence in the Thames Valley; and that the Great Eastern was extolling the merits of Broxbourne and Bishops Stortford. The GNR had opened an Inquiry Bureau which was dispensing information about homes in the 'Northern Heights', and were even trying to sell Hatfield and Letchworth. Ticket facilities were extended; the GER, for example, whilst continuing to restrict season tickets to First and Second Class passengers in the inner zone, introduced Third Class seasons at Harold Wood and Romford in 1909. Yet despite all this effort, rather less than 10 per cent (a little more than one million passengers a month) of the railways' traffic in 1911 was derived from the 12- to 30-mile zone.

The South Eastern's branch westwards from Purley, which had reached Kingswood in 1897, was extended one-and-a-quarter miles to Tadworth in 1900, serving pleasant, undulating country soon to become peppered with comfortable villas. In the north-west, the Great Western's new Birmingham line reached Greenford from Old Oak in 1904 and High Wycombe (much of the way jointly with the Great Central) in 1906. Branches from Greenford to Ealing and Denham to Uxbridge were opened in 1904 and 1906. The connecting Great Central line through South Harrow to Neasden was ready in 1906. Very little new housing appeared round these GWR and GCR lines before 1914. In the same area, the District's line from South Harrow to Acton Town received an electric train service in 1903, the first regular above-ground electric railway operation in London. These trains went on to Uxbridge in 1910, using the Metropolitan's Harrow to Uxbridge branch (opened in 1904 and electrified from 1 January the following year). Here again housing developments before 1914 were more talked of than achieved. Also in the north-west was the LNWR's 'New Suburban Line', alongside the main line from Euston as far as Bushey, with a loop to Watford High Street and a new branch to Croxley Green, all opened in 1912–13. The GNR extended its Enfield branch to Cuffley in 1910, but this was the first section of an alternative main line, with suburban traffic only a secondary interest. In the east, beyond the Cheap Train suburbs, the GER opened in 1903 a loop line from Ilford to Woodford through Fairlop, to be referred to again later.

Existing suburban lines were electrified by the Metropolitan, the District and the LBSCR. As already mentioned, Metropolitan electrics were running to Uxbridge in 1905, and the District's electric service to Hounslow, Ealing, Wimbledon, Richmond and East Ham dated from the same year. Electric operation of the Hammersmith and City line began in 1906 and the District electric trains reached Barking in 1908. On the South London line of the LBSCR, the 'Elevated Electric', from Victoria to London Bridge via Peckham Rye, started in 1909. This company went on to electrify its services from Victoria to Streatham Hill and Crystal Palace in 1911 and from London Bridge to Tulse Hill, Crystal Palace and Norwood Junction a year later.

With one notable exception, the five tube railways constructed between 1900 and 1907 barely penetrated the suburban zone. (We shall see later that the Charing Cross, Euston and Hampstead Tube's Golders Green line was to prove an extremely powerful agent of suburban growth.) These capital-intensive tube lines, with their deep stations reached by slow-moving lifts, suffered serious losses in short distance traffic to the motorbus a few years after they had opened, so that before 1914 serious thought was being given to suburban extensions in search of extra traffic to succour the central area investment.

Including those on the new lines which have been mentioned, thirty-four new stations were built in the London suburban area between 1900 and 1914, whilst many others were enlarged and improved.[1] On existing lines frequency of service was built up to meet suburban expansion, as for example on the GER Chingford branch, which received a fifteen-minute slack hours service in 1909. Line capacity was increased in several places by widening, notably the Metropolitan line out to Harrow, which was quadrupled, with automatic signalling, in 1911–14, the GER quadrupling as far as a point just west of Romford in 1902, and the extra tracks provided between Victoria (LBSCR) and East Croydon in 1903–7.

The New Suburban Man

Long before the public transport explosion just described, the number of people able to contemplate suburban life had begun to increase significantly. The last quarter of the nineteenth century had seen a steady rise in real incomes, accompanied in many occupations by reductions in working hours. At the same time, there was strong growth in the number of administrative, clerical and skilled manual jobs available, all of them offering good pay and regular hours. And the education facilities were being expanded to meet the demand; even in the poorest areas of London, children were given the opportunity to reach standards which opened the way to white-collar employment. After the Elementary Education Act of 1870 there was intense building activity by the School Boards of London and urban Middlesex and Essex. Between 1904–5 (its first year of responsibility for elementary education) and 1919–20, the London County Council's education expenditure rose from just under £3·5m. to almost £9m., and this in a period when the population of the LCC area was declining slightly.

In all the large cities, but particularly in London, where there was a tendency for wealth to concentrate, the white-collar class, so essential to the expanding public services and the booming activities of commerce, increased rapidly. The accumulation of social legislation and the enlargement of the armed forces led to a more

[1] *See* Appendix 4.

1. Laying tram tracks, Carshalton Road, Carshalton, 1906. (From a commercial postcard.)

The colonising tramcar: London United car 242 on Wimbledon-Hampton Court service at West Barnes Lane, Raynes Park, 1907. (From a commercial postcard.)

2. South Eastern Railway Suburban: Tadworth station about 1912 with new housing in evidence. (From a commercial postcard.)

Commuters at New Malden station, LSWR, 1908. Only four women can be seen. Some of the men are taking flowers and plants. (Courtesy: G. L. Gundry.)

than twofold growth in central and local government staffs in the years 1891–1911 (the cost of the civil service, stationed mostly in London, jumped from £22·5m. in 1895 to £61·5m. in 1914). In the commercial field, the development of joint stock limited liability companies, the boom in trade, shipping and overseas investment, and the opening up of new retail outlets at home all required a supporting salariat. With the new multitude of clerks came an increase in directors, managers and senior officials of all kinds, and the banks and professions serving government and commerce prospered proportionately. The collectivist policy imposed by war-time conditions spilled over into the following decades, leading to further growth of the public services, and the influences nourishing the growth of the salaried classes were to operate with even greater power in the twenties and thirties; the process was given a boost after the mid-twenties with a big expansion of service trades and the development of new consumer industries, mostly concentrated in and around London. Thus whilst incomes from salaries formed 10½ per cent of the total of national income in 1911, the proportion grew to 20½ per cent by 1924 and 24 per cent by 1938.

Here indeed was a vast army of customers for suburban houses of all types. Of course by no means all were able to start their married lives in brand new suburban homes, but for the many obliged to make do with something cheaper at first, there were, ever present, desires to climb the social scale and to exchange the congested, grimy and often rowdy atmosphere of inner area streets for the quiet clean respectability of a new suburb. An additional spur to centrifugal movement was the heavier rate burden in the inner areas, which had already prompted many of the middle class to go further afield. Tradesmen too, for similar reasons, were beginning long before 1914 to desert the traditional rooms above the shop for a new house and garden.

Meeting the Demand

During the closing years of the nineteenth century there had been a surge of activity in the building trade, not only in London, but over the whole country, and this had spilled over into the early 1900s. But around 1905 the pace seemed to slacken, the tide turned, and the trade entered a period of depression. This continued to such an extent that in 1909 there was more unemployment in the building industry than at any time since 1881. Despite some recovery immediately before 1914, there was by that year a national housing shortage.

To some extent this falling-off in building activity may be explained by the high price of capital in a period when investors preferred the substantially higher yields, if higher risks, of overseas projects. And, although their effect has been exaggerated by some economic historians, the Land Taxes of Lloyd George's People's Budget of 1909 may have introduced an element of uncertainty into suburban development. There was also the Town Planning Act of the same year, which enabled local authorities to buy and develop land likely to be built on, to limit the number of buildings to the acre, and to determine the general form of buildings and the direction of new roads. Although this Act was only adopted by one council in the London area in the period before 1914, it may well have acted as a check to some building enterprise. A more significant discouragement to those building houses for renting was the fact that the extensive provision before 1905 caused rents to remain fairly steady right through to 1914.

Despite a general atmosphere of depression, certainly evident in at least some parts of London, the special influences at work in the metropolitan area were sufficiently powerful to ensure continuous building activity at most points around the suburban fringe, with particularly vigorous growth at one or two especially favoured places. In London there was a higher demand for houses to purchase rather than to rent arising from the concentration of the middle class, and by reason of the city's vast size, there was a greater chance of building land coming into the market fortuitously than in smaller places.

It is time to investigate London's Edwardian suburbs in some detail.

Chapter 2
SUBURBIA
1900–14

Future Respectability Assured
During the fifteen years preceding the outbreak of World War I, the outward growth of London went forward steadily, if patchily. The appearance of some of the new areas was not markedly different from the late Victorian suburbs, but elsewhere, new features were emerging: a more open layout, tentatively a little closer to nature than the rigid precision of the byelaw streets; and brighter looking houses, of less substantial construction. Most new property was still built for letting, but there was a growing tendency to erect speculatively for sale. In some measure this was a response to relaxations by certain building societies, but it also reflected the increasing prosperity and size of the middle classes. And it was in the houses built for sale that the new designs were most apparent. No doubt investors were conservative, preferring solid-looking property, whilst potential owner-occupiers were vulnerable to icing on a lighter cake.

An *Evening News* advertisement feature of 1909 described the period as one 'when people are buying their houses in preference to renting them', adding,

'it is greatly to a purchaser's advantage to purchase a house in a district where this system prevails, because the future respectability and stability of that district is assured. When a district has a majority of individual owners in it, a far greater interest is taken in local government and needless or reckless expenditure is avoided.'

Wembley was the area which stimulated these comments.
At this time, most building firms were still small in size. The easy credit obtainable from builders' merchants, together with the possibility of financing work in progress with advance payments from

estate developers, discouraged company organisation, and it was still rare for builders to act as principals. Estate companies formed by landowners and entrepreneurs provided the necessary capital and organisation, and most builders remained content to work under them, co-ordinating the various trades involved in road and house construction. Development was on a modest scale, generally concentrated in one locality at a time.

The Edwardian Fringe

North of the Thames, the working-class and lower middle-class areas which had seen such rapid growth in the late nineteenth century were now entering the final stages of their development. West Ham, almost filled up by 1901, increased its population by a mere 8 per cent in the following decade. Its neighbour, East Ham, which had seen a 194 per cent increase in the nineties, grew by 39 per cent in the same period. Walthamstow, Tottenham, Wood Green, Edmonton, and Willesden, all broadly similar in character, showed increases of between 31 and 44 per cent in 1911, but Acton, another of this group, saw a growth of 52 per cent to 57,500. Here, and in some others of those mentioned, the establishment or expansion of local industries contributed to population growth.

It was in these areas that the 'half-house' flourished. Sometimes also known as the 'one up, one down', this was an ingenious design which provided complete and self-contained accommodation for one family on the ground floor, and for another above, at low rents. Street doors were sometimes shared, or placed side by side in the same porch. On the Warner and Winn estates around Pretoria Avenue and Forest Road, Walthamstow, in 1905, a ground-floor half-house could be had for 6s 6d a week. There were two bedrooms (11 ft. by 10 ft. 6 in. and 8 ft. by 9 ft.), a parlour (11 ft. by 10 ft. 6 in.), a kitchen (12 ft. by 11 ft. 3 in.), and a scullery. The slightly more desirable first floor, with similar, but marginally larger rooms, cost another 6d a week.

Predominant among the growth areas in north-east London was Ilford, to be examined in detail later. Here the 1911 population exceeded that of 1901 by almost 90 per cent. Strong growth was also shown at Chingford (86 per cent, to 8,184), Wanstead (51 per cent, to 13,830) and Woodford (34 per cent, to 18,496). Other districts newly opened up in this sector included Upminster, Emerson Park and Romford. The 450-acre Gidea Park 'Garden City', designed by

Garnett Gibson and Reginald Dann, was begun in 1910, when John Burns laid the foundation stone of the first house. Within two years of the opening of the GER station on 1 December, some £30,000 worth of plots had been sold. A 3,750 sq. ft. freehold plot could be had for £100, or 36s 6d a month, and purchasers were encouraged to start laying out their gardens as soon as they had paid the first instalment.

Development at Highams Park, Chingford had started in the nineties, receiving an extra boost with the arrival of the British Xylonite Company from Homerton in 1898. Growth was sufficient to justify reconstruction of the station two years later and by 1908 there were 5,000 residents (without a public house, allegedly because they preferred it so, but probably because it was precluded by restrictive covenant). O. H. Watling, the principal builder, was at this time erecting red-brick houses with white stone facings, including some in Beech Hall Road on 21 ft. by 90 ft. plots, at £300 leasehold (£425 freehold).

Along the new electric tramways between Wood Green and Enfield and Wood Green and Finchley, new housing spread over the fields and parklands of Palmers Green, Winchmore Hill and New Southgate. Southgate grew rapidly, its 1911 population reaching 33,612, 124 per cent higher than 1901. At Enfield there was a 32 per cent increase in the same period. In November 1909, the 311-acre Grovelands Estate was sold for development with detached houses priced from £500 to £2,500 freehold, to be served by a new station and shops at the foot of Bourne Hill, which never materialised. On their Hollyfield Estate at New Southgate's Friern Barnet Road in 1910, Messrs. Betstyle were selling three-bedroom terrace houses for £295 leasehold (£32 rent) which included such delightful extras as a fretwork screen to the staircase, a tiled floor in the hall and decorated lead lights in the front door. There was a 'massive' wooden mantelpiece in the 13 ft. by 14 ft. dining-room, whilst the 16 ft. 6 in. by 13 ft. drawing-room included tiled stove and hearth and leaded windows either side of casement doors to the garden. A 'combined gas and coal range' was to be found in the 12 ft. by 11 ft. kitchen, and upstairs there was a white porcelain-enamelled bath and lavatory basin in a room decorated with an embossed dado. Front gardens were ready-planted with shrubs, every window fitted with a blind. More expensive houses were not easy to sell in this area around 1908. One builder announced somewhat breathlessly:

'Builder bankrupt – houses sacrificed – under stress of depressed property market, houses with large gardens, four bedrooms, two reception, bath, semi-detached in open position, good views, five minutes from trams and 15 minutes Church End (GN) station, letting at £40 per annum, are for sale at £485, absolutely freehold.'[1]

A little further west, in Hendon, the 1901–11 population growth was 73 per cent, most of this at Golders Green. Here the Edwardian era saw the appearance of a completely new suburb in the five years after the opening of a tube railway terminus in 1907, an important development given detailed consideration in Chapter 4. Electric tram services linked the tube terminus with Finchley, an already well-established middle-class suburb, whose 1911 population was 39,419, an increase of 78 per cent on 1901.

The electrification of the Metropolitan Railway in 1905 encouraged expansion of the existing residential settlement at Harrow and stimulated the birth of suburban Wembley and Ruislip, but the early arrivals in these places were merely the scouts of the great invasion that was to follow in the 1920s and 1930s. Harrow's population increased by 67 per cent to 17,074 in 1911, but nearby Wealdstone's growth in the same period was 102 per cent to 11,923. In the autumn of 1913, the Metropolitan Railway board was recommended to approve the opening of a halt at West Harrow 'having regard to the development of the district', the general manager reporting that there was an increasing demand for 'small villa houses' in Harrow and a large area of suitable building land near the railway line.[2] The halt was duly provided at a cost of £1,122 and opened on 17 November 1913. Three years later, it was handling 40,000 passengers a month, and lavatories 'male and female' had to be provided at a cost of £200 in response to pressure from the local authority.[3]

With less than two people to the acre in 1909, Wembley was served by six railway stations on the lines of four different companies (LNWR, GCR, Metropolitan, District). Marylebone was only eleven minutes away, the City twenty-four. With such facilities, it was hardly surprising that the 1901 population of 4,519 had reached 10,696 in 1911, a growth of 137 per cent, mostly in the last few years of the decade and in the southern part of the district.

[1] EN 14 November 1908 (the houses were in Princes Avenue, Finchley).
[2] BTHR MET 1/32.   [3] BTHR MET 1/33.

Plots on the Wembley Park Estate were advertised in 1901, but there was little activity until 1909, when Sidney Gatling had six different designs ready at £300 upwards. With frontages of one-and-a-half miles to the Harrow Road, the 220-acre Wembley Hill Garden Estate was promoted by its owner, Sir Audley Dallas Neeld, Bart., who laid out roads, including the two main 80-foot-wide avenues, which flowed together to form a broad entrance just south of Wembley Hill station. When this estate was formally opened on 20 June 1914, Callow and Wright had 20 houses under construction. Sir Audley preserved the Oakington Manor as a library and institute, and presented 44 acres alongside the river Brent to the Wembley Council as an open space. Further north, the 280-acre Wembley Park Estate had originally been purchased by the Metropolitan Railway in 1890 with the intention of setting up a sports ground and pleasure park to attract traffic. This had not proved a great success (a replica of the Eiffel Tower was started but left unfinished), and in 1898 most of the land had been sold to the Wembley Park Estate Company, mortgagees of the railway company.[1]

Although the population of the Ruislip-Northwood urban district remained small, the 1911 census figure of 6,217 represented an increase of 72 per cent on 1901. Houses were being built in 'Ruislip Manor Garden Village' in 1912 on 1,300 acres of land owned by King's College, Cambridge. Associated Garden Estates Ltd, the agents, were advertising plots close to Ruislip station for as little as £100, but were careful to see that apartheid was properly maintained:

'. . . although the Company aims at introducing all classes into the community, it is not intended to indiscriminately mix all classes and sizes of houses together; different portions of the estate lend themselves to different types and sizes of houses. Thus one of the neat village houses which are being erected near Ruislip station would be completely lost amid the wooded heights of Northwood, which demand more stately architecture, with its more massive setting.'[2]

About 200 houses had been erected at Ruislip Manor by the end of 1914.[3]

[1] BTHR MET 1/28; Wembley Transport Society Publication no. 3: *The Early History of the Metropolitan District and Metropolitan Railways in Wembley*, 1963. [2] EN 6 May 1912. [3] RCLG, evidence, 17 May 1922.

Aided by the arrival of the LUT electric trams and the electrification of the District Railway, Ealing, the classic Victorian middle-class suburb, showed further expansion in the Edwardian years, including the establishment of Brentham Garden Village, an early example of co-partnership housing.[1] The population increase here between 1901 and 1911 was 85 per cent, to a total of 61,222. Nearby Hanwell had 19,129 inhabitants in 1911 (83 per cent increase), and Southall went up by 99 per cent to 26,323. In both places, the growth was associated with the opening of the tramway along the main road and the arrival of industries from inner London. Other developing districts in the west were Chiswick and Heston-Isleworth, the latter with an increase of 40 per cent in 1901–11. Twickenham, also on the LUT system, expanded at the same rate, reaching 29,367 in 1911.

South of the river, the Edwardian and early Georgian years saw much building activity; on the eastern side of Wimbledon; at Raynes Park; along the LCC tramway from Balham to Tooting; eastwards along the Mitcham Lane and Streatham tramway; and around Streatham. Unlike the LUT tramways, which acted mainly as feeders to railway stations, the LCC electric cars, with their very cheap fares, soon encouraged a healthy through traffic between such points as Tooting and Streatham and the central area. There was also a good deal of development along the Croydon and Epsom railway, around the stations at Wallington and Carshalton, and filling out the Victorian settlements at Sutton and Cheam. The urban districts of Beddington & Wallington and Carshalton showed increases of 70 and 73 per cent in the 1911 census. Further south, the valley sides at Coulsdon and Purley were spattered with red-tiled villas, so much so that by 1911 the 8,277 population in 1901 had become one of 18,872 (128 per cent).

Wimbledon had become well established as a middle-class suburb in Victorian times. Its 1911 population was 54,966, an increase of 32 per cent over 1901. The Wimbledon Park Estate, partly in the metropolitan borough of Wandsworth, opened up from 1901 onwards, was served by the stations at Southfields and Wimbledon Park, which provided steam trains to Waterloo as well as District electrics through to the West End and City. Three-bedroom houses here were selling at £350 leasehold (£500 freehold) in 1908, four-bedroom ones at £425 (£600). At Barnes, to the north, the 1911 census found a population of 30,377, an increase of 71 per cent in the ten years.

[1] See Appendix 5.

But the largest increase in all Greater London between 1901 and 1911 has yet to be mentioned. This occurred at Merton and Morden, where the count was 14,140, no less than 156 per cent higher than the previous census. Most of the new housing was south of the LSWR main line, between Raynes Park and Merton Park, forming the south-western tip of continuously built-up London. Across some open land to the west, served by the electric trams of the LUT and frequent trains to Waterloo was New Malden, which accounted for most of the 12,137 population of Malden and Coombe, almost double that of 1901. And nearby, to the east, Mitcham grew from 15,015 to 29,606 (97 per cent increase); here again much of the new housing was to be found close to the electric tramways.

Costs of Suburban Living

In the Edwardian years, the clerks at the Railway Clearing House were advised not to contemplate marriage until their income reached at least £90 a year. They could then just about afford a two-bedroom Victorian cottage or a new half-house, at a rent of between 7s 6d and 9s a week, leaving enough over for the other necessities of life. With the advantage of subsidised travel, railway clerks had a wide choice of area, but for others, fares were by no means an unimportant consideration. Workmen's trains and trams were not always a convenient alternative for the office worker, and as Third Class season-tickets ranged from £6 to £10 or more a year, the minimum 'safe' salary for marriage in the white-collar class was probably about £100.[1]

A family man requiring four bedrooms would need to find £30

[1] Trams were the cheapest form of public transport; workmen's cheap fares for early morning journeys, with return at any time in the day, were the rule on most routes, sometimes at rates as low as half the ordinary fare, even lower on the LCC system. From 1 January 1901 the LCC fare for all inward journeys completed by 8 a.m. was a mere 2d return irrespective of distance, providing single rides of as much as 9½ miles for one old penny. By 1912, the LCC was operating 1684 workmen's cars every weekday, equivalent to five-and-a-half million car-miles a year. On the Tooting route, the number of workmen's tickets issued rose from a little more than half a million in 1902–3 to more than four million in 1909–10. For early rising suburbanites equipped with iron lungs and insensitive posteriors, there was no better bargain than the LCC tram; thus in 1913, between West Norwood and London Bridge, the return fare was 6d by bus, 4d by workmen's train and 2d by LCC tram (to Blackfriars). The early morning cheap fares offered by the railway companies ranged from the Great Eastern's philanthropic 0·16d a mile to the LNWR's 0·31d. Thus, in these Edwardian years, a daily return journey from the suburbs to the City might be made for a very few pence (Abbey

to £40 a year rent plus another £10 or so for local rates and water. Three-bedroom houses were generally available at between £25 and £30 rent. Gas varied from 2s 2d a cubic foot (say a little under £4 a year if used only for cooking) in Catford and Wandsworth to 3s 6d at Woodside Park and 4s 3d at Bexley. Electric light, still un-common even in new suburban houses, cost from 3½d a unit (say £2 10s a year) in Norbury to as much as 6d a unit in Catford and Purley. Allowing for food, solid fuel and other expenses, a salary of about £150 was necessary before a three-bedroom or modest four-bedroom house was within reach. This was at a time when the average clerk or shop assistant rarely received more than £120 to £130 and the skilled worker at most £110 to £120.

Nor were these easy years for those with limited incomes. Be-tween 1896 and 1910 the average real wage rates declined, despite booming trade and industry, a reduction which could not be met by increases in money wages because British exporters were obliged to keep their prices down in the face of increasing competition. Al-though the wind was tempered by the free-trade policy and reduc-tions in retailers' margins, it remained true throughout the period that a difference of a shilling or two in the white-collar worker's

---

Wood 6d; Ealing 4d; Richmond 9d; Penge or Crystal Palace 5d; Barking 3d). Although ordinary Third Class return fares on the District and North London railways were only about 0·4d a mile, the main line companies charged between 0·62d and 0·92d. Later risers could avoid these rates by purchasing season tickets, but what they paid depended to some extent on where they lived, for Third Class seasons were not issued from all suburban stations and the LCDR issued none at all. Typical annual Third Class season ticket rates in 1912 were:

Streatham	£7 2s
Ealing (to Charing Cross)	£7 14s
Southfields	£7 14s
Norbury (to London Bridge)	£7 15s
Bowes Park	£8
Lewisham	£8
Harrow	£8 8s
Tooting Junc.	£8 10s
Eltham Park	£9
Hither Green	£9
Bexley	£9 10s
Sidcup	£9 10s
Malden	£9 12s
Sutton	£10

There were no Third Class seasons issued at Ilford, but the Second Class rate to Liverpool Street was £7 10s. To encourage suburban settlement, most main line companies sold seasons at 50 per cent discount to the wives of season ticket holders and at rather less generous discount to other members of the family living in the house.

weekly outgoings really mattered. Around the turn of the century, the author's grandfather moved from Bowes Park to Tottenham because by so doing he could obtain an identical two-bedroom house at a rent of 6s, saving 1s 6d a week.

Some of the costs just mentioned have been extracted from an interesting correspondence in the *Evening News* of 1912 on the subject of the cheapest suburb. As might be expected with so many variables, the discussion was inconclusive, although some areas emerged with poor reputations. Twickenham was not recommended because the roads were indifferent and badly lit, electricity and gas were expensive and the dustmen, roadsweepers and lamplighters were excessively importunate with regard to their summer outings and Christmas Dinners. Another very disillusioned gentleman wrote from New Southgate, where the trams were always crowded on Saturday evenings with people who found Wood Green's shops much cheaper, where the smell from the gas works was at times most distressing and a nearby glass works kept its furnaces smoking night and day all year round; and, a final touch of unwelcome reality, where children could be seen playing in the gutters at the end of the High Road every evening, *in naked feet*.

Those a little higher up the social scale, the managers and the professional classes, could look further out, with the idea of outright purchase. Prices for three-bedroom houses varied between £215 leasehold for a terrace location to £450 or more for the better type of semi-detached (corresponding freehold prices would be about £330 to £600.[1] Four-bedroom villas ranged from terrace property at £250 to semis at £475 or more, say £360 to £675 freehold. Advances from building societies were available, on a somewhat restricted basis, although there were signs of a more relaxed approach (in 1904 the Halifax Building Society raised the level of its advances from 75 to 90 per cent of valuation on freehold houses up to £300.[2] Interest rates for mortgages fluctuated a little but were generally around 4½ per cent. Some examples of purchase terms can be quoted: a four-bedroom house in Wood Green, with a 20 ft. frontage, was offered at £250 leasehold in 1904 or £20 deposit followed by £1 19s 6d a month, whilst a three-bedroom house on

[1] For example, a house selling at £225 leasehold could be had for £340 freehold; in another case the relationship was £295:£445; in another, £350:£500.
[2] Oscar R. Hobson, *A Hundred Years of the Halifax* (Batsford, 1953). For houses valued at £301-£400 advances were 85 per cent, for those valued at £401-£600, 80 per cent. Advances for approved leasehold properties were set at 5 per cent below freehold level.

Cameron Corbett's St German's Estate at Muirkirk Road, Catford, in 1907 was £275 leasehold or £20 down and £2 3s a month, plus 9s 2d ground rent.

Some London building societies operated 'appropriation' systems, a periodical ballot among depositors with an interest-free loan on the security of a house as the prize. The author's grandfather contributed to the Third St James's Mutual Building Society, and although lacking any professional qualifications, inspected houses for them. In 1906 he won the quarterly ballot. He was at once offered £50 for the prize by another depositor, but refused; with his £100 savings and the £300 interest free loan, he purchased an almost new three-bedroom plus boxroom terrace villa in one of Tottenham's best areas, overlooking open country to the north.

The Edwardian Villa

The typical two-storey London house of the 1880s and 1890s was still being built in large numbers through the Edwardian era, especially in such districts as Tottenham, Walthamstow, Ilford, Willesden and Catford. The ground plan, based on a narrow frontage of 16 to 20 feet, enabled the builder to cram as many as forty or more to the acre and had as principal feature the so-called 'back addition', an extension into the garden from the main block, containing scullery and kitchen, with bedrooms over, back to back with that of the house next door. Roofs were of slate, usually topped with ornamental ridge tiles, and walls of dark red, grey or yellow stock bricks. There were ponderous bay windows, up and down, heavily decorated with stone sills and copings. These houses were let or sold with venetian blinds and curtain rods fitted to their sash windows and often with their pocket handkerchief front gardens already planted with yellow or dark green privet hedges. Patterned cast-iron railings set on a low brick wall established the boundary with the street and the houses either side. Other features commonly occurring were tiled forecourts, stained glass lights in and around a heavily varnished front door, and anaglypta dados to hall and staircase. Larger versions had both sitting- and dining-rooms behind one another off the hall and the passage leading through to the kitchen, scullery, coal store and outside w.c. in the back addition. Upstairs there was a main bedroom at the front stretching the full width of the house, with two or three smaller ones behind it as well as a bathroom and perhaps a second w.c. Many were arranged for convenient occupation by two families, one upstairs, one down. In the more select areas such as Sutton and New Malden, semi-detached versions could be found, whilst elsewhere the end houses of the terrace often sported the gothic extravagance of a turret, sometimes containing a tiny room.

The most serious defects of this design were the dark internal passages, the fact that the most frequently used rooms faced each other across the narrow yard between the back additions (earning the name 'tunnel backs'), which made them dark and sun-starved, and the absence of outside access for refuse collection and solid fuel deliveries. Even so, with their simple bathrooms, adequate sanitation and reasonably spacious accommodation, they represented a considerable advance and were often quite well built. In Tottenham, around 1901, such a house might be had for between £300 and £350 leasehold, or £450 freehold.

By the turn of the century, another house type was appearing in the London area. Sometimes in terraces, but more often semi-detached or detached, it was of lighter construction and more cheerful appearance. Roofs were of red tiles and the elevations featured irregular patterns of window and gable, perhaps with catslide projections at the front. Outside walls were constructed of light red bricks or covered with cement or rough-cast. There was much outside woodwork, usually painted white, and many had useless little balconies with wood palings. Windows were of the casement rather than the sash type and the bays were of timber on a brick base, or tiles hung on a timber frame, instead of brick and stone throughout. This new style could be traced back to Bedford Park and the small houses of C. F. A. Voysey and Norman Shaw. In its various forms, it was found in most Edwardian suburbs. Golders Green had little else, and large numbers can be seen at such places as Purley, Norbury, Palmers Green and Southfields.

As early as 1901 a speculative builder at Ilford was providing houses ready-wired for electric light, but the availability of this facility in the new suburbs was restricted for a few more years by the vagaries of early electricity supply networks. Other developments included in the new houses of the 1900s were porcelain-enamelled baths instead of painted cast iron, and slow combustion stoves for water heating. A noticeable trend was the combination of kitchen and scullery, reflecting the shortage of servants, and a general reduction in the number and size of rooms. These changes were not always popular:

'Anyone can see today at Hampstead Garden City what miserable tiny boxes, so-called rooms, are now being built, viz., in Willifield Way and Wordsworth Walk. In the kitchens you can practically stand in the middle of the room and touch the sides.'[1]

But standards generally were improving. In his report for 1908, the Hendon Medical Officer of Health recorded the erection of 498 houses, almost all in Golders Green and Hampstead Garden Suburb, noting with approval that each had a bath and upstairs lavatory of the pedestal type (the closed box was on the way out); and that all drains were roddable, without the necessity of breaking open the ground.

Maid, Piano and Park

Edwardian suburban life was characterised by the long daily round of housework. There were innumerable things to be dusted, scrubbed, polished, or stoned, clothes to be washed, mangled, dried, starched and ironed (a week's laundry for a small family would take two women most of a day), coals to be carried, grates to be blacked, fires to be laid, heavy meals to be prepared, and numerous children to be kept tidy, cared for and amused. Even in quite humble middle-class households much of this load was borne by one or two female servants.

In the wealthier establishments a cook and one or two maids would be kept, perhaps also a children's nurse and a gardener/groom, though not all would necessarily live-in. As late as 1919 two ladies living alone at Hadley Wood required (and were able to secure) the support of a personal maid, four house servants, a gardener, and a gardener's boy.[2] Formally, the minimum was a 'cook-general', who would command £20 to £26 a year in the London area in addition to her accommodation and keep, but there existed an even more humble creature known as the 'maid of all work' who was offered as little as £16 in the London advertisements at the turn of the century. Such girls were the helpmates of the lower middle-class family with an income of at least £150 to £200. Below that level, the wife bore the full burden, sometimes assisted by her mother if she lived nearby.

[1] Letter in EN 5 September 1910.
[2] Nancy Clark, *Hadley Wood, Its Background and Development* (Ward Lock 1968).

Not surprisingly, the maid in a small house had a long day. Suburban housewives were advised in a London evening paper of 1901 not to let the maid of all work lie abed later than 6 a.m. A 'rising bell' operated from the mistress's bedside was recommended as it was unwise to rely on the girl getting herself up. The younger female servants provided a fairly secure outlet for the sexual boredom or frustration of the men in the household (a topic not ignored by the comic postcards of the period), and they were also vulnerable to tradesmen callers. Infanticide among girl servants was common enough in an era when discovery of an illegitimate child would result not only in instant dismissal, but exclusion from all further employment as a domestic. Female servants were also not infrequently the targets of neurotic or inconsiderate mistresses exercising feminine cruelties of varying types and intensity. In such circumstances it was almost impossible for a girl to leave because she could not obtain another position without a good reference.

Other avenues of employment for girls and women were opening up, so that in the decade before 1914 domestic assistance became increasingly difficult to secure on a London suburban income. However, this change was not really marked until the war years; as many as one third of the girls leaving Middlesex elementary schools in 1913 went into domestic service.[1]

With two or more servants, the wealthier suburban matrons had time on their hands. This they occupied by paying and receiving social calls, and organising charitable or church work. Lower down the social scale there was little difficulty about finding something to do; even when a girl was kept, there was still plenty of work, because husbands normally gave no assistance in the house and there were no labour-saving devices. Some light is thrown on this aspect of domestic life by a letter from the wife of a bank clerk in the *Evening News* in 1913. This described a change made in the weekly routine. Although her husband earned £150 a year, this housewife affirmed they could not afford a servant to help with their house and two children (perhaps a sign of the growing shortage). Until a short time before writing the letter, her weekends used to begin with the husband's return from work about 3 p.m. on Saturday, followed by a high tea or 'scanty dinner'. Much of this day was spent shopping and preparing for Sunday's 'big meal' whilst her man pottered about the garden or went to watch football or cricket. On Sundays they had risen at 9.30. After breakfast, the husband

[1] HFT 5 December 1913.

had gone for what she described as 'a depressing morning walk' returning too early for the Sunday dinner. After that generous meal she had not finished washing and drying the dishes and dressing herself in her Sunday finery until 3.30 p.m., when she managed a rest until tea. In the evening they would go out together for a walk or to church. Sunday had been the hardest day of her week. Now all was changed. She shopped on Friday, gave the husband his 'big meal' on Saturday and enjoyed freedom all day Sunday, when they got up earlier and went out if the weather were fine. This arrangement was of course not possible for the weekly paid, who did not get their wages until after they had ceased work at 1 or 1.30 p.m. on Saturday.

Indoor entertainment in the Edwardian suburb centred round the piano; ballads and music hall songs on weekday evenings, hymns on Sundays. A piano was almost an essential for those who wished to climb the social ladder, taking pride of place in the 'front room' (sitting room) among the best furniture. Even the poorest families, if they had some ambition, would scrimp and save to amass the necessary £20 or so – hence the contemptuous description of the working-class Conservative: *Pride, Poverty and a Piano*.

On summer evenings, the tennis club was the great social centre of the middle-class suburbs, with its teas in the pavilion, its annual gymkhana, its regular weekend 'flannel dances' to music from the piano or gramophone.

Sunday would see the suburban family dressing in their best clothes, mother in her tightest corsets, the children prickly, stiff and uncomfortable in starched frocks, blue serge and stiff collars. Thus attired, they would process to church, morning and evening, but usually without mother in the morning unless there were servants. In between, they would visit the local park to admire the floral displays and study the dress and manners of their neighbours. Competition for the best seats on the main promenade was keen. An alternative diversion was a visit to the cemetery, where the graves of close relatives were tidied and bedecked with fresh flowers. By no means all the deceased were elderly; many families had lost youngsters to diphtheria, scarlet fever or tuberculosis.

Churches were quickly provided in new suburbs, as in Victorian times, the ubiquitous 'tin chapel' or parish hall often preceding the construction of the permanent building. In middle-class suburbs, money for new churches was still extracted with ease. Nancy Clark records that in 1911 an average of £15 per household was raised in a very short time to purchase a site and church room at Hadley Wood.[1]

The Electric Palace

Although the music hall still flourished, alternatives were appearing and few halls were built in the new suburbs of 1900–14. Roller-skating, first popular in the eighties, enjoyed a brief revival in 1908–10 when many rinks were opened in London by the American, C. B. Crawford, and others. Typical was that at Cricklewood, which started life in February 1910 with an entry fee of 6d and three sessions daily (10.30, 2.30 and 7.30). But this was a passing craze, never approaching the potential of its near contemporary, the moving pictures.

Film shows had for some years been held in makeshift premises, often converted shops, with inadequate exits and few fire precautions. As the cellulose nitrate film stock was highly inflammable, there was growing concern about public safety in these 'penny gaffs' and 'flea pits', culminating in the Cinematograph Act, 1909. Coming into force on the first day of the following year, this required county councils to issue licences for entertainments using inflammable film, the exhibitors having to conform to rigorous safety regulations made by the Home Office. The Act, which was contemporary with a period of expansion in the film production industry, brought into being the first purpose-built cinemas.

But such buildings could not be provided overnight on the scale required, and the roller-skating rinks, now a less profitable undertaking, could be converted quickly to halls suitable for the new requirements. Some survived in their new role for several decades; one such was the Finchley Rink, which opened as a cinema on 26 December 1912, claiming to be the first picture house in Britain with a sloping auditorium. It had ten exits, 'double fauteuils' in the balcony, and showed a coloured film in its first programme.

As demand for 'regulation' cinemas soon exceeded the number of buildings suitable for conversion, the years 1910–12 saw a small boom in the construction of picture theatres with names like the Imperial, Empire, Gem, Picturedrome, Bijou and Electric Palace. Small by later standards (200–500 seats), their elevations were often exotic, with an element of fantasy brushed off from the films

[1] Nancy Clark, op. cit.

themselves. Inside, for a very low entrance fee, the 'patrons' were flattered and cossetted with thick carpets, bevelled mirrors, softly-shaded lights, red plush tip-up seats and free afternoon teas. The suburbs were not neglected: the Coronet at Wealdstone, probably the first new cinema in Middlesex, and one of the first in London, was quickly erected in 1911 and soon followed by others at Golders Green, Hendon, Sutton, Kingston, Colliers Wood, Putney and elsewhere.

Before long the self-appointed guardians of public morals were in a great state of excitement, troubled not only by the subject matter of some of the films, but also by the conditions in which they were viewed. Building upon their licensing role, the local authorities eagerly assumed the task of censorship, aided from 1 January 1913 by the British Board of Film Censors, set up to guide the industry. In conformance with the prevailing tone, when the Hendon Cinema opened on 15 February 1913, the management promised they would 'always aim at giving a clean and popular performance'. But such high-mindedness was not enough. What young people might be up to in the semi-darkness whilst they watched a moral film hardly bore thinking about, especially if they had found one of those 'double fauteuils' which seemed deliberately designed to facilitate petting. In some London districts 'decency supervisors' were appointed to keep an eye open for unseemly behaviour in the gloom, and steps were taken to ensure that the armrests of seats offered discouragement to cuddling; other measures included raising auditorium lighting to what was called 'decency level', or even more disconcerting, arranging for full lighting to be switched on without warning from time to time. Such precautions were not always well-received, or profitable: when J. P. Martin's improved bioscope showed *The Drunkard's Reformation* (a 'great moral picture') at West Hendon in 1909, in 'full light, the dangers of darkness thus being avoided', patronage was distinctly disappointing.

In November 1909, the *Evening News* carried an article about the rapid development of these 'neat little theatres' which might bring their owners profits as high as £100 to £150 a week; adults could enter without fuss or formality for as little as 3d sitting through as many performances of the hour-long programme as they wished, whilst the children had their Saturday penny matinees. The piano accompanists were trained to produce every kind of sound effect as a background to the silent films, and many picture theatres had apparatus to simulate such noises as thunder, the closing of doors or

the sound of horses' hooves. Less than three years later, the same
paper recorded that there were some 500 cinemas open in London
and suburbs with an average staff of eight, and almost all built since
1906. By the end of 1914, the suburban county of Middlesex had
80 licensed picture houses.

Chapter 3
COUNCIL COTTAGES (1)
1900-14

A Duty, but not an Obligation

Thomas Courtenay Theydon Warner was able to boast in 1901 that he was the second largest builder, next to Cameron Corbett, of artisans' dwellings near London:

'. . . it will be some years before the County Council scheme will come up to what I have done: and I have done it for profit and not for public purposes.'[1]

Until the end of World War I, local councils were under no statutory obligation to provide housing, although various measures passed in the second half of the nineteenth century allowed them to build to meet overcrowding or replace cleared areas if they felt inclined to do so, at their own expense. London's first central authority, the Metropolitan Board of Works, possessed specific powers to provide working-class housing, but made no use of them.

In 1890 the Housing of the Working Classes Act consolidated and modified earlier legislation. Part III of this measure gave councils power to acquire land compulsorily for building additional housing, as well as by agreement. About twenty London local authorities adopted the 1890 Act, notably Battersea, where 408 dwellings had been erected by 1907; West Ham (401); and Hornsey (308). Other councils using the Act to build around the fringes of London were: Barking, Barnes, Brentford, Croydon, Ealing, Finchley, East Ham, Erith, Southgate, Heston-Isleworth, Camberwell, Woolwich, Richmond, and, surprisingly, Esher.

Two examples can be quoted as typical. Croydon purchased 3 acres just east of Woodside station for £1,500 in 1903, erecting 86

[1] To the Joint Select Committee of Lords and Commons on London underground railways, 1901. Warner, who was M.P. for Lichfield and a former member of the Essex County Council, owned 300 acres in Walthamstow, inhabited by 2,184 weekly tenants, almost all 'artisans and clerks' employed in central London (965, 969-70).

houses and a shop. The houses were of two types, costing £190 and £250 to build. The cheaper had a living room and two bedrooms, the other five rooms, as follows:

Living-Room:	11 ft. 8½ in. by 12 ft.
Parlour:	11 ft. 7¾ in. by 9 ft.
Bedroom 1:	11 ft. 10½ in. by 10 ft. 2 in.
Bedroom 2:	11 ft. by 8 ft. 2½ in.
Bedroom 3:	8 ft. by 6 ft. 4 in.

Rents varied from 6s 6d to 8s a week. Barking, which had six separate schemes finished before 1914, managed to reduce the rents for three-bedroom cottages to as little as 5s 6d a week without placing any burden on the rates.

But by far the most extensive builder of low-rent housing under 1890 Act was the London County Council, which had succeeded the Metropolitan Board of Works in 1889. In December 1898, the LCC decided to erect additional housing under the Part III powers, provided this would raise no additional charge on the rates. At this time land prices in inner London were rising, as were the cost of materials and labour. Private speculators and investors were turning to more lucrative commercial and industrial building, often using land obtained by clearance of small houses.

In the years up to 1915, the LCC established large cottage estates at Tooting, Norbury, Tottenham and Hammersmith, erecting in these and smaller developments some 3,400 cottages and cottage flats, accommodating about 12,000 people. Not all these estates were within the county of London. The Housing of the Working Classes Act of 1900 had extended the land purchase powers to areas outside the authority's boundaries, a move which enabled the LCC to obtain suitable land with less difficulty, at considerably lower cost.

In phase with the development of the cottage estates, the ruling Progressive Party on the LCC furthered a policy of cheap fares on the newly acquired and extended tramway system, whilst continuing to fight in Parliament and before the Board of Trade and the Railway Commissioners for the maximum spread of workmen's fares on the railways and privately owned tramways. Some trouble was taken in siting the estates to ensure that there were reasonable facilities for cheap fare travel to and from London, although this was of course more difficult outside the county boundary, where the LCC had no transport powers.

Totterdown-on-Tramway

It was at Totterdown Fields, just within the southern boundary of the county, that the LCC set up the first of its cottage estates. The site was on the south-east side of the Upper Tooting Road, served by the Council's first electric tramway. Here, in a district touched by horse-trams since 1890, and already under the builder, land values were rising. For its 38¾ acres, the LCC was obliged in 1900 to pay the very high price of £1,150 an acre.

Between June 1903 and August 1911 work proceeded on laying out roads and erecting 1,299 houses and 4 shops, to the designs of the Council's architect, W. E. Riley, In his evidence to the Royal Commission on London Traffic, Riley said that the land for a three-room cottage at Totterdown cost the Council £28 15s, the associated road and sewer works, £20, and the building itself, £214 15s, a total of £263 10s, compared with £761 12s (including £454 for land) for a three-bedroom flat in inner London (Leather Lane, Clerkenwell). He claimed that the Tooting cottage would be self-supporting at a rent of 7s or 7s 6d a week.[1]

Lined with plane trees, the uninteresting 45-foot and 40-foot roads at Totterdown were not landscaped. Cottages in terraces of up to twenty were set back 5 to 15 feet from the roadway. Each house had a small garden and a scullery, and some were provided with a bath. Sizes varied from 'three rooms' (living-room, two bedrooms and scullery) to 'five rooms' (living-room, parlour, three bedrooms and scullery with bath), rents from 6s 6d to 13s 6d.

Some of the five-room houses were let at 10s 6d, a rent said to be up to 3s 6d cheaper than that for comparable accommodation in inner London. As the tramway workmen's fare was but 2d return daily, the financial benefit could be as much as 2s 6d a week, to which must be added the unquantifiable advantages of clean air and a garden. For three rooms, the money savings were less impressive at under a shilling a week.[2]

Totterdown filled up quickly. Of the first seventy-five tenants, almost half worked in central London and their wages ranged from 25s to 50s (average 32s).[3] After the First World War, the estate population settled down to around 4,500.[4]

The popularity of the development was no doubt in large

[1] RCLT *Minutes*, 7005–7022.
[2] RLTB 1909, *Appendix E*; EN 17 February 1911.
[3] RCLT *Minutes*, 5835, 5876.
[4] e.g. 4,589 on 31 March 1938 (*LCC Statistics* Vol. 41).

measure attributable to the convenience and cheapness of the Council's electric tramcar service, which started on 15 May 1903. Within a year, there were 229 tramcars each way daily on the Blackfriars Bridge route and 200 on the Westminster Bridge, both totals including the all-night service. There were also 188 journeys each way between Tooting and Waterloo. The 5·9 miles to Westminster were covered in 44 minutes, the 6·4 to Blackfriars in 48, and any journey completed before 8 a.m. could be made for 2d return.[1]

But the efficiency of the new tramway was soon threatened by its success. The number of workmen's tickets issued increased from just over half a million in 1902/3 to over four million in 1909/10.[2] This traffic was not, of course, entirely derived from the LCC estate. All around, the remaining open land was quickly covered with byelaw streets lined with the more solid type of private housing for the lower middle class.[3] Early in 1911, the LCC was berated for its enterprise:

'I have used the Tooting and Westminster service for six months and have rarely been able to travel thereon with comfort. Last week, at Nightingale Lane, Balham, I was twice turned off a full car for Westminster at 9.30 a.m. and have had to board one for some other place and change to the tube at Clapham. ... At Westminster Bridge, the Tooting cars at 5 o'clock were already full upon arriving there every evening but one last week. . . . It is on the Tooting and Streatham routes that conditions are the worst. The official mind must be brought to realise the remarkable rate at which the suburban and residential districts are springing up in the neighbourhood around and beyond their termini, where lately there was nothing but green fields and waste land. . . .'[4]

So fierce were the struggles to board the last workmen's cars in the morning at Tooting that there were troubling allegations of rough handling of women and girls. To put things right, the kindly LCC began in 1908 to operate 'women only' tramcars on this line, a move soon suppressed by the Commissioner of the Metropolitan

[1] RCLT, *Appendices*, 77 (Vol. III).   [2] RLTB 1910, *Appendix F*.
[3] e.g. five- to seven-room houses in and around Eswyn Road, Tooting Bec, with bathroom and scullery, anaglypta dado to hall and staircase, picture moulding to principal rooms, stained-glass windows, tiled hearth and forecourts, venetian blinds, electric or gas lighting, could be had for £220–250 leasehold or 12s. upwards rent in 1906 (EN, 28 January 1906).
[4] EN 17 January 1911. At this time standing passengers were not allowed on tramcars or buses in London.

Police who alleged that it was illegal. Queue shelters were introduced in the following year at Blackfriars to alleviate the evening
loading congestion on this and other south London routes.

Bricks of Clay at Norbury
It was just south of Streatham, another fast-growing area, that the
LCC built the first of its so-called 'out-county' estates. This was on
the west side of the main Croydon road, south of Norbury station,
where 30 acres were bought in February 1901 at £600 an acre, a
little over half the price paid at Tooting. Apart from a few large
villas sprinkled alongside the main road and one or two roads hopefully laid out for building, the area was still largely rural.

Between 1906 and 1910, the council put up 498 small houses,
using only 17½ acres. As at Tooting, the cottages had from three to
five rooms. All but the smallest type had baths, and, for the first
time, a large number were given a separate bathroom. Rents for
three rooms ranged from 7s to 8s 6d, for four rooms, 8s 6d to 10s,
and for the largest house, 10s 6d to 11s 6d.

Just before the council elections of January 1907, unsuccessful
attempts to manufacture bricks from the local London clay at
Norbury provided the Tory *Evening News* with useful ammunition
on the extravagant follies of the wicked Progressives. Experts were
invited to comment on the futility of the experiment and readers
prevailed upon to visit the estate to view the vast pile of cracked and
crumbling bricks manufactured at their expense. No mention was
made of the fact that at nearby Croydon bricks had for many years
been made from local clay.

Unlike the residents of Totterdown, the pioneers in Norbury
had no direct and cheap tramway service into London. An electric
line had opened along the road into Croydon on 26 September 1901,
but this terminated at Hermitage Bridge, the county boundary,
well over a mile's walk from the LCC tram terminus at Streatham
Library, served by electric cars from 19 June 1904. An extension
thence to the boundary was opened on 31 July 1909, but although
through fares were available between the two systems, passengers
were obliged to change cars and walk some way in the open until
the tracks were finally connected on 7 February 1926. At Norbury
station, about a quarter of a mile from the estate, a limited number
of workmen's fare facilities were available to London Bridge and
Victoria. The Third Class daily return fare to these inner stations

was 1s, but about 1911, Third Class season tickets became available, reducing the travel cost to about 3s a week. After the completion of the widening to four tracks between Windmill Bridge Junction, Croydon, and Balham Junction on 6 July 1903 the train service through Norbury was increased.

Private building in the Norbury area was well under way by 1908. In June that year, the *Evening News* contained advertisements for Craignish Avenue ('bring your own surveyor to inspect') and Ederline Avenue ('balconies, overlooking cricket ground').

Tennis at Tottenham

A much more ambitious out-county enterprise was the White Hart Lane estate at Tottenham, just over half a mile north of Bruce Grove station on the GER's 'twopenny train' line. Land here was obtained in 1901 at the low price of £400 an acre, but to achieve this, the council were required to take 226 acres when they needed only 177 for immediate use. Later, some of the northern section beyond White Hart Lane was sold. The first part of the estate, about 40 acres fronting Lordship Lane, was filled in 1904–15 with 963 cottages and 5 shops with flats above. As on the other two estates, the layout and designs were the work of W. E. Riley, who tried here some deliberate variations in the alignment of the blocks, but was otherwise unimaginative, setting the cottages in a grillage along Lordship Lane and Risley Avenue, or in a series of parallel lanes between those roads. Some of the houses had walls of stock brick, with slate hanging and gables, others were in less formal garden suburb styles, in red brick. Almost all had a bath, and rents for two to five rooms varied from 6s to 13s.

Tower Garden, at the eastern end of the development, provided facilities for tennis, bowls and general relaxation. A nearby farm, together with open views to the south and north, contributed an almost rural setting, disturbed only by the electric tramcars on the main road.

Fares to the City ranged from 1s to 4s a week, according to route and time of departure. The GER cheap facilities were supplemented by the tramcars of the MET, which connected the estate with Bruce Grove station and Wood Green after 20 August 1904. Later, LCC cars serving the City and East End through-worked over this line.

With the election of the Conservative Municipal Reformers in

1907 there were second thoughts about the Tottenham estate. It was decided that as the area was already predominantly working class in character (in contrast to Norbury and Tooting), it would be wrong to cover the whole site with low-rent housing. Accordingly powers were obtained in the council's 1912 Act to develop part of the land as a garden suburb for all classes, the building of non-working-class houses to be left to private enterprise. Another part of the same Act gave the council powers to grant long leases to its tenants. Following in the wake of the LCC, the Peabody Donation Fund constructed 154 five-room terrace cottages in Lordship Lane, immediately to the east, completed in 1907.

The last of the pre-1914 LCC estates was at Old Oak, in the borough of Hammersmith, at the south-west corner of Wormwood Scrubs and about one mile east of Acton GWR station. The 54¼ acres were obtained from the Ecclesiastical Commissioners in 1905 at £550 an acre. As a recognition of its origins, the estate's streets were given the names of former bishops of London. Later, 8 acres were sold to permit the construction of the Ealing and Shepherds Bush Railway by the GWR, eventually to become the Central Line from Ealing Broadway to White City. For this land and the damage caused to the estate, the LCC succeeded in recovering £10,500 of its original expenditure of £29,858.

West of the new railway, 319 cottages and cottage flats and 5 shops were built in 1912 and 1913. Roads were laid out in the eastern part of the estate, but development had to await the conclusion of World War I.

The early tenants of Old Oak had to walk almost a mile to find any public transport, the nearest being on the main Uxbridge Road. With the opening of a passenger service on the railway on 3 August 1920, the estate had its own station (East Acton) with through services to the West End and City, as well as to Ealing and Acton.

These suburban estates of the LCC and other local authorities did not differ greatly from those of private enterprise. Their occupants were for the most part commuters to central London, especially in the early years; their streets, when new, looked much the same; and the houses, although plainer in design, both inside and out, were of the same general pattern. But the passage of time brought a widening difference. On the whole, the gardens received less care and attention, fewer trees and shrubs were planted, and the streets and house surrounds were frequently left untidy and unkempt.

Chapter 4

CASE STUDIES 1900–14
ILFORD AND
GOLDERS GREEN

Land of Griggs and Corbett

As the century opened, one of London's fastest growing suburbs was to be found 7½ miles east of Liverpool Street on the GER main line to Ipswich. There had been a railway station at Ilford since the opening of the line in 1839, but for fifty years the quiet village, amid market gardens famous for their onions and potatoes, had seen little change. Accessibility from London, and the slightly elevated, gravelly soil, gradually attracted a few moderately wealthy residents who set themselves up in large houses placed in extensive grounds. In 1888 Ilford became a civil parish separate from Barking; two years later it was a local government district, and in 1894, an urban district. Additional trains were provided in 1893, further improvements following very shortly afterwards as a consequence of the enlargement of Liverpool Street and Ilford Stations, and the completion of four tracks to Ilford in 1895–8. These facilities encouraged the building of small houses, and from a population of just under 11,000 in less than 2,000 houses in 1891, the town grew in the following decade to 41,240, in almost 8,000 houses. By 1906 the number of houses had reached 14,000, 1,300 of them unoccupied, and the 1911 census showed that the 1901 population had almost doubled.

From the late 1880s, streets of cheap cottages had been built south of the railway, and soon afterwards an estate of large villas was started by J. W. Hobbs and Co. in the 150-acre grounds of Ilford Lodge, between Cranbrook Road and Ley Street, just north of the station. When this firm sank with other Balfour companies in the Liberator Building Society collapse of 1892, development was continued by the Ilford Park Estate Company.

These pioneer efforts were to be overshadowed by those of the

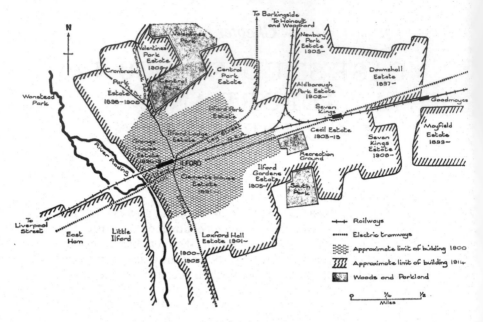

II Ilford estates 1900–14

great founders of suburban Ilford, W. Peter Griggs[1] and Archibald Cameron Corbett.[2] Griggs purchased most of the 215-acre Cranbrook Park Estate, between Cranbrook Road and the River Roding, and between 1898 and 1907 covered it thickly with substantial-looking houses set along monotonously straight roads whose names sought to impart tone (Kensington Gardens, Mayfair Avenue, De Vere Gardens, Empress Avenue, etc.). Griggs' single-fronted houses with four main rooms were selling in 1906 at £260, £270 and £395 leasehold, whilst the four-bedroom, double-fronted

[1] Griggs (1853–1920) was a typical example of the Victorian 'self-made man'. An orphan at seven, he had amassed a small fortune from work on the Thames by the age of thirty. He became an Ilford councillor in 1899, a county councillor in 1901. In 1905 he was elected chairman of the Ilford council. Knighted in 1916 for his war efforts, he became Ilford's first M.P. in December 1918.

[2] Corbett (1856–1933) was created first baron Rowallan in 1911. He married the daughter of John Polson, the cornflour magnate, and was Liberal M.P. for Glasgow, Tradeston, from 1885 until receiving his baronetcy.

versions were £375 and £395. There were even some with five bedrooms, at £450 and £495. Similar prices obtained at Griggs' second estate, Central Park, around Valentines Road, from 1900. By the end of 1904, Griggs had contributed some 2,000 houses to Ilford, but the pace was then slowing down. Three years later he was prospecting new fields, further east, opening up the 'Upminster Garden Suburb' of some 850 acres north of the railway.

Corbett was probably the most prolific of London's suburban developers in the 1890s and 1900s, responsible for many thousands of dull, stereotyped, but reasonably well-built houses which brought the white-collar class in strength not only to Ilford and its eastern outskirts, but also to Catford and Eltham in south-east London. His father, Thomas Corbett, had built most of the southern part of Forest Gate, just west of Ilford, starting in 1877, and when he died in 1880, his rows of roads named after royal residences were carried to completion by Cameron. Encouraged by the success at Woodgrange Park, Corbett bought 93 acres known as the Clements House Estate south of the Ilford High Road, on which he built over a thousand houses from 1893. A year after this purchase he secured the Ilford Cottage or Grange House Estate at £430 10s an acre, close to the station on the north side of the GER main line. This was covered with 450 double-fronted villas, each with servants' annexe alongside, to a design also used at Seven Kings, Catford and Eltham.

Next came the Downshall Estate, 107 acres of market gardens north of the Seven Kings High Road, just the east of Ilford. This was planted with several thousand small houses, their bay windows in monotonous line, each front porch with its little figurehead, all arranged in 'a vista of apparently interminable roads'.[1] Lastly, Corbett bought the Mayfield Estate, a 330-acre site immediately south of the railway at Goodmayes, a little further east. Work here began in 1899 but development was slower as the situation was more remote than that of the other estates. By 1903, Corbett had sold over 3,000 houses in the Ilford area, and the major part of his effort there was spent.

Corbett's houses had frontages ranging from 21 to 48 feet. The smallest type, with only one reception and three bedrooms, was priced at £217 (£225 at end of terraces). For two reception rooms and three-bedrooms the cost went up to £264 10s, whilst four-bedroom houses varied from £265 to £385 according to size and

[1] A. E. Davis, and E. Gower, *Tramway Trips and Rambles* (1907).

position. A six-bedroom villa with frontage of 48 feet sold at £520. (All prices leasehold).

After 1900, other builders and developers worked over the low-lying land east and west of Ilford Lane, south of the railway. Here, on the Uphall, Loxford Hall and Ilford Gardens Estates, the houses were in general cheaper and smaller than those on the higher ground to the north of the suburb. Often there was only one bay window, on the ground floor. Between Ilford Lane and the river, £200 would secure a 99-year lease of a house with one reception room and three bedrooms, complete with venetian blinds in the main windows and a 50-foot back garden (Madras and Hamilton Roads, 1902). Three years later, a little further east, a man called Ranson was offering houses with 21- to 25-foot frontages on the Ilford Gardens Estate (around Gordon Road) at rents of between £22 and £28, just within reach of a newly married clerk earning around £90.

By 1904 the Ilford housing boom was showing signs of collapse. The 5½-acre Old Vicarage Estate failed to attract offers at the reserve price, and was withdrawn. On the Aldborough Park Estate, to the west of Corbett's Downshall, J. T. Smith and J. H. Pavitt had paid £500 in 1897 and were finding it difficult to dispose of houses built from 1901 onwards along roads with Boer War names. When 142 house plots on the nearby Newbury Park Estate were offered in 1904, only four (in Hertford Road) were sold, at £42 10s each. Even the great W. P. Griggs was feeling the cold wind. At the annual employees' dinner in November 1904, he complained 'It has been very difficult to keep things going in the building trade. The firm has to give even more to the people in the shape of improvements and extras to induce them to buy.' Two years later, there was further evidence that the market was temporarily saturated when 129 acres at Barkingside, quite near the new railway, failed to find a buyer at the very low reserve price of £300 an acre.

But although the pace slowed, building did not stop. An average of 334 houses a year were built by private enterprise in Ilford between 1911 and 1915. Griggs worked northwards, gradually updating his styles, using more and more wood externally. From 1909 a 22-acre 'garden suburb', designed by H. Clapham Lander and owing little to the principles of Unwin, was developed east of the Cranbrook Road on the Valentines Park Estate. The Town Planning and Garden Cities Company's houses are of some interest as they are in a transitional style approximately halfway between the heavy solidity of the Grigg and Corbett estates and the lightly built semis which appeared in North Ilford after 1920.

Propriety by Easy Purchase

Ilford's popularity derived from its excellent train service to the City, the good value offered by its new houses, and the facilities available for easy purchase. The UDC was among the first in London to adopt the Small Dwellings Acquisition Act of 1899, which enabled the council to borrow capital from the Public Works Loan Commissioners at $3\frac{1}{2}$ per cent to lend on the security of house property at $3\frac{3}{4}$ per cent, repayable over fifteen years. In his evidence to the Royal Commission on London Government in 1922, F. H. Dane, the vice chairman of the Legal and Parliamentary Committee of the council, said that 524 loans had been made and £101,957 borrowed from the Commissioners. Although this represented only a small proportion of the total number of houses built in Ilford since 1900, he claimed that it gave 'a nucleus of folks who take an interest in the town's affairs'.[1] Corbett made things even easier, providing loans to cover part of the initial cash deposit for his houses. Thus in 1901, a three-bedroom house of 29-foot frontage on the Mayfield Estate, priced £308, could be had by borrowing £240 from the council and £45 from Corbett, leaving only £23 to be found in cash. The annual payment to the council in this case was £22 4s 1d for fourteen years, and that to Corbett, £8 2s 8d for eight years. With a ground rent of £6 18s a year, this produced a total monthly outlay of just over £3, to which rates (7s 10d in the £) must be added. Including rates, taxes and some allowance for repairs, a Corbett six-room house (one reception room, three bedrooms, kitchen and scullery) would be obtainable under this scheme for 18s a week for the first fourteen years and 15s for another seven, payments lower than the rent of many similar houses in inner London.

Griggs built his own houses, but Corbett, the Ilford Park Estate Company and others employed builders on a contract basis. One of Corbett's main contractors was Robert Stroud (1856–1925), who had moved into this field after acquiring valuable experience laying Ilford's first main drainage in the 1880s. He subsequently entered public life, eventually becoming chairman of Ilford Council. Many less substantial men were attracted to this kind of work during the

[1] RCLG, 11 June 1922, evidence of F. H. Dane.

boom period, some of them to end up in the bankruptcy courts. One such, Walter Horace Cole, was said in 1900 to have liabilities of £1,275 and assets of £30; starting as a jobbing builder in 1897 with a capital of £250, in October of that year he began 5 houses in Morland Road, on a contract worth £1,757 10s. On this he lost £90. He then contracted to build 15 houses in Wellesley Road at £5,700, but received only £5,522 17s as he could not complete at the contract price and was unable to obtain further credit from the builders' merchant. Finally he undertook to build 10 houses in Brisbane Road for £3,813 19s, but was paid only £2,612 15s 11d before the houses and materials were seized by the Ilford Park Estate Company under the terms of the contract. He explained to the court that the Estate Company did not care whether or not he made a profit, as they received all the houses and materials left on the ground; if there were any profit, he took it, any loss fell on his creditors. Another man, T. F. Crabb, came to Ilford in 1897 with no capital at all, and obtained a contract to build 13 houses on the Ilford Park Estate. When he was six months in default, the freeholders foreclosed, and he joined Cole in the bankruptcy courts in 1900.

The new residents of Ilford were in the main clerks, skilled workers and officials of various kinds, with a sprinkling of the better-paid shop workers; most travelled to central London every day. In the smarter areas north of the railway there lived people who liked to describe themselves as 'something in the City', who could in many cases afford a servant or two. The social division was sharp enough:

'Ilford, albeit of mushroom growth, has a pretty conceit o'itself, and rightly so. Let me explain at the outset that Ilford is not a unity, but a duality. The line of severance is the railway. I shall be guilty of no exaggeration when I say that the difference between the two districts is almost as the difference between Kensington and Notting Hill. Who will marvel then when I say that the leading ambition of every rightminded Ilfordian is to migrate as speedily as possible from one side of the line to the other? Arrived at the desired haven, he will find that Ilford proper is proper in the very best sense of the term. The pattern of houses is spendidly uniform; its street vistas are beautifully monotonous; every front garden is a replica of its neighbour; while the names of the thoroughfares have a poetry and distinction that will be found hard to beat elsewhere.'[1]

[1] EN 3 October 1907 (reader's letter).

3. 'Our Suburb: We used to cycle to the station; but now we have the bus.' (A Frank Reynolds drawing from *Punch*.)

By Electric Train to the new Suburban Hinterland. An Underground poster of c. 1912.

4. House construction on the outskirts of London c. 1900. (From *Living London*, 1901.)

Venetian blinds and lace curtains, Winchester Road, Highams Park, soon after completion, c. 1900. (From a commercial postcard.)

Propriety was indeed carefully preserved. Both Corbett and Griggs were strong advocates of temperance, refusing to allow public houses or even off-licences on their estates. Churches were promptly provided in all parts of the new Ilford to foster the spiritual well being and morality of the prudent white collars.[1] In 1898 the vicar of Ilford had wistfully remarked:

'The Downshall Estate will soon be stretching out its hands to us to make some sort of spiritual provision . . . I have no craze for bricks and mortar, but estate owners have, and it is they who compel us to continue church building whether we will or no.'

But not all was respectable and proper. In 1906 two widows were prosecuted for operating what the police described as a disorderly house in Fairfield Terrace, and in the same year a stationer at Goodmayes was found guilty of selling 'improper' postcards. Worse still, a baby farm was set up in two adjacent new houses on the Downshall Estate in 1900, to be closed down only after a vigorous correspondence in the local press and the personal intervention of a greatly shocked Corbett.

New schools and shops appeared with remarkable speed. The School Board appointed in November 1893 certainly lost no time. Horns School (264 places) opened in 1895, Cleveland Road (1,800) and Chadwell Street (450) three years later. Two other large buildings, Christchurch Road (1,408) and Downshall (1,640), were ready in 1900 and 1902, but there had been a temporary school on the Downshall Estate since 1899. Last of the series was Loxford, (1,380) in 1903-4. All these were junior and primary schools. The Park Higher Grade School (600), the first of its kind in Essex, was erected near Christchurch Road in 1900. Nor was adult education neglected. A public library and lecture hall, presented by Andrew Carnegie, was opened in the High Road, near Goodmayes station, in April 1909.

Shopping parades were built in the High Road at Seven Kings and Goodmayes about the time the big estates were going up. When these later proved insufficient, further shops were erected in the front gardens of houses along the main road.

[1] St Clement (1200 seats, 1892); St Chad, Chadwell Heath (1895); Ilford Wesleyan Church (1895); Ilford Congregational Church (1895); Ebenezer Baptist Chapel (1898); Baptist Chapel (1899); Roman Catholic Church (1899); St John, Evangelist (1902); St John, Seven Kings (500 seats, 1904); St Alban (700 seats, 1906); St Luke (1915).

Some care was taken that the flood of houses did not occupy all the ground. With a measure of afterthought, Dane suggested that Ilford's success in this direction had had a social effect:

'We have rather town planned our area from the parks point of view ... we have seen the awful example of our neighbours between us and London and have tried to set up a community ... we have a better class resident, perhaps, in consequence of providing parks and open spaces, we have attracted a better class population, although we have got an ordinary working class population who thoroughly enjoy the parks the same as the other folks.'[1]

But perhaps not in the same way?

Pride of Ilford was Valentine's Park, the first section of which was opened as Central Park in 1899 on 29 acres purchased from Mrs Holcombe Ingleby's Valentine House Estate at £320 an acre. Building activity soon increased land values; later additions were charged at £650 (7½ acres) and £850 (11 acres). When Mrs Ingleby died in 1902, the remainder of her estate was sold off; the public park was enlarged by the purchase of another 37½ acres and a gift of 10, including her American Gardens; finally, in 1912, the council bought 22 acres from the Town Planning and Garden Cities Company at £600 an acre, bringing into the park Valentines House itself, and enlarging the total public area to 117 acres. Corbett showed his public spirit in 1900, donating 9 acres to make a park either side of Seven Kings Water, and again later when he gave 14 acres off Green Lane to provide a public park on his Goodmayes estate. The 32-acre South Park and 12-acre Moss Green Recreation Ground dated from 1902, the land in both cases being acquired at £350 an acre.

Ilford had no theatre at first, but three were available in Stratford, easily reached by train or tram. Cinematograph entertainments were held occasionally in the town hall from 1906 onwards, and the first cinemas and a music hall came a few years later.

Electricity was supplied by the council's own generating station, opened in Ley Street in May 1901. From the beginning, Cranbrook Road and the streets on the Grange and Clements House estates were electrically lit, and electricity was offered to domestic consumers through penny-in-the-slot meters, of which some 500 were in use by 1906. By 1912 the undertaking had over 4,000 consumers

[1] RCLG 11 June 1922, evidence of F. H. Dane.

on its books. A larger number of houses and other premises were however lit by the Ilford Gas Company's town gas, selling in 1901 at 3s 8d a cubic foot.

Flood, Flies and Mud

As with all human enterprise there were teething troubles in the new suburb. In June 1903, after three days of almost continuous rain, the River Roding overflowed its banks, creating a small inland sea between Ilford and Wanstead Park. In some houses the water reached the fourth stair as furniture was carried up to the bedrooms. Paterfamilias, returning from the city, was seen wading homewards, trousers rolled above white knees. Subsequently there was much criticism of the authorities responsible for embanking the Roding, and of those who had built houses below the flood level. An embarrassed Griggs hastened to erect a wall to protect the houses in Wanstead Park Road from further wetting. The Seven Kings Water also proved troublesome, as in August 1906 when the inadequacy of the storm drainage was fully demonstrated. Water poured down to the Seven Kings High Road, causing the trams to throw out bow waves as they coursed along.

Most of the new estate roads lacked a proper surface, and many were the complaints about winter mud. Conditions were so bad that cyclists resorted to the pavements where these existed. In November 1902, Ingleby Road was described as a mixture between ploughed field and quagmire, and Corbett's Downshall estate, known without affection as Klondyke for its complete lack of amenities, suffered from similar troubles. The unlit roads were made almost impassable by thick mud in winter, and in summer, the early settlers were blinded and soiled by grey dust. 'We carry all Seven Kings with us', wrote *Mud Pusher* to the *Ilford Guardian* in January 1900. 'It is really grievous to see ladies struggling through the mud', complained another correspondent. Refuse disposal was also a source of grumbles. At first it was carried out somewhat infrequently by private contractors. A Windsor Road resident wrote in 1901 that dustbins had not been emptied for a month, and house refuse was strewn all over the road; he cast dark hints that things were managed better in the Cranbrook Park area, on the other side of the tracks, where the councillors lived. Four years later, Downshall ratepayers were plagued by flies and unpleasant smells from the Council rubbish dump to the north of the estate.

Providing the Arteries

Although Corbett relied upon others to bring amenities to his estates, he was very much alive to the value of good transport facilities in securing the necessary initial sales of his houses. His first move at Ilford was to make a contribution in 1898 towards the cost of a northern entrance to Ilford station which would serve his Grange House Estate. When negotiating the purchase of Downshall, he entered into an agreement with the GER which secured the construction of a new railway station. He undertook to build new houses if the railway for their part would open a station by 31 March 1899, guaranteeing them a minimum of £10,000 in season tickets for the first five years, and depositing £1,000 as security. As good as their word, the GER opened Seven Kings station on 1 March 1899, serving it with twenty-eight up and thirty-two down trains on weekdays, whilst Corbett's pledge was soon more than honoured. When the Mayfield estate was started, Corbett reached a similar arrangement with the railway, and Goodmayes station opened its doors on 8 February 1901. Two extra running lines were provided from Ilford to the new Seven Kings station and on to Goodmayes when that was ready. In the busiest morning hour' 8.30 to 9.30, there were then fifteen trains to the City, six coming from further out, one starting from Chadwell Heath, six from Goodmayes and two from Ilford itself. The best time from Ilford to the City was fifteen minutes.

Ilford station, rebuilt with three platforms in 1893–5, with two more added on the fast lines in 1898, had some 250 trains and booked over 1.1 million passengers daily at the beginning of the century, compared with 671,500 passengers only three years earlier.

A 4½-mile loop line between Ilford and Woodford, opened for passenger traffic on 1 May 1903, was provided with twenty trains each way daily between 6.54 a.m. and 10.59 p.m. The substantially built, closely spaced stations had 600 ft. platforms and all facilities. Constructed in fulfilment of a promise to a parliamentary committee after the suppression of an independent scheme, the railway was expected to encourage further building to the north of Ilford and east of Woodford, but the boom was fading away by the time it was ready and the new stations heard few footsteps. Indeed so sparse was custom that Hainault station was closed, together with its goods yard, from 1 October 1908, not to be revived until 3 March 1930, when the area was at last showing some signs of life. In 1911, the GER general manager told a parliamentary committee that the line suffered greatly from tramway competition (an exaggeration, as trams touched but two of its six station catchment areas), and was worked at a loss of £8,000 a year.

Ilford's municipal trams had started operation on 14 March 1903, running from the Broadway to Barkingside via Ley Street (2½ miles), to Chadwell Heath via Seven Kings and Goodmayes (2¾ miles) and to the East Ham boundary at Ilford Hill (¼ mile). A fourth line, to the Barking boundary at Loxford Bridge opened on 22 May, completing the system (Ilford cars ran over this into Barking from 6 June 1905, but the joint service was shortlived). Although their tracks were joined to those of Barking and East Ham, Ilford cars never ran through to London; East Ham Corporation provided a service, however, from Ilford Broadway to Manor Park in 1905, extended to Bow Bridge four years later and through to Aldgate, at the edge of the City, in 1910, jointly with West Ham and the LCC.

As the northern flanks of his Cranbrook Park Estate were rather remote from the station and shops, and consequently sold less readily, Griggs organised a three-horse bus between the station and Endsleigh Gardens in 1903. This ran every ten minutes via Cranbrook Road and The Drive at a fare of 1d. After being cut back to Belgrave Market and reduced to fifteen minutes interval, the facility was withdrawn when only a few weeks had elapsed. Unkind correspondents to the local papers pointed out that the bus had moved very slowly once clear of the busier part of the route and that the crews wasted much time chatting with servant girls at the outer terminus. Later there were several proposals to extend tramway service into the Cranbrook Park area, no doubt supported, if not suggested, by councillor Griggs. However, at public meetings, residents of the estate voiced strong dissent, evidently fearing that tramcars would lower the precariously preserved tone. After some years of argument, during which the tramway came very near to construction, the arrival of the less intrusive motorbus solved the dilemma.

On the main road east to west through the town, the electric cars were by now under increasing pressure from the motorbus. In 1908, the fast, electrically-lit Great Easterns, bright in their yellow livery, were operating an excellent service between Ilford and the Bank, on which season tickets were available at 15s a month or 35s a quarter. This eventually succumbed to fierce competition from the General's service 8, which worked along the main road to London from Seven Kings, and the two companies merged from 1 January 1911. A year later, the General started a seven-minute service between Barkingside and Barking station via Cranbrook Road and Ilford Broadway, at the same time extending their main road buses eastwards into Romford. A General garage was opened at Seven Kings in 1913 to shelter and service vehicles of the Ilford area routes.

Edwardian Ilford, with its large estates of small houses built for sale, its parks and its sports clubs, its sponsored railway stations and its rows of busy shops, was in many ways the precursor of the host of new suburbs that were to flash into life around London in the twenties and thirties. But for all that, it was in some senses already old-fashioned when new, particularly in the design and appearance of the majority of its houses, with their heavy construction, stone facings and slate roofs, and their environment of monotonously long straight roads. Only on the northernmost edges, towards Gants Hill, was there any suggestion of the new suburban house styles that were to become standard in the third and fourth decades of the century. We have to look elsewhere for the true model of the coming suburban era, the new suburb where the lighter, brighter type of house was built to the absolute exclusion of all others, where the streets were less dreary in appearance, and where light bulbs outnumbered gas mantles.

Quite in the Country

At the close of the nineteenth century the outward spread of London was lapping around the sides of Hampstead Heath, reaching on the west as far as Childs Hill and the Midland Railway workers' settlement at Cricklewood. To the north, below Hendon and Finchley, lay an extensive tract of open country unmarked by railways, sealed off by the natural barrier of the Heath. Almost in the centre of this area was a straggling little settlement of a few large houses, some cottages and a farm, known as Golders Green, 'a place within three miles of Regent's Park where there are roses in the hedgerows and the larks are singing . . . a place almost unique in its rural character'.[1] Aside from the opening of the famous crematorium in 1902, the only events thought worthy of report in the local newspaper at the beginning of the new century were an

[1] Evidence before the Light Railway Commissioners in opposition to a proposed tramway between Golders Green and Hendon, 1901.

outbreak of rick fires, a burglary or two at the big houses and a little horse-stealing in the pastures bordering the Hendon and Finchley Roads.

A visitor to the spot in 1906 would have seen at the crossing of these two roads a single house in the south-east corner, The Hawthorns, with Hodford Farm behind it, home of James Raymond, dairyman, whose son, Walter Leslie, just beginning a successful career as an estate agent, has several mentions later in this book. Towards Hendon, the green-swarded road was bordered by some ten substantial villas, prettily set in large grounds. In one of these, The Elms, dwelt Count Righini and his wife Madam Ella Russell, the well-known soprano, who had been attracted there 'because they thought it would be quite in the country'.[1]

But already there were portents to threaten the 6½-acre seclusion of Madam Ella and her Count: gas lamps along the Finchley Road, casting a yellow glare across night fields; a hoarding or two indicating that building land was available; and, against a tumbledown pig shed near the cross roads, a more modest board announcing that the Underground Electric Railways Company of London Ltd had acquired the site for a station. Here was the fuse to light the explosion that in a few years would transform this rural backwater to a bustling suburb of over 20,000 people.

An Entirely Fresh District

Proposals for opening up the district around Golders Green with electric tramways coming before the Light Railway Commissioners from 1897 onwards, had met with much opposition; only one line, from Cricklewood to Finchley was sanctioned.[2] This left the radial link with central London open to other possibilities, predetermining to some extent the type of housing development at Golders Green.

A scheme for an underground railway from Charing Cross to Hampstead had been approved by parliament in 1893, but, unable to attract capital, it had lain dormant until rescued in 1900 by an American syndicate led by the financier Charles Tyson Yerkes. The

[1] Ibid.
[2] There was strong opposition on amenity grounds to tramways through Hampstead village and similar opposition, combined with doubts as to the need, destroyed all prospects for lines from Golders Green to central Hendon and West Hendon, a route submitted on several occasions up to 1902, the year in which the Cricklewood to Finchley tramway was finally agreed.

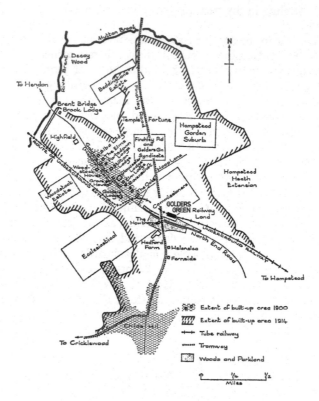

III Golders Green estates 1900–14

new owners surveyed the route and decided to go on from Hampstead into the open fields north of the Heath where there was ample space for car sheds, power station and sidings. Nor was this all; the Americans knew from home experience that given favourable conditions, a frequent service of electric cars to places just beyond the edge of towns or cities, soon caused the fields to disappear under bricks and mortar. Application was made to parliament for the extension, and a separate bill, not in the railway's name, was sponsored by Yerkes and his group for the construction of 5.15

miles of electric tramways, tapping Hendon and Finchley to increase the traffic at Golders Green station. At the railway terminus, a syndicate was formed through agents to develop the nearby fields for building, and the Americans were thus involved in options to buy land before the railway and tramway schemes were publicly announced at the end of October 1900. All this activity closely followed a pattern already familiar in the U.S.A. A few months later, the promoters' hopes were openly voiced by their consultant engineer:

'There is at present a district lying beyond Hampstead which has been almost unapproachable. . . . The railway accommodation is at present by the Midland Railway on the one side and by the Great Northern branch on the other, and we have endeavoured to place our terminus as nearly as possible midway between those two railway systems, so as to open up an entirely fresh district for building and for development.'[1]

Although the tramway feeder proposals failed to get through parliament, the railway extension from Hampstead to Golders Green was authorised in November 1902, linked with another scheme for a surface railway in continuation as far as Edgware. Construction of the underground line began late in the same year, but the extensive tunnelling required was not finished until April 1906, and the line from Charing Cross (later Strand) was eventually opened on 22 June 1907. Two-car trains left Golders Green every twelve minutes from 5.17 a.m. to 12.31 a.m., taking twenty-four minutes to reach the inner terminus. Traffic at Golders Green was heaviest on Sundays, when Londoners went out to enjoy the rural ale and the band which sometimes played in the station forecourt (official Sunday licensing hours were restricted to lunchtime and from 6 p.m. to 10 p.m., but the *Royal Oak* at Temple Fortune, like other suburban pubs, enjoyed much patronage from 'travellers' who were able to demand alcoholic refreshment at any time provided they had slept more than three miles away the night before). So popular did this excursion become that the service had sometimes to be strengthened to six-car trains every four minutes.[2]

Meanwhile, preparations for the 'entirely fresh district' had gone ahead rapidly. Late in 1904, Hendon UDC had passed the first

[1] Sir Douglas Fox, joint engineer of the Charing Cross, Euston & Hampstead Railway, to the Joint Select Committee on London Underground Railways, 14 May 1901.
[2] *Pennyfare*, August 1937.

plans, a scheme for new roads and drainage submitted by H. J. S. Adams which included the planting of plane trees along the Finchley Road. This road was lit and drained in 1906 and that summer the owners of the large villas were beginning to move out with their profits. The Oaks passed to the Finchley Road and Golders Green Syndicate, which held a large area north of the crossroads and west of Finchley Road. To the north was Beddington's Estate, astride Bridge Lane, and to the east, the large tract belonging to the Eton College Trustees, later to become the Hampstead Garden Suburb. The southern flanks of Golders Green, from the north side of Childs Hill to the east side of Finchley Road just north of the station were held by the Ecclesiastical Commissioners.

Gold in the Green

Two firms of estate agents were early at work. Ernest Owers[1] was entrenched in the Hawthorns, whilst Raymond and Crump were installed in a small wooden hut in the station approach; both establishments stand out clearly amid open country in photographs taken in the autumn of 1906. The following summer saw prospectors thick upon the ground: 'within sight of the Golders Green terminus of the Hampstead Tube, half a dozen estate agents' pavilions may be counted dotted about the fields'.[2]

With the sole exception of the proprietors of the new railway which had sparked it all off, everyone concerned with the development of Golders Green was to gather substantial profits. As soon as work began on the railway, agricultural land which had formerly sold at £150 to £250 an acre increased in value eightfold or more. In the classic pattern of such situations, some of the land changed

---

[1] Owers (1860–1938), now almost a legendary figure in the world of estate agents, started business life as a solicitor's clerk. After some experience in the Stock Exchange and his father's small estate agency at Shepherd's Bush, he set up an agency, with virtually no capital, in 1879, living frugally above his office adjoining West Hampstead Metropolitan station. His vitality and financial acumen brought sufficient success to enable him to secure a strong position in the Golders Green bonanza in which he made his name and fortune. A small hut opened at the station site in 1905 was replaced by an office in 'The Hawthorns' and later by more palatial accommodation in the new shopping parade, directly opposite the station, on a fine corner site. In 1920 Owers formed a limited company with his partner Charles Death and with Charles Handman, and this firm participated in the rather less dramatic Edgware development after 1924. Retiring from daily business in 1931, Owers sold his interests three years later to Handman and to W. Charles Williams, Hospitals benefited from generous bequests out of his estate of £400,790 (over £2m. at today's values).

[2] HFT 23 August 1907.

hands several times before builders' materials were seen on it, often broken up in the process into smaller and smaller parcels at higher and higher prices. In the summer of 1906, before the station had opened, land nearby was sold for shops at the rate of £5,500 an acre, and two years later, other plots in the same area were retailing at prices equivalent to £10,000 an acre; this was land which had been let for agricultural use at £3 or £3 10s a year per acre. Half a mile from the station, the Woodstock House estate, with its 500-yard frontage to the main Hendon road, was sold in May 1909 at £1,000 an acre, after passing through several hands.

When a second parade of shops was opened between Hoop Lane and the station in 1911, the *Hendon and Finchley Times* dryly observed that the freeholder had incurred no expense in laying out the main road, making it up or laying sewers, and assuming that the annual rent was equal to that for the earlier block of shops opposite, the 30 new shops might realise for him some £3,000 a year, a gold-mine of £75,000 at twenty-five years purchase, all on land which was once 'waste' (the green at the sides of the road), and obtained from the lord of the manor by paying off certain nominal 'fines'.

A Continuous Hammering

The earliest roads to appear in the fields were those on the Wood-stock estate (The Grove, The Drive, and the eastern end of High-field and Woodstock Avenues) and on the Syndicate's land (Temp-lars Avenue and Wentworth Road), and the first of the new houses were completed on the latter estate in October 1905, at the corner of Hoop Lane and Wentworth Road.[1] In that year only 19 houses were finished and only 14 followed in the next twelve months, but 1907, the year of the underground railway, saw the completion of 73 and thereafter the accumulation was impressive:[2]

1908	340
1909	461
1910	562
1911	744
1912	486
1913	514
1914	477
1915	432

[1] F. Howkins, *The Story of Golders Green and Its Remarkable Development* (1923).
[2] From the Reports of the Hendon Medical Officer of Health (Childs Hill and Hampstead Garden Suburb).

These figures are from the annual reports of the Hendon Medical Officer of Health, who for the year ended June 1909 recorded completion of over 2 miles of new roads and 6 miles of sewers, and for the following year, $2\frac{1}{4}$ miles and 5 miles, almost all at Golders Green. At the new station the first full year of traffic yielded $1\frac{1}{2}$ million passengers, but by 1915 the total was over 10 millions,[1] a figure which was to grow by only 3 more millions in the next twenty years.

So intense was the building activity that the Golders Green to Edgware railway, unable to secure its authorised right of way, was obliged to return to parliament in 1909 for what was hoped would prove a cheaper deviation through the area, avoiding some of the already completed roads, Even so, when this line was eventually constructed just after World War I, a number of residential roads had to be stopped up and some new houses had to be demolished.

'All day long there is a continuous hammering which reminds one of distant thunder', recorded the editor of the local newspaper in February 1910. The builders worked to such good effect that a year later, the *Evening News* was publishing a full-page feature on the suburb including advertisements by six firms offering houses in eight separate locations at prices ranging from £400 to £1,000. Quality was emphasised; on the West Heath Drive estate, Arthur J. Reynolds boasted of site concrete 6 in. deep, of walls up to 14 in. thick, and stressed that no zinc was used. A name seen in this and many hundreds of Golders Green advertisements was that of Edward Streather (1875-1936), one of the area's most prolific builders. Streather, who had arrived in 1906 from the Midlands, began building on the Ecclesiastical Commissioners' land. He was joined in 1911 by his brother, William Turner, and these two men, together with their sons, Reginald and Cecil Turner, built thousands of houses in Golders Green and Hendon, moving on to Edgware and Mill Hill in the twenties and thirties. Edward, who lived in one of his own houses in St John's Road, Golders Green, was founder and first secretary of the Golders Green Lodge of the Freemasons (1909), becoming Master in 1913.

Half-timbered, tiled and gabled, and cottagey in appearance, the Golders Green houses set the trend for the next three decades of London suburban exteriors. Although most were of fair size for speculatively-built property, their prices, reflecting the inflated land

[1] Howkins, op. cit.

values, were on the high side. For the same reason, back gardens were short, rarely more than 80 feet. Owers was selling three-bedroom semis five minutes from the station in 1908 for £450 leasehold, whilst Edward Streather's slightly larger ones in Finchley Road and St John's Road were £600 freehold. On the Woodstock estate at Montpelier Rise, Brady was charging £425 leasehold, whilst at Golders Gardens, on the site of Golders Lodge, F. Bastable was completing three-bedroom semis for sale at the same price. Bastable also had semis in The Grove on 25 ft. by 160 ft. plots at £600 freehold. In The Drive, W. Bristow's 'Quaint Houses', with four bedrooms, and halls with fireplace, sold at £550 upwards in 1909.

As the warclouds gathered in the hot summer of 1914, activity was still intense, 'All round we see the builder going forward; wood, stone, sand and other materials on the roads in transit until one can compare the Hendon of today with a city that has practically been destroyed and is being reconstructed.'

Haymills were starting their 300-house Decoy Estate, served by a new road from Golders Green to Bell Lane, and at the main entrance, a principal of the firm, H. A. Bernstein, was having a large villa built for himself in a setting of terraced gardens. Owers was 'raising up crescents' on the Golders Green Manor Estate, whilst in Garrick and Ambrose Avenues, E. Wright sought permission for 59 houses, 5 to have motor garages.

No overall plan had been laid down for Golders Green, nor was there any local authority control beyond the usual requirements regarding road widths, drainage, and conformance to the basic building byelaws. Street layout was very largely determined by the desire to pack in as many houses as possible and by the pattern of land ownership. Little regard was paid towards amenity or convenience, many roads leading to nowhere in particular, often ending quite abruptly at the boundary of the land and ignoring obvious links (as at Wentworth Road and Leeside Crescent and the series of 'Gardens' running from the Finchley Road to dead ends against the Hampstead Garden Suburb boundary). Plot sizes were small owing to the high cost of the land, and although the overall effect was decidedly less dreary than at Ilford, there was little sense of space, no reminders of the fields and hedgerows so recently overwhelmed, no large areas left for recreation. Most of the mistakes and omissions of Golders Green were to be repeated many times over in the new suburbs that were to come after 1920.

Living Together in the Garden Suburb

Close by the speculators' paradise of Golders Green, and in high contrast to it, was the Hampstead Garden Suburb (so-called, but in fact entirely inside the Hendon Council's boundaries). Established through the inspired efforts of the social reformer Henrietta Barnett,[1] the Suburb was a planners' arcadia with many laudable objectives, not all of which were fulfilled in practice.

When the underground railway to Golders Green was under construction, a station was proposed at the Hendon–Hampstead boundary, on the site of Wylde's Farmhouse, and the general expectation was that the land immediately to the north of Hampstead Heath would quickly succumb to the builder.[2] Henrietta, who rested from her East End social labours in a cottage on the Heath, was active in a successful campaign to prevent this development and rescue the land as an open space. Whilst this was going on, she conceived a plan for a new community to be established around and to the north of the new recreation area. She knew Ebenezer Howard, and had been much influenced by his Garden City Movement and the success of the earlier garden villages at Bedford Park, Port Sunlight and Bournville. Her idea was for a landscaped settlement of houses, cottages and flats, each with a garden, where all classes, from the artisan to the upper middle 'would live together under the right conditions of beauty or space'. Or, as Alfred Lyttleton later interpreted, a place where 'the poor shall teach the rich, and in which the rich, let us hope, shall help the poor to help themselves'. It was all a little muddled in conception but fiercely idealistic and blue-eyed.

Assiduously lecturing and pamphleteering, Henrietta eventually raised enough capital to see the Hampstead Garden Suburb Trust safely launched in March 1906. Negotiations with the freeholder, the Eton College Trustees, started at once, and in May the following year the Trust bought 243 acres for £112,000. The very next day, Henrietta was in a field turning a ceremonial first sod, and six months after that, a thousand men were at work, their number

[1] 1851–1936: born Henrietta Octavia Rowland, of wealthy parents. She became interested in social work in the East End of London through the property management movement of Octavia Hill. Her husband, Samuel Barnett, was appointed vicar of St Jude, Whitechapel in 1873 and she assisted his social work in Stepney, where they founded Toynbee Hall. Mrs Barnett was made Dame of the British Empire in 1924.

[2] Although partially constructed below ground, this station was never opened. See Alan A. Jackson and D. F. Croome, Rails Through the Clay (Allen & Unwin, 1964).

including 400 navvies, whose spiritual welfare was watched over by a representative of the Navvies' Missionary Society. Down came the old wooden tower used for pigeon shooting, and the rabbits, hares and pheasants of the woods and farmland retreated north-wards. During October 1907, the first two cottages were completed near Asmons Hill.

On the original plan, the most expensive houses, costing up to £3,500 leasehold, were to be grouped around the newly acquired Hampstead Heath Extension, at the southern end of the site, whilst the middle value ones, from £425 upwards were to be placed at the western end of the land. Revenue from ground rents of these houses was intended to subsidise the ground rents of 70 acres of workmen's cottages to the north, to be erected by Hampstead Tenants' Ltd, operating on co-partnership principles.[1] A portion of the overall revenue was allocated to upkeep and amenity of the estate.

The democratic intentions of the Trust were evident in the first published plan (March 1906), which showed a hostel for 'Working Lads' and 'barns' for 'tools' and 'coster barrows'. But despite the 2d return workmen's fare from Golders Green station to central London, costermongers and working lads were never a very obvious element in the Suburb. In 1912 only 166 of the thousand or so flats and houses by then completed were let at rents less than 10s a week (although the Trust did have another 131 flats let to its own work-men at 3s 3d to 5s 9d a week). Any members of the hoi polloi who did venture into the Suburb soon departed. Its convenient location, the enhanced environment jealously maintained, and the nucleus of distinguished residents, steadily pushed house prices and rents well out of the reach of the lower orders. Nowadays the accommodation originally intended for artisans and workmen sells or lets at levels beyond the resources of wage earners, or at any rate beyond the proportion of income they are prepared to allocate to housing.

Protected by its own legislation, the Trust was able to limit in perpetuity the number of houses to be built and to over-ride Hendon UDC byelaws which forbade cul-de-sacs and streets less than 50 feet wide. Its passage through parliament eased by an undertaking that the overall density would not exceed 8 houses to the acre, the Garden Suburb Act enabled architect Raymond Unwin to indulge his theory that T-shaped closes and cul-de-sacs, and blocks of houses grouped around little 'commons' were a more economical and more spacious form of layout than an extravagant

[1] See Appendix 5.

number of byelaw streets set in rows. Unwin tried to create an atmosphere of safety and enclosure, and his road system for the Suburb was designed for internal movement rather than through traffic. Unfortunately, his concept was sadly wrecked in the northern part of the Suburb, torn open in 1928 by the construction of the Hendon By-Pass (Falloden Way), to become soon enough the scene of many fatal accidents.

Unwin was assisted in drawing up the general plan by his fellow architect Barry Parker, who had worked with him on the layout of Letchworth, the first garden city, from 1903 onwards. From his house at Wylde's Farm, Unwin acted as resident partner and supervising architect until 1914. Purchasers of plots in the Suburb were allowed to employ their own architects, but designs had to conform with the general scheme, the objectives of which were to retain an open setting, to maintain as close a harmony with nature as possible and to create a mood of rural peace and security. Groupings and rooflines were most rigidly controlled, special care being taken to produce a satisfying blend of roofing materials and roofscapes. As no boundary walls or fences were allowed, the divisions between properties were marked by hedges, which extended through to the front gardens after Mrs Barnett had found the American open front system not to her liking. Many of the houses and flats built in the years up to 1915 were designed by Unwin; other architects working in the Suburb during this period were Edward Lutyens, M. H. Baillie Scott, C. Cowles Voysey, Geoffrey Lucas and W. Curtis Green.

Lutyens also contributed some of the larger buildings, notably those in the Central Square. Here, at the summit of the site, were the Anglican church of St Jude on the Hill, the Free Church, the Institute, and two schools, all of them rather too large and monumental to harmonise successfully with the small quiet houses they served. The Square itself emerged sedate and lifeless, all emphasis on soul and intellect; there were no shops, bars, restaurants or places of entertainment to give it attractive power as a true centre of the Suburb's life. Access to the tube station, the natural hub of Golders Green, was devious from most parts of the Suburb, and the road system looked towards Temple Fortune, a place of little significance, especially in the early days.

Building in the first five years was concentrated in the northern section between Temple Fortune Lane and Asmons Hill. Over a thousand houses and flats, accommodating some 5,000 people, were finished by the summer of 1912, and further land had been acquired, bringing the total area to 652 acres (later additions brought the Suburb to almost 800 acres). As well as the larger buildings already mentioned, a Club House was built at Willifield Green, and the Orchard, 'a Quadrangle for the aged and lame', was completed to the designs of Unwin in 1909. The Club House (Parker and Unwin), provided in 1909–10 by Hampstead Tenants Ltd, contained a 'tea and games' room, accommodating over 200, a reading-room, a smoking-room and ladies' rooms. Baillie Scott's Waterlow Court, 50 flats for 'working women', was finished in July 1909, but the Quadrangle planned for blind people was never built. There were no shops anywhere until a small block was completed in 1910 on the western fringes, at Temple Fortune. Within the boundaries of the Suburb, public transport was lacking (the road design was hardly conducive to bus or tram operation), but those walking to reach it had the consolation of passing some of the 33 open spaces and tennis courts.

There was an active social life of a sort from the earliest days. A dramatic society was quickly in operation, holding its rehearsals in a builder's hut in Hampstead Way. In September 1910, the society put on an open-air play, *The Masque of Fairthorpe*, in which the residents portrayed the Spirits of the Fields in state of alarm at the imminent arrival of Jerry Builder, who threatened to despoil the beauty of their surroundings but Templar came to their assistance, driving away the intruder with his sword. Fairies, Leaves, and Flowers then revelled in their restored freedom.

Such simple delights did little to appease the grumbling of the malcontents. In December 1913 a man in Addison Way was complaining that the new houses there had four or five living-rooms and a boxroom, 'accommodation of the most meagre description' for which he was obliged to pay the 'exorbitant rental' of some £50 a year plus excessive local rates. But this was the least of his worries. Shortly after moving to his new house in the previous summer, he and other residents were 'astonished to hear in the rear of our gardens unearthly yellings and screamings'. Investigations revealed that the hubub arose from two charitable institutions erected by the Trust, one a Home for Boys (for the Hendon Workhouse), the other a Salvation Army Shelter for Destitute Girls. 'The unearthly noises continued all through the summer months unchecked . . . the boys seemed to be possessed of incredible lung power and frequently made use of their sanitary dustbins to swell their vocal efforts'. There were then no jet aircraft to swamp all ground noise at frequent intervals, so the poor fellow lacked even the solace of variety. Strangely ignorant of the Suburb's origins, he ended his lament:

'an extraordinary feature of this lucrative property is that it is managed by a benevolent old lady, the widow of a clergyman, who seems obsessed with the idea that the residents should be grateful to be placed in such close touch with these rescue homes, although paying more than an economic rent for their holdings.'[1]

Colonisers of Golders Green

Our friend was perhaps untypical of the Suburb's residents. Most of them were middle-class intellectuals, professionals with artistic and cultural leanings, commercially successful artists and writers, liberal or even socialist in their political outlook. In contrast, those of Golders Green itself, with incomes at much the same level, were more likely to be businessmen, managers, and other senior white collars, Tories almost to a man. Some theatrical people found Golders Green a convenient place to live; prominent among them was Marie Lloyd, who moved into a large white house built for her by Edward Streather at the corner of Wentworth and Finchley Roads.

The high price of property and the character of the new suburbanites quickly earned the area a reputation for petit-bourgeois snobbery which stayed with it well into the thirties; a 1922 Royal Commissioner was moved to remark 'there are very superior people in Golders Green',[2] and the suburb frequently featured in music hall and radio humour. Few of the houses were large enough to accommodate servants, but many families hired a maid, making sure that she was in attendance at least for the evening meal, which would be taken at the front of the house, with curtains drawn well back and lights blazing.

Among the early arrivals were a few Jews, who, having amassed enough capital to secure a comfortable suburban home, found Golders Green convenient for their London workplaces, and not too remote from the established outposts of Jewish settlement at

[1] HFT 5 December 1913.
[2] RCLG, evidence, 26 April 1922.

Hampstead and St Johns Wood.[1] These early settlers were soon joined by others, and in 1913 the first Festivals were held in a house in West Heath Drive. Two years later, when it was estimated that there were some 300 Jewish families in the area, it was decided to establish religious classes and prepare for a synagogue. The first section of the synagogue was consecrated in 1922, making further Jewish settlement certain.[2] A strong community was established in Golders Green and Hendon during the twenties, continuing to grow, and pushing further outwards to Edgware in the next decade. Many of the Jews fleeing from the Hitler regime in Europe found their way to these areas of London after 1933, so much so that in October 1939, it was estimated that there were over 14,000 aliens in the Metropolitan Police 'S' Division (covering Hampstead, Golders Green, Edgware, Hendon and Mill Hill), almost a quarter of the entire alien population of Great Britain at that time.

Transport Facilities Built Up
As the new houses were occupied, the Underground service was improved. The twelve-minute interval of 1907 became ten minutes in the following year. A three-minute peak hour service was introduced in 1909 with the opening of the electric tramway to Finchley. From 114 trains each way daily at the beginning, the number operated grew to 318 at the end of 1910. A special 'Theatre Express' was started on 11 October 1909, leaving Leicester Square at 11.24 p.m., passing several stations on the way, and reaching Golders Green in fifteen minutes. There an electric tramcar was waiting outside the station to take the theatregoers home to Temple Fortune and Finchley, whilst for those who lived in central Hendon, there was a three-horse bus. By 1912 Golders Green residents could stay in town very late; in February that year the last departure was advanced to 1.4 a.m. from Charing Cross, connecting with the last trains on the Bakerloo and Piccadilly lines. At the beginning of the twenties, Golders Green was the fifth busiest station on the whole Underground system, with 35,000 passengers on an ordinary weekday, or about one million each month.

[1] The pattern of Jewish middle class settlement along the easy transport routes to places of business in the City and East End, notably in linear form outwards through north and north-west London, is carefully examined in Dr Vivian D. Lipman's paper, *The Rise of Jewish Suburbia*, (Transactions, XXI, Jewish Historical Society of England).
[2] The Rev. I. Livingstone, *History of Golders Green Synagogue* (1947).

Before the railway came, Birch Brothers worked a half-hourly horse-bus between Tally Ho Corner, Finchley and Oxford Circus, via Golders Green, whilst the Atlas and Waterloo Association had an hourly bus between Hendon and Oxford Circus via the crossroads, 'the prettiest omnibus route in London'.[1] The second route was closed as unremunerative on 29 September 1906, replaced by another operator's shuttle service to and from Childs Hill, where a London bus was available. After the tube railway had opened, the Underground Company sponsored a Birch Brothers motorbus between the station and Hendon (The Bell), running every twelve minutes in the rush hours and every twenty-four at other times. This service, which operated with through tickets to and from stations of the Underground, started on 28 July 1907, and when the motor vehicles proved unreliable, a fifteen-minute horse-bus service was substituted (from 1 December).[2] A request in 1908 that it be extended further into Hendon met with a refusal accompanied by the information that the average loading was only 30 per cent of capacity.

The General entered the area in October 1909 with a motorbus service operated on behalf of the Underground between the station and Finchley. LGOC's service proper started on 30 March 1911 with an extension on route 13 (London Bridge–Childs Hill) via Golders Green to Hendon (The Bell), worked every five minutes with 'the new silent B-type bus'. This duplicated the Underground's horse-buses to the station which were accordingly withdrawn on 31 August. With the entry of the General into the Underground group in 1912, Golders Green station received further bus services. Before that year was out, 2 and 28 were extended to the station from Childs Hill and West Hampstead, providing service to Victoria and Wandsworth Bridge; a new route 83 was started between Golders Green station and West Hendon (Station Road) via Hendon village, and the long route 84 (Golders Green station–St Albans), which began as a Sunday service in August, became a half-hourly daily working from 9 December.

To accommodate the growth of bus traffic at the station, the forecourt was widened in 1913 to form a bus station, with queue positions for the various services. Three years later, the suburb was served by seven General routes.

[1] H. C. Moore, *Omnibuses and Cabs* (1902).
[2] London Underground Railways Joint Circular No. 20, 26 July 1907 and HFT 22 November 1907, 6 December 1907.

Electric tramcar operation started on 17 December 1909 with the MET service along the Finchley Road to Finchley, Tally Ho. This went south to make connection with the MET western system at Edgware Road, Cricklewood, on 21 February 1910.

These transport improvements, the lifelines of the new suburb, were something of a revolution for the older residents of the area. Towards the end of 1912, an editorial note in the *Hendon and Finchley Times*, describing a fifty-minute journey on a 5d through ticket from the Elephant and Castle in south London to Hendon, with not more than three minutes spent waiting in the open, made the point that a similar journey a few years previously would have taken two hours at almost three times the cost.

One of the transport newcomers proved a mixed blessing. Unlike the tramway undertakings, motorbus operators had no obligation to repair the roads they used, and the rapid increase in bus services soon had its effect. In the financial year 1912-13, Hendon Council's road estimates were exceeded by a rate of almost 2d in the £, all of it attributable to 'excessive motor omnibus traffic', principally on the road from Hendon to Golders Green. After several years of patching up the bus-torn macadam, wood paving was eventually laid in 1914, at a charge to the ratepayers of £28,000. The road was then carrying an average of 631 solid-tyred buses daily. The *Hendon and Finchley Times* asked angrily why 'private adventurers for money making purposes' should add £5,000 to £10,000 a year to the cost of this road and 'get off free'. Nor was this all. At night, life in the still rural village of Hendon[1] was at this time made miserable by the opening of a garage for the new buses on the site of Ravensfield Manor. Returning up the hill around midnight and setting off again before dawn, the 'new, silent B-types' created a din to which the ears of Hendon's favoured residents were quite unaccustomed. A K.C. called Romer made much of the motorbuses' impact on Hendon when seeking an injunction in February 1914 in respect of noise and nuisance at the garage:

'Having finished their foul work in the streets, the motor omnibuses return to the garage at night . . . a good deal of shunting is necessary before they find a resting place. The omnibuses frequently suffer from some sort of indisposition and will be carried

[1] At the close of 1907 Hendon had no telephones, electricity or full-time fire brigade.

to the dock for the disease to be diagnosed, and if possible cured. I do not know what is done whilst First Aid is administered, but an appalling noise is made. I suppose that the motor, when put into the hands of the doctor, has to take a deep breath and count ninety nine (laughter). There is much hammering and shouting, and rags are burnt. . . .'[1]

The garage, which had opened on 3 March 1913, and was extended in the following year, accommodated 100 buses, served by 400 drivers and about 50 greasers and washers. Staff amenities, good for the period, included a canteen, and billiard, concert and reading-rooms.

Bus crews whose journeys terminated at Golders Green station were less fortunate. There were no refreshment facilities for them, or for the railwaymen, both were 'famishing in a land of plenty. Golders Green is too aristocratic or too aesthetic to provide a coffee house for the worker'. (Note the careful distinction, in this remark by the local paper, between the residents of Golders Green and those of the Suburb). The need for some facilities of this kind was increased when a six-cab rank was established outside the station on 27 October 1913.

Completing the Suburb

Amenities of various kinds quickly followed the houses. The first part of what was to become a monumental series of shopping parades was ready in 1908. Post Office facilities and the first branch of a joint stock bank (Parr's) arrived in the next year together with Sainsbury's, who found trade so slack at first that they closed promptly at 4 p.m. each day.[2] A second block of shops and flats was finished in 1911, the year which saw the old-established drapers of Broadhead and Co. sufficiently confident in the future of the new suburb to remove themselves bodily from Camden Town to the Promenade, as the shopping centre was now called.

Anglican worship started in September 1909 when 150 seats and hassocks were ready in what was eventually to be the parish hall of St Alban's Church, near the station, in North End Road, but the church itself was not completed until 1933. In the Garden Suburb, after some use of a builders' hut, the Anglicans dedicated the Lady

---

[1] HFT 13 February 1914.
[2] Sainsbury's advertisement, *Daily Telegraph*, 19 April 1969.

Chapel of St Jude on 27 October 1910, the complete church opening three years later. The nearby Free Church came into use on 25 October 1911. At St Michael's, Golders Green Road, worship started in a temporary 'iron church' of 200 places in October 1910. The building was destined to serve for some fifteen years; the present church of 750 places was consecrated in February 1914 and enlarged ten years later.

Covenants imposed by the Ecclesiastical Commissioners forbade the sale of alcoholic drink unless it was part of a meal, so the new suburb had no pub. Other relaxations were well served. Golders Green's first cinema, the Ionic, opened on 1 May 1913 by the ballet dancer Madame Pavlova (a local resident), was designed and built by William James King, a Hendon builder and councillor. In Finchley Road, just south of the station, and still open at the time of writing, the Ionic derived its name from the style of its elevations, executed in Monk's Park Stone. A related theme was used in the 700-seat auditorium, which had a double roof and was heated by gas. Wall panels by Wilfrid Walker depicted Grecian and Italian lake scenery, also the Borghese Gardens. The foyer was in 'Adams style', with draperies of Rose du Barri tint, and the 'patrons' walked over a Turkish carpet to their Rose du Barri corded velvet seats. Surprisingly, all this splendour cost King only £3,518 to assemble, but when his takings flattened out to a mere £50 a week a few months after opening, he successfully obtained a substantial reduction in the rate assessment.

Grander by far was the £50,000 Golders Green Hippodrome, next to the station. Bertie Crewe gave this a 'modern English Renaissance' exterior and an internal theme of 'French neo-grec'. Built by F. G. Minter of Putney, the theatre was opened to the public on Boxing Day 1913. From an entrance hall with panelled walls and ceiling and marble mosaic floor, wide marble staircases led to the fauteuils and grand circle. The 90-foot-wide stage, with one of the largest proscenium openings in London, (40 feet wide by 30 feet high) was built over a 20,000-gallon water tank. Under the coppered dome, the 3500 seats were priced at 3d to 7s 6d for twice-nightly performances which featured music hall and a film show. On Sundays, the entertainment was films, accompanied by 'full grand orchestra', much to the annoyance of the Middlesex County Council, who discussed taking legal action against the licensees for desecration of the Sabbath.

There was no school in the main part of Golders Green until

the completion of the 1,000-place Wessex Gardens primary in 1914–15, but a 900-place infants and elementary school was established in the Garden Suburb early in 1913 when the children moved over from classes which had been accommodated in the Institute. Situated in Child's Way, the new school was a £16,000 single-storey building by W. G. Wilson, which included cookery, laundry and manual training centres. A few months after it had opened, the Hendon Council's health statistics recorded that Garden Suburb boys were three-quarters to one inch taller than the average elsewhere in the district, a characteristic no doubt attributable more to the middle-class origins of the parents than to the healthy air of the Hampstead ridge. Secondary education facilities arrived with the opening of a County School for boys and girls in September 1914. This handsome £22,000 building by H. G. Crothall, with its tiled roof, purple-grey bricks and red brick and stone dressings, stood in 6 acres of playing fields off Golders Rise, on the site of Hendon House.

Not long after the opening of the tube station there had been calls for more police 'to curb the unruly crowd which assembles there'. But this problem was only apparent at holiday times and weekends, and Scotland Yard did not deem it necessary to provide a permanent police station until 1916, when the building at Temple Fortune was completed. To cope with the increasing business from the new area, a Petty Sessional and Children's Court House was provided at The Hyde, Hendon in December 1913, replacing the Edgware Court, which had operated since the sixteenth century.

Hendon's volunteer fire-brigade, a 'retained' brigade since 1895, achieved full-time status in 1907. A Merryweather motor fire-engine with a 50 ft. telescopic ladder was purchased in June 1914, to operate from a new £7,000 fire station in the Burroughs, Hendon, alerted by 24 street alarms. This sufficed for the entire urban district of 8,382 acres until 1929.

Among the many problems faced by the Hendon UDC was that of providing adequate sewage disposal facilities for the expanding population at Golders Green. Connection to the LCC's main drainage system proved too costly, as it required the construction of a 4½-mile tunnel under Hampstead Heath. Instead, in 1911, the council resolved to embark on their own project, purchasing 200 acres in the Brent Valley, north-west of Golders Green, for expansion of their existing works. Interrupted by the war, the £50,000 scheme was finally completed in 1922. After precipitation and double filtration the effluent of the new suburb was discharged into the once pretty river Brent.[1]

As the new district filled up, eyes were turned northwards towards central Hendon and the land between, which it was expected would soon be served by an extension of the Underground railway towards Edgware. After the passing of the deviation bill for this railway in 1911, there was a renewal of activity. In 1912 5 acres of land near the proposed Hendon Central station changed hands and plans were passed by the council for a £50,000 crescent of 45 shops to be built there. But although some £40,000 was spent in acquiring land for the railway, and the Underground Company had new houses built to replace those which stood in its path, the necessary capital for the work could not be raised. Hendon had to wait until the early 1920s for its tube, when financing would be facilitated by the government's desire to create work for a large army of unemployed.

In contrast to the eager activity of the private sector, Hendon Council's own building efforts were unimpressive, emerging in 1914 after almost twenty years of discussion. Some of the delay was attributable to the difficulty of finding suitable land at a price the council could afford. In 1903, when one councillor was describing housing at Childs Hill as a 'disgrace to civilisation', it was declared that if more than £500 an acre had to be paid, the scheme would be a burden on the rates. Eventually completed in 1915, the 50 houses on the Childs Hill allotment gardens, together with land, cost the council £9,960. They were let at rents of 8s and 9s 6d a week.

By the end of 1914, Golders Green and the Garden Suburb were firmly established communities, although by no means completely filled up. The rapid growth of Golders Green around a new railway facility efficiently fed by frequent road services set a pattern for many of the new London suburbs which were to follow after the war, districts whose street layouts and house designs were often almost unrecognisably degraded versions of those in the Edwardian section of the Garden Suburb.

[1] RCLG, evidence 14 June 1922.

Chapter 5

SOME HOMES FOR
HEROES 1919-25

'*What is our Task ? To make Britain a fit country for heroes to live in*'
In the years immediately following World War I, housing assumed
importance as a political issue, and these words, spoken by Lloyd
George at Wolverhampton in November 1918, quickly became
translated to an election slogan: *Homes fit for Heroes.*

During the war, building workers had been drained away into
the fighting forces or emergency work, and materials had become
scarce, or even unobtainable. After the middle of 1915, there was
almost no new residential construction in the London area for
nearly five years, apart from government schemes for housing war
workers at Woolwich and Kingsbury.[1] This freeze, combined with
higher wages and concentration of workers in areas of war production, quickly forced up rents, so much so that in some places public
resentment threatened to erupt into civil disorder. An anxious
government responded by pegging the rents of smaller houses at
the 1914 level, a decision easier to make than it was to undo.[2]

Although we have noticed some change in the general trend in
the London area before 1914, private house building up to this time

[1] The Housing Act of August 1914 gave the Local Government Board and the
Commissioners of Works powers to buy land and provide houses for those
employed by or on behalf of the government. An Order of March 1915 under the
Defence of the Realm Act allowed the government to take possession of land for
housing purposes. In London, the largest scheme was the Well Hall Estate at
Eltham (on the tram and bus route to Woolwich) where over 1,000 houses and
flats were built on 96 acres in ten months of 1915 to accommodate workers at
Woolwich Arsenal and neighbouring war factories. A large number of temporary
bungalows ('hutments') was also erected in the Woolwich area. At Stag Lane,
Kingsbury, 250 houses and flats were provided for workers at the nearby aircraft
factories, which dated from 1916. Their tenants were brought from Scotland,
Lancashire and the Midlands, and the scheme, designed by Sir Frank Baines,
was completed between 1917 and 1919.
[2] Rent and Mortgage Interest (War Restrictions) Act, 1915. (Mortgage interest
was restricted to protect the landlords who had borrowed capital to purchase
houses for letting).

had in the main been restricted to properties for renting. The incentive motivating developers and builders lay in the profits they could secure by covering parcels of relatively cheap land on the suburban fringe, using capital provided by building societies, landowners, trust funds and banks, and selling the houses as an investment ('as safe as houses'). The money thus obtained was used to finance further developments. At the end of the war, with materials and labour at a premium, with interest rates at a high level, and with higher standards of amenity demanded, it cost four or more times as much to build a small house as it had in 1914. Thus the economic rent was not only beyond the reach of those for whom it was designed, but would compare most unfavourably with the controlled rents charged for existing properties. In this situation investors deserted the housing market.

The decline in housebuilding during the years leading up to 1914, the virtual suspension of all construction during the war and the collapse of the small property investment market were not the only aspects of the post-war problem. Demand for small houses had increased enormously. Ever since the last years of the nineteenth century, the improved expectation of life, a rising marriage rate and a decline in the birth-rate had tended to swell the number of separate households and the growth of this factor was now outpacing that of the population. In the emotional hothouse of wartime and the subsequent demobilisation the number of marriages accelerated and the average age of marriage fell. The increased familiarity with contraceptives occurring in wartime conditions may have played some part in sustaining the shrinkage of family size already apparent before 1914. A conservative estimate made by Marian Bowley[1] was that in the immediate post-war years the housing deficit in England and Wales was between 600,000 and 800,000, mostly in small property for the lower income groups.

Those few builders able to secure adequate financial backing faced many difficulties. Thousands of skilled workers had been killed or maimed in the war, whilst others were still trapped in the fighting services (demobilisation was not completed until 1920). Such men as could be found required higher wages for a shorter working week; bricklayers, for example, were receiving an average wage in 1920 of £5 0 7d compared with £2 2s 10d in 1914. Trade had been dislocated, and materials, ruthlessly devoured in the

[1] Marian Bowley, *Housing and the State 1919-44* (Allen & Unwin, 1945).

gross appetites of war, were in short supply at inflated prices. By the autumn of 1920 wholesale prices of building materials were three times the 1913 level. As always in such situations there were some who found a way; the author of a 1920 book about East Ham recorded the building of a number of cinemas, 'where the material comes from is a mystery, for the local builders and merchants are unable to procure but a very small supply'.[1]

In April 1919, an editorial entitled *Have You Seen That House?*, in the London *Evening News* referred to the wide feeling of uncertainty and the coyness of once enterprising housebuilders, who now preferred to hang back until the level of prices and the supply of labour returned to a more normal state. A year later the same paper published a photograph of a woman patrolling the pavements of Oxford Street bearing the message on her back 'House Wanted. If you know of one, please stop me.'

Land, at any rate, presented no problems. Around London many cheap building sites were on offer as soon as the war was over. Agriculture was in a depressed state and many acres once devoted to the needs of London's vanished army of horses now lay idle. Some ex-servicemen, heady with postwar euphoria, used their gratuities to buy smallholdings in Essex and Kent, erecting surplus army huts as living accommodation. Others invested their wartime savings in plots of land and waited for building prices to fall. 'Choice Woodland Sites' within a mile of Dorking station were advertised at £40 an acre freehold in the summer of 1922, whilst at nearby Great Bookham a 300-square-yard plot 'off the clay' could be had for a mere £12 in 1921. Nearer London, the Monks Orchard Estate at Croydon was sold off in the latter year for £100 an acre.

Even before the war had ended, the seriousness of the housing problem, with its underlying threat of social unrest, had been appreciated in Whitehall. A circular of July 1917 called upon local authorities to prepare schemes for housing the 'working classes', promising assistance from the Exchequer. This was followed in March 1918 by another which advised a maximum density of 12 houses to the acre in urban areas and mentioned that a study of construction and design standards had been commissioned from Sir Tudor Walters. Housing was to become a social service as those in power saw the necessity of legislation on a national scale, changing the voluntary basis of local authority provision to an obligation.

[1] Alfred Stokes, *East Ham* (1920).

Houses by Act of Parliament

Dr Christopher Addison, Minister of Health in the Tory-dominated coalition government, introduced a Housing and Town Planning Act in 1919 which placed the responsibility for supplying low-rent housing firmly upon the shoulders of the local authorities, who were encouraged by a guarantee that any loss above a penny rate would be met by the Exchequer, an open-ended arrangement soon to be regretted. Rents were to be fixed according to capacity to pay, the highest not be substantially above the controlled rent level, certainly nowhere near enough to be economic. All plans were to be approved by the Ministry of Health which had assumed the responsibilities of the now defunct Local Government Board, and the Tudor Walters' standards, not least the inclusion of baths, were obligatory. In practice the central government made little or no attempt to control the extravagance of the feather-bedded local authorities, the overriding objective being to obtain the maximum number of new houses in the shortest possible time. As we shall find later, such matters as the inadequacy of public transport facilities and the local building byelaws were swept under the carpet in the rush to build.

Virtually free of financial restraints, the councils pressed ahead with great enthusiasm, building over 60 per cent of the total of new housing provision in 1919–22 compared with under 6 per cent before the war. During 1922, the London local authorities erected more houses than in any other year up to 1939 with the exception of 1927 and 1928, their output reaching nearly three times that of private firms. So intense was the activity that there was soon some concern at the drain on the Exchequer, and in June 1921, it was decided to limit the number of houses subsidised to only a few more than had been built or approved at that time, 170,000 in all.

In Greater London, 34,330 houses were erected under the 1919 legislation, including the private enterprise subsidies to be mentioned in a moment. Of these 27,441 were council houses, 32 per cent of them built by the LCC. The final plans were approved in July 1921, and by 1923, as prices were falling at last, local authority building had almost dried up. Waste there undoubtedly was, but in the inflationary conditions of the period, Addison's Act had proved an effective instrument, producing a substantial contribution to the nation's housing stock.

For London, some typical experiences may be mentioned. Wandsworth's Housing Committee was set up in May 1919 in response to the request from central government that the problem merited urgent attention. Between January 1920 and May 1922, the landowners of Magdelen Park, Earlsfield, erected 376 cottages on 24 acres, all of which were purchased by the council at £1,099 and £1,013 each inclusive of land and paving charges (the cheaper ones were without a 'parlour'). A similar arrangement was made with the owners of 4¼ acres in Topsham Road Upper Tooting, (Elmwood House Estate), where 91 parlour-type houses cost the council £1,021 each from 1920 onwards. Compulsory purchase powers were invoked to secure the 42 acres of the Furzedown Estate at Tooting, where 88 cottages were built from 1920 onwards at a cost of £973 each including land and paving. Finally, at Southfields, 66 acres were acquired compulsorily from the Watney Estate, sixteen to be used for building; only 24 houses had been erected before the Ministry of Health shut off the cash flow in 1921. A conference with the ministry secured approval for a further 83 at Southfields and 60 more at Furzedown, but Whitehall later advised restriction to 20 in each case, in view of the fall in prices. This proved wise. The cost of building fell from over £500 a house in March 1922 to £378 later in the same year, when tenders for the balance came in.[1]

Hendon's 1919 Act houses at Mill Hill, with only two bedrooms, one reception room and a tiny 8 ft. 3 in. by 6 ft. 9 in. scullery cluttered with bath, copper, gas cooker, sink and draining board, cost as much as £1,100 each without land. The rent of these little cottages, whose appearance was described as 'barrack-like', was 11s 6d or 14s.

Over 8,800 houses were erected by the LCC under the Addison Act, on new estates at Dover House, Roehampton, Becontree, and Bellingham, all to be noticed later, as well as on the pre-1914 developments at Norbury, Old Oak and Tottenham. At Norbury, 218 cottages were added, bringing the estate population to some 2,600 Old Oak gained 736 houses, the finished estate eventually accommodating about 4,600. After 1919, the White Hart Lane Estate at Tottenham more than doubled in size, benefiting from the Addison and later subsidies. A further 1,266 cottages and flats were provided together with another 16 shops. By 1938 the estate had a population of just over 10,000.[2]

[1] Information from the *Wandsworth Official Guide* (1939).
[2] Details of the LCC completions mentioned are:
   Norbury: 60 three-room, 116 four-room, 42 five-room.
   Old Oak: 235 three-room, 338 four-room, 163 five-room.
   White Hart Lane: 108 two-room, 313 three-room, 596 four-room, 249 five-room.

Private Houses – at a Price

Private builders were not overlooked in the 1919 housing drive. A separate Housing (Additional Powers) Act granted lump sum subsidies to a maximum of £160 for houses of 920 feet super., (increased in 1920 to £260 for 1,400 feet super.), irrespective of whether they were for sale or rent. For reasons already suggested, private building made a slow start and there was virtually none for renting. Builders expected prices to fall much more than the amount of the subsidy and believed the period of high demand would prove short lived. A typical example of the caution shown was seen at Merton Park, where an estate purchased for building in 1920 was left untouched until 1925.

No advertisements for new houses were seen in the *Evening News* until 21 November 1919. For some while after that the choice remained very limited. These first post-war houses from private firms were beyond the reach of all but the better-off elements of the middle class, for not only were the prices artificially high, but facilities for easy purchase remained undeveloped. High bank-rates prevailing in 1920 and 1921 pushed the repayment rates up and it was normally necessary at this time to find legal charges as well as a cash deposit of as much as 20 per cent. During 1920, just under 1,500 houses were built by private enterprise in the Greater London area, only 348 more than the combined total of the local authorities.

Among the first of the districts receiving the resumed attention of the private firms was Golders Green. Late in 1919 Owers was able to announce that he would have some detached houses ready in the following March. During 1920, builders in the suburb managed 375 completions, almost as many as 1914. The total fell to 249 in the following year, rising to 420 in 1922. Houses on the Vale Estate were selling in 1920 at £1,000 (three bedrooms) and £1,250 (four bedrooms), both leasehold. In 1922 Streathers' £1,000 leasehold three-bedroom semis at Golders Green and Mill Hill required a £300 deposit and repayments of £69 6s a year for sixteen years, but £150 of the deposit could be borrowed at 5 per cent repayable over five years. To some extent these high prices also reflected the value of the land in what was now a very popular residential area. In 1922, the Metropolitan Railway were able to get £850 an acre from Messrs Haymills for the remaining 22½ acres of land they had bought many years earlier on the north bank of the Brent (the Shire Hall Estate) for a proposed branch railway to Hendon.[1]

[1] BTHR MET 1/36.

Some strange sights were seen at Golders Green at this time. Using legislation promoted to relieve unemployment,[1] the Underground Company had obtained a Treasury guarantee of interest and principal on a loan of £5m. for fifty years. The capital was raised by public issue of 4½ per cent debentures and some of it went to finance the long-planned extension from Golders Green to Hendon and Edgware. When in the summer of 1921 the engineers began to cleave a path through the suburb their own railway had germinated, semi-detached houses became detached, others disappeared, and a few more lost their ground-floor outlook as the roadway was humped up to cross the new line. In July 1922, the *Evening News* illustrated a complete staircase and a bath taken out of one of these relatively new houses and offered for resale as the walls came down.

The excellent service on the original line and its new extension combined with the drive and enterprise of the builders and developers made the district north-west of Golders Green station one of the fastest growing areas of the twenties. Between 1921 and 1925 the population of Golders Green increased from 10,500 to 13,400 and that of central Hendon from 11,880 to 15,730. When costermongers' stalls appeared in the Golders Green shopping centre on Saturday afternoons in 1925, this was taken as a sign that the district was losing its suburban status and merging into central London.

In other areas prices were just as high as at Golders Green. At Beech Avenue, Sanderstead in December 1920 a three-bedroom house required £1,200, a four-bedroom one £1,350, and both prices were net of the government subsidy. New houses were also to be found for sale at this time (1920–22) in Mill Hill, Sudbury, Wembley Park, Potters Bar, Enfield and Croydon, almost all on developments started before August 1914. During 1921, 3,231 privately built houses were completed in the Greater London area, rather less than one third the inflated 1919 Act output of the local councils. 1922 figures were 4,860 private, 12,047 council.

Almost the only place around London where a relatively cheap house could be had in the immediate postwar period was in the first garden city, but as Letchworth was 34½ miles from Kings Cross, just about the only workers to benefit from this were the railway clerks and officials, who enjoyed concessionary travel to work. A small colony of them formed there during 1919–21.

Wages and material prices began to drop at last in the summer of

[1] Trade Facilities Act, 1921.

5. Edwardian solidity at Fox Lane, Palmers Green, c. 1907. (From a commercial postcard by E. F. Tournier.)

The new style emerges: Dalmeny Road, Carshalton, soon after completion, c. 1909. (From a commercial postcard, Staines Photo Series.)

6. Villas across the hills: Furze Lane, Purley c. 1910. (From a commercial postcard by W. H. Burdekin.)

Transitional styles: Grigg houses of c. 1907 in Ranelagh Gardens, Ilford. (Photo: Alan A. Jackson.)

1920. The fall continued, bringing the cost per foot super. down from just over £1 in early 1920 to 9s 4d in 1922. July of the latter year saw bank rate returning to its early 1914 level of 3 per cent (it had reached seven in April 1920). The Ministry of Health's Reports revealed that the cost of the standard 'non-parlour' three-bedroom house had fallen from £930 in August 1920 to £436 in March 1922.

More Legislation

Bonar Law's Conservative administration resumed subsidies on a more prudent scale in the Housing etc. Act, 1923. On the assumption that if private building were encouraged it would become possible to relax rent control,[1] this government offered payments to private enterprise, witholding them from local authorities unless they were able to satisfy the minister that private activity in their area was inadequate. To qualify for the subsidy of £6 a year for twenty years (or lump sum of £75) the house had to be within 620–950 feet super., with fixed bath, and completed by 1 October 1925. Builders received their cash in lump sums from the local authorities, who claimed back annually from the Treasury.

A provision of the 1923 Act giving local authorities power to guarantee payments by house purchasers to building societies stimulated the construction of large numbers of unsubsidised private houses. Under the arrangement, the Halifax Building Society, for example, were able to advance 90 per cent of their surveyor's valuation instead of the normal 75 per cent, and the interest on such a mortgage would be 5 per cent over a twenty-two-year repayment period.[2] Leading insurance companies also began to guarantee building societies by offering single premium policies to house purchasers. But these measures were of benefit only to the better-off white-collar class and the middle class, for even with the easier purchase terms, the prices of privately built houses remained beyond the reach of the lower income groups. Some 46,000 subsidised houses were completed in the Greater London area under the 1923 Act, 28,216 of them by private firms, almost all for sale.

[1] Rent control was removed on change of tenancy by another Act of 1923, but apart from this, it continued for many more years. Acts of 1933 and 1938 excluded houses above certain rateable values; in London the last left controlled rents in being for houses of £35 rateable value and below.
[2] O. R. Hobson, *A Hundred Years of the Halifax Building Society 1853–1953* (Batsford, 1953).

With the election of a Labour government the following year, the emphasis changed again. John Wheatley, the Minister of Health, put through a Housing (Financial Provisions) Act which restored in full the local authorities' powers to provide housing, extended the 1923 Act subsidies to houses completed by October 1939 and increased the Exchequer grant to £9 a year for forty years for urban area houses built by local authorities to let at restricted rents. All subsidy houses were now required to have a fixed bath in a separate room. Wheatley encouraged the productivity of the industry by persuading trade unions and employers to revise the apprenticeship rules so that more skilled men could be brought into the various building trades.

As most councils preferred to let at rents which, with the subsidy, would keep the housing account in balance, Wheatley's act, like its predecessors, produced nothing for the lower paid. But the output of 1924 Act houses was creditable: 64,000 in Greater London (37,600 by the LCC alone), plus another 2,373 assisted private enterprise houses.

It is convenient to mention here the remainder of the subsidy legislation up to 1939. When the Conservatives came back to power in 1925 they cut the 1923 and 1924 Act subsidies for all houses finished after 20 September 1927, reducing the 1924 subsidy further and abolishing the 1923 one for those completed after 30 September 1929. In the latter year the Labour Party returned, cancelling the reduction in the 1924 subsidy. The last round of musical chairs came with the Conservatives' Housing (Financial Provisions) Act of 1933 which abolished subsidies for all houses completed after 30 June 1934. Subsequent legislation concentrated on rehousing and the clearance of overcrowded areas.

Chapter 6

SPECULATORS'
SUBURBIA 1923–39

Private Building in Earnest
With the stimulus of subsidy legislation and improvements in the supply of both labour and materials, private builders were soon able to make significant advances in their output, although high prices for materials continued to inhibit activity until about 1927. Apart from other factors, costs were kept artificially high by the existence of rings in building supplies which had maximum effect whilst housebuilding remained largely in the hands of small firms. Thus until the end of the twenties average house prices were beyond the reach of people earning less than £3–£4 a week, a group containing a high proportion of those with genuine housing need.

In this first decade after the end of World War I, Greater London was attractive for estate developers. Demand was at a very high level, and still growing, and the ability to pay was above average. From February 1923, the *Evening News* was able to fill a weekly page of illustrated housing announcements, entitled 'The Homeseeker's Guide'. Before the end of the year, the selection of houses shown was already extensive. Prices ranged from £1,150 to £685, but the latter was for leasehold property in Welwyn Garden City, and the average freehold sale price was nearer £1,000. Locations advertised in September 1923 were Norbury (the most expensive houses of the month), Streatham, Coulsdon, Godstone, Addiscombe, Sanderstead, Cheam, Orpington, New Malden and East Molesey in the south, Hanwell in the west, and Welwyn Garden City, Finchley, Hendon, Mill Hill and Wembley in the north. Bungalows were much in vogue, and in the same month were advertised at prices from £975 (at Orpington) to as little as £450 and £475 for two-bedroom types at Greenford, Hillingdon, Uxbridge and Sunnymeads.

From 1923 onwards the rate of building climbed steadily, apart from temporary setbacks in 1927 and 1928, the number of privately

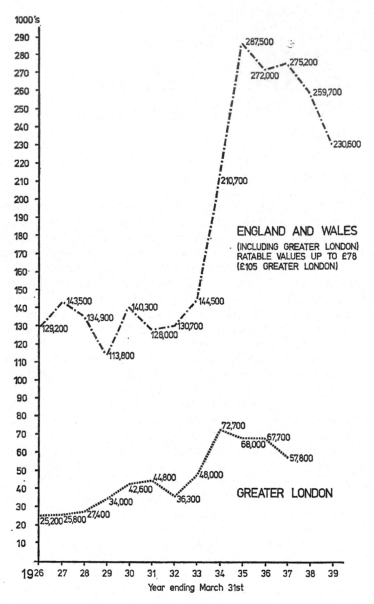

1000's

290 — 287,500
280 —
270 — 275,200
272,000
260 — 259,700
250 —
240 —
230 — 230,600
220 —
210 — 210,700
200 —
190 —
180 — ENGLAND AND WALES
170 — (INCLUDING GREATER LONDON)
RATABLE VALUES UP TO £78
160 — (£105 GREATER LONDON)
150 —
140 — 143,500
144,500
134,900 140,300
130 — 129,200 130,700
128,000
120 —
113,800
110 —
100 —
90 —
80 —
72,700
70 — 67,700
68,000
60 — 57,800
50 — 48,000
44,800
40 — 42,600
36,300 GREATER LONDON
34,000
30 —
25,200 25,800 27,400
20 —
10 —

1926 27 28 29 30 31 32 33 34 35 36 37 38 39
Year ending March 31st

I Private enterprise house construction, England and Wales,
and Greater London, 1926–39

built houses in the Greater London area increasing by an average of 6,000 or so a year, until an annual output of 34,118 was reached in 1929. In some parts of London private firms were so active that by the beginning of 1926 supply had outstripped demand; this was the case at Golders Green and Hampstead Garden Suburb, which together had 5,400 houses, more than one third of the total in the 8,382-acre Hendon Urban District, and almost all of them less than twenty years old.

In the mid and late twenties the greatest private building activity was seen at Croydon, Coulsdon and Purley, Carshalton, Beckenham, Merton and Morden, Sutton, and Wandsworth in the south, and at Ilford, Edmonton, Finchley, Harrow, Hendon and Wembley north of the river.[1] Merton and Morden UDC found themselves advancing £500,000 to 800 house purchasers in the years 1925–9.

No Depression for the Builders
Throughout the twenties a generally depressed economy, marked by a slump in the exports of the staple industries, had kept unemployment well above pre-1914 levels. Towards the end of the decade there was a sharp rise, the national total reaching 1.3m. in 1929. Against a background of world depression and financial crisis moving from America through Europe to Britain in the following three years the figure was to reach almost 3 millions. Protected by the diversity of its industries and by the high proportion of non-manufacturing occupations, London escaped the worst. From such setback as it did suffer, recovery was rapid, assisted by the continuing prosperity of the consumer durable industries, the expanding distributive trades and uninterrupted growth in service and administrative jobs. And it was the workers in these groups who placed most importance on the acquisition of good housing. Almost without exception they remained employed throughout the depression years, enjoying increased purchasing power because in general money wages remained stable in a period of falling prices. Thus the high level of demand already arising from the housing shortage and the growth in the number of households was further inflated in the London area. Then, from 1932 onwards, as the building societies introduced various measures to facilitate house purchase, demand was whipped higher still.[2]

[1] Based on an analysis of advertisements in the *Evening News*.
[2] The role of the building societies as a permissive factor in the growth of owner-occupation is considered in Chapter 11.

As demand was brought to a peak, various factors converged to increase supply. Through the twenties, the private builders had done well, but their output had been restrained by the slow fall in costs, the low level of investment and high interest rates. Now the forces required to open the dam emerged, springing directly from the economic depression and the financial crisis. Building costs which had started to decline after 1926 (pausing only briefly in 1929–30) continued to fall until they reached their between-war lowest level in 1934. Interest rates went down after 1932 with the government's introduction of a cheap money policy, whilst building trades wages remained stable, even in some cases dropping slightly. Private investors abandoned gilt-edged securities after the drop in interest rates, finding increasingly restricted opportunities for attractive investment at home and overseas. Building was to benefit, and the money flowed in. Each year from 1929 to 1938 investment in residential construction absorbed half the aggregate net figure; in 1932–33, residential investment jumped by more than 30 per cent. The switch in investment patterns also increased bank deposits, causing the banks to become more generous with loans for residential construction. To some extent additional labour became available to London builders as the younger men sought work outside the depressed areas of heavy industry. Another feature of the slump, with its high unemployment levels, was the readiness of the government to assist public transport undertakings in raising capital for new projects, such as the electrification of existing railways and the construction of new lines and stations, much of it benefiting the London area. This increased the number of readily disposable sites available to housing developers.[1]

In the Greater London area, private enterprise housing output rose from just over 34,000 in 1929 to almost 45,000 in 1931. After a brief check in the following year – aftermath of the immediate financial crisis – output climbed steeply until 1934, when nearly 73,000 houses were built, the highest total of any of the between-war years.

It would be misleading to imply that all builders in the London area enjoyed financial success in the worst years of the depression. The figures of houses built are deceptive in this respect, for if the price or situation was not right, new houses could remain unsold for a very long period. Some firms, particularly those who had special-

---

[1] The various ways in which the railways were assisted, and the development of transport facilities in the period, are dealt with in Chapter 13.

ised in higher priced property, had a hard time. W. T. Streather, an experienced builder, and his son, Cecil, found that the financial crisis and general uncertainty of 1931 caused sales in Mill Hill to drop 'almost to nothing' and cited this as a contributory factor to their bankruptcy in 1936.

As the immediate shortage was met for those able to afford a private enterprise house, the speculative builders endeavoured to sustain demand in two ways: by reducing costs and prices to attract the bottom end of the market; and by encouraging dissatisfaction among those still living in pre-1914 property. This discontent was fed by the progress of the electricity industry and the spread of new standards of domestic hygiene. For their part, the builders kept it simmering by increasing the cover and tempo of advertising. By 1930 domestic electricity was readily available all around London's outskirts, and during the nine years that followed, electric labour-saving devices, principally irons, vacuum cleaners, and cookers, poured on to the home market in quantity. Sales of electric cookers trebled between 1930 and 1935, and the 1938 sales of vacuum cleaners were double those of 1930. None of these delights was available to the housewives still living in gaslit Edwardian and Victorian inner suburban houses, mostly rented from landlords who had no incentive to install electricity. Above all, those in such houses longed for a smart bathroom, an inside w.c., and a modern kitchen. Another smaller group easily persuaded to move to the more manageable new houses were the now virtually servantless metropolitan middle class, whose women were entering outside employment in increasing numbers.

The private enterprise output of 72,756 houses in 1934, an increase of almost 25,000 on the previous year, was the peak figure for the period 1919–39 and was over 27 per cent of the total number of houses built in England and Wales that year by all organisations, public and private. During 1935 and 1936, private output in Greater London remained around 68,000, but after that, the rearmament programme began to take effect; in 1937 the figure dropped to just below 58,000 and next two years produced totals a little below that. By the end of March 1938, private firms had finished 618,571 houses in the Greater London area since the end of World War I, handsomely beating the local authorities' 153, 188.

As in the previous decade, almost all the private building was for sale and accessible only to the middle class, the white-collar group and the highest paid manual workers. By 1939 the number of houses built had more or less satisfied the demand of these groups. Between 1921 and 1937 almost 1,400,000 people had moved into outer London, the central area figure falling in the same period by almost 400,000. Centrifugal migration of this type was a feature of all the major urban areas, but showed most strongly in London. Although regional migration (from the depressed areas to London and the south) added significantly to the capital's population during the period, it did not at first provide many customers for the new suburban houses; most of the migrants were single men and women, and if families did make the move, their first London house was likely to be a rented one in the inner suburbs, quite possibly evacuated by a family moving to a new semi further out.

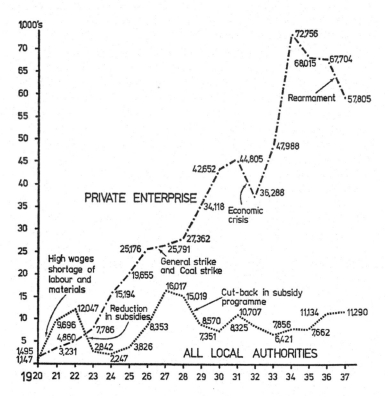

II Houses built in Greater London, 1920–37

The Providers

During the greater part of the period, the building industry in general remained poorly organised, its costs high compared with those of the new industries such as motorcar manufacture (1932 figures for product costs, taking 1914 as 100, were 180 and 88 respectively). There were very few changes either in construction methods or in the type of labour and materials used. With plentiful labour, the traditional conservatism of both builder and house buyer was encouraged and sustained.

Many small firms employed only bricklayers and concreters to fashion the shell of the house, leaving the rest of the work to craftsmen supplied by subcontractors. Both large and small firms engaged the abundant unskilled labour, much of it Irish, on a weekly or even a daily basis, and on the larger developments it was not unusual for the men to live and sleep rough in and around the site, as their navvy forebears had done in the previous century. There was also little difficulty in finding skilled labour of high standard for much of the period, although some shortages occurred in the peak years of construction, especially in areas where large numbers of firms were working in close competition. In 1931, when £108 was paid for bricking out a four-block, at Hayes, Middlesex, Taylor Woodrow could expect their bricklayers to lay at least 1,000 bricks a day, and many of the men engaged could do much better than that.[1]

In the fiercer competition of the new decade, the high profits which had been gained during the twenties from small developments near good transport facilities shrank perceptibly. At first the London building boom attracted all sorts of 'extraordinary people . . . very young and inexperienced builders' labourers . . . an ex-milkman erected several houses'.[2] Young estate agents' clerks moved into full-scale estate development with virtually no experience. A bankruptcy report of 1937 records the former occupations of two Edgware building partners as 'maker of silk ties' and 'gown manufacturer', whilst another in similar straits had been a Liverpool iron and steel merchant and haulage contractor. Soon enough such amateurs and adventurers found the going hard, likely as not ending in financial disaster. Conditions in the boom years of the late twenties and early thirties favoured the establishment and growth of larger units, and also saw the entry into the residential

1 Alan Jenkins, *On Site 1921-71* (Heinemann, 1971).
2 Letter to the Editor in TEG, 1 July 1933.

field of several firms hitherto specialising in civil engineering or general contracting. These larger firms were able to buy land in bulk, find materials in quantity in the cheapest market, maximise their sales effort and go after profits by taking a relatively small percentage on a large turnover. Capital came to them at low rates of interest and they could make production economies by using plant intensively and deploying a large labour force in the most efficient manner. They assembled technical and professional staffs so that they provided from within the organisation all the services and skills necessary to purchase, develop and sell off large building estates.

Something should be said at this point about the principal firms operating in the Greater London area between the wars, many of them names which occur elsewhere in this book. In the front rank were a group of large- or medium-sized companies active in several districts simultaneously, most of them very much alive today: Costain, Crouch, Davis, Laing, Nash, New Ideal Homesteads, Taylor Woodrow, Wates, Wimpey. Of these, Costain and Wates had been building small houses since the early twenties, and Nash had begun at Kenton about 1925. Taylor Woodrow started in Blackpool in 1921. All the others were either new, or new to residential construction, entering the field from 1929 onwards. Similarly, those large firms which restricted their building to one particular sector of the suburbs mostly dated from the late twenties or early thirties.

Pioneers of large-scale estate development in post-war London were Richard Costain and Sons Ltd, a firm originating in Liverpool. Their first venture, a high-value estate at Kingswood, opened in 1923. Every house was carefully sited on its plot in a rural-romantic environment with many trees preserved. During the next few years, with Kingswood slowly filling, Costain started new estates at Selsdon Garden Village (1925), Addington (1925), Caterham (1926), Croham Heights (1927) and Brent Water (1927). The last, on a short piece of the North Circular Road near Cricklewood opened in that year, was a fresh departure. The houses, small and low priced, were designed to attract the better paid manual worker. Other developments followed in the thirties, including two more for the lower income group, Rylandes Farm, near Dagenham (1931) and Elm Park, Hornchurch (1934). It may not have been deliberate policy, but this firm, almost alone among the major London developers, succeeded in providing for most income groups other than the low-paid workers. By 1935 they were entering new territory, opening the first part of Dolphin Square, a 7¼-acre complex of 1,250 service flats on the riverside at Chelsea, in November 1936. Beginning in a small way with bungalows at Walton-on-Thames around 1928, G. T. Crouch went on a year later to develop estates at Strawberry Hill and Sutton Common. A large number of sites, mostly south of the river, acquired in the thirties, were to be covered with small houses in a strong mock-Tudor style. By 1937 the firm was beginning to diversify, helping to construct stations on the new suburban railway between Motspur Park and Chessington.

A. F. Davis, later Davis Estates Ltd, started at Kingsbury in 1929 with two estates, soon spreading their activities all round Greater London and further afield. Some twenty sites in the London area were being advertised in 1935.

An old-established general building and civil engineering firm, John Laing and Sons, entered the speculative building field in 1930. From the beginning, their specification included cavity walls, by no means a universal feature even ten years later. Most of the Laing estates were in the north-western sector of Greater London, a choice of ten being available in 1935. Something of a speciality was made of modestly-priced three- and four-bedroom detached houses, with plain elevations of facing bricks on all four walls. Laing designs, which have aged well, were the work of Geddes Hyslop ARIBA, Arthur W. Kenyon ARIBA, Frances Barker ARIBA and others. The firm did not confine their suburban activities to housing; most of their estates were provided with shopping centres, and from 1934 onwards, at Queensbury, they included two factory estates in a large housing development, a rare contemporary example of balanced planning. This was followed by the 'industrial garden city' at Elstree, mentioned later in this chapter.

T. F. Nash were first active in the Harrow area in the twenties, building much of Rayners Lane and erecting cinemas there and at Harrow in 1936. They went on to develop sites in other parts of London, purchasing in 1937-8 large acreages at Collier Row (Romford), Hayes (Middlesex), Sevenoaks, Northolt and St Albans. Much of this ambitious enterprise, on sites often remote from public transport, was rudely interrupted by the outbreak of war.

Perhaps the most prolific of all the London developers of the thirties was New Ideal Homesteads, formed in 1929, and opening its first estate at Dartford a year later. It was founded by Leo P. Meyer, formerly assistant surveyor to the Erith UDC, and partner in the building firm of Blackwell and Meyer of Bexleyheath. Meyer tirelessly worked the fastest selling portion of the market. By 1932 he had pared down his costs so successfully that he was able to offer a three-bedroom, two-reception room semi for the remarkably low price of £395 (£295 leasehold on some estates). An agreement concluded with the Halifax Building Society in June that year enabled the company to dispose of houses for a cash advance of only 5 per cent of the sale price. Two years later, 16 estates were open around the suburbs of London. Some 5,700 houses were sold that year, nearly one twelfth of the total private sector output in Greater London. In 1936 London estates totalled 25 and remained at this figure until 1939. The carefully standardised NIH range of semis, chalets and bungalows of the thirties can be found in almost every London suburb of the period, but the main concentration was in the south-east. In addition to the basic building organisation, the firm operated subsidiaries or departments which handled house design, sales, road construction, insurance, legal work and the supply of electrical equipment.

An ambitious 25-year-old Blackpool builder named Frank Taylor decided in 1930 to try his luck in London, bringing with him his best workmen and a friendly estate agent. He selected a 120-acre site off the Uxbridge Road at Hayes for his initial venture, the Grange Park Estate. The first houses, in four-blocks, were on sale in 1931 at £445 and £550 and by April 1933, 860 houses of the planned 1,248 had been built and sold. The firm also constructed 23 shops on the main road, together with an 808-seat cinema, the Corinth, opened in August 1933. Two years later, when Taylor Woodrow became a public company with the intention of expanding into the public works field, some 6 estates were under development, mostly in west and north-west London, and there were others in the provinces.

The Wates Brothers, Norman Edward, Ronald, and Allan, expanded the building firm established by their father, Edward, in 1901. Active throughout south London in the twenties, the firm were selling on 15 estates in 1935, 20 in 1939, by which time some 30,000 houses had been built. In 1935 operations were expanded to embrace public works and general contracting.

Returning from the war in 1919, G. W. (later Sir Godfrey) Mitchell bought the Hammersmith road building firm of George Wimpey and Co., established in 1880. Large-scale estate development started with a 130-acre scheme at Ealing in 1928 after some earlier ventures by Godfrey Mitchell in a personal capacity. The Ealing estate was a success and others were begun in the next three or four years all round London. Houses on about a dozen sites were being advertised in 1935–7 and some 10,000 had been completed by 1939. During the thirties the firm's policy was to have 8 or 9 estates under construction simultaneously.[1] A virtually self-contained organisation was built up, including facilities for buying land, road and sewer construction, house design, financing of estate development and house purchase, a sales force, and a legal department. Like some of the other large firms, Wimpey were moving into civil engineering and large-scale public works contracts by the middle of the thirties.

Close behind these major enterprises were other well-known names. Although not dispersing their activities widely around the London area, these were firms which nevertheless made a substantial contribution to the housing stock. Frank H. Ayling, of Thornton Heath, working in south and south-east London, developed some 20 sites between 1927 and 1939. Henry Boot was early on the scene, with houses at Elstree in 1924, going on to open up a dozen or so estates in the thirties, mostly in west and north-west London, as well as building many cottages for the LCC. John and Sydney Cronk specialised in lower-priced blocks of houses, completing about a dozen estates south of the river after 1930. The brothers Ellis and Lawrence Berg began quietly at Sunbury-on-Thames in 1924, expanding to build about half a dozen estates in south and south-west London after 1930. At first, almost all Berg houses were either detached or very large semis, all of strongly individualistic design with imaginative touches, and Bergs were among the pioneers of the integrated garage and the hall-to-hall semi. Later on smaller semis, chalets and one or two bungalows were built on some estates. James White Comben and William Henry Wakeling sold off their Fulham grocery business and started to build in Wembley about 1913. During the twenties Comben and Wakeling worked Wembley very hard indeed, moving on to Eastcote, Hatch End, Finchley, Kingsbury, South Kenton and Greenford in the thirties. F. and C. Costin started at Harrow in 1923, restricting a substantial output to the Wembley and Harrow area. Another very prolific but highly localised builder was Albert Cutler, active in the Harrow area from 1922 and a regular advertiser in *Metro-land*.

A name even more well known today is M. J. Gleeson, who

started with some 750 semi-detached houses on the Park Farm Estate, North Cheam, about 1933, all sold at £550–£600. Another section of the market was tackled in 1937–9 on the Nonsuch Court Estate, east of Ewell village, where 400 garaged detached houses were built and sold for £980–£1,365. There were a number of other smaller developments, mostly around Ewell and Sutton.

One of the few firms able to trace their origins back to the years before 1914 was Haymills, who began at Golders Green about 1909, building mostly in Hendon and Wembley after 1920. Like some of the other large London builders, they turned to public works and general contracting in the mid-thirties, contributing to suburban development in other ways, building schools at Hendon, Ruislip and elsewhere, and the Underground station at Park Royal. A substantial contract secured in 1939 was for the erection of the Underground works and car sheds at Aldenham, on the never-to-be-completed Bushey Heath extension of the Edgware tube line.

The brothers Morrell, Cyril Herbert, and Stanley Charles, were responsible for launching several ambitious projects in south-east London in the thirties. Extensive users of the builder's pool system, they had arrangements with two large building societies, one of which was to receive wide publicity as a result of the Borders case (Chapter 11). Another well-known south-east London firm were Tysoe and Harris, who started at Addiscombe in 1923, going on to establish over a dozen estates in the following twenty years.

A good number of the better-managed small firms survived into the thirties, but there were noticeably fewer small fish in the suburban sea during the second decade. A small builder often began by putting up less than a dozen houses, using the profits obtained from these to finance a subsequent larger venture, proceeding to something larger still on the third round, and so on. Some would run too fast, having tasted initial success, falling into financial difficulties, their houses standing half finished until another firm came on the scene to complete the estate. One south London firm was brought to bankruptcy no less than three times in the thirties by trying to go ahead too fast: some of its estates were completed, some hardly begun; all were lavishly advertised.

Successful local builders often played a prominent part in the affairs of the districts they had helped to create. Griggs and Curton, mentioned elsewhere in this book, were examples of this; another was Arthur J. Reynolds, who started building at Golders Green in 1905, continuing through the twenties and thirties at Hendon and

Edgware. Elected to the Hendon UDC in 1919, he was made chairman in 1927-8 and was mayor of the new borough from 1935 to 1937. Also a Middlesex County Councillor from 1922 to 1928, he was a prominent Freemason and president of the Golders Green Conservative Association.

A Formless Suburbia

Almost without exception, the low-density housing estates provided by the building firms between 1923 and 1939 coalesced uncomfortably into new communities which were little more than haphazard accretions of residential roads around a railway station or main thoroughfare. As there was virtually no serious attempt on the part of the multifarious planning authorities to ensure that housing development was balanced with industrial or office building, many of the new areas assumed the character of dormitories from which the earning adults moved into the metropolitan core for their daily work, and to a lesser extent, for evening recreation. Thus much of the suburban growth of the interwar years contributed to daytime congestion in the central area of the capital and placed highly concentrated strains on the public transport system twice a day.

But not all the new districts were of this type; industrial development, impressive in its pace, particularly in the thirties, appeared around the sites of the war factories in west and north-west London; also along the Great Western Railway's Bristol and Birmingham main lines; at West Hendon and Wembley; along the Lee Valley; at Croydon; and at various points along the 210 miles of new arterial and bypass roads built in the London area in the twenties. Factories employing twenty-five or more workers increased by a net figure of 532 in the Greater London area during the years 1932-7, offering employment to 97,700 workers, or two fifths of all the additional employment created by the 664 factories opened in the whole of Great Britain in this period. In one year, 1934, of 478 new factories opened in Great Britain and an associated 37,200 jobs, no less than 209 with 15,750 jobs were in Greater London. Similarly of the 1,057 factories enlarged in these years, 307 were in the Greater London area.[1]

London's excellent rail and road communications with all parts of Great Britain, its very large local market and the generally

[1] Board of Trade, *Survey of Factories*, 1934, and RCGDIP. For a competent survey of London Industrial development in the period, see P. G. Hall, *The Industries of London since 1861* (Hutchinson, 1962), pp. 121-171.

attractive living conditions made suburban industrial sites very attractive, especially after the 1929 derating of industry, which encouraged factory building in low rated areas. Some large factories in these outer areas contributed less to local rates than the cost of the services which the local authority had to provide for them.

Most of the new suburban industrial nodes were soon surrounded by streets of speculative builder housing, much of it of the cheap block type. Some was taken by the workers in the adjacent factories, thus reducing the daily movement between these mixed development suburbs and the centre, but significant numbers of the workers were compelled by financial circumstances to stay in their low-rent housing in inner London. Travelling daily against the main traffic stream, they might, with overtime, spend as much as twelve hours a day away from home. By no means all the factories were of course completely new; many were set up by old-established firms moving out from inner London to get more floor space and re-equip with mass-production plant.

The new motor roads, most of them on routes recommended by the London Arterial Road Conferences of 1912–16 and then agreed by the local authorities, would have remained much longer on the drawing boards had it not been for the severe unemployment of 1920. Achievement in the early twenties was commendable; the Ministry of Transport London Area programme for 1920–4 involved expenditure of £4,288,000 and 190 miles of construction, mostly new roads, but including some widenings, were completed or in progress in March 1926. This work included Eastern Avenue (Wanstead–Romford and Ilford–Woodford, 10¾ miles), Sidcup–Wrotham (11 miles), Watford Bypass (North Watford–Hampstead, 15½ miles), Barnet Bypass (Hatfield–Mill Hill, 14 miles), Great Cambridge Road (Tottenham–Cheshunt, 11 miles), Great West Road (Gunnersbury–Hounslow–Hanworth, 8 miles), Western Avenue (East Acton–Greenford, 5 miles), part of the North Circular Road (9½ miles) and bypasses for Kingston (9½ miles), Sutton (4½ miles), Croydon (3¾ miles), Eltham and Sidcup (6 miles), Bexleyheath (5½ miles), Orpington (6½ miles), Farnborough, Dartford, East Ham and Barking. The projects selected were those crossing relatively undeveloped land and therefore capable of being started with least delay; others of equal merit, such as the South Circular Road and a link between the Old Kent Road and Catford were left for future generations.

A follow-up programme in the thirties included the completion of most of the remaining 9 miles of the North Circular, extension of Western Avenue from Greenford to Denham (7 miles), 12 miles of a North Orbital Road (Denham–Rickmansworth and North Watford–Hatfield), part of the Great Chertsey Road from Richmond to Hanworth (4 miles), a Hampton Court–Esher spur for the Kingston Bypass and bypasses for Ewell, Leatherhead, Dorking, Egham, Harrow and Guildford-Godalming. This period also saw the widening of many miles of the twenties roads, either by providing a second 27-foot carriageway or by broadening the original one from 36 feet to 44 feet.

Once built, these raw concrete strips were quickly supplied with bus services and soon became lined with low-value speculative housing, petrol stations, garish public houses in mock Tudor style (often termed 'road houses'), shopping parades, and factories. For much of this haphazard and restless ugliness, the 1935 Ribbon Development Act[1] came too late. Describing how the Kingston Bypass had been cut through open country 'at great cost', a 1936 speaker remarked that soon after its opening in 1927, it became 'the mecca of the land speculator and the speculative builder of the small house' and for part of its length was cluttered up with a jumble of factories and small houses, converting it to a traffic artery serving a new chain of communities, which detracted from its value as a through route. Factory traffic flowed out on to it and slow traffic debouched into the main stream from the service roads alongside.[2]

Surrey County Council learned the lesson. Anticipating the Ribbon Development Act, it took powers as early as 1931 to restrict access to new main roads and to limit roadside building. Middlesex and Essex County Councils did the same. Surrey's new policy was first practised on the Guildford and Godalming Bypass, which had been started in 1929. Faced with the restrictions, many landowners gave land, or sold it at a discount, enabling much of the immediate borders of the road to be left free of building. At the opening ceremony in July 1934 James Chuter Ede, chairman of the county council, spoke of the mistakes made with the Kingston and Sutton Bypasses which had accumulated 'devastating strings of ribbon development', and promised that the council were determined to prevent 'the perpetration of further horrors'.

[1] See Chapter 17.
[2] J. A. Rosevear in a speech to the Auctioneers and Estate Agents' Institute, February 1936 (TEG, 8 February 1936).

Towards the end of the thirties there was at least one attempt to integrate housing and industrial development in a rational manner around a new motor road. At Elstree, John Laing and Son acquired from Lord Strafford a 470-acre site around the Barnet Bypass for a 'Garden City Estate'. Wallis Gilbert and Partners and C. M. Crickmer drew up plans which included a clear space of 380 ft. between the building lines along the main road. By the end of 1938 6 factories had been built together with some 40 houses, all west of the Bypass. Work was overtaken by the war and the scheme was subsequently much modified by planning restrictions (some of the land was used for council housing).

At its widest in the north-west and south-west, the ragged belt of inter-war suburbs, with their characteristic red-tiled roofs, mock-timbered elevations and redbrick and pebbledash walls, lies almost entirely outside the boundary of the former County of London, beginning at points 6 to 10 miles from Charing Cross and ending, often quite suddenly, at the Green Belt, some 10 to 15 miles further out. Within the Green Belt, and usually associated with very good radial railway services, there are many large islands of twenties and thirties housing, as for example either side of Leatherhead, around Watford and Rickmansworth, at Reigate-Redhill, Sevenoaks, Brentwood and Potters Bar. Although planning decisions since 1945 have allowed infilling and completions of pre-war estate starts, the edge of continuously built-up London remains in general very much where the builders downed tools in 1939–40. Occasionally, as at Edgewarebury Lane, Edgware, or Church Road, Malden, the transition from suburban street to country lane is startlingly abrupt.

Several distinct groups of suburbs can be distinguished. Some nucleated around railway stations (as at Stoneleigh, Elm Park, Edgware, Queensbury, Rayners Lane, Motspur Park, Hinchley Wood, Petts Wood) or around an old village high street or green (Banstead, Cheam, Ewell, Ruislip, Orpington, Stanmore, West Wickham, Old Malden); others, utterly dependent on the motorbus or private car, clung only to a section of main road or a road junction (North Cheam, Collier Row, Gants Hill, Tolworth, West Molesey). Some of the last group eventually acquired a railway station.

The focal points were marked by concentrations of shops with flats above, either in the same mock Tudor as the houses, or, less appropriately, in debased classical styles. Often there was a large cinema, maverick in its elevations, shouting for attention. Local councils made no attempt to control or harmonise the appearance of these buildings, nor was any thought given by the developers to the relationship of one to another in streetscapes from which every trace of rustic beauty was ruthlessly expunged. In the larger shopping centres the chain stores and multiples imposed their standard shopfronts and elevations everywhere, irrespective of surroundings. The Post Office contributed a standardised Georgian design which usually put everything else to shame but became boring as it appeared in such large numbers.

Malden demonstrates well how rural charm was overwhelmed. Here discordant house and shop designs were allowed to creep close around the village inn, pond and green. The Building Estate Development and Town Planning Committee of the Malden and Coombe UDC sanctioned 11 more shops and flats in the summer of 1937, averring that their appearance would 'in no way destroy the amenities of the district' (possibly true, in that irreparable damage had already been done). One member, more sensitive than his colleagues, suggested that Old Malden was 'a little bit of England worth preserving', something that could not be brought back once it was destroyed. Today you can still see The Plough, the pond and the green, but you'll need blinkers.

Lacking other associations, the new districts often acquired names chosen by their major developers, labels which stood more chance of survival if they were also attached to a railway station (Albany Park, Falconwood, Stoneleigh, Brookmans Park, Queensbury, Oakwood, St Helier, Elm Park). F. R. Absalom, who covered the area east of Carpenders Park station (opened in 1914 for the convenience of golfers), named his creation St Meryl, after one of his daughters, but this has not endured. Because they filled up vacant land between existing centres or clustered around railway stations especially built for them, or populated hitherto remote places, many of the new districts straddled the boundaries of two or more local authorities, a circumstance which led to all sorts of difficulties. Thus Edgware was in both Harrow and Hendon, Kenton in Wembley and Harrow, Chadwell Heath in Ilford and Dagenham, Becontree in Ilford, Dagenham and Barking, Motspur Park in Malden and Coombe, and Merton and Morden, Worcester Park in Malden and Coombe, Sutton and Cheam and Epsom and Ewell. At the last, the railway station was sited at the intersection of the three council boundaries.

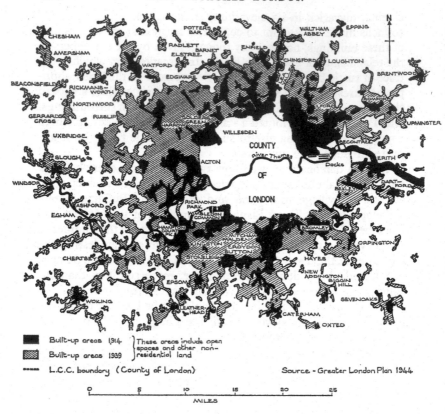

Built-up areas 1914 ⎤ These areas include open
⎦ spaces and other non-
Built-up areas 1939 ⎦ residential land

L.C.C. boundary (County of London)   Source - Greater London Plan 1944

0   5   10   15   20   25
MILES

IV Built-up area of Greater London, 1914 and 1939

The new growth was not evenly distributed around the edge of
1914 London, nor was the attack mounted in full strength in all
directions at the same time. Many factors influenced the pattern
and pace: the price and availability of suitable building land; the
existence of good radial transport services, or the promise of them;
the appearance of new factories or main roads; even fashions for
certain districts among the more favoured potential purchasers.
Deliberate planning rarely intervened to spoil the variety and un-
predictability of the process. The one universal characteristic was
wasteful use of land.

An interesting feature, not always obvious on first examination, was the broad perpetuation of suburban social zones established in the late nineteenth century. The cheaper property tended to spread outwards to the east, north-east and north, and to the south-east, often punctuated with pockets of higher value housing on radials from the First and Second Class ticket-holder settlements of 1880–1914. Entirely new areas of low-price housing elsewhere can sometimes be associated with new industrial areas or convenient access to the older ones. The south-west and north-west, receiving the clean country air from the prevailing winds, remained the favoured sectors, but even these did not escape large patches of cheaper development on the flatter, less attractive sites.

Middlesex Swamped

Middlesex, already in 1900 much flooded by London on its eastern side, was to bear the brunt of the tide. At the close of the twenties many hundreds of acres of its cheap, flat claylands lay waiting the builder in the centre and on the western side. No longer needed for the supply of forage to London's once numerous horse population, this area had been given ready accessibility by railways constructed in the opening years of the century. To the south of the clay was the Thames market-gardening plain, opened up in the twenties by the Great West and Great South West Roads, its deep loams no longer nourishing the city's fruit and vegetables in an era of cheap long distance transport.

The census of 1931 showed the Middlesex population as 1.64 million, an increase of 385,700 or 30.8 per cent, since 1921, five times the increase in England and Wales as a whole, and the highest of any county. Between 1931 and mid-1938 there was a further increment of 419,000.[1] In the years 1921–38, the Middlesex district of Harrow received the largest influx of any local authority in Greater London, a total of 134,480. Although this was a growth of 275 per cent, it was exceeded by Wembley's impressive 552 per cent, from 18,239 in 1921 to 121,600 in mid-1938. At Hayes and Harlington, the 1931 census revealed a 154 per cent increase, from 9,842 to 22,969, and there was a further increment to 50,040 by summer 1939. Ruislip-Northwood leapt from 9,112 in 1921 to

---

[1] All 1938 and 1939 figures in this chapter are from the Registrar General's estimates; other figures are taken from the census returns. Detailed population statistics will be found in Appendix 1.

16,035 in 1931 and 47,760 in mid-1939. Other large increases were registered at Friern Barnet (275 per cent 1921–38), Potters Bar (273 per cent), Feltham (167 per cent), Hendon (152 per cent), Heston and Isleworth (114 per cent) and Uxbridge (107 per cent).

In 1937 the county's Medical Officer of Health was confidently predicting its future; with population growing at an average of a thousand a week, he thought building would continue 'until all available land is covered with streets of houses'.[1] It very nearly came true. By 1939 all but the northern and north-western marches were built over. The huge accretion in west Middlesex had required an ambitious main drainage scheme, completed in 1936. Feeding into a sewage disposal and purification works by the Thames at Mogden (near Isleworth), this scheme, which replaced twenty-eight local sewage plants, served a territory of 160 square miles.

Much of the Middlesex housing was of the cheaper type, selling at prices below £1,000, a particularly large concentration of these being built for about 4 miles all round Harrow. More expensive houses were found in substantial numbers in Edgware, Southgate, Finchley, Northwood and in parts of Wembley.

Along the Electric Rails of Surrey

The north-western corner of Surrey, served by frequent and regular electric trains after the mid-twenties, expanded with equal vigour. In the ten years after 1921 that part of the county within the Greater London area[2] showed an increase of 33.2 per cent (198,013). The major growth point was the Merton and Morden urban district, which also had the benefit of Underground railway service to the City and West End after 1926. Between 1920 and 1937 this area gained no less than seven new railway stations. From 17,532 in 1921, population grew to 41,227 in 1931 (135 per cent); by mid-1938 it was 68,980, a 223 per cent increase on 1921. A similar level of growth was seen at Carshalton: 13,873 to 28,586 in 1921–31, and on to 59,510 in 1939. Other Surrey areas with increases over 100 per cent in the period 1921–38 were Malden and Coombe (168 per cent), Epsom and Ewell (161) Sutton and Cheam (154), Coulsdon and Purley (138). Surbiton (131) and Banstead (121). The number

[1] Annual Report of the Middlesex Medical Officer of Health, 1936.
[2] Banstead, Barnes, Beddington and Wallington, Carshalton, Coulsdon and Purley, Croydon, Epsom and Ewell, Esher, Kingston, Malden and Coombe, Merton and Morden, Mitcham, Richmond, Surbiton, Sutton and Cheam, Wimbledon.

of houses in Malden and Coombe almost doubled between 1921 and 1931 (3,444 to 6,015).

The most conspicuous concentration was on the claylands between Sutton and Kingston, where almost all the houses were priced under £1,000. The cheaper type of house was also to be found in quantity east and west of Croydon, and at Mitcham. Property over £1,000 appeared further south, on the northern slopes of the Downs between Epsom and Croydon, and along the railway between Epsom and Effingham, where the older settlements on the higher chalk were carried down over the clay to the railway stations. The attractive heathlands south of Esher and Weybridge were also favourite sites for higher priced housing.

Essex, Kent and the Rest
Metropolitan Essex[1] saw an accretion of 159,147 (17.8 per cent) in the decade 1921–31, an important part of it concentrated in the LCC new town at Becontree (chapter 16). Much of the council settlement was within the boundaries of Dagenham, which experienced a prodigious intercensal increase of 879 per cent (9,127 to 89,362). By mid-1939 the latter figure had grown to 109,300. Another fast-growing area was Chingford (9,506 in 1921; 22,076 in 1931; 39,460 in 1939), but here most of the new residents were owner-occupiers. Strong growth was also seen at Hornchurch (335 per cent 1921–38), Romford (163 per cent), and Barking (116 per cent, mainly from Becontree). Ilford acquired another 84,600 inhabitants in the period 1921–39, the largest numerical increase in London Essex after Dagenham.

Almost all the Essex housing was in the cheaper class, but there were patches of over-£1,000 development around Wanstead and Loughton and at north Chingford, partly an extension of the pre-1914 GER First Class season ticket zone, but also owing much to the amenity value of the carefully preserved Epping Forest.

Coverage of the Kentish sector was slower to start, but nonetheless impressive. That part of the county in Greater London[2] saw an increase of only 57,018 in the decade after 1921, but the addition in the next eight years exceeded 200,000. In 1922, Bexley still had

[1] Barking, Chigwell, Chingford, Dagenham, East Ham, Ilford, Leyton, Walthamstow, Waltham Holy Cross, Wanstead and Woodford, West Ham.
[2] Beckenham, Bexley, Bromley, Chislehurst and Sidcup, Crayford, Erith, Orpington, Penge.

3,300 acres of agricultural land, Bromley had 2,040 and Chislehurst and Sidcup 2,790,[1] and for another five years or so there was little change. Then the builders arrived in force, determined to fill the Southern's new electric trains. Bexley was the main growth point, its population rising from 21,104 in 1921 to 32,626 in 1931 and 77,020 in 1938 (264 per cent over 1921). Close behind were Chislehurst and Sidcup (22,351 to 27,182 to 61,750; 176 per cent) and Orpington (18,628 to 25,858 to 46,320; 149 per cent). At Bexley, and Chislehurst and Sidcup much of the new construction was the product of a single firm, New Ideal Homesteads. In Bexley, 4,000 houses were erected by all firms in 1934, 2,400 in 1935 and 2,000 in 1936. Other significant increases in London Kent were at Beckenham (104 per cent, 1921–38), and Crayford (100 per cent). A clear indicator of the expansion of north-west Kent, and of its nature, was the heavy increase in rush hour arrivals at Charing Cross station (see page 234). Places farther out in Kent did not escape the attentions of developers; the ambitious plans for Lullingstone are noticed in chapter 13; at Sevenoaks, New Ideal Homesteads were building at Bradbourne Park as early as 1932, and this town also attracted T. F. Nash, who purchased 300 acres of the Montreal Estate five years later.

Lower-value housing predominated in metropolitan Kent, with a notably large concentration north, west and south of the original settlement at Bexleyheath. More expensive development occurred at Petts Wood, Bromley, Keston and south of Sevenoaks.

Other areas on the edge of London showing significant growth in the twenties and thirties were East Barnet and Elstree in Hertfordshire and Slough in Buckinghamshire; at the first, the 1921 population of 13,514 went to 18,549 ten years later and 32,830 in 1938 (143 per cent on 1921). Elstree which had only 4,122 inhabitants in 1921 reached 9,089 in 1938, an increase of 121 per cent, thanks in part to the setting up of some film studios and a number of factories. Slough, a self-contained industrial area rather than a suburb of London, saw a 150 per cent leap from 20,285 in 1921 to 50,620 in 1938.

[1] RCLG, evidence, 2 May 1922.

Chapter 7

BUILDING ESTATES
1920-39

Methods of Development

Until the end of the twenties it remained common practice for areas of 'ripe' building land to be bought up by developers, often land or estate agents, acting either for themselves or for a third party. Such purchases were often made from a land speculator, perhaps the last of a chain, who had bought the site to 'hold for a rise', that is to wait for the increment that would follow building on neighbouring sites, the opening of a new transport facility, or some other favourable influence. Having acquired his building site, the developer would proceed to lay out roads and arrange the provision of main services before offering building plots to individual private purchasers, or disposing of groups of plots (or whole sections of the estate) to builders for erection of houses on a speculative basis, the latter method being more usual in London. Occasionally the land speculator, or the original landowner, would arrange development himself, employing a firm of agents who specialised in laying out and selling-off of building estates.

To get an estate started it was often essential for the developer to have a few houses erected by contract at his own expense; to entice builders, it was frequently further necessary in the twenties to offer them substantial financial assistance, a sideline which could prove quite remunerative for the developer.

Ideally, an estate developer would aim to restrict his capital outlay to the initial price of the land, and the laying out expenses, disposing of all the plots in five years at most, and recovering all outlay plus interest and a profit of at least 10 per cent of actual cost. Thus in 1926, when the Metropolitan Railway Country Estates Ltd proposed to develop $7\frac{1}{2}$ acres near Hillingdon station, it was estimated that the outlay on land, drains, roads, main services and the construction of tennis courts would be £3,250, and that the 20 house plots would realise a total of £4,700.[1]

[1] BTHR MET 10/327; *Metro-land*, Metropolitan Railway, 1928.

After laying out an estate, some developers went on to fill it with houses under their own control, hoping to profit from both the land and property sales. Another method, frequently used in London from about 1930, and not unknown before then, was for a large building firm to handle all aspects of estate development from the time a site was selected. Closely-knit groups of companies were sometimes found, operating in a similar way; a basic development company, another working as sales agents, a third as builders, with fringe companies handling finance and other activities such as purchasing. Thus at Queensbury, on the Stag Lane aerodrome site, over 1,000 houses were erected in 1934–6 by Metropolitan Builders Ltd for the Sharon Development Company, with Hilbery Chaplin and Co. acting as agents. Other building firms handled most things themselves, but preferred to rely on estate agents to sell and publicise their houses.

Drains, Gas and Water
The developers' costs embraced all expenses involved in soil drainage, the construction of roads and connections to the main sewers, and the provision of water, gas, and electricity services. Drainage was often a serious problem on the lowlying claylands which were used for much of London's new housing after 1919, not least in the arrangement of levels to achieve the correct fall on what was often flat ground. When he surveyed the Southall-Hayes area for his first London venture in 1930, Frank Taylor (of Taylor Woodrow) settled upon a site spurned by other developers because of drainage difficulties. Exercising a little ingenuity, he solved the problem quite cheaply by pumping up to the main sewer, thus making profitable use of land otherwise ideally placed alongside a main road with good cheap transport facilities to the Southall industrial area.[1]

Unless they were fortunate enough to discover a suitable site adjacent to a main sewer connecting earlier development to the outfall, developers would be involved in linking their drains to the existing system, which could mean carrying pipes through neighbouring land at the cost of easement payments. Lack of main drainage facilities was sometimes an inhibiting factor in the development of large districts otherwise attractive and accessible. Thus the pace of building in Bookham and Fetcham, and in Ban-

[1] Alan Jenkins, *On Site 1921–71* (Heinemann, 1971).

stead significantly increased after drainage schemes were completed by the Epsom Rural District Council in 1927–32.

During the twenties and thirties, the electricity companies serving the London area were very sales conscious, imposing few conditions before agreeing to lay their mains. The more conservative gas companies usually required the developer to agree that a specified number of rooms would be 'carcassed' for gas, or, if the cost of carcassing was met by the builder, they might provide mains and services free. Water authorities often sought a sizable deposit, equivalent to their outlay on mains, and returnable after a stated number of water rates were in payment, or they would lay mains against a guarantee of 10 per cent return on capital.

With the increasingly rapid pace of development, adequate sanitation was not to be taken for granted. In the lowlying clayland areas such as north-east Surrey, sewers, sometimes newly installed, were not always able to cope with the flow, surcharging from their manholes when subsoil water infiltrated after heavy rain. Local authorities were reluctant to meet such trouble by re-laying with larger diameter pipes because the waterladen nature of the subsoil made this a difficult and expensive operation.[1] It was not unknown for polluted water to contaminate well strata. An epidemic of 'gastro-enteritis' in Ewell, Sutton, Carshalton and Wallington in July 1936 was traced to sudden and severe pollution of a well at Cheam, where a second well was found to be below the highest standard of quality. The water company hastily appointed a resident chemist and installed a chlorine and ammonia plant, whilst the Epsom and Ewell Medical Officer of Health concluded that the incident was 'a reminder of the extreme vigilance necessary on the part of those responsible for the production and distribution of water, more necessary than ever with increasing centralisation and increasing population.'[2]

Roads, Made and Unmade
Road widths were prescribed by local byelaws or town planning requirements, the latter also influencing the direction and layout of streets. Although existing rights of way had to be preserved, diversions were possible if they clashed with the estate plan. Should

[1] Epsom and Ewell Urban District Council, *Report of Medical Officer of Health*, 1936; Leatherhead UDC, ditto 1936 and 1937.
[2] Epsom and Ewell UDC, *Report of Medical Officer of Health*, 1936.

there be any doubts about the legal status of an old path, the temptation to overbuild before any arguments could arise was seldom resisted.

In the London area an estate or builders' road of 20-foot width cost from £1 10s to £3 a foot including sewers.[1] Such roads were made of gravel, flint or granite chips laid over hardcore, and were bordered by footways of slag, clinker or hardcore. Kerbs, if provided at all, were usually creosoted deal beams. At first they looked reasonably tidy, and some were undoubtedly better than others (Laing claimed a minimum 5-year life for theirs at Colindale in 1931), but in most cases the process of disintegration started by the building operations was quickly completed by street traffic. Dusty wastes in summer and rutted quagmires in winter, the worst of these roads grew more and more intolerable until they were 'adopted' and 'made up' by the local authority. This might not be for 5, 10 or even more years after the estate had been completed, but unless the cost had been collected in the original sale price of the houses (seldom done), the frontagers would have to find the money.

Although permanent concrete roads were built in advance of house construction on a Surbiton estate as early as 1926, developers were slow to appreciate the advantages of this practice, which did not become widespread in London until the early thirties. Such roads were not only quickly and easily made; they improved access to the building sites in bad weather, and they required virtually no maintenance. Moreover, they assisted sales by imparting a finished appearance to the estate. Around 1930 a number of local authorities began to insist on the construction of approved permanent roads before any houses were built. Surrey County Council was a pioneer in this respect, acquiring powers for the purpose in its 1931 Act.

Many developers sought to minimise road and drainage costs by acquiring strips of land alongside main roads. Such sites had the further attraction of free publicity so that they usually sold quickly. In the twenties and thirties many people considered it an advantage to live on a main road, and would happily pay a little more for the privilege. The practice of ribbon development as it came to be called, much encouraged by the growth of motorbus services, eventually caused such blatant damage to amenity and the function-

[1] G. Cross, *Suffolk Punch* (1939); F. Howkins, *An Introduction to the Development of Private Building Estates and Town Planning* (1926).

ing of through roads that it came to be controlled by special legislation.[1]

Constraints

The Ribbon Development Act was by no means the only restriction encountered by the developer. Writing as early as 1926, Howkins[2] listed over twenty statutes affecting estate construction. Of equal importance were the local building byelaws, which regulated width and construction of roads, drainage, depth of foundations, airspace around buildings, sanitation, fire precautions and other aspects of public health and safety. And, because most London area local authorities had a town planning scheme in some stage of evolution by the end of the twenties, the estate developer needed to ensure that his ideas fitted into this.[3] Lastly, restrictive covenants running with the land usually stipulated minimum prices of houses to be built or the maximum density to the acre. Sometimes these had become unrealistic in the context of the area's general development, or would threaten the profitability of the site if strictly observed. After 1925 it became possible to have such covenants modified or removed, but legal expenses were involved in bringing the case before the Official Arbitrator.[4] Before this, builders would often erect houses of smaller size and ground area, leaving the balance of the land uncovered in the hope that the density restriction might eventually be lifted.

In some districts the local building byelaws were both stringent and strictly enforced; a few councils went as far as requiring a certificate of habitation to show that the house was fit for occupation. It is possible that the nature of the byelaws and the manner of their administration in different local authority areas had some influence on the patterns of building development.[5] One place where byelaws were most conscientiously enforced was Ilford, so much so that the Council's Surveyor refused to pass houses erected in 1919–20 by the LCC and the City Corporation. This action, which may have had political undertones, was overruled by the Ministry of Health,

---

[1] The Restriction of Ribbon Development Act, 1935, see page 321.
[2] Howkins, op. cit.
[3] See Epilogue.
[4] The Law of Property Act, 1925, s. 84.
[5] A view advanced by F. M. Elgood, chairman of the National Housing and Town Planning Council to RCLG, 21 June 1922.

obsessed with the urgency of getting as many houses as possible built in the immediate post war period.[1]

Despite all these seeming complications, the constraints on the developers of the twenties and thirties were as paper chains compared with those which came after 1945. In practice there was very great freedom to indulge in personal whims and fancies, both in layout and design, and little difficulty in covering with the minimum of delay almost any parcel of land offered on the market.

Defects in Estate Design

Most of the estates built by private firms paid scant regard to the precepts of the Garden City and Garden Suburb movements. With imagination lacking, or suppressed in the anxiety to maximise profit in the shortest possible time, most developers cleared away all trees and shrubs on the site, and rarely bothered to make use of natural features in their scheme. Existing viewpoints were ignored; attractive situations such as the northern flanks of Shooters Hill at Woolwich or the valley slopes around Purley received the same blanket treatment as the flat and featureless fields of Rayners Lane.

Estate roads were laid out in aimless, wandering fashion, or followed the irrelevant meanderings of old farm tracks, sprouting tiny cul-de-sacs in all directions, until in extreme cases, one close led off from another in frantic effort to cover every corner of the land. Such thoughtless layouts rendered even moderately direct access to the outside world impossible and often encircled backland under separate ownership so that it could not easily be developed at a later date.

In the thirties, some planners favoured highly symmetrical patterns of roads which looked satisfying on the drawing board but frustrated easy communication on the ground, both within the estate and exits and entrances. And these very formal plans, coupled with the regular building lines almost universally adopted, served only to underline the tedious similarity of the houses.

Grass verges of between 3 and 10 feet in width were fairly common in these later estates. Sometimes this strip between road and footway was planted with shrubs and trees; Laing's beshrubbed verges still survive at Oakwood and Canons Park, but Bergs' rhododendrons at Ashtead lasted only a few years. In this, at least,

[1] RCLG, 11 July 1922, evidence of F. H. Dane, Ilford UDC.

we can detect some slight homage to the garden suburb. Howkins thought trees at 6s to 10s each 'well worth the expense' to an estate developer, citing a case of quicker sales in a tree-lined road.[1] At Edgware, A. W. Curton preserved some trees, adding silver birch, mountain ash, Spanish chestnut and Copper beech along his frontages, but mostly Howkins' advice was ignored, especially in the earlier part of the period. Until about 1935 it was common practice to fell all existing trees, even when these were not in the way of the new houses, and attractive avenues, such as that at Whitchurch Lane, Edgware, were sacrificed to road widening. A writer in an Edgware paper in 1936, bemoaning the large-scale destruction of trees in the district, remarked upon the short-sightedness of the developers, unable to see that apart from their intrinsic value, trees would 'keep up the class of the neighbourhood . . . and thus keep up the value of the property'.

On the typical estate of the twenties and thirties, each road would be lined with its full quota of houses, every one set squarely to the building line, staring straight into the windows of another on the opposite side. Plots were usually of standard size, varying from 20 to 35 feet wide according to whether side entrances or garage spaces were included. A restless monotony emerged, with no suggestion of space, despite the wasteful use of land.

Road layouts were not only extravagant of space, but also of road materials and public utility mains, particularly on undulating sites. Usually it was only the local authorities, on their own housing estates, who followed Unwin's theory that T-shaped closes and groupings around little greens provided the most economical and aesthetically satisfying results.[2]

Occasionally a developer who had purchased a well-timbered private park would make some use of its careful landscaping, duly ensuring that such reckless extravagance was adequately reflected in the selling price of the houses. At the Woodcote estate, near Purley, every house was given a most generous garden, and the development was planned around a large 'village green' complete with stocks, inn, and goose pond. After purchasing Canons Park, at Edgware, George Cross decided to preserve the two lakes and as many fine trees as possible, to form a worthy setting for houses which were to include such treasures as 'faithful reproductions of old Kentish black and white sixteenth century farmhouses by Mr

[1] Howkins, op. cit.
[2] Raymond Unwin, *Nothing Gained by Overcrowding* (1912).

Love of Canterbury, making perfect pictures in the rural surroundings'. (Prices started at £1,450.)

By the middle thirties, the more enlightened members of the architectural profession were expressing concern at the appearance of the speculators' estates, even making some impression with their protests. As in other matters, the larger firms sometimes set a good example. John Laing and Son early adopted a policy of preserving trees, spending up to £100 if necessary to retain a good specimen. If the estate were level and without natural features, they would provide a central garden.[1] Privets were planted along the house boundaries, and purchasers were given a leaflet on the care of this shrub. The firm maintained nurseries and a staff of expert gardeners to keep their estates in order, although of course this care was withdrawn once the development was completed and handed over to the local authority.

Much in a Name

'Attractive names will prove very helpful in disposing of both land and houses' suggested Howkins.[2] In the naming of roads and estates, developers intuitively sought to evoke the old suburban daydream of *rus in urbe*, preferring 'Gardens', 'Drive', 'Rise', 'Way' (even 'Waye') to the traditional Street, Road or Avenue. Occasionally only one word was used, as at Ashtead Woods, where Berg gave his roads field names. A glance at one small sector of the map of between-wars suburban London (Keston-Shirley) shows less subtle efforts to impart a rustic tone: Beech Dell, Pine Glade, The Glen, The Vale; such names can be found with equal ease elsewhere. 'Park', with its suggestion of aristocratic acres, retained its nineteenth-century popularity in estate and road names. It was especially dear to New Ideal Homesteads, who at one time attached it to all their London estates. The Southern Railway narrowly escaped having four consecutive stations with names ending in Park (Raynes Park, Motspur Park, Worcester Park, Stoneleigh Park). Names were indeed important; Howkins mentions a Moat Estate renamed Manor Park Estate 'with good results';[3] a whole essay could be written on that. Aristocratic connotations were always helpful. When a developer bought a Victorian house called Kynaston Lodge at Harrow in 1932, he prudently dubbed the building estate Kynas-

[1] John Laing, *House Building 1934–6* (1934).
[2] Howkins, op. cit.
[3] Ibid.

7. Corbett house with servants' annexe, Aldborough Road, Ilford. (Photo: Alan A. Jackson.)

Corbett houses in Kirfauns Avenue, Goodmayes. (Photo: Alan A. Jackson.)

8. Golders Green cross roads in 1904 and 1913. In the lower picture note the partially built bridge across the Finchley Road for the Underground Railway extension to Edgware. (From a commercial postcard by W. Schroder.)

Golders Gardens, Golders Green, when new c. 1911. (From a commercial postcard by Gordon Smith.)

ton Court. Laing even used names to distinguish house types (Olympia, Malvern, Filey, Jubilee, Coronation), which was rather more imaginative than the usual 'Type A5' or 'Plan B'.

On estates of any size it was common practice to set aside sites for shops, cinema, public house, churches and (more rarely) library, school and social centre. With the exception of the first, the original developer was not usually involved in the supply of such amenities, the plots often remaining vacant for many years after the completion of the houses. A lack of community services was apparent almost everywhere in the suburbs because local authorities struggling with large expenditures on such essentials as schools and drains were reluctant to raise rates to pay for anything more, well aware that their average ratepayer was mortgaged to the limit of his income. Harrow, with a population of well over 144,000, thus had no public library as late as 1935 and Hendon's 134,000 did not get their first branch library (at Golders Green) until that year. Throughout the thirties, Hendon Council successfully resisted all pressures for a library in the extensive new district of Edgware, one councillor suggesting that the several twopenny libraries in the shopping centre gave sufficient reading service. Similar sentiments were voiced at Guildford, a Surrey town with very large areas of suburban-type housing for London commuters; here the council managed to reach the end of the thirties without a professional librarian or a permanent library building.

A very small number of estate developers encouraged and supported the formation of social centres. One such was F. C. J. Ingram, whose 'Woodside Park Garden Suburb' of the early thirties boasted a social hall and playing fields. At Pavilion Gardens, Staines, in 1935, every house was said to overlook the tennis courts, with their tea gardens, shrubbery and pavilion, all furnished by the builder. Some other developers included tennis courts as an attraction, or gave land to clubs formed by the new residents. Awkwardly-shaped plots or lowlying ground unsuitable for building would be used in this way, or might be donated to the local authority as an open space. An example of the latter was the gift by George Wimpey and Co. of 1½ acres at the rear of Clarence Avenue, New Malden, in 1937.

Suburban Shops
Although most movement in suburban streets was on foot, the town planning schemes of the twenties and thirties tended to

proscribe dispersal of shops. Concentrated in designated areas, the parades of shops, with flats above, were to be found along the most important new or existing main road, often near the railway station, a weary trudge from many parts of the surrounding estates. This policy arose partly from a desire to keep the residential areas 'select' (trading and tradesmen were still regarded as not quite respectable) and partly from a recognition of the increased earning potential of shops situated in groups. Its effects were much ameliorated by the willingness of most tradesmen to deliver goods to the house, a process greatly facilitated by the availability of a cheap telephone service, actively canvassed by the Post Office.

A common rule of thumb was that a small shopping centre required a minimum of 200 houses in support and should contain at least the six 'essential trades' – butcher, baker, grocer, greengrocer, dairyman and newsagent/tobacconist/confectioner.[1] But it was not always easy for a developer to persuade the local council that shops were necessary on his estate. In 1935 Fairway Homes had 200 houses in occupation on the Mimms Hall Estate at Potters Bar, and 700 more under construction or planned. Nearby were 238 houses on a shopless council estate. Although promising to reconsider the application when the estate was complete, the Potters Bar UDC opposed the shops. At the subsequent Ministry of Health Inquiry it was suggested that the Council was trying to protect existing shopkeepers in the district, an allegation which was of course denied.

If conditions were right, shops could reap handsome profits for the developer, so provision was usually adequate, if not excessive. Cross[2] mentions that in the average London suburb, house plots might sell at £5 a foot frontage, but good shop sites would command between £50 and £100 a foot, with up to £500 realisable on what he called 'partly-matured' sites (shop frontages were normally 15–20 feet with a depth of 40–60 feet, and rear access was virtually obligatory). Among the builders who developed their own shops were G. T. Crouch, who were advertising them on the Hinchley Wood and Feltham estates at £1,100 freehold in 1936, and two years later at £1,625 (£150 rent) at Morden Park. In each case the price included a flat above. At Ewell Road, Tolworth, in 1930, a builder was offering shops with two reception rooms and three bedrooms above for £1,825 freehold. In general prices for a com-

[1] Howkins, op. cit.
[2] Cross, op. cit.

bined small shop and flat ranged from £1,000 to £2,000 according to site and size of accommodation.

Other developers preferred to retain the freehold, knowing that the value would appreciate. A survey of advertisements shows that rents for flatted suburban shops in the thirties fell within the range £100–£250. As we shall see later, the Underground Railways, with lucrative sites at their new suburban stations, let some profits of this type fall through their fingers. One firm well alive to the potential of shops on their estates was John Laing and Son, who erected parades for almost all their developments in the thirties, retaining the freehold in every case. The largest of the Laing retail centres was at Queensbury, where about 80 shops and flats were built at the west end of the wide boulevard approach to the new station between 1934 and 1939. Each was 40 feet deep, with 40 feet of yard space at the rear, widths being 16, 17 or 18 feet. Rents, which were scaled upwards in 7-year steps over a 21-year lease, ranged from a minimum of £180 to £290 for a corner site at the end of the lease period. Similar shops at the Laing Woodford estate were let for £125–£220 a year (plus £25 for a corner site), and Laing were at pains to point out that the estate contained, 'a good class of residents that takes pride in its home, furnishing, clothing and food, and has the money to spend on both necessities and luxuries'.

Developers holding good main road sites would try very hard to secure two or three of the well-known multiples, even at some sacrifice. Once it could be stated that one of these had bitten, others came quickly. Cross demonstrated this with his Premier Parade of 21 shops alongside the Edgware Underground terminus.[1] He was so impressed by this success that he went on to develop shop sites all round suburban London.

The increasingly powerful multiples soon found it convenient to use one central London agent who could provide them with a wide choice of sites in the new areas. One firm specialising in this work was Hillier, Parker, May and Rowden, another was Edward Lotery, whose suburban shopping parades bore the trade mark of a herring-bone design in the brickwork above first-floor level.

In general, tactics were similar to those which Cross had found so effective. After securing an option on a plot, plans would be drawn up for a parade of shops and the best position quickly offered to one of the big multiples, often with low rent or free shopfitting as bait.

[1] See Chapter 14.

Sometimes, when seduction proved especially difficult, the shop might be offered rent free for a few years. Not all the multiples were content with tenant status. Sainsbury and W. H. Smith in particular insisted on freehold possession, the latter employing their own architect and requiring special fittings and features. Once a multiple was secured, half or more of the other plots could be 'let off the plan'. Construction of the development was then begun, financed by a bank loan, with mortgages from insurance companies. After a time, the multiples woke up to their pulling power and drove harder bargains; Lotery met this by encouraging the expansion of new multiples such as the Tesco cut-price grocery chain, arranging finance and throwing in free shop-fronts and fittings.[1] Tesco's impressive pre-war expansion was largely oriented towards the suburbs. From the opening of the first retail shop on the Watling estate in 1932 until 1939 this firm set up over 100 branches, many of them serving new districts such as Tolworth, North Cheam, Elm Park, and Hornchurch.[2]

Older shopping centres conveniently accessible from the new estates also prospered from the housing boom. Thus at Sutton a single drapery shop opened in the High Street in 1899 by George Shinner was able to expand by the purchase of neighbouring properties culminating the process in 1934 by the acquisition of a corner site occupied by a church. By the end of the thirties the establishment was a thriving departmental store.

[1] Information on Lotery from Oliver Marriott, *The Property Boom* (Hamilton, 1967).
[2] Information on Tesco Stores from Maurice Corina, *Pile it High, Sell it Cheap* (Weidenfeld & Nicolson, 1971).

Chapter 8

HOMES FOR THE MORTGAGED: The Suburban House and Garden 1920–39

Semis and Others

Whether they realised it or not, many of the Londoners dreaming of a new house in the suburbs were seeking to renew contact with the rural environment which their immediate ancestors had deserted in the hope of attaining higher living standards in the Metropolis. They were willing to make many allowances, but looked for at least a suggestion of the country cottage in their new suburban home. They also sought greater privacy, more living space, the latest in domestic amenities and, as often as not, some measure of social improvement.

New houses built in blocks, no matter how convenient or modern, had about them a certain urban flavour, whilst the detached ideal was too greedy of land to be generally available at an attractive price. It was the semi-detached house[1] which provided an acceptable and very popular compromise, allowing the developer to fill his land at 10 or 12 to the acre, yet presenting certain advantages to the purchaser, some more real than others. The extra plot width allowed a fair amount of garden, and with its complete break on one side providing room for a garden entrance for tradesmen and dustmen, the semi imparted an illusion of privacy combined with a slight basis for snobbery. It offered white collars and artisans the chance of escape from the often intrusive gregariousness of the inner suburban terraces and more than a suggestion of the detached privacy so long the prerogative of the middle class. The design

---

[1] Semi-detached houses were first seen in London just before the opening of the eighteenth century, but for the following 200 years or so they remained the exception rather than the rule.

allowed some scope for individuality in decoration, and proved amenable to the rural romantic treatment which was to be carried over with such enthusiasm from the suburban villas of the Victorians.

Because the drive for individuality was so strong there was no attempt to plan pairs of semis to look like single houses; it followed that the external impact was restless and never quite right. Perhaps the most successful arrangements were those in which the entrance halls and stairs were placed together in the centre, reducing the contiguous rooms to two in each house. The firm of E. and L. Berg was among the first to use this design, in the early thirties.

Occasionally very large semis were built, as at Sanderstead in 1932, where Costain came up with four double bedrooms, maid's room and integral garage in a spacious design priced at £1,180. Ultra-large semis were rather a speciality of the A. W. Curton Edgwarebury Lane Estate, Edgware, which offered in 1935 a design with six bedrooms, three reception rooms and a breakfast room, all for £1,785. But the ultimate in semis was to be found at Wood Lane, Osterley, in 1928, each one in a ¼-acre plot; only three bedrooms and one garage, but very special features included a 'cast stone porchway', a panelled hall, and a 'roof garden with balustrade'. The price was £2,500.

Many building estates included a small number of detached houses, usually placed on corner sites or along the main frontage (the isolated ones were often taken by doctors or dentists). Several builders were willing to provide semi-detached or detached versions of the same plan to choice, complete privacy costing around £100 extra. Sometimes estates were built with a very high proportion of detached designs, or even entirely of this type, but the economics of the exercise caused the houses to be so tightly packed together that they seemed to be little more than severed versions of the standard semi. Only in the very highest price ranges of the speculative market, at or above £2,500, was it possible to find well-designed detached houses pleasingly set in their own plots.

In those districts where the local authorities were tolerant about density, some builders reduced sale prices and increased their profit by erecting blocks of 4, 6 or even 8, always charging slightly more for the end houses. This arrangement led to certain awkwardnesses; it was difficult to avoid monotony, and service lanes had to be cut along the backs of the gardens to facilitate fuel delivery and refuse collection. As car ownership increased in later years, garages of various shapes, sizes and materials sprouted in the back gardens, the service lanes affording tortuous, potholed access for their cherished contents.

Another product of the pressure for lower selling prices was the 'chalet', a development of the bungalow, via the 'semi-bungalow' with its single bedroom in the roofspace. Chalets usually followed a standard plan which included one very small bedroom on the ground floor and two fairly large ones in the roof, either side of a central staircase. Semi-detached designs with the main entrance at the side were the rule. With their steeply pitched rooflines, chalets looked more interesting and pleasing than the cheaper standard semis, but became tedious enough when repeated *en masse*, as they were on some estates.

Bungalows were most frequently encountered on cheap land, which meant that they occurred in quantity in suburban Essex and the lowlying outer fringes of Middlesex around Uxbridge and Staines. Offering obvious benefits in ease of maintenance, they were sold in both semi and detached versions and were attractive to invalids and the elderly, although they were spurned by those who experienced the irrational, perhaps primeval, fear of sleeping at ground level.

Whilst some of the bungalows and a substantial proportion of the houses built around London in the twenties and thirties had but two bedrooms, most of the speculative output provided two double and one small bedroom, enough for the average family, but excessive for the childless couple or the unmarried living alone or with one dependant. These 'minimum households' received more attention as the house market reached saturation point in the middle thirties. With many blocks of self-contained service flats going up in central London, suburban counterparts in the form of flats or maisonettes began to appear from about 1934. On casual inspection, the maisonette looked rather like a substantially built semi, but on coming closer, fireproof staircases would be seen against the outer walls, leading to the front and rear doors of the upper unit. Each section had two bedrooms, a kitchen and a bathroom, even a tiny back garden, half the usual width. New Ideal Homesteads' maisonettes of 1938, in eighteen different suburban locations, could be had from £355 upwards. Neither the idea nor the name were new. 'Maisonettes' were mentioned in advertisements at least as early as 1902, but at that period entrance staircases were often internal and the more usual description was 'half-houses'.

Blocks of self-contained flats, frequently with the name '——— Court', were erected in completely new areas such as Edgware and Cockfosters as well as on the sites of large Victorian villas in the older suburbs. In return for rents ranging from £70 to £150 a year, the tenants enjoyed central heating, the services of a resident porter and the maintenance of the communal gardens, in addition to the accommodation, which usually comprised one reception room, two bedrooms, a kitchen and bathroom.

Architects Are We All
Because the average speculative builder tended to look upon an architect as something of a luxury, the involvement of the profession in the vast output of suburban houses between the wars was insignificant and usually indirect. Many builders, familiar enough with the standard layout of a small house, would proceed by practical experience and rule of thumb, saving fees of around £150 for an estate of 100 houses of three basic types. If an architect were employed by a small developer, he would be a man at the outset of his career, or one not particularly successful in the mainstream; his designs, once acquired, would be used over and over again with only the slightest variation.

The larger firms, probably without exception, employed professional architects to prepare series of designs which they could repeat on different estates. Some firms changed their designs but little over the years, others brought out one or two new types of house each year in the thirties, usually introducing them at the Ideal Home Exhibition. Rarely were architects named in advertisements. A 1928 announcement mentioned that the houses in Strawberry Hill's Walpole Road, 'all different', were the work of Sir Henry Banister Fletcher, RIBA, FSI, and on Crouch's Coulsdon Vale estate in 1933, the £995 and £1,000 houses were to the designs of G. R. Hamsdorf, 'an architect of European reputation'. Laing employed three or four architects, occasionally naming them in advertisements, and between them they produced enough designs to allow, for example, up to seventeen different types or variations on one estate started in 1935.

With or without architect, most developers knew exactly what their potential customers required. Assiduously, often clumsily, they strove to evoke at least a suggestion of that rural-romantic make-believe which was the very spirit of suburbia. One typical

1937 estate was thus, 'almost a dream city, with its old style gables and lattice windows, its trim gardens and pleasant closes.[1] External appearance assumed great importance, for it often made the sale; there had to be the strongest possible contrast with the drab, uniform terraces of the inner area streets, a little show, and a hint of the country cottage. Inside, the new houses were to be full of light, their fittings and arrangement designed to ease the domestic chores. Alas, the desired objectives were difficult to achieve at the price levels the mass of buyers could afford, so the ideals and the daydream became sadly diffused, and the little that remained of them was often provided at the sacrifice of hidden quality.

All attention focused on the superficial; decorative features were paramount. Cottage styles, more or less loosely based on designs conceived by the Garden Suburb and small house architects of 1890–1914, were a common starting point, but whereas the originals had the virtues of simplicity, the speculator went overboard with decoration: roofs were broken up by barge-boarded gables, verges and valleys; windows were given leaded lights and even bottle glass, with small rooms sprouting oriels and staircases deserving 'cathedral windows' often in coloured glass; brickwork was multicoloured, textured, shaped, even deliberately fissured; and porches with red-tiled roofs sheltered front doors of oak with gothic panels, iron hinges and ring knockers.

Harmony was at a discount, symmetry was disguised to the point of absurdity (except in the semi repetition); variety, at least in the superficial, became a major selling point. 'No pair of houses alike in road' boasted a 1927 announcement of Bury Avenue, Purley; 'semi-detached, but each pair of a different design' was the promise of Firsby Avenue, Finchley in the same year. On a small estate at Grange Park, Winchmore Hill, in 1929, there were 'eight different elevations', whilst 'every house different' was the theme for Bergs' all-detached Hinchley Wood estate of 1931 (here there was some harmony of design, as one architect was used). In that year, at Southend, Catford, A. J. Glock was offering the Farm Estate, with the mind-boggling choice of 'Queen Anne, Jacobean, Georgian or Tudor' styles (yes, in that order). At Rayners Lane, in 1933 there was at least variety of promise: 'the Honeymoon Cottage' (£950), 'the Monk's House' (£1,050) and 'the Sunshine House' (£1,100).

Despite all the effort devoted to external attractions, monotony

[1] Advertisement for Crouch's Morden Park Estate, EN 6 July 1937.

was not avoided; variety of detail there was in plenty, but the basic size, shape, height and plan were pretty well the same everywhere, and, as we have seen, imagination was not much in evidence in the general layout. Most of the speculative building was rightly considered unattractive, even ugly, by those who could afford to employ their own architect. Nature and time have done much to soften the impact, although there are still places where the effect is as stark and garish as it was when the houses were new. Perhaps outward appearance would have been more pleasing if the pace had been slower and the majority of developers had not striven to build down to a price; certainly the worst examples occur in the areas of the most hectic activity. Yet to those who came to them from the dreary greyness of the inner area, the new houses always looked wonderful; and once bought, each house became a home, its outward design soon assuming little importance to the owner.

Most popular of the elevations was that variously described as 'Tudor', 'Elizabethan', or simply 'Old World' (with or without the final 'e'). Its bogus romanticism and picturesque touches had a very strong appeal, for there was nothing quite like it in Willesden, Harringay or Deptford, and it suggested the country cottage ideal. Even the cheapest houses paid some homage to the style with a dash of mock timbering in the gable and a few leaded panes. On many estates, the 'Tudor' houses were matched by shops, public houses, even petrol stations executed in the same manner. And for those prepared to pay, the faking could be carried to a high degree of perfection:

> 'The Tudor is one of the easiest architectural styles to make blatant and over picturesque and is easily marred by an all too obvious "newness" in the materials employed. All these evils Consolidated Property Trust Ltd know how to avoid. They know the value of old bricks mixed with new ones, of old timber, and of exact adherence to the genuine Tudor tradition.'[1]

Modernism Spurned

There was but one mild, brief, and largely unsuccessful revolt against this obsession with the picturesque, The back-to-fundamentals Modern Movement in architecture initiated in Germany and Holland by Walter Gropius and others in the 1910s came to

[1] TEG 6 August 1930.

public notice in London principally through Dr Charles Holden's Underground stations of the twenties. In that decade Gropius was building small houses at Dessau and elsewhere and English architects were providing designs in the new style for wealthy clients. With its flat roof, smooth white walls and large steel-framed windows, 'Modern' fitted well with the contemporary sun-cult.

London's speculative builders took up the fashion around 1932, when a little rash of flat-roofed, plain-walled houses, in both angular and flow-curved styles, began to appear. At the Ideal Home Exhibition two years later all the show houses were of this type, grouped into a 'Village of Tomorrow', with examples submitted by Wates, Laing, Bergs, Morrells, Davis, and Crouch.

One of the pioneers was the old-established firm of Haymills, who announced in January 1934 that at Forty Avenue, Wembley Park: 'Haymills capture the Modern Spirit. Great Advance in house design. Flat roof, soft grey facing bricks'. Similar houses by the same firm at the Downage Estate, Hendon in the same year had wall-panel electric fires instead of the normal mantelshelves and tiled surrounds to a coal fireplace. On the flat roof was to be found a glass-enclosed 'sun parlour'. Contemporary with these, at Elmbridge Avenue, Surbiton, another builder had 'The Modern Style. The House of 1950', with flat roof, cavity walls and a rubber floor to the bathroom.

At first the new trend was confined to the medium to high price range, but a firm called Howard Houses were astute enough to realise that its simple elevations provided opportunities to pare down costs. On their Upper Farm Estate amid the flatlands of West Molesey, from March 1934, they offered a £395 semi with sitting-room, kitchen, '2–3 bedrooms' and a bathroom. Certain advantages were suggested:

'This flat roof offers you a whole floor of extra space, and delightful means to revel in the out-of-doors . . . easy access to the roof can be arranged. There your children can play in safety and in unrestricted sunshine. There you can take your meals in the open, entertain your friends, enjoy the peace of the moonlight and sleep al fresco if you wish.'

Yes, all this at West Molesey. Another advertisement for the same estate depicted the proud owner performing his physical jerks on the roof, limbering up, no doubt, for the long trek to Hampton Court station. Gropius would have approved; among the advantages he had listed for flat-roofed houses was 'the chance to make roof gardens'.

Soon all the large firms were on the bandwagon. In the spring and summer of 1934, Davis, Morrells, Bergs and New Ideal Home-steads were each advertising their versions of the 'Modern Style'. Bergs even ventured a few houses on a circular plan, with a large living room lit by a window occupying almost half the circumference. Those too timid, or too shrewd, to break away from tradition fought back. In June 1934, £685 houses in Oak Road, Kenley, were advertised by F. W. Thomas as '100 per cent modern houses, but not modernistic . . . substantially built to last centuries'.

Before long, the novelty palled. The ordinary house-buying public, conservative in their tastes, did not welcome designs that advanced too far from their concept of what a house should look like. Many were still seeking the rural-romantic, to which the new styles made no concessions at all. By April 1935, Howard was advertising the Upper Farm Estate with sketches of pitched roof houses and nary a mention of al fresco life or physical jerks. and the prices were up to £425 and £495. The end of that year saw the fashion for flat roofs and suntrap houses almost over as far as the London speculative builders were concerned.

In one respect modernistic offered a valuable practical advantage. The traditional elevations, with their superfluity of decoration, large areas of exposed softwoods, broken-up roof lines and variety of wall treatments, were costly and irksome to maintain in good order. In contrast, the smooth plain surfaces and neat steel-framed windows of the new style required but little attention. Builders quickly found that the uncluttered modernistic elevations would sell well enough if they were set under the familiar pitched roof, and an increasing number of these compromise designs appeared after early 1933, sometimes with shiny green roof tiles instead of the usual red. Among the first of these were semis and detached houses designed by Welch, Cachemaille-Day and Lander at the Old Rectory Garden and Mill Ridge Estates, Edgware for Roger Malcolm Ltd in 1933-4, all selling at over £1,000. External modernism was restrained, more so than that of a house designed by J. E. Newberry, FRIBA, for Streather and Hogan at the corner of Broadfields Avenue and Hale Lane, Edgware in 1934. Hendon Council refused planning permission for this on the ground that the unrelieved white-walled elevations presented too violent a contrast against the adjacent houses in traditional styles. The builders successfully appealed, explaining to the Ministry of Health Inspector that their architect was merely attempting 'simplicity without eccentricity', trying to get away from useless ornamentation and 'flummery'.

Insecure Foundations

As much of the new construction was on London clay of the heaviest type, sound foundations were necessary if structural troubles were to be avoided. In some parts of Surrey and Essex there was the further danger of sulphates in the clay which attached foundations prepared from conventional concrete mixes, a problem not fully appreciated until the late thirties. Subsidence, accompanied by extensive cracking of walls, followed the shrinkage of clay beneath shallow foundations after long spells of dry weather. As always, the wording of advertisements gives a clue to what was happening elsewhere:

'This estate is on gravel, not clay' (Rice, Watford, 1934)

'Gravel subsoil! Solid foundations!
'Not adversely affected by dry weather!' (J. J. Fleming, Shortlands, 1934)

'On footings reinforced over whole of site, which prevents cracks and subsidence.' (Connaught estate, Carshalton, 1934.)

Only the better builders concerned themselves with such matters. After all, long dry summers were not all that frequent. So the 30 in. by 30 in. solid concrete advertised by J. C. Derby on his Beckenham Manor Estate was pretty rare, as was the 5-year guarantee against settlement offered by A. W. Curton at Edgware in 1937. Indeed some advertisers saw merit in announcing '9 in. of concrete', 'site concrete 6 in. deep', 'reinforced footings' and 'reinforced concrete foundations', an indication that even such minimal solidity was not to be taken for granted.

One could be more confident about damp courses, as these were required by local byelaws and subject to inspection by the council's officials. It followed that even in the cheapest houses they were adequate, although few bothered to go as far as Berg's 'double slate' (Shirley, 1934), or the belt and braces policy of J. C. Derby's 'slate and bitumen'. Damp courses in chimneys, however, were often absent or poorly placed.

Coke Walls and Cathedral Windows

With good quality facing bricks costing half as much again as other types, builders looking for economies were tempted to resort to the cheapest grades of brick, which they would cover with pebbledash or roughcast. This offered fairly adequate weather protection until it cracked, as it inevitably did. A few facing bricks would sometimes be placed prominently at corners in such houses, conveying the sly suggestion that all the covered bricks were of the same type.

The cheap mass-produced Fletton brick achieved rapid popularity after about 1925, and in its more expensive textured and coloured forms was increasingly used as a substitute for the traditional facing bricks. Builders took much trouble with the brickwork of the higher priced houses, perhaps because it was given exaggerated attention by amateur surveyors. Multi-coloured, red, and other expensive hand-made facings were liberally used in such houses on all four outside walls. Otherwise, the best bricks were usually confined to the street frontage unless there were some special circumstances, as at Stoneleigh, where the backs of show houses could be seen from the station platform.

The stone facings which had been widely employed in Victorian and Edwardian suburbia disappeared almost completely after 1920, although we do find a 1934 advertisement for Glebe Gardens, New Malden talking about 'superior stone elevations', and a year later, Cotswold stone porches appeared at the Links Estate, Sundridge Park. Houses in Cotswold stone at Kenton Lane, three-bedroom semis selling at £875 in January 1935, were advertised as the first of their kind in London, and probably were, at any rate since before 1914.

Until the mid-thirties, most houses sold below £1,000, and not a few above that price, had only 9 in. of brickwork in their outside walls, a form of construction always vulnerable to driving rain if left unprotected. The best answer to this problem was the 11 in. cavity wall, recommended by the Building Research Board in 1932 and pioneered in low-cost houses by the larger firms, notably Costain, who were using it at Selsdon as early as 1924, and Laing, who included it in their 1930 'Little Palaces of Colindale' and all subsequent estates. Wimpey announced in 1938 that all their houses had this form of brickwork.

Local byelaws prevented the use of the wooden partitions found in many pre-1914 houses; non-load bearing internal walls were usually built of the cheapest grades of brick or blocks of coke breeze. Floors in the cheaper houses were normally made up from imported deal over the ventilated air space required by the local authorities, but pine strip, parquet and oak block floors were often found in houses priced above £850, particularly in the entrance hall.

Bay windows were an almost obligatory feature if the houses were to sell quickly, if only because they were rarely included in council 'dwellings'; indeed they became so popular that the expression was used to describe an acquired middle-class accent or way of life. In origin this detail was respectable, with endorsement from none other than Raymond Unwin: 'Windows facing the street are much less depressing if slightly bayed to invite a peep up and down as well as across.'[1] And they had practical advantages, offering the builder a cheap means of making rooms appear larger (measurements were frequently taken into bays) and of providing the house owner with a lighter room admitting the sun in different directions through the day. Mass-produced joinery for bay and other windows was one of the few advances in building methods adopted in the boom of the late twenties and thirties. Steel-framed windows were introduced about 1919, but were not widely used by speculative builders until the mid-thirties. Neater in appearance than the heavy wooden frames, easier to paint, and generally more weathertight, they were however apt to rust under paint if not very carefully maintained.

Builders were fond of decorating windows with square or diamond-shaped lead lights which contributed much to the desired country cottage effect. Some went to extremes having secured the appropriate craftsmen on the site, placing lead lights in the lavatory, in internal glass doors, even in the doors of kitchen cabinets. Burglars loved them as they allowed quiet and easy entry to a latch-opening hand. Unless well made, which was rare, their weather resisting qualities eventually deteriorated, but they proved an asset in wartime as they had some resistance to blast.

A 'large landing light of church window design' was to be found in 'Castle Homes' at Walton-on-Thames in 1934. Arched windows of this kind, of varying heights and widths, were often found lighting stairs and hallway. Fitted with amber glass, they imparted an illusion of perpetual autumn afternoon tranquility, exactly right for the ambience of peace and stability so many looked for in suburbia. Standing quietly in his parqueted, panelled hall, bathed in this amber glow, breathing in the subtly mixed aromas of Pear's soap, Mansion Polish and toast, the proud owner would feel the sacrifices

[1] *Cottage Plans and Common Sense*, 1901.

he had made to secure a £1,000 house well worth while.

Not all window design was backward-looking. About 1930 some windows were fitted with 'Vita Glass', admitting the ultra violet rays of the sun, which were thought to be beneficial to health, but like the flat roof, this proved but a passing phase. Glass walls or 'picture windows' occupying most of one outer wall of a room appeared in many commissioned houses of the period. Although they offered a means of saving construction costs which could be sold as an amenity they were generally spurned by the speculative builder, who rightly judged his customers to be as firmly wedded to privacy and cosiness as their Victorian predecessors.

Roofwork offered opportunities for economy. In houses selling below £1,000, the timber frame was often lightly made, of cheap woods. Boarding or felt beneath the tiles was frequently omitted with the result that lofts would be filled with several inches of snow after a hard blizzard. But it is fair to add that even the lowest priced houses of the larger firms had close-boarded roofs by the early thirties, when Wimpey and Laing, for example, were advertising this feature as universal on their estates. Tiles, first seen on London suburban villas in the 1870s, had become virtually universal by 1920, with reds predominant. Cheap concrete tiles came into general use in the mid-twenties, almost entirely ousting clay tiles as well as the last of the slates. Tile quality varied greatly; that it was often not good was evident in the number of 1920–39 houses that had to be retiled after about thirty years.

Behind the Front Door

Inside, the new houses reflected social change. Few of the designs built for sale after 1920 contained any provision for servants, for these were no longer obtainable at the low wages prevailing before 1914 (resident servants per hundred families in the London suburbs fell from 24 in 1911 to 12 in 1921.[1] Many of the purchasers of new houses in the twenties were leaving behind middle-class villas built on the assumption that at least one servant would be kept. 'Labour-saving' was the catchword of the period, indicating a trend which had already started before World War I (as early as 1911 some South Harrow houses were advertised as 'specially designed to meet the requirements of a small family not wishing to incur the worry and expense of keeping a servant'.

[1] *New Survey of London Life and Labour*, 1931.

By leaving out the 'back addition', the post-1920 designers achieved more light and air within, but despite wider frontages, a penalty had to be paid in space. With smaller rooms came lower ceilings (though not so low as they became after 1945), and, eventually, furniture shrunk to match the new scale.

Most houses in the lower price range had tiled kitchens and bathrooms, the tiling moving higher up the wall with the price, even reaching the ceiling in some cases. All post-1919 construction in the London suburbs had at least one inside w.c., often placed in the bathroom for economy's sake. Although some of the very cheap houses had only gas or electric water heaters at kitchen sink and bath, the vast majority were fitted with a hot water system operated by a back boiler in the living-room fireplace or a slow combustion stove or gas circulator in the kitchen. Heated towel rails were found higher up the price scale, whilst an airing cupboard warmed by the hot water tank was standard. Central heating as we know it today was very rare, even in the largest types, although these might have a single radiator in the hall (bedrooms were given coal fireplaces until the mid-thirties when they were gradually ousted by wall-panel electric fires or fitted gas fires). At Edgware, in 1935, A. W. Curton was offering central heating as an extra at approximately £9 a radiator.

Electricity was universal in new houses around London after World War I, but its use was as yet confined to lighting, irons, and small fires. In houses selling at less than £1,000 it was rare to find more than two or three 'power' points and about the same number of 5-amp points for radio or table lamps. A £635 house by Davis Estates in 1937 was exceptional in offering four 15-amp power points (in the kitchen, small bedroom and two main living-rooms) and panel electric fire in the second bedroom (the main bedroom had a coal fireplace). On the same estate, the purchaser of a £975 house got a little more; power points in the three downstairs rooms and three of the four bedrooms, and 5-amp points in each of the two main bedrooms. Yet at Edgware, in 1935, in houses costing between £1,000 and £1,800, there were only three power points (one in the kitchen). Electrical oddities such as newel post lamps in the hall controlled by two-way switches from upstairs or down, sometimes proved helpful to sales staff dealing with hesitant customers.

Another feature found in even the cheapest houses was some form of fitted kitchen furniture, usually at least a 'cabinet' (a descendant of the dresser), a larder, and perhaps cupboards under the sink.

These rather simple amenities were enthusiastically welcomed by the thousands of Londoners able to achieve the transition from inner area working-class property without bathroom or inside w.c., heated by coal fires, and lit by gas, oil lamps and candles. Although the new suburban homes and estates were all too frequently an aesthetic catastrophe, they invariably brought such people dramatic improvements in standards of hygiene, health and wellbeing. In particular the possession of a bathroom seemed almost dreamlike luxury to those accustomed to bathing in galvanised steel tubs before the kitchen stove or washing in cold or lukewarm water at a bedroom washstand. Salesmen worked hard on this part of the package. 'A beautiful Roman Bath' suggested Rice of Watford in 1934; 'bath floodlit by flush-fitting lamp' proposed Castle Homes of Walton-on-Thames in the same year, Others offered sunken or square baths, even 'marble bathrooms' (Edgware, 1931, Oakleigh Park, 1935). Unless cloakrooms were included in the design, a second, downstairs w.c. was rare, but most builders would oblige for another £10 or so.

Period styling was carried indoors. Oak-panelled halls (often with china rails) and panelled dining-rooms were not difficult to find in houses priced above £900; they were a standard feature in Curton's Edgware houses, selling at £1,140 upwards. A 'Queen Anne staircase' and panelled walls were available for £1,275 at Reddons Road, Beckenham in 1923, whilst the 'Bijou Baronial Halls' of the Merrylees Estates at Endersleigh Gardens, Hendon and Copt Hall Gardens, Mill Hill were described in 1930 publicity as having 'Tudor Lounges'. At Hinchley Wood, Bergs thought buyers might be attracted by an 'old world' fireplace with inglenook seats, a feature also found in later Berg estates, and at Petts Wood, where in 1932, Noel Rees was enthusing over 'old-fashioned ingle-nooks' in Oregon Pine, with fire surround of old bricks, 'an extremely attractive and cosy spot for winter days'. These inglenooks were suggested by those found in Parker and Unwin houses of the Edwardian era.

Among the many thousands of houses available at prices between £400 and £1,000 there was very little variation in interior arrangement. The entrance hall, rarely more than 6 or 7 feet wide, with barely enough space to stand a pram, stood in front of a small kitchen, originally dubbed the 'kitchen-scullery', later the 'kitchen-

ette'. Here, in somewhat cramped conditions, amid much con-
densation, all the cooking and laundry would be undertaken by the
servantless housewife, within sight and sound of the children playing in the garden or living-room. This little room, much smaller
than its pre-1914 equivalent, just managed to accommodate a
cooker, gas washing boiler, wringer, sink, hot water boiler and
storage cabinet. (Later generations were to have much difficulty in
finding room for refrigerators and washing-machines.) Alongside
the kitchenette were the two main living-rooms, one behind the
other. The dining-room, usually smaller than the sitting-room,
was at the back, often with a serving-hatch to enable food and
crockery to be passed through from the kitchen. French doors gave
access to the garden. Parallel to the side wall of the house were the
stairs, leading to a tiny landing serving the two main bedrooms
directly above the living-rooms, also the bathroom and w.c., over
the kitchenette, and, at the front of the house above the hallway,
the third bedroom, usually referred to as the 'boxroom', just large
enough to accommodate a single bed, small wardrobe and chest of
drawers.[1]

House buyers wanted the largest possible rooms for their money,
so if the builder could contrive living-rooms and main bedrooms
at around 144 sq. ft. each, within a selling price of £650–£750, he had
at once achieved a lead on his competitors. Most builders of the
cheaper houses (under £1,000) found themselves obliged to adopt a
basic rectangular plan, which kept construction simple and costs at
the minimum. These pressures produced four main rooms of more
or less equal size, leaving the third bedroom and kitchen to be
somehow squeezed into the remaining space. Thus the third bedroom was quite often only between 5 ft. 9 in. and 8 ft. wide and 7 ft.
6 in. to 10 ft. in length, whilst the kitchenette would be 5 ft. to 8 ft.
wide and 9 ft. to 10 ft. 6 in. long. Local planning authorities were
not much concerned about the small cooking and laundry area, but
the idea of bedrooms little bigger than large cupboards caused some
to pause. When approving typical house plans for West Ewell and
Stoneleigh in March 1937, the Epsom Council commented adversely
on the pokiness of the third bedrooms without requiring any change
to be made. In some designs there was so little room left for the
kitchen that it had to be attached to the back of the house, with its
own tiny roof, looking for all the world like an afterthought (e.g.
Appendix 6, plan 7).

[1] *See* plans in Appendix 6.

Only a few builders perpetuated the pre-1914 and Continental European device of folding doors or glass doors between the principal downstairs living-rooms. Bergs had some designs at Coombe Hill, Hinchley Wood, Ashtead and elsewhere in which glazed double doors opened back to merge the two downstairs rooms, or the hall and one of the living-rooms, When advertising their 1934 houses at New Malden, Wates enthusiastically suggested that with the folding doors open, one could 'make a ballroom'.

Extra rooms were rarely found in property costing less than £900 but a small 'cloakroom', with w.c. and tiny lavatory basin, entered from the hallway, might be included in a £1,000–£1,200 house. At the Glebe Gardens Estate, New Malden, in 1934, the somewhat discriminative facility of 'Gents' Cloakroom' was offered in houses selling at £850. Bergs would add a cloakroom to their hall-to-hall semis[1] for a small extra charge, building out the porch and using up part of the hall window space. When roofspace was accessible from the first floor, the more imaginative builders provided large walk-in cupboards, usually described as 'boxrooms', The New Ideal Homesteads £745 chalet of the thirties (Appendix 6) included a boxroom with 100 sq. ft. of floorspace alongside the two upstairs rooms. Integral garages were similarly used, one builder advertising the 'room' as suitable for 'maid's room, bedroom, children's playroom, office, or workshop' (to have had the maid in a room which could be reached only via the master bedroom would surely have led to complications). Few builders used the term 'breakfast-room' after the mid-twenties, although A. W. Curton's 1935 brochure for the Edgwarebury Lane Estate, Edgware showed such a room at the back of the house between kitchen and drawing-room in all the more expensive designs. Later the third room on the ground floor was usually referred to as the 'study', 'morning room' or 'maid's sitting-room', and in one solitary example (Highams Estate, Woodford Green, 1930), it was described as the 'day nursery'. Three rooms on the ground floor were available at prices as low as £695 to £995 at Spring Park Farm Estate, Shirley, in 1933. In these the third room, the 'breakfast-room' (varying in size from 8 ft. 9 in. by 7 ft. 7½ in. to 10 ft. 7 in. by 7 ft. 6 in.), was placed between the dining-room and the 'scullery'. Some builders included 'lounge halls' in their more expensive houses, a room entered directly from the front door (or via a very small vestibule) and containing the staircase and a fireplace. Most of Curton's Edgwarebury Lane

[1] See plan in Appendix 6.

houses over £1,390 had this feature, and above £1,605 it was in addition to dining-room, drawing-room and breakfast-room.

Deprived of a spare room, with no excess space in the hallway, the owners of the cheaper houses soon acquired unsightly garden sheds (often assembled from wood left behind by the builders), in which to shelter their bicycles, perambulators, tools and garden implements.

The Hallowed Plot

A major attraction of suburban life had always been the opportunity it seemed to offer of enjoying the pleasanter aspects of rural life whilst remaining in touch with the amenities of urban civilisation. The garden was an essential part of the life style, assuming new importance in the twenties and thirties as a result of two changes which came during and immediately after the war. Extra evening daylight in the main gardening season arrived with the introduction of 'Daylight Saving' (Summer Time) in 1916. The second change was a reduction in working hours; before 1914, office hours of 9 a.m. to 6 p.m. or even 6.30 p.m., with a 1 p.m. or 1.30 p.m. departure on Saturdays, had not been uncommon in central London, but after 1919, 9 a.m. to 5 p.m. or 5.30 p.m., with a 12 p.m. or 12.30 p.m. Saturday finish became usual. Well-groomed gardens were seen everywhere in the new suburbs, an outlet for creative drives suppressed in the routines of office life; many of the new house owners devoted almost all their leisure daylight hours to them, growing vegetables and fruit as well as mounting a floral display for nine months of the year. Prowess was encouraged by office gardening societies, which organised shows and competitions, obtaining seeds and other goods at wholesale prices.

Except at corner sites, gardens were usually an unimaginative standard rectangle 80 to 200 feet long and 20 to 40 feet wide. Although there would have been little or no extra cost, no builder seems to have thought of adding interest to the gardens by providing interlaced curved plots or irregular shapes. More land was available in some outer areas, mostly with houses in the higher price range; thus at Tadworth in 1934, Costains provided a 300-foot garden with their £1,180 detached houses, whilst at Bookham in 1939 there were £1,150 houses in 250-foot gardens. Sites of half an acre, with gardens up to 400 feet in length, were on sale at Pinner Hill in 1923, and in the same year, gardens of equal length came with £900 houses at Taplow, Few were deterred by challenges of this kind.

Some new gardeners found houses built on old market gardens or orchards, with well fertilised topsoil or trees and fruit bushes still in position, as at the Broadlands Estate, Ponders End, in 1935 and the £775 houses in Mill Lane, Oxhey in 1938. The latter, on 200-ft. plots, had the further attraction of 'overlooking a mill stream'. Less content was the keen amateur who acquired a patch of heavy clay lightly scattered with builders' debris, the more usual case. Later, the topsoil removed during the building operations was sold back by the local garden supplier, and everyone was happy.

Fences were frequently skimped. Cheap softwood, or chicken wire strung between poorly galvanised stakes, was considered adequate to divide plots. For a little extra on the sale price, some builders took more trouble; Bergs for example used close-boarded cedar wood, topped by a squared trellis in the same material, much of which still stands after almost forty years. At the front, the houses were separated from the street by gardens rather larger than those found in many Edwardian and later Victorian lower middle-class suburbs. Here boundaries were established by low walls of up to six courses of bricks or of crazy stones, sometimes topped by wooden posts carrying ornamental iron chains or low wooden palings, altogether flimsier barriers than the iron railings and high walls favoured by the Victorians. These low walls and fences fore-shadowed a breaking down of the separation between house and street, a tendency also seen in the planting of grass verges and roadside trees and shrubs, suggesting an extension of the gardens to the edge of the highway.

A House for the Car

The space demands of what was to become the most popular adult toy of the century were recognised as early as 1906 when houses on the Hale Brook Estate, Edgware, were advertised as having 'room for motor'. Garages, at that time more often described as 'motor houses' or 'motor sheds', were included with some specula-tively built London houses from about 1912, but the greater part of the twenties construction still lacked this feature. Indeed, until the early thirties it was sometimes found that the houses with garages, because they were that much more expensive, sold more slowly than those without.

'Garage space' was increasingly available between pairs of semis from about 1926 and after the end of the twenties many builders would be ready to provide brick garages as an extra for between £30 and £60. In this final decade, more and more detached and semi-detached houses above £850 or so in price were designed with integral garages, though these were often uncomfortably tight for anything but the smallest cars.

Caveat Emptor

All new residential building, as explained earlier, was subject to local byelaws under the Public Health Acts. These were principally concerned with such points as drainage, sanitary arrangements, ventilation around the structure, dimensions of rooms, and construction of walls, foundations, chimneys, and staircases, and were directed at ensuring basic standards of health and safety. They made no attempt to impose a general specification in regard to materials and workmanship and ignored many important aspects of construction and finishing. In those areas where large numbers of houses were going up at the same time it was physically impossible for the surveyor's department of the local council to maintain adequate byelaw supervision, though no doubt these usually most conscientious officials did their best to keep a sharp eye open. In practice it was rarely possible to manage more than one inspection of any house and the builders, through ignorance or intention, had ample opportunity to proceed by their own methods and then cover up. Another difficulty occurred in some of the more rural areas where the local authority used part-time surveyors and building inspectors otherwise in the employ of builders and developers for whom they were preparing housing plans and giving advice on construction. Clearly this was a situation which created opportunities for slackness of supervision.

Nor did the inspections carried out by the building societies exercise any particular influence on quality. These inspections were undertaken primarily for the purposes of valuation and were normally made soon after completion, when faults in construction were concealed and it was too early to notice their outward effects.

With competition forcing prices down to rock bottom, skilled labour diluted by sheer weight of output, and a general scamper to complete and sell as many houses as possible whilst the boom lasted, it would have been surprising if standards had not slipped. A contemporary commentator outlined the picture:

'Small houses are on average much more lightly built than in prewar days. The roughcast can and does hide a multitude of faults – the timber work is lighter, the roofs not nearly so well tiled, and the joiner's work, plywood and the like, not nearly so satisfactory.'[1]

The use of inadequately trained workmen could lead even the best builders to produce unsatisfactory houses. Not every firm could boast with W. H. Wedlock Ltd of Bexleyheath, 'All labour by skilled Trade Union craftsmen. No piecework.'[2] There just weren't enough experienced men to go round.

But the picture was not entirely black, and those prepared to pay a little above the average prices could still find a fairly high order of quality. Three-bedroom houses with garages in Kent House Road, Beckenham, advertised by Messrs Wisdom in 1930 for £1,050, certainly had slightly larger rooms than similar houses selling elsewhere for £600–£800, but the extra money also purchased a meticulous specification: solid concrete foundations of 2 ft. 6 in. square section; $4\frac{1}{2}$ in. iron gutters; $2\frac{1}{2}$ in. iron down pipes; $\frac{1}{8}$ in.-plate water tanks; brass mortice locks in all internal doors; joists 9 in. by 2 in.; stairs wedged and screwed; 1 in. floor boards; and a double damp course. Most of the larger firms took trouble to maintain high standards. Laing, for example, imposed the following standard specification throughout their estates of the thirties: cavity walls; oversize timbers in roofwork; tiles laid over roofing felt; foundations excavated wider and deeper than local authorities' byelaws required; concrete foundations under partition walls; ballast concrete over the site; copper hot water cylinders and pipes; insides of gutters painted; all hidden woodwork primed before being placed in position; steel joists inserted above window bays. In themselves, these items provide a useful checklist of the vulnerable points in the cheaper houses of the less reputable firms.

Builders with fairly clear consciences frequently included in their publicity an invitation to 'bring your own architect or surveyor', even in some cases offering to pay all expenses and provide him with detailed plans and specifications. Others, anxious to reassure

---

[1] TEG 24 June 1933, from a paper read to the International Congress of Building Societies by J. G. Kitchen.
[2] Advertisement in *Southern Railway Suburban Timetable*, 1937.

worried enquirers, merely laid claim to 'pre-war quality'. There was also a rather special attribute known as 'northern quality': 'Mr Boothman is a Northerner. He believes that the sturdy, solid building in the northern counties will be appreciated in this mushroom capital. He has brought his own workmen hundreds of miles to build these houses.' (*Briar Hill Estate, Northolt, 1930*)

But the mediocre, if not the downright bad, generally outweighed the good, and by the early thirties, concern was being expressed in the professional journals at the quality of the vast output then in progress, 90 per cent of it, according to one writer, without the supervision of qualified professionals.[1] The employers' association, the National Federation of Builders, began in 1935 to investigate methods of raising the standard of small house building, and in the following year a Standards Board was set up under the chairmanship of Sir Raymond Unwin. This body had the task of prescribing standard specifications and it included representatives of the Royal Institute of British Architects, the British Standards Institution, the building societies, and of course, the builders. Eventually it produced a voluntary scheme, announced by the Minister of Health in January 1937. A National Housebuilders' Registration Council with Unwin as chairman, was to administer the registration of builders who were prepared to guarantee that their houses were built to the standard specification. The register would be available to purchasers and the houses subject to inspection by the NHBRC officials at various stages of construction, after which the builder would give a two-year warranty to remedy any defects. Within eight months it was claimed that over a quarter of the housebuilders in the United Kingdom had supported the scheme, though this may have been an overstatement; at any rate, 1,138 firms had by then registered and by 1939 many of the big London firms such as Wates, New Ideal Homesteads, Laing and Wimpey were advertising the guarantee.

In almost every new area around London it was not difficult to find examples of the sort of thing which had brought about the formation of the NHBRC. Wet walls and floors, cracks and tilts caused by inadequate foundations; leaky roofs and windows; insecure ceilings; weak, creaking staircases; ill-fitting doors; warped windowsills; and smoky chimneys – all these were common enough. In some cases the houses were so bad that the unlucky purchasers

[1] TEG 10 August 1935, letter from the secretary of the Incorporated Association of Architects and Surveyors.

were moved to warn potential customers by putting up notices in their front gardens; DON'T BUY WITHOUT SEEING US FIRST appeared at West Molesey, and COME AND SEE MY HOUSE BEFORE YOU SEE THE SHOW HOUSE at Orpington, the last painted by a professional signwriter. One builder sought legal advice about this knocking of his product, but was told he was powerless to stop it.

Even the larger firms occasionally lapsed during the peak of the boom. Lead pipes which had burst because they were unsupported for 6 ft. were discovered in 1934 houses of one of the major companies, who received some unwelcome publicity when the matter was discussed in court four years afterwards (they had long before made good at their expense). A house built in Feltham in 1933 by the same firm was described in another court as 'disgracefully built. The workmanship was bad. The materials were bad. The byelaws in many respects had been ignored.' This house had cost the unfortunate purchaser £475 and the remedying of the defects had required a further £110.

Builders and developers were sometimes taken to court by purchasers for breach of contract. An early case of this type occurred in 1930 when a resident of the Cannon Hill Estate at Raynes Park obtained judgement for £91 7s with costs at the City of London Court after alleging that his £915 house, purchased new in 1928, was not weatherproof. It was stated that rain penetrated the walls, running down the inside until it soaked into the floorboards and caused fungus to appear. An appeal court upheld the award, stating that if a purchaser contracted with a builder to erect a house for him, or if he agreed to buy a house in the course of erection intending to occupy it when ready, there was an implication in law that the house was fit for human habitation, which this house was not.[1] A similar case in 1932 concerned a house bought the previous year in Stafford Road, Waddon for £785. A week after occupation, rain penetrated the ceiling of the upper front bay, damaging furniture, and ceilings cracked and fell. On grounds of breach of warranty, a sum of £50 was awarded.[2] Ceilings also gave trouble in a house in Tillingbourne Gardens, Finchley, bought new in 1933. One of the owners was injured when they collapsed. The judge found a breach of warranty and awarded the cost of repairs plus £340 damages and legal costs.[3]

[1] TEG 5 April 1930, 10 May 1930, 24 January 1931.
[2] TEG 23 July 1932.   [3] TEG 18 April 1936.

When a firm of builders brought an action against a purchaser for the balance of a second mortgage advanced to him in 1927, it was alleged by the defendant's counsel that the new house, in the High View Estate, Beddington, was a 'ramshackle collection of bricks', neither windtight nor watertight. The man's wife and child fell ill as a result of the dampness of the house, and were forced to vacate it early in 1932. An architect who examined the property on behalf of the court thought it fair value for £995 at the time of purchase, although cheaply built. Sir Francis Newbolt, giving judgement for the defendant, said that the houses had been built without an architect and shortly after occupation it had become clear that the property in question was not habitable. Huge patches of damp formed on the walls, nurturing fungus; bedclothes had to be dried out every day, and the furniture was damaged.[1]

Builders were also sued or warned by the local councils after infringement of the building byelaws. In 1926 the Hendon surveyor found that the floor of a new house had been completed without any concrete being laid over the site, and the builder had not sent in the required notice for inspection. The local newspaper, reporting that the builder had been warned of prosecution in the event of further offence, commented that the houses in question were by no means cheap; 'many of the new houses seem to be erected with phenomenal rapidity and one is not really surprised to learn that in the hurry a most important byelaw has been broken'.[2] At Dartford Police Court in 1933 a builder was accused of failing to give the Bexley Council notice of completion of houses, and of contravening building byelaws by constructing roofs so that woodwork extended across party walls, and placing a wooden bressumer in a party wall. The houses concerned were part of an estate of 900 at Welling, and the builder admitted discharging some of his carpenters for carelessness. Council inspectors gave evidence that work was often covered up before they were able to look at a house. Conviction was obtained on each of the summonses and a fine imposed.

Even council houses, built to a careful specification under proper professional supervision, were not always free from serious defects when those concerned were under pressure to provide large numbers as quickly as possible. Some of the cottages on the LCC Watling estate at Edgware showed signs of subsidence cracking by 1930, whilst others were found to have rotten floorboards which had

[1] TEG 1 April 1933.
[2] GGG 12 March 1926.

to be ripped out and replaced in 1930–1. The Council heard that 'owing to the urgent need for the houses', the foundation and erection work had been hurried through without the usual interval to let drains and watercourses settle; and the winters of 1926 and 1927, when construction was going on, had been abnormally wet. The dry rot affected no less than 1,561 houses, almost one third of the estate, requiring an expenditure of £39,000 to put right.[1]

Owner-occupiers could not expect thorough renewals on this scale. Most of them were too heavily committed to afford the luxury of legal action, even if the builder was still accessible and solvent, and their only recourse was to patch up and cover up, perhaps selling and moving elsewhere if they were able to do so. Others defaulted on the mortgage as soon as the small cash stake they had handed over could be written off as rent. But the problem diminished; as the pace of building slowed after 1934 and as the influence of the larger firms and the NHBRC spread, the likelihood of purchasers securing adequate quality gradually improved.

[1] EG 7 April 1933, 22 September 1933, TEG 8 April 1933.

Chapter 9

COUNCIL COTTAGES
1920-39

One Fifth for the Lowly
Only about one fifth of all the new housing erected in Greater London between the wars was sponsored by the local authorities. Of the 771,759 flats and houses completed between 1919 and 1938, 76,877 were for the LCC and 76,311 for the other councils. Reflecting the changes in central government policy outlined in chapter five, local authority output in the Greater London area rose to peaks of just over 16,000 dwellings in 1927 and more than 15,000 in the subsequent year, falling each year thereafter until 1931 in the face of uncertainty about subsidies and costs. Apart from a minor peak of almost 11,000 in 1931, the output did not exceed 10,000 again until 1936. The final withdrawal of the Wheatley subsidy was followed by legislation emphasising slum clearance rather than additional housing, and when the graph began its slow upward trend after 1933, work was concentrated on the most pressing need – blocks of flats in inner London. This change shows clearly in the LCC figures: between 1919 and 1927, cottages comprised over 85 per cent of the output (over 90 per cent in most years), but in 1931-2, the percentage of cottages began to decline, so that by 1939-40, of the 4,922 dwellings completed in the year, only 323 were suburban houses.

When abolishing the subsidies on council houses in 1933, the Conservative government was assuming that with falling prices and interest rates and the saturation of the middle-class market, private builders would erect houses to let for the working class. They had been encouraged in this hope by the National Federation of Housebuilders, who had assured them that this change would follow the withdrawal of subsidies. As we shall see, London private builders and developers did move into the cheaper end of the market in a substantial manner, but most of their houses were still beyond the reach of the ordinary worker; even the few built to rent could not be let at rents which fitted comfortably into his wages.

In London, as elsewhere, the council houses erected in quantity in the twenties proved beyond the means of all but the most highly paid workers, despite the fact that post-1919 local authority rents were failing in general to recoup full costs. Indeed the LCC suffered some embarrassment when it was revealed that one of its own employees had been refused a council house because his wages were regarded as insufficient to support the rent liability.[1] There was also some evidence of selection at the other end of the social scale. Not all councils encouraged white-collar applicants; a clerk in the Post Office Engineering Department, with four children, demobilised after four years in the army, was told by a Lambeth council official in 1920 'we are not building houses for your class', but was eventually included in the waiting list after making a strong protest.[2] Even those who managed to get a council house because they were regarded as capable of meeting the relatively high rents often found it a hard struggle to make ends meet. They not only had to find money for the many expenses of keeping up appearances on a brand new estate, but also for extra fares to their work in inner London.

It is not surprising that in the early days of the big LCC cottage estates, many soon gave up and drifted back to their old environment. Becontree, with its particular transport difficulties, was especially unpopular, so much so that with many houses empty in the first few years, the LCC were obliged to advertise the estate on their tramcars. Other factors contributed to the drift back and the unpopularity of the estates with those who stayed. Spaciously laid out, on the very edges of the metropolis, these new developments were somewhat bleak reflections of the suburban estates of the more enlightened private builders. As such, they presented a stark contrast to the gregarious warmth of the crowded tenements or close-packed terraces their tenants had known since childhood. Relatives, especially mothers, remained behind in inner London, and the close kinship ties of urban working-class life were disrupted. White-collar suburbans, apart from the occasional mild neurosis of the housebound wives, did not find the isolation and loneliness of the new areas too difficult to endure; with them, kinship ties mattered less, and they were accustomed to 'keeping themselves to themselves'.

[1] A. Emil Davies, *The Story of the LCC*, 1925.
[2] Recalled in a letter to the author by G. T. Moody.

It was not easy for the manual workers and their families to adapt. The men missed the accessible street corner 'bookie' and pub, and the vast inhuman halls of the LCC's 'Improved Licensed Refreshment Houses' were no substitute for the latter. Their wives found the shops farther away, the prices higher, the credit less easily obtained, the assistants cold, the stock lacking variety. The average suburban shopping centre had little appeal for women accustomed to friendly banter with street stallholders and owners of street-corner shops who lived in a room behind the counter. These strains bore most heavily on the earlier residents because life on the council estates eventually assumed many of the characteristics of that of inner London and relatives gradually moved out to be near their kin. In her study of the LCC Watling Estate, Ruth Durant tells how in the autumn of 1927, shortly after the first houses had been occupied, a woman banged loudly on her neighbour's door, and when it was opened, cried out 'What's happened?' When asked what should have happened, the woman, who was quivering with fright, replied 'Everything is so terribly quiet'.[1]

Later, as social organisations developed and the houses filled up, compensations appeared, and these great estates settled down to a way of life uniquely their own, quite distinct from that of the private enterprise suburbs, which they resembled only in layout and superficial appearance.

For almost all the tenants, the houses represented a great advance on what they had known before. Standards of local authority housing were significantly higher than those of the pre-1914 era; almost without exception, the recommendations of the 1919 Tudor Walters Report to the Minister of Health were followed, notably in its emphasis on a good proportion of 'parlour houses' (two reception rooms) and a living-room of at least 180 square feet to relieve congestion in the kitchen/scullery. A separate bathroom was now the general rule.

There was, however, some underestimation of the requirement for larger houses to meet the lower income group's tendency to produce large families. As a result, the LCC were somewhat shocked to learn after the 1931 Census and a survey carried out following the 1935 Housing Act that a fair number of the houses on its new suburban estates were overcrowded by the accepted definition of more than two persons to a room.

[1] Ruth Durant, *Watling: A Social Survey of the LCC Estate at Watling*, 1939.

The LCC: Problems and Achievement

Overshadowing the output of all other local authorities was that of the LCC, who built over half the council houses and flats erected in Greater London between the wars. Lacking sufficient building land within its own area, the County Council had to place almost two-thirds of its new construction on so-called 'out-county' estates, assuming the role of 'a colonising power, like Ancient Rome, pouring out the treasure and labour of her citizens in order to make new homes for them in foreign lands'.[1]

As coloniser, the LCC encountered many difficulties, brushing constantly against the insularity of the numerous outer London authorities responsible for providing the schools, clinics, libraries, street services and other amenities and utilities needed on the new estates. Bringing in its train an enormous influx of working-class Londoners, the powerful interloper met with much resentment born of social and financial foreboding. Most councils rightly guessed that it would cost them more to provide services to the LCC estates than they would recover from the additional rate income. There was also a fairly widespread suspicion that the admission of an LCC estate was somehow the first step towards annexation of the whole district into the County of London. Fairly typical was the reaction of the *Golders Green Gazette* to a 1924 proposal by the LCC to purchase land at Edgware:

> 'As is inevitable in such cases, this will lead to a big slum development, impairing the good work already in hand in the north of the Chandos Estate, and completely "knocking out" any chance of residential development at Burnt Oak. Workmen from all sorts of localities, and attached to work in all sorts of directions, i.e *not by any means local workmen*, will invade and pervade the whole district from Edgware to the Hyde and Hendon. This is a serious matter, not by reason of any thought of antagonism to the workmen, but for the destruction it will involve to the original most praiseworthy and necessary aims of the Railway and needs of the district.'[2]

Local councillors had learned a few tricks by 1935, when the County Council's eyes were upon 700 of the 1,000 acres of Crown Lands known as Fairlop Plain, east of Barkingside. Ilford Council quickly

[1] W. A. Robson, evidence to RCGDIP, 15 June 1938.
[2] GGG 12 September 1924.

9. The shopping centre, Golders Green Road, looking towards Hendon, c. 1923. (From a commercial postcard, M. Series.)

The first house to be built (October 1907) in the Hampstead Garden Suburb at Asmons Hill. (Photo: Alan A. Jackson.)

10. Estate construction at Queensbury on 25 September 1935. The Metropolitan Railway Stanmore branch is in the foreground; the roads immediately beyond the railway are Dean Drive, Taunton Way and Honeypot Lane; the new roads without houses at the top left are those later used for the LCC Kenmore Park Estate. (Photo: Aerofilms Ltd.)

Estate construction for New Ideal Homesteads at Mossford Park, north Ilford, May 1934. Mossford Lane and County High School (under construction) at right of picture. (Photo: Aerofilms Ltd.)

decided that it would prefer the site to be used as an aerodrome, and sought loan sanction from the Ministry of Health to achieve this. After this rebuff, the LCC turned to a site at Chigwell, a little farther north, of which only a small part had to be acquired by compulsory purchase. At the inquiry, one lady resident vented her wrath on the establishment:

'*Mrs Bastard*: You haved ruined my home! (*turning to LCC officials*) Do any of you gentlemen live near an LCC estate?
(*receiving no answer*)
No, I don't suppose you do,
(*addressing the Ministry's Inspector*):
Do you live near an estate?
The Inspector: They have just bought some land near my house.
Mrs Bastard: Do you like it?
The Inspector: No.'[1]

About the same time, a great storm had blown up in Chingford, where the LCC were trying to acquire the 220-acre Friday Hill Estate, which they proposed to cover with 2,000 houses at an average density of 12 to the acre. In the local town planning scheme, the area had been zoned for residential development at 8 to 10 houses to the acre, but on the very same day that the LCC decided upon compulsory purchase, the Chingford UDC met to agree compulsory purchase orders on 50 acres of the land for 'open spaces and highway improvements'. At the subsequent inquiry, a witness for the residents of the adjacent Whitehall and Endlebury districts expressed the opinion that the LCC's tenants would come mostly from the East End, and that 'many of them would not even be of British origin'. An Ilford chartered surveyor contributed the information that certain houses fetched an average of £920 at Ilford, but those similar in date and design on the edge of the LCC estate at Goodmayes realised only £726. Despite the strength of the opposition, the LCC won their way and the purchase of 179 acres was completed in 1938.[2]

The County Council were also successful in acquiring 142 acres just north of Headstone Lane station for development at between 10 and 12 to the acre. This was in a typical middle-class suburban area and in August 1935 at the Ministry of Health Inquiry, E. Comben, of Messrs Comben and Wakeling, builders, complained

[1] As reported in TEG, 10 October 1936.
[2] TEG 5 October 1935; 26 February 1938.

that sales of £875–£1,200 houses on the opposite side of Uxbridge road had fallen from 12 to 3 a month since the publication of the LCC's plans.[1]

Such devaluation of overlooking property was no doubt inevitable, but once the newcomers arrived, social fears were soon seen to be exaggerated. For the reasons already given, the LCC's 'out-county' tenants of the period were confined to the better-paid and, in general, the more presentable members of the lower orders; some were even civil servants.

The difficulties which faced the LCC in establishing its suburban colonies were aggravated when, as sometimes happened, the chosen site overflowed the boundaries of one or more local authorities. Many of the problems might have been resolved more easily, even avoided altogether, had the County Council accepted a 1918 proposal that a Joint Housing Authority be set up for Greater London with the task of distributing the LCC housing evenly around the outer districts as an alternative to concentration in large estates. But County Hall was suspicious and distrustful of the concept of an *ad hoc* body which might tend to undermine its hard-won power.[2]

As the LCC had no statutory authority to operate public transport services outside its area, this important matter had to be left to chance and persuasion. Yet good transport connections to inner London were vital to the existence of most out-county estates because the County Council was equally bereft of powers to establish or foster industrial development.[3] In more than one case the LCC would have built tramways to serve suburban estates, but was prevented from introducing the necessary legislation without the consent of the local authorities through whose areas the line would pass. Opposition was encouraged not only by the fears we have mentioned, but by the increasingly powerful road transport and motorcar lobbies, who sought to establish the electric tramcar as an unpopular anachronism. Parliament, for its part, refused to relax its standing orders to allow the LCC to override local opposition.

As well as completing the pre-1914 estates at Tottenham, Hammersmith and Norbury,[4] the LCC constructed 8 new cottage

[1] TEG 17 August 1935.
[2] E. R. Abbott, evidence to RCLG, 17 May 1922.
[3] For example, 2.2m. workmen's ticket passengers used Burnt Oak Underground station (on the Watling Estate) in 1936, forming 38.5 per cent of the station's total traffic. At Morden, which served the LCC's St Helier Estate, the figures were 3.9m. and 43.3 per cent (*LPTB Annual Report, 1937*).
[4] See chapter 5.

estates between 1919 and 1939, most of them of considerable size. In the late thirties 7 more estates were started, some of them to be largely complete by 1940. All 15 developments will be reviewed in a later chapter. The sum of this not insubstantial contribution to London's suburban growth in the interwar period was about 61,000 cottages and flats, 26,000 of them at Becontree alone.[1]

For most of this time, the man in charge of the design, layout, and construction of the council's vast housing enterprise was their Chief Architect, G. Topham Forrest,[2] who favoured plain and simple Georgian styles with backward looks at Hampstead and Letchworth. Practical and hardwearing, if a little dreary, his cottages and flats featured square-paned sash windows, plain front doors with tiny canopies, tiled roofs, and honest brick exteriors. Garden Suburb influences were also seen in the studied informality of estate layout, the little greens, and the careful groupings at intersections. Yet, despite these efforts, and attempts to retain as many trees as possible, the overall impression remained institutional and lacklustre. In a contemporary publication, the LCC appeared to acknowledge this, explaining that financial stringency had 'enforced not only simplicity of design, but also a considerable degree of standardisation'.[3] At St Helier, and later estates, some attempt was made to lighten the general effect by importing from private enterprise developments such design features as tile hung bays and rough-hewn cedar planking under the gables.

Inside, these little houses were grimly utilitarian. To save money, many of those built in the twenties had no proper hot water system. Water for baths had to be heated in a washing copper in the scullery and then transferred to the bath by means of a small semi-rotary pump or syphonic apparatus. In many designs, the bathroom was inconveniently situated on the ground floor. Another economy was the abandonment of the secondary means of access, which meant that dustbins had to be carried through the

[1] This figure, taken from Table 13 in *London Housing Statistics 1946–48*, (LCC), includes a small number of wartime completions.
[2] 1872–1945. After service with the Leeds and West Riding Councils, Forrest became county education architect for Northumberland, and later, county architect for Essex. He was appointed architect to the LCC in 1919. His LCC work also included educational buildings and hospitals, the post graduate medical school at Hammersmith, and the architectural treatment for the Chelsea and Lambeth Bridges, the latter in partnership with Sir Reginald Blomfield. He retired in 1935 and was succeeded by E. P. Wheeler (*LCC Minutes*).
[3] *Housing: With Particular Reference to Post-War Housing Schemes*, LCC, 1928.

house to the street, although the designers did see to it that this was not done across the living-rooms.

Other Councils' Housing

Only two authorities within the LCC area managed to provide housing outside the county boundary. The City Corporation's estate at Gants Hill, Ilford, was born of the 1919 Act. An ambitious development of 2,000 cottages was planned, to cover a site stretching from just west of Cranbrook Road across to Horns Road, but work was suddenly stopped when the government cut off the subsidies in 1921. At that time, only 220 houses had been built, and the remaining land, some of it already covered with footings, reverted to the farmer. Eastern Avenue was slashed through the estate area in 1922, and six years later, as bus services were bringing the district to life, the City's lands were sold off to Charles Henry Lord, of Bradford.[1] Before long, some of the cottages facing the main roads had been profitably converted into shops.

Special statutory powers allowed Hampstead Borough Council to erect 122 houses and flats in Cricklewood, just outside its boundary, in 1935. Most of the other metropolitan boroughs confined their housing activities to large blocks of flats, making maximum use of what little building land they had. Exceptions were Woolwich, Greenwich and Wandsworth, where some open land remained.

Using a good deal of direct labour, Woolwich built more flats and cottages between 1919 and 1938 than any other metropolitan borough. Almost 4,500 dwellings had been completed by 1939, most of them on 3 large estates. Situated just north of Eltham Green, the 334-acre Page Estate, which was started in 1920, eventually contained 2,306 cottages and flats, 4 primary schools, 3 churches, 2 clubs, a welfare centre, a shopping centre, and a children's playground. Completed in 1937, this development was served by Eltham Well Hall and Kidbrooke stations on the Southern Railway's Bexleyheath line, and, after 1932, by the LCC's final tramway extension, which ran along the wide Westhorne Avenue, affording direct connection to Woolwich town centre and Lewisham. The Middle Park Estate, between Eltham Hill and Sidcup Road dated from 1931–36, and contained 1,517 houses and flats, a school and a church (both provided by 1933). Here there were houses with

[1] Information from the Deputy Keeper of the Records, Corporation of London, in a letter to the author.

half-timbering and tiled porches, almost indistinguishable from speculative building of the same period. Woolwich's last inter-war estate, Horn Park (south-east of Westhorne Avenue and west of Sidcup Road) was begun in 1936 and had 544 dwellings by 1939.

Wandsworth, already mentioned in chapter five, completed 1,764 cottages and flats by 1938. The Greenwich total in the same period was 1,111.

Outside the LCC area, housing provision was the responsibility of the county and municipal boroughs, and the urban and rural district councils. In Middlesex, the Harrow, Enfield and Edmonton councils each built around 1,800 houses and flats between 1919 and 1938. Ealing, Hayes and Harlington, Twickenham, and Heston and Isleworth were close behind, all with totals exceeding 1,400. In Essex, Walthamstow, with very little suitable land left uncovered, managed a creditable 1,740 dwellings between 1920 and 1939. South of the river, the county borough of Croydon had 3,519 properties on its rent roll by 31 March 1938, most of them built after 1919 on 3 large estates: Norbury (1920–27), east of the railway between Thornton Heath and Norbury stations (792 dwellings); Mitcham Road, east of Waddon Marsh station (1928–31; 832); and Waddon, just south of Waddon station (1925–6 and 1931–4; 1,205). In June 1935, the Croydon Corporation approved a 'garden city' scheme for 569 acres of farmland south-east of Addington village. To be known as New Addington, this was to be developed by the First National Housing Trust, with assistance from the Ministry of Health. Some 4,000 houses, with rents as low as 10s and 11s were to be provided, together with 2 churches, a cinema, and open spaces. Work began in 1937, and by 1939 about 1,000 houses (mostly semis) had been finished. Over 650 were occupied. After World War II, the estate was completed by Croydon Corporation and the population rose to 27,000. As this isolated outpost was remote from any railway station, it was linked to the centre of Croydon by a sponsored bus service, to be mentioned later.[1]

It is surprising to find that some Surrey councils did better than those of rather more plebian Middlesex. Mitcham had achieved the respectable total of 4,520 houses by 1938, Kingston-on-Thames 2,908, Merton and Morden 2,570, and Sutton and Cheam, 2,613. Even such predominantly middle-class areas as Esher, Epsom and Ewell, Carshalton, Beddington and Wallington, and Coulsdon and Purley each managed over 1,500 in the period.

[1] TEG 29 June 1935; *Croydon, the Story of a Hundred Years* (ed. J. B. Gent), 1970.

Chapter 10

LIFE IN THE NEO-GEORGIAN SUBURBS

London Suburban Man
Quite the largest element among the inhabitants of the new suburbs were the white collars: civil servants and other public sector officials; bank, insurance and finance house employees; railway office staff; sales and advertising men; journalists; schoolteachers; technicians; and the higher echelons of the retail trade. In the smaller houses and the cheaper bungalows, would be found a significant section of the top layer of the working class: skilled tradesmen; postal, transport and newspaper workers; foremen; and the uniformed ranks of the public services.

Most of these new suburbans originated in the Victorian and Edwardian suburbs, making place as they moved outwards for regional immigrants and less fortunate Londoners coming from even older and more crowded property nearer the centre. When choosing a new house, Londoners tended to look along the transport routes long familiar from Sunday and Bank Holiday excursions. Thus residents of East and West Ham would favour Rainham, Hornchurch or Upminster; whilst Walthamstow and Leyton would look at houses in Chingford, Woodford and Buckhurst Hill; Tottenham, Edmonton and Wood Green would tend to move out to Enfield, Cheshunt or Broxbourne; Malden and Earlsfield would go to Epsom, Ashtead or Hinchley Wood; and so on. Of about a hundred members of a Camden Town firm, over half had moved to new houses at Watling, Hendon, Colindale, Kingsbury, Edgware and Mill Hill by the summer of 1934; not all were newly married – in some cases, grown up sons and daughters had persuaded their parents to move to be near them.[1] This may be taken as reasonably typical, but of course the migration was not entirely radial, although it was rare for a Londoner to cross the river (that was foreign territory, with a quite unfamiliar, distinctively different transport

[1] HTBG 21 September 1934.

system). Associated with the radial migration was the influence exercised by the location of workplace; a man whose office was on the eastern side of the City would be most likely to choose somewhere served from Liverpool Street or Fenchurch Street stations; civil servants working in the Whitehall area patronised new developments which could be reached directly from Waterloo, Charing Cross or Victoria.

Still close to their working-class origins, white-collar families practised frugality and financial prudence almost instinctively, but their large-scale conversion to owner-occupation did not come about by deliberate choice. If they wanted a new house, they had virtually no alternative but to buy. And the safety conscious building societies for their part made sure that mortgages went only to those with secure jobs and regular salaries.

Returning his monthly tribute to the building society, the typical London suburban man of the period had regular habits and pursued a self-contained, somewhat devitalised existence of security and respectability. Everything in his life centred around the new home, which he sought to make a shelter from the harsh realities of the world, a controllable, predictable environment for himself and his family. Sensitive copywriters sometimes struck just the right note, 'the Estate possesses everything that could be desired for a well-ordered and comfortable life'.[1]

For the family, social life was restricted, the deprivation often self-imposed. Housewives in particular led a strangely isolated, lonely existence during the time the rest of the family was away at work or school. Few married women had outside jobs and if there were no children of pre-school age to look after, they quickly became bored with their own company in the tranquil, blank surroundings. Their upbringing, frequently reinforced with natural shyness, hindered communication with others in like straits. Women who had lived in a Surrey suburb for over a year hardly knew their neighbours' names and contacts were minimal: 'People just nod, and pass on'.[2] Not surprisingly, mental and spiritual well-being was sometimes undermined, some women succumbing to a state social workers of the thirties began to call 'suburban neurosis'. The causes of this malady were said to be threefold: lack of social contacts, leading to boredom; worries about money and the home; and a false set of values derived from novels and films which implanted

[1] E. and L. Berg advertisement in HF 12 December 1936.
[2] *The Resident* (Stoneleigh Residents' Association), July 1938.

expectations of thrills and excitements not likely to be found in the suburban environment. On the large LCC estates, the Pilgrim Trust and similar bodies worked hard to provide social facilities, often with the enthusiastic co-operation of a nucleus of residents. In 1938 the London Council of Social Service and the newly formed Federation of Community Associations initiated a survey of leisure activities in selected suburban areas with a view to the establishment of more community centres. But such work was only in the pioneer stage as our period ends.

As suggested earlier, many of the new suburbans in any event wished to 'keep themselves to themselves', for although all the inhabitants of any suburb of the twenties and thirties would be in much the same social group, they had little in common which individuals considered worthy of the effort involved in making contacts. They chose instead to sink into the comfortable anonymity which still remains a strong feature of London suburban life, rarely extending their acquaintance beyond immediate neighbours.

It followed that the men evinced very little interest in their environment outside the home and were distinctly apathetic about local politics and affairs, an attitude strengthened by daily work in completely different surroundings. And if this were not enough to dilute local allegiance and interest, many of the new districts found themselves part of not one but several older communities. An example of this confusion of loyalties and responsibilities was the housing estates which appeared in the early thirties on the Chipstead side of the Woodcote Park Golf Course. Served by Woodmansterne station, the residents paid rates to Carshalton UDC, but obtained their water from Sutton and their gas from Croydon; some lived in the parish of St Andrew, Coulsdon, whilst others were in Woodmansterne parish; if their house caught fire, the first brigade to be called was Coulsdon, that being the nearest to hand.[1]

Snobbery and Status
Many felt that a house in the suburbs constituted at least one step upwards in the social ladder and indeed this was one of the several factors motivating the centrifugal migration. Once established in their new houses, the fear of losing the new status (even if that were imaginary) provided sufficient incentive for keeping up appearances.

[1] TEG 17 September 1938.

All the new residents were in this game together. Astute advertisers incorporated the theme in their copy: 'Novean Homes are offered to families of good breeding who wish to acquire a house to be proud of at a cost of less than £1 a week'.[1] And, as if the possession of ready cash had some cleansing power all of its own, the Surrey Downs Housing Company of Great Tattenham insisted upon a 10 per cent deposit when others were content with less, just 'to keep the estate select'.[2] Discrimination also reigned at Petts Wood, where Basil Scruby and Co. allowed no terrace blocks or bungalows, and tried their best to keep each road to properties of a 'definite class'.[3]

Further support was given by careful naming of roads and estates, a subject touched upon earlier in this book, and by inclusion in restrictive covenants of prohibitions on keeping poultry, laundry displays on Sundays and bank holidays, or the use of houses for trade or business purposes. Sensitivities were easily upset. A country lane at Mill Hill, known for centuries as Dole Street, supplied the name for a school built there in 1939 by the Hendon council to serve suburban growth. But the protests were such that within a few weeks the council were driven to free it from the taint of a word also associated with state assistance to the unemployed.

In this atmosphere, subtle gradations of class, imperceptible to the outsider, were taken very seriously as the Stoneleigh Drive incident mentioned in chapter 15 illustrates. A young widow or separated wife obliged to go out to work or take in a 'paying guest', the family who allowed their children to play in the road on Sundays (or indeed at all), the man who went to work (rather than to the station) on his bicycle . . . matters of this kind were a constant source of anxiety and gossip. 'There's always one in any road' was almost the only consoling thought that could be exchanged.

After moving in, accents would be 'improved' in attempts to match those of neighbours regarded as higher up the social scale, and any tendency to swearing would be checked. A wife would try to refer to 'my husband' rather than 'my Bill' and to remember to take off her apron before she crossed the road to see a friend.

Most new suburbs quickly acquired a private school or two, successfully competing with the often distant and overcrowded

[1] Advertisement for Stoneleigh, HF 2 June 1934.
[2] Advertisement in HF 1 June 1935.
[3] TEG 22 November 1930.

facilities of local education authorities overwhelmed by the rapid pace of housebuilding. These little schools, often set up in the large villas left behind by the Victorian or Edwardian proto-commuters, nurtured class distinctions by cultivating middle-class accents and attitudes for 3, 4 or 5 guineas a term. Their staff not infrequently included unqualified amateurs and discontented or clouded professionals, yet they managed to ease many of their pupils into minor Public Schools when the time came. Snobbery and publicity were served by deft touches, as at Edgware, where the headmaster of one of these schools stood prominently in the doorway, adorned in his university gown, to see the boys off to lunch each day. Some were sufficiently profitable to move into purpose-built accommodation after a few years.

Imitation was prevalent in suburban life. Should one family manage to send their child to a private school, neighbours would follow suit as soon as they were able to achieve the necessary financial sacrifice. If one man began to mow his lawn, others would soon be heard at work all around. And a few weeks after Mrs Jones had proudly whispered about her pregnancy, neighbours would be happily attempting conception.

Yet, amid all this emulation, individuality of a sort was asserted in such things as garden design, house decoration and house naming. The latter was to an extent related to the lack of permanent numbers, a state of affairs which usually lasted until the road was adopted by the local authority; with the increasing construction of concrete roads by builders, adoption speeded up and names were on the wane by the mid-thirties. As might be expected, the all-pervading rural-romantic daydream provided the most popular theme: *Meadowside*, *Woodsview*, and *Fieldsend* were alas, all too soon misnomers (*Crossfoxes* and *Woodlawn* were more prudent); honeymoons were commemorated at *Petit Bôt*, *Lyme* and *Lynton*; lower down the social scale the narrative and the whimsical found favour, together with linked first names – *Dunromin*, *Bakome*, *Idunno*, *Gladroy*, *Lesrene*. . . .

Another aid to snobbery was the ability to employ at least some semblance of domestic help. Maids living-in were still found in the larger houses, but were increasingly rare as the thirties faded (many were Welsh and Irish girls unable to find employment in economically depressed areas and grateful for a cosy domestic base in a strange environment). At the next stage down the social ladder, the maid gave way to the 'daily', a woman offering an hour or two of help each day during school hours. These were more easily obtained if there were a council estate or working-class cottages within walking distance; they were usually women in their late thirties or older, whose eldest children could look after the others and help in the home.

Health in the Suburbs

If the publicity were to be believed, new house owners and their families were certain to gain great physical benefits from their move. The country air of the new districts was much mentioned. In announcing his 'soundproof' houses of 1935, W. Greville Collins advanced the modest claim that 'A summer at Feltham has the health value of a trip round the world'. Southgate had other merits in the mind of Hugh Davies, one of its estate agents, in 1937; it was not only 'high above the fog belt and the probability of floods' but 'you could retain your holiday tan' if you bought a house there. Also 'above the fog belt' was Costain's Croham Heights Estate, where children would grow up in 'healthy air'. But the same firm's nearby Selsdon Heights Estate seemed even more desirable for the health faddist:

'the highest home centre within easy reach of the metropolis, 500 ft. above sea level. Free from fog and dampness. When neighbouring lowlands are shrouded in mist, the Selsdon Heights stand out in clear, brilliant air . . . chesty people find new relief on this naturally-drained chalk soil.'

Not to be outdone, the equally elevated Surrey Downs Estate at Tattenham Corner was advertised as 'amid the fairyland of Surrey, 600 feet above sea level on dry chalky soil swept by sweet air direct from the SOUTHERN SEAS'. Here, 'where illness is unknown', the medicinal pines were constantly on guard in an atmosphere free of fog. No doubt all this was some compensation for a journey to town so circuitous that the train first headed south.

Only a small part of the new suburban development was on the high chalk, a subsoil not without disadvantages. Most were on clay, which not everyone found congenial. At certain times of the year, in some of the clay areas, a musty-smelling mist hung low over the surrounding fields, its aura pervading the houses and gardens. The houses themselves often felt damp, especially when new, for there was virtually no central heating. Some chesty or rheumatic people found anything but an improvement in their health after settling into inadequately dried-out houses surrounded by waterlogged roads, ill-drained gardens and mist-shrouded meadows. Perhaps with such thoughts in mind, a doctor writing about suburban health matters in the *Evening News* in 1913 had expressed the opinion that clay soil might contribute to repeated attacks of sciatica and neuralgia, and could be a cause of rheumatism, bronchitis and pneumonia in the elderly, of tuberculosis in young adults, and rickets and diptheria in young children.[1] A formidable, and in the light of modern knowledge, false catalogue.

To combat any such thoughts, advertisers looked on the brighter side. A clayland suburb (Field End Road, Eastcote) was seen in rosy light by a 1936 copywriter:

> 'in an area limited to about 50 acres of an estate there have been mystifying elements which have produced some extraordinarily beneficial changes in the health of many of our workpeople and residents. For example, most of our staff, whose ages range from 15 to 55 years, have increased in weight, and those of them who have been martyrs to rheumatism and kindred ailments declare they have never felt so fit in their lives.'

Perhaps it was the healing waters of the Yeading Brook, or it may have been the manurial odours of the Harrow Sewage Farm, when the wind was right; one hesitates to suggest that the idea was put into their heads.

In truth, given dry, well-heated houses and modern sanitation, clay offered no serious hazard to health; and no matter what the subsoil might be, there was prevalent benefit from the more open layout of the new suburbs, the relatively clean air, and the much improved living conditions offered by the houses themselves.

Despite fairly widespread research it has been possible to find only one advertiser using this as a theme. Costain's publicity for the 1928 Brentwater Estate on the North Circular Road (near Cricklewood) contained a kind of strip cartoon contrasting in vivid sketches the squalor of a tin bath in the kitchen with the neat bathroom of their houses.

Seasoned Travellers
It was the wives and children who stood to benefit most from the cleaner air and the improved living conditions. Breadwinners were

1 EN 22 March 1913.

obliged to endure the strains of daily journeys to and from work in central London. Returning on Saturday afternoon for an all too brief weekend break, husbands would bring themselves to the margins of physical exhaustion as they strove to make gardens from rock hard clay or thinly disguised chalk. For a man accustomed to a sedentary life and around forty, as many were, this could be calamitous.

Regular railway travel to town had its compensations. By no means all the trains were uncomfortably full, and those who selected their line carefully would be able to put the daily train time of between one and two hours to good use. There was opportunity for reading, even for writing, whilst travellers with no inclination for either after a brief glance at the newspaper were able to indulge in congenial conversation, exchanging gossip and advice with social equals sharing similar problems. Most trains had one or two little groups of 'regulars' who secured for themselves each day a particular compartment, scowling any intruders away. Similar behaviour was evident among the card schools as they gathered to pursue relentlessly their solo whist upon newspapers spread over swaying laps. But these train groups were thinly spread; for reasons already sketched, most preferred to travel alone or perhaps with one comfortable and longstanding acquaintance.

Arrived at the station, the daily travellers, dressed to a man in dark suits, white, stiff-collared shirts, and bowler or trilby hats, with their tightly furled umbrellas held as elegantly as they were able, would quickly assemble in their respective and habitual positions along the platform, for they knew exactly where 'their' compartment would come to rest. As advanced amateur gardeners, they would, whilst they waited, offer unsolicited advice on the station gardens, tended lovingly by an abundant uniformed staff with little to do between the rush hours. By unspoken arrangement, those who preferred to travel in silence were left alone when they had received and returned a nod of acknowledgement from their closest neighbours.

Once inside the train, any conversation that did take place would range over the weather and the headlines, sport, holidays and family activities. Problems of the children's education, gardens, house maintenance or (more rarely) office life, would be mulled over. Even if, as was often the case, the company was exclusively male, blue jokes and anecdotes were frowned upon. Crossword puzzles in *The Times* and the *Daily Telegraph*, sufficiently challenging to last the whole journey, were sometimes worked through on a mutual basis.

If he cared to make use of it, station and train fulfilled the role of a social centre for the suburban male, a forum for the exchange of news, the making of new acquaintances and contacts, the publication of requirements, even the collection of money for charities. Station staff knew everyone worth knowing in the suburb apart from the few tradesmen who made no use of the railway for carriage of goods.

At Home for Admiration

Once settled in his new house, the new suburban man spent most of his waking hours outside its walls. In good weather he was in the garden; otherwise the cinema offered a pleasant alternative occupation, especially popular on winter evenings and Saturday afternoons. Younger people spent many hours at tennis and dancing. Pleasure motoring and golf were in the main confined to the more expensive suburbs. On Saturday afternoons in winter, when the First Team were at home, devoted soccer enthusiasts were to be observed returning to give voice to inner suburban loyalties.

Indoors, leisure time was occupied in reading or 'listening-in' to the radio; only a very small number of men indulged in specialist hobbies such as stamp collecting or model railways. The 'do-it-yourself' home decorations and repairs so widespread today were virtually unknown, for new houses required very little attention of this sort, and when they did, there were usually plenty of professionals available to put things right at modest cost. Such men often remained behind after taking part in the original building work, setting up one-man businesses operating at low profit margins. In the early thirties, a full redecoration of the exterior of a medium-sized semi could be had for less than £5, a revarnishing of the front door might cost 4 or 5 shillings.

An important activity in the first year or so after moving in was the display of the new house to admiring relatives and friends, a ritual usually performed on Sunday afternoons.[1] Supplied with the names of road and house on a letterhead printed at cut price by the newly established local stationer, the tourists would find themselves veering wildly around the maze of rutted builder's roads, stepping

[1] The author is indebted to Mr A. J. Kennet for recalling these details.

between piles of bricks and prefabricated window frames, trying not to trip over the plankways used for running wheelbarrows between the dumps of materials at the roadside and the building plots. In vain would they make enquiries about their destination from the equally disoriented and widely scattered inhabitants of the new estate busily clearing their front gardens. Eventually the bright and clean new semi would be found, stark and clinical in its treeless, shrubless setting, a carpet of browning turf beneath its proud window bays.

Once the ladies of the party had placed their coats on the best bed and rearranged their hair in the mirror of the Drage's or Times Furnishing dressing-table, the first item was a tour of the gardens. Any plants that the new residents had encouraged into sustained life would be meticulously indicated, and the phrase 'a great deal to do yet' was heard more than once. During the walk towards the back fence, the boast would be made, 'they can't build at the back of us', accompanied by a sweep of the arm towards distant woods and meadows precariously glimpsed between other houses. Next came the internal tour, accomplished quickly enough, accompanied with much wall-banging and floor-stamping to emphasise the soundness of construction (politely the visitors would pretend not to notice that the furniture wobbled somewhat during these demonstrations).

Inspection completed, a large tea would be taken: cold meats, or tinned salmon and lettuce followed by many many cakes, sponges and tarts, with perhaps some jelly, trifle or blancmange; a meal so lavish that the whole family would be on a restricted diet for days afterwards to establish financial equilibrium. Afterwards the party would move into the sitting-room (self consciously referred to as the 'lounge') for a demonstration of the new superhet. radio. This was soon made to interrupt the ripple of feminine chat with snatches of symphonies, jazz, contraltos and sopranos, intermixed with a great gibberish of foreign tongues, all to the proud owner's shouts of 'That's Berlin', 'Here's Hilversum' or simply, 'Beromunster'.

A couple of hours after tea, as conversation flagged and the guests talked of leaving, they were invited to return to the dining-room for a second, almost equally enormous meal, washed down with coffee instead of tea. By now it might well be raining; there was no bus, and the muddy trudge through roads lit only by the occasional uncurtained window was sufficiently prolonged by navigational difficulties to ensure that the selected train was missed.

Suburban Screens

For the lonely uprooted housewife, or wife and husband together in the evenings and on Saturday afternoons, the cinema offered comforting warmth and brief escape from dull routine at low cost – 'this loving Darkness, a fur you can afford'.[1] By the thirties, it had become the main leisure activity outside the home. Essentially a personal, rather than a communal experience, it provided something for the whole family. Most adults went at least once a week, and almost always, children could go with them (the censors saw to that). Saturday matinees were also held for the children, who watched selections of cowboy, cartoon and comic films, shouting themselves hoarse the while. But above all, the picture house was the resort of the 16–30 age group; in its friendly murk, couples could embrace with abandon, whilst those without partners lost themselves in the romantic dreamland brought to life on the screen.

It was in the years 1915–18 that the cinema took its place as a social institution. Affording everyone the opportunity of a few hours' relief from the worry, horror and pains of war, its cosy privacy was especially welcome to servicemen and their girls, kissing and fondling through precious leave hours. Cinema-going habits acquired in the war years did not fade in the twenties, but few large picture houses were built in the suburbs of that decade. With the arrival of the sound film in 1928 the cinema was launched into its golden age and simultaneously into the suburbs. This renaissance also fostered the first authentic cinema architecture to be seen in London, 5 years or more after its birth in Germany.

The new buildings, most of them 'supercinemas' with seats for a thousand or more, electric organ, and a stage for variety acts, were scattered on a generous scale through the London suburbs from 1930 onwards. Costing between £50,000 and £100,000, they were frequently completed in as little as five months, their steelwork and other fittings providing some relief for the depressed areas. Middlesex, the suburban county, which had 82 cinemas in 1920, ended the thirties with 138, offering a total of some 190,000 seats, or one for every ten inhabitants; over 19,000 seats were provided in 1936 alone.[2] Golders Green had the first of London's talkie-equipped suburban supercinemas, the Lido, designed by W. J. King, and

[1] C. Day Lewis' poem, 'Newsreel', 1938.
[2] Based on reports in *Cinema and Theatre Construction*, 1939 and Middlesex CC statistics reported in the issues of January 1937 and December 1938.

opened on 1 October 1928. There were 1,959 seats, a Christie-Unti organ, a café-lounge and space for parking a hundred cars; in every respect it set the trend.

Before long, plots were being set aside for cinemas on most large suburban developments and a good site in a suburban shopping centre, with road access on at least three sides, might fetch between £10,000 and £50,000, in addition to the building cost already mentioned. A prominent developer of suburban cinemas was Oscar Deutsch, who fulfilled his promise to ring London with Odeons. In July 1933, only three years after the circuit had started life in the Midlands, Deutsch opened his first London Odeon at Kingston; others quickly followed – South Harrow, in September, Tolworth and Worcester Park the following January and Weybridge and Surbiton in March. From then onwards, the pace was hot; one growing suburb (Kingsbury) receiving two in eight months (May 1934 and January 1935). London's suburbs sprouted 9 Odeons in 1934, 10 in 1935, each with 1,000–1,500 seats.

'Redundancy', or overprovision of cinemas, was a constant fear of investors after 1929, but the rate of construction around London, after making a rapid recovery from the depression year of 1931, did not begin to abate until 1939. Kingsbury's double in rapid succession was repeated elsewhere; 2 cinemas, with a combined total of 3,128 seats, were opened in Purley within one month in 1934, whilst over 4,000 seats were available in Bromley's Gaumont and Odeon, both completed in the second half of 1936.

As almost everyone could regularly afford the very low entrance charge, the council estates proved no less attractive to developers than the owner-occupier areas. Thus residents of the LCC estate at Becontree had 4 cinemas to choose from by the end of 1934, including Robert Cromie's 2,750-seater Princess, built by Costain in 1932. Before the talkie era had begun, Watling had the substantial Regent, Edgware Road, opened in 1929 and much enlarged in 1932. St Helier was served by the Morden Cinema, opposite the Underground station (December 1932) and by Harry Weston's 2,000-seat Gaumont, Rose Hill, completed in June 1937. At Downham, there was W. J. King's Splendid, opened in July 1930, with 2,244 seats set in highly-decorated splendour.

Few suburbs were too select to manage without a cinema, although when one was proposed for Claygate in 1927, it was coyly justified as a means of putting the housewife 'on equal terms with the housewife of more urban localities in the matter of securing the domestic treasure of which she dreams'. But whether they were for servant girls or their employers, cinemas appeared at places like Haslemere, Cranleigh, Esher and Godalming (the latter with elevations approved by Lutyens, no less) as readily as at Rayners Lane and North Ilford. And they came soon after the houses, often enough before the churches; they were part of the very fabric of the new suburbia. There can be few illustrations of the impact of suburbanisation more dramatic than the replacement of a sixteenth-century farmhouse at Pinner by the Langham Cinema in the space of little more than six months in 1935–6. Designed by T. C. Ovenston, the 1,500-seat Langham contributed beige Rainfordware elevations relieved by horizontal bands of green, all under an otiose rooflet of green tiles, to Bridge Street.

Aside from the ubiquitous Odeons, Gaumonts and Astorias, the favourite names for the new suburban temples were those with connotations of opulence (Ritz, Plaza, Mayfair), or splendour and importance (State, Royal, Regal, Rex, Paramount, Majestic, Capitol, Dominion, Embassy, Ambassador, Commodore). The exotic, although less in vogue, was still encountered (Granada, Savoy, Florida, Havana, Rio).

Some of the architects have already been noticed. The most prolific were George Coles (who began his London work with the 1929 Burnt Oak Regent and later worked mostly on Odeons), Robert Cromie (who also started in the twenties), William R. Glen (staff architect for the ABC circuit), W. J. King (a pioneer of the supercinema), Andrew Mather and A. Percival Starkey (designers of suburban Odeons), W. E. Trent (a worthy pioneer of authentic cinema architecture) and Harry Weston.

These men shaped and designed their buildings to underline the self-importance of movie entertainment, seeking also to infuse in the cinemagoer a deep sense of luxury, relaxation and comfort, which, together with the films, would lift him temporarily from the dullness of his everyday life. They could have taken as their text these words, which appeared in the March 1933 issue of *Cinema Construction*:

'The really successful cinema is far more than a mere house of entertainment. It is part of the life of the people. It is a place where brightness takes the place of gloom and an atmosphere of hope and cheer accompanies a trip to a cloudland of romance and beauty.'

What High Church had done for the slumdwellers of nineteenth century London, the cinema could do better for the office slaves and housebound wives of the thirties.

The architects and decorators went into it with enthusiasm, but, because the American influences were too strong and the pressure too high, only rarely achieved the elegance found in Germany and some other Continental countries. Exterior and interior design explored a variety of Egyptian and Mexican motifs, or loud geometric patterns, with much use of indirect tinted lighting and neon tubes. For the street elevations, large uncluttered surfaces of glazed terracotta faience were favoured, with white, cream and biscuit the most popular hues; these facades not only remained bright and attractive to the eye in the worst of English weather, they formed an ideal base for neon and floodlighting and publicity display. In some areas the local authorities insisted on quieter treatment, as at Epsom, where the 1937 Odeon was required to harmonise with the other High Street buildings by using narrow bricks and stone dressings, although a stunted version of the usual Odeon tower was admitted, 'a valuable concession to modernity and one which also gives the theatre the publicity which it requires'. This last point was an important one for the architect to bear in mind; above all, he must make his building *stand out*. Not surprisingly, the otherwise popular Tudor style was completely rejected (the odd exception was the 1930 New Kinema, Oxted). As the unsuccessful experiments with the 'modern style' had shown, domestic architecture was imbued with the idea of permanence, a house was regarded as something to pass on to future generations, something which would outlast new styles. The cinema, in contrast, was not built to last for ever; the owner would have his outlay back, with profit, within a few years and could afford to allow his architects off the leash.

Interior decoration was exuberant. Here architects were frequently subservient to decorators and designers who sought to create 'atmosphere', filling the auditoria with all sorts of clutter, often following a theme, usually Spanish-American or Egyptian. Miniature churches, turrets and floral gateways, back-lit in changing colours, provided 'recreative relief when the curtain falls'. Occasionally the decorators were frustrated by over-fussy municipal bureaucrats. An old-world gate with iron hinges, weatherbeaten timbers and mossy cracks painted on the walls of the Splendid, Downham, had to be removed because council officials thought a panic-stricken crowd might assume it to be a means of exit, crushing themselves to death against its solidity. The artist was surely flattered.

Almost all the larger cinemas had spacious 'café-lounges' or 'tea-lounges', usually over the entrance 'foyer', and furnished with wicker chairs and attentive waitresses. These rooms were easily converted into dance halls, and at Harrow and elsewhere, regular *thé-dansants* were held. Some supercinemas even had separate ballrooms. No longer were the waiting patrons made to shiver outside; instead they used deep-carpeted, mirrored vestibules and crush halls large enough to take a high proportion of the seating capacity. There were ladies' rooms which evoked something of the film stars' luxurious way of life: a 'cosmetic room for the convenience of lady patrons' at the 1936 Grosvenor, Rayners Lane, must have bolstered the spirits of many a tired housewife relaxing there in the emotional aftermath of a Great Romance vicariously enjoyed.

But for some the excitements and luxuries of suburban cinemas and dance halls were not always enough, and these would 'go up West' as often as they could afford. Such traffic was encouraged by the railways with cheap fares and return trains at late hours. A typical selection of south London suburbs are shown in the Southern Railway timetable of January 1937 as having last trains from West End termini between 12.02 a.m. and 12.35 a.m., with cheap day return tickets ranging from 1od. to 2s. From most of these places there were at least two trains an hour outside the peak hours. Excellent facilities like these also encouraged the suburban housewife to window-shop in the West End, or even, in Ascot week, to travel up to Waterloo just to stand and stare at the feminine finery boarding the race trains.

West End cinemas, showing films before suburban release at slightly higher prices, with thicker carpets, softer seats and plushier powder rooms as a bonus, were a special favourite with suburban lovers, and were also a venue for family treats. A trip to one of these large cinemas or to a theatre would be rounded off with a visit to a Lyons' Corner House, establishments which provided the impecunious suburban with a fine illusion of luxury at remarkably low prices; their exuberant décor, live music, efficient service and well-furnished powder and washrooms offered superb value for money. At Lyons' Regent Palace, entrance to the tea or supper dance was obtained for only 2s, less than half the sum required at the Café de Paris or the Savoy.

Superhet. and Twopenny Library

As indoor entertainment, the radio (generally referred to as 'the wireless') had edged out the piano. Regular daily broadcasts had begun in 1922, reaching the suburban sitting-room via 'cat's whisker' crystal set and earphones. Valve receivers and horn loudspeakers were available from the middle twenties, but many homes were without them until the end of the decade. At this time, sets were not cheap, and might cost the equivalent of two weeks' pay or more for the white-collar worker. To meet this, many built up their own from parts, or, if they lacked the patience or skill, would commission one from an office colleague who found the construction of sets a congenial means of supplementing a low salary.

By the early thirties, most London suburban homes had a radio of sorts, fed from an aerial strung from the roof to a tall pole at the far end of the garden, the wire coming into the house through a formidable switch which had to be opened in thundery weather.

Eventually mass production brought prices down. A three-valve all-mains set selling at £15–£17 in 1931 was replaced by such models as the famous circular Ecko superhet., with its four valves and integral loudspeaker, sold for £8 8s in 1934. Five years later, the price of battery radios was down to £6. Increased ownership created a domestic problem as the party walls of the new semis were too flimsy to smother the sound. At least one London builder paid some attention to this; Baldwin and Co.'s £875 houses at Mill Hill (Thornfield Avenue) were advertised in 1934 with the slogan 'the next-door wireless cannot be heard.' Increased power and better design in the later thirties allowed listeners to escape from the sobriety of the Reithian BBC Sunday (programmes, which did not start until lunchtime, were mainly composed of religious matter and serious music); most popular of the Continental stations broadcasting English commercial programmes was Radio Luxembourg, with Normandie a close second.

Television from London's Alexandra Palace began in 1937. When the service was suspended at the outbreak of war two years later, there were some 20,000 sets in use. most of them in and around London. But with the price of a combined T.V. and radio at around £50, or a small table T.V. at £24, most residents of suburban semis were obliged to confine their viewing to the sets in the local radio shop, or the cinema café.

If radio palled, the suburbanite would turn to light reading, usually fiction. As mentioned elsewhere, the new areas had few public libraries at first, but the need was met by the shop libraries found in most suburban High Streets. Lending novels of all kinds at 2d a book a week, these were heavily patronised by housewives and single women, many seeking a little of the romance so sadly lacking in their dull lives. Stoneleigh, a typical new area of the thirties, had two of these twopenny libraries, one supplied by Foyles' ('100 new books every month'), and both opened long before any public library facilities were available within easy reach. Apart from this hired fiction, few books were to be seen in the new suburban home; if there were a bookcase or shelf, it would be most likely to contain a dictionary, some instruction manuals on gardening cookery and sex, a holiday guide or two, and cheaply bound classics and other works offered at bargain prices in the newspaper circulation war of the early thirties.

Outdoors in Suburbia
Tennis retained its popularity as the suburban game, partly because it was a sure avenue to pleasant flirtation. Private clubs existed long before courts were available in the public parks. Edgware had three as early as 1931, when building was still far from complete. The clip-clop of bat and ball, accompanied by boyish shouts and girlish laughter, floated over summer gardens, mixing with the gentle surge and retreat of the hand lawn-mowers to create a suburban music long since replaced by the intrusive drone and roar of aircraft and the spluttering of petrol mowers.

Developers of the more expensive estates were fond of advertising that the gardens were large enough for a tennis court, whilst others left land for courts between the backs of gardens, or in corners unsuitable for a house plot. Occasionally tennis facilities were provided as an estate amenity; more frequently, the fact that houses overlooked or were close to tennis courts was quoted as a sales bait (at Maybank Avenue, Sudbury, in 1926, a builder claimed that his houses overlooked 'select tennis courts' but alas, by 1931, these had disappeared under another estate).

A good deal less 'select' for the suburban environment was greyhound racing, introduced from the U.S.A. in the late twenties. Indeed it was virtually unacceptable in a new suburb, as the Edgware row demonstrated. Most of the new tracks were therefore set up on such waste land as still remained in the Edwardian or Victorian zones, or in those new suburbs where housing co-existed with new factories. Like the cinema, 'the dogs' were to some extent family entertainment, and an all-weather one, the average track providing sheltered viewing for 20,000 or more, with strong flood-lights for evening races. By 1934, 25 tracks were open in the London area, including one at Wembley Stadium (1927), one on the semi-industrial eastern fringe of Wimbledon (1928), another serving Becontree LCC estate and the Ford Works, and the Hendon Stadium, near the North Circular Road industrial area (1934).

Motoring was still outside the economic reach of most suburbans. Apart from a few imported Fords, modestly powered cars sold in the early twenties at prices around three times the average suburban income. After 1930 mass-production techniques and a concentration of manufacturing resources brought prices down until 9- and 12-horsepower cars could be had at £145 upwards. In 1933, the Dagenham-built Ford Popular, a two-door, 8-horsepower saloon, was selling at £100 ex-factory. This car could be run at an annual cost of £8 tax and £7 10s comprehensive insurance, on petrol cheaper than it had been in 1914. Even so, cars were few and far between in suburban roads, for, with mortgage and furniture hire-purchase payments claiming a substantial slice of his disposable income, the average suburban householder could accumulate further capital only with great difficulty. At Tolworth in 1937, the only car owner in a ¼-mile road of new houses was a civil service Clerical Officer. Those living half a mile or more from the station frequently used a pedal cycle to save time and energy in the morning and evening. Publicans and others with suitable accommodation near the railway would slightly undercut the company's storage rate, taking the machines into their care for 9d to 1s a week.

Behind Suburban Curtains
Social gatherings in private houses were perhaps most frequent in the wealthier suburbs, but elsewhere women would occasionally congregate in sitting-rooms over tea or coffee, often with the pre-text of organising some church or charity function. Thus met together, they would eagerly exchange scandal and gossip, sharing medical and other intimacies. At evening meetings, when men were present, conversation soon flagged, to be replaced by card-playing or dancing to gramophone records or radio. Again, only the larger houses were suitable for this type of function; in the humbler suburban areas such events would be held in the more formal atmosphere of the tennis club pavilion or church hall.

Other social opportunities were offered by the tennis clubs already mentioned, and by the dramatic, operatic and literary societies. These groups were the resort of the lonely and unappreciated, an outlet for those with real or imagined artistic gifts. Romantic themes were popular for amateur dramatics; staged embraces could, and occasionally did, lead to other things, for this was almost the only environment favourable to extra-marital diversions in otherwise 'respectable' communities.

For those fond of organising others, or of giving vent to their aggression in public action, there existed in almost every new area a residents' or ratepayers' association, not infrequently established in the first place by the builder or developer, with an eye to maintaining the standing and status of the estate as an example of his enterprise. Essentially inward-looking and selfish, but none the worse for that, these organisations strove, with varying degrees of enthusiasm and success, to preserve and improve the amenities and facilities of the new areas, and to monitor the expenditure of the local authorities. Favourite targets for attention were the railway and bus services, education facilities and street services. Some associations were sufficiently enterprising to attain substantial representation on the local councils, where their candidates provided a healthy counterweight to the preponderant property, trading and other business interests. The associations were also active in organising social events such as whist drives, garden-produce shows, dances, cricket matches, various kinds of mutual aid, and generally establishing a basis for social coherence in the absence of any other influence.

They thus assumed some of the community functions of the churches, whose sway in the neo-Georgian suburbs was a good deal weaker than it had been twenty years earlier. Support now came most strongly from the women, who formed the majority in many suburban adult congregations. Although sites for churches were still allocated in most large developments, the finance came less quickly. Small brick halls, even wooden huts, often had to suffice for ten or fifteen years; many suburbs of the thirties had no permanent church building until after World War II.

Leading his well-regulated, predictable life, his security at stake if he erred too far from the path of conventional morality and behaviour, the new suburban man gave but little trouble to the police (or, indeed to his employer, for with most of his income pledged to house mortgage and hire purchase of furniture, regular monthly pay cheques and 'permanency' of employment were highly valued). On the surface, and for most of the time beneath it, the 'respectable' suburbs lived up to their name; the owner-occupier husband's off-beat activities seldom went beyond mild bilking on the railway, occasional inebriation, or surreptitious reading of *Silk Stocking Stories* or *London Life*. These last helped to fill out the usually somewhat narrow sexual experience; only the more adventurous would risk the spicy draught of an office affair.

Crime was almost always the work of outsiders. Most suburbs suffered periodical epidemics of burglary and house-breaking which led to agitation for more police. More than half the detected house-breaking offences in the Metropolitan Police District occurred in the newly built areas, a state of affairs the police ascribed to the spaces between the houses, which allowed easy access to the rear, where entry could be made at leisure in privacy, and to the multiplicity of windows and the low elevations, which facilitated entry.[1]

Once or twice in a decade there were incidents which caused the most violent shock to the respectable image of the suburb. One such was the Golders Green affair of 1927. After a number of complaints by residents which had not been very actively followed up by the police, Hendon Council hired private detectives to establish exactly what was going on in a house in Golders Gardens. At the subsequent police court hearing, it was stated that the windows of this house, especially those of the upstairs rooms, were always heavily curtained; wines and spirits were delivered two or three times daily, and there was a great deal of noise, especially after dark, with frequent comings and goings of taxis and chauffeur-driven cars. The hired detectives carefully described performances of an indecent nature given by six young ladies, including a dance by one of their number upon the top of a piano, for which she was attired only in her silk stockings and garters (an allegation which sparked off some learned discussion about the height of the ceiling). Eventually the occupier's wife received a six months sentence of imprisonment for assisting in the management of a 'house of ill-fame' in which 'a very large amount of immoral trade' had been taking place.

Golders Green had grown up.

[1] Report of the Commissioner of Police for the Metropolis, 1937.

Chapter 11

SUBURBAN MONEY
1925–39

From Loan to Profit

Developers proposing to work up building land in the London
suburbs of the period had little trouble in securing short-term credit
from a bank. Larger and older firms could usually get working
capital at 1 per cent over bank rate but the less experienced would
be charged rather more. This process was especially easy in the
early thirties when economic conditions made unusually large
amounts of capital available for risk investment. At this time, a
builder holding some land or otherwise reasonably well secured
could normally persuade a bank manager to allow him a substantial
initial advance with up to £300 or so to follow in respect of each
house finished.

Small builders could also get help with finance from developers
selling off plots, and some building societies were willing to provide
money for development. Builders' merchants continued their
traditional practice of issuing large quantities of supplies on a credit
basis.

An estate developer's profit was of course the amount ultimately
realised by the sale of all the plots less his outlay on the land and
the cost of working it up, including an allowance for interest on
capital, usually 6 per cent. His aim would be to maximise return by
disposing of all the plots in the shortest possible time. Some idea
of the handsome profits obtainable on the edge of London during
the twenties and thirties can be derived from the detailed statements
given by George Cross[1] and from disclosures made in the courts. In
a 1936 action for example, it was demonstrated that the appellant
builder, after a not inconsiderable outlay on publicity, had secured
net profits averaging £79 a house on an estate of 462 plots at Feltham, where most houses had been sold at only £425 or £550.[2]

[1] Cross, op. cit. See also Chapter 14.
[2] TEG 15 August 1936, report of Wilfred Greville Collins *v.* Feltham UDC.

Notoriously difficult to estimate with accuracy, the full cost of building a house was the sum of a very large number of items, with labour accounting for about one third of the total. Incidentals which had to be considered when arriving at a selling price included interest on working capital; legal charges; insurance; stationery and other office overheads; advertising; sales commission; and net profit (usually assessed at between 7 and 15 per cent of the outlay).[1] Sometimes profit would be cut well below this level to meet competition from surrounding estates or from other builders on the same site, or, if other factors allowed, it would be inflated to cover risk.

Causes of Disaster
The arrangement of a speculative building enterprise required financial skill and careful budgeting to ensure that cash flowed in as fast as it moved out; this meant that activity had to be cut back if sales fell off, and many were reluctant to do that. Bankruptcies were a common enough event, sometimes affecting the same principals twice or more in a decade; injudicious decisions brought down the experienced as well as those who jumped on to the bandwagon from other occupations.

Many of the smaller firms wisely stayed in the district they knew best, where they could form sound judgements of the market, but as the pace quickened between 1932 and 1934, the prospect of quick profits in new areas was too much for some to resist and the result was often calamity. A common source of difficulty was the purchase of badly placed sites far from shops or transport facilities, whilst others erred in buying too much land at once, only to find their sales dropping off as competitors set up around them. Some were over-ambitious, extending their risk by developing too many estates at the same time, accumulating liabilities until they were unable to repay money borrowed at high rates of interest. Other traps awaiting the inexperienced came from misdirection of effort; too much spent on publicity, on organisation, or on staff; or misjudging demand by erecting the wrong type of house or layout for the area.

Even highly experienced and well-organised firms could become enmeshed in expensive litigation over such matters as covenants, title, boundary disputes, easements and drainage, not to mention

[1] General overheads of a Wimpey estate in the London area were said to average £66 a house in 1935 (TEG 17 September 1938).

compulsory purchase of their estate land by local authorities requiring it for open spaces or other purposes. And, as we have seen, litigation, not to mention the consequent bad publicity, could follow slapdash construction.

Price and Choice

Although the second half of the twenties produced a good selection of houses priced at £600–£850,[1] and most over £700 were semis with the usual two reception rooms and two-and-a-half bedrooms, the sizes of the main rooms in this bracket were commonly less than 150 sq. ft., often as low as 140 sq. ft. Between £850 and £1,000, room size might reach 250 sq. ft., or even a little more, but there were few detached houses at this price, and only a small number had four bedrooms. To acquire the extra bedroom, it was normally necessary to pay at least £1,200 (say £1,250 for a detached house). Few builders in these last years of the twenties were constructing houses for speculative sale above the £1,300 level.

At the other end of the scale, there was very little to be had below £600 apart from shoddy bungalows in the less attractive, lowlying parts of south Essex and west Middlesex. One remarkable exception was Costain's 1927 Brentwater Estate on the North Circular Road, already noticed. Here three-bedroom terrace houses sold at £575 (£650 less £75 government subsidy), inclusive of gas hot water system, and occupation could be secured for £57 down and 18s a week. Over 700 of these houses had been sold by the beginning of 1929.

During the thirties, fiercer competition and (until 1935) falling costs of materials and labour brought greater variety to the lower price ranges, although quality was often sacrificed in the race to cut prices to the minimum. All around London there was now a wide selection at £550 to £1,000, but below £650/£700, the average size of the main rooms settled around £140–150 sq. ft. Up to another 30 sq. ft. in each room could be had in the £650–£800 group and between £800 and £1,000 room size varied from 180 to 200 sq. ft. Almost all houses selling at £850 and above (and a fair number below this figure) were of the standard two-and-a-half bedroom semi type,[2] now frequently with garage space at the side. From

[1] All prices quoted in this chapter are freehold. The reader is referred to the specifications and plans in Appendix 6, which fill in the general picture given here.
[2] Appendix 6, plan 3.

£950 upwards, integral garages were increasingly seen, even in semi-detached designs. Four bedrooms were now found in houses priced between £800 and £1,000 and three-bedroom detached types were available at £750 upwards (John Laing were pioneers in this, showing at the 1933 Ideal Home Exhibition 'the only detached house available in the London area at £775 freehold all-in, with three bedrooms and garage space'). Detached houses with four bedrooms could be found at £1,000 or £1,100, and the higher limits of speculative building extended to £3,500 or even £4,000. Houses in the top price range, detached, with four to five bedrooms, two to three reception rooms, cloakroom, and 'maid's room' were built in such areas as Wimbledon Park, Edgware, Mill Hill, Cheam, Banstead, Roehampton, Purley, Clapham Park, Woldingham, Leatherhead and Guildford.

To qualify these general comments on prices, it is necessary to mention some notable exceptions at the lower end of the scale. In 1935, G. T. Crouch produced a four-bedroom house for only £512 (on the Harlington Road Estate at Feltham) and a year later, New Ideal Homesteads had a £535 four-bedroom house (the fourth bedroom was 7 ft. 9 in. by 6 ft. 6 in.) at Barnehurst. NIH also managed to sell a detached house with two reception rooms, three bedrooms and separate lavatory for as little as £599 (at Falconwood Park, Welling, 1935).

But the achievement of which New Ideal Homesteads were most proud at this time was a three-bedroom, one-reception-room terrace house at the rock bottom price of £395 freehold. This was first seen towards the end of 1932 on the Penhill Park Estate, Sidcup, but was later included in the Park and Hillcrest Estates, Barnehurst, the Albany Park Estate, and in estates at Feltham. One feature of this type was 'a solid oak overmantel'.

The £395 mark was soon attained by other firms: at Romford (in 1932); at Copt Gilders, Chessington (1933); at West End Road, Ruislip (1934); at West Molesey (1934); and at North Cheam (1934). All these had three bedrooms (the third of course very small) and one or two main rooms downstairs.

In a few isolated instances even this was beaten. C. W. Goodchild, a Romford builder, was selling three-bedroom, one-main-room houses for £385 in September 1932, whilst a year later, also at Romford, and at Hillingdon, Hilbery Chaplin were advertising two-bedroom houses with a single 14 feet by 8 feet downstairs main room at £345. The well-known firm of Taylor Woodrow also produced £345 houses at their Grange Park Estate, Uxbridge Road, Hayes, in 1933 and 1934.

Each to His Means

Over 75 per cent of the new houses bought in the twenties and thirties were obtained by building society mortgage. Showing increasing strength in the first post-war decade as investors found other parts of the capital market unattractive or hazardous, the societies were well prepared to play a major role in the housing boom.

Although the initial cash deposit required from purchasers was a factor to be reckoned with in the twenties, it assumed less importance later, as we shall see in a moment. Above all, the prospective purchaser had to be able to maintain regular payments ranging from about 15s (10s after the early thirties) to £2 or more a week, according to the purchase price, the amount of cash deposited, and the length of repayment period chosen. Building societies promulgated a 'safe rule' that total outgoings on house purchase, including local rates (3s to 6s weekly on the small to medium house), should not exceed a quarter of the net income. It was therefore highly unlikely that anyone earning a basic rate of less than around £3–£3 10s a week would be able to manage the commitment, and of those that could, only a very few would be able to show that they had an assured, secure income.[1]

From about 1932, with mortgage interest rates coming down, and building costs at their lowest since 1914, a fair number of houses appeared on the market in the price range £350–£550. Repayments for these were as low as 10s to 13s, opening up the possibility of house ownership to those earning £3 10s to £4 10s a week, touching for the first time the better-paid manual workers. In this wage bracket were the higher grades of uniformed railwaymen, bus and tramcar crews, and a large number of clerks in secure pensionable employment, all of them categories which could satisfy the building societies' requirement of ability to repay. Some developers build estates to attract this new group of potential owner-

---

[1] The gap was recognised by the National Federation of Housebuilders in 1930. They suggested to an unresponsive government that private builders might erect houses for renting by lower paid workers at 7s 6d to 9s 6d a week if builders were given a subsidy of £100 a house and allowed to build 20 houses to the acre, in blocks of eight.

occupiers. In 1936, Costain advertised their £500 'Arcadia' houses at Elm Park, with repayments of 13s a week, as being within the reach of those earning the 'normal workers' wage of £3 15s'. These semis had one 17 ft. 6 in. by 11 ft. 2 in. main room downstairs and three 'double' bedrooms (11 ft. 2 in. by 10 ft. 6 in.; 11 ft. 2 in. by 10 ft.; 9 ft. by 7 ft.). They were certainly popular, even if the claim that they were accessible to 'normal workers' was a little over-pitched. Early in January 1937 the firm announced that 1,272 had already been sold. The New Ideal Homesteads £395 house mentioned earlier was obtainable in 1932-3 for 9s a week plus rates, whilst the repayments for the Hilbery Chaplin £345 house were only 8s 5d. But such low figures were exceptional and the number of very cheap houses built was not large in proportion to the total; the average price in the thirties around London was nearer £650-£750, with repayments from 18s to £1.

Until interest rates and building costs fell in the early thirties, the lowest paid among the owner-occupiers were those in the £4 10s to £5 10s group, which included newspaper linotype operators and a few other favoured and highly skilled technicians, some foremen, supervisors and inspectors, and clerks in the civil service, local government, railways and banks, who were at the marrying age of twenty-six to thirty. All these were able to make repayments of 18s to £1 a week which in the late twenties would secure houses priced at £500 to £575. When mortgage rates came down in the early thirties, this group could raise their sights to the £750 house. Home buying for those at the lower end of the practicable earnings range required careful management of resources and the long term stability of local authority rates was an important factor in their calculations. To maintain financial equilibrium, many house buyers resorted to subletting or taking in a lodger, practices which were forbidden on council estates. A 1935 report in a Hendon paper mentioned that families leaving the LCC Watling Estate to purchase private houses nearby had been astonished to discover the high incidence of multi-occupation in roads where they had expected to experience a rise in status.

Those receiving between £6 and £10 a week included qualified schoolteachers, senior bank and insurance officials, Executive and Higher Clerical Officers in Government offices, the middle and upper strata of local government officials and the lower ranks of the professions. These people could afford repayments of between £1 and £2 a week which extended their range of choice in the thirties to houses costing up to £1,100. Many members of this group were quite prepared to make initial sacrifices, pitching the weekly repayment on the high side in the knowledge that they would progress steadily up an incremental salary scale and could as often as not hope for at least one promotion. A qualified male teacher earning about £6 15s in 1928 had no difficulty in meeting repayments of £1 8s for an £850 house and after 1935 the same outlay would see him settled in a house costing £1,000 or a little more. The average earnings of the basic grade in the civil service Executive Class were about £7, with the assurance of increments to a maximum of £10 weekly, pay which allowed access to houses selling at around £900 and after 1935 to those priced at £1,100 or slightly more.

It was from the salaried class earning upwards of £260 a year that the vast majority of the new London house owners came. Their needs were more or less met by the middle thirties and, from then until the outbreak of war, the builders increasingly turned their attention to the minimum cost house, to maisonettes and to self-contained flats in large blocks. There was also some return to the building of houses for renting.

Mortgage Rates

A little more must be said about mortgage rates in the twenties and thirties. Although loans up to 90 per cent of valuation could frequently be had from local authorities, especially after 1925,[1] and some insurance companies were prepared to advance money for houses on the security of a life insurance policy, the major source of finance for purchase was always the building society movement.

Several factors increased the flow of investment into the societies in the twenties: the disappearance of rented property as a worthwhile investment; the upward trend of income tax; and, most

[1] Before 1923, local authority loans were limited to houses already built and were made only to occupiers, over a maximum period of fifteen years, by those few councils which had adopted the Small Houses (Acquisition of Ownership) Act, 1899. These loans were extended by the Housing Act 1923, to houses to be built for the borrower's occupation, maximum market value £1,200, and sited in the lending authority's area. The Housing Act 1925 enabled local authorities to lend for purchase of houses in any area, maximum repayment period thirty years, maximum market value £1,500. In all cases the rate of interest was fixed, and usually below the prevailing building society rate, but the loans were not available from all authorities, and some imposed restrictions such as residence in the area. The 1925 act also allowed local authorities to lend money to people unable to find the initial down payment required by the building societies, and to guarantee payments to be made to building societies by purchasers.

11. Tudorbethan shops at Motspur Park station (built 1926). (Photo: Alan A. Jackson.)

A typical suburban shopping centre of the 1930s: Banstead Road, Carshalton Beeches c. 1939. (From a commercial postcard by E. A. Sweetman & Son.)

12. Butchered oaks and Twenties Tudor at Long Lane, Finchley c. 1927. (From a commercial postcard.)

Concrete and bricks to the edge of the woods: T. F. Nash estate, Balmoral Drive, Hayes, Middlesex, 1937. (From a commercial postcard.)

The Laing Estate, Purley (north side of Mitchley Avenue) 1937. (From a commercial postcard.)

important of all, the increase in real incomes after the mid-twenties. Following the 1929 financial collapse in the U.S.A. and its repercussions in Europe, uncertainties of the capital market accelerated the diversion of funds towards the building societies. One London society, the Woolwich Equitable, whose assets had grown only by £1.6m. from £2m. in 1920–5, found them swollen to almost £17m. in 1930 and £30.1m. in 1935.

Although some societies cut the rate of investment interest from 5 to 4½ per cent in 1931 in an attempt to slow down the embarrassing inflow, the attitude of the movement in general was one of great caution; many of the sober-sided directors and managers thought cheap money to be but a transient phenomenon. But the trend continued and in July 1932, the main London societies, no longer able to contain their misgivings at an accumulation of investment unmatched by a correspondingly higher demand for mortgages, decided to restrict increases in existing investments, to reduce the interest paid to new investors to 3½ per cent, and to limit new investment to a maximum of £50. This move, which coincided with the conversion of interest rates on government stock from 5 to 3½ per cent, at once created a demand for reduction in the borrowing rate. The London area mortgage rates, which had fluctuated between 5 and 6½ per cent since 1924 were generally reduced to 5½ per cent in the late summer of 1932 and to 5 per cent a year later. This rate then came to be regarded as the minimum and was included, together with the 90 per cent maximum advance, in a code of ethics drawn up by the National Association of Building Societies. The code was planned to operate from 13 April 1935, but on 27 March, New Ideal Homesteads made the surprise announcement that they would be able to arrange mortgages at 4½ per cent. Forced to come in to line, the Co-operative Permanent and the Halifax Societies lowered their rates in April, and other major societies followed suit. With payments spread over twenty-one years, a £400 house could now be had for only 11s 8d a week, a £500 one for 14s 7d. In the continuing atmosphere of tense competition between the building societies, the National Association and its 1936 successor, the Building Societies Association, never did succeed in obtaining the complete agreement of even the major societies to a standard code of ethics and procedure.

Bolstered by the continuing strong flow of investment, the societies expanded rapidly, and other relaxations accompanied the fall in mortgage interest rates. Repayment periods were extended from the previous norm of fifteen or sixteen years to twenty-five or even thirty, reducing the monthly payments by as much as one third. And, by various devices to be mentioned in a moment, the initial cash deposit was to all intents and purposes removed from the transaction. Competition between the societies kept the interest rate at 4½ per cent (in some cases it went down to 4¼) for the remainder of the thirties, precluding any adjustment when the interest rates of government securities began to rise again after 1936.

In these conditions, the societies' role in house purchase evolved impressively. Over the nation as a whole, they had advanced £32m. to mortgagors in 1923, in 1928, £69.85m.; in 1933 the figure was £103.2m., and in 1936, the peak year of the twenties and thirties, it reached £140.3m. Borrowers in 1928 numbered just over half a million, but by 1936 the total had grown to 1.3m. One society working in the London area, the Abbey Road, registered a 700 per cent increase in borrowers between 1926 (9,300) and 1936 (82,000).

Cash down ? No worry
Traditionally, the building societies had required an initial cash stake by the borrower of at least 20 or 25 per cent of their valuation of the house or of the purchase price, whichever was the lower. Coming on top of the legal charges and survey fees, which might total from £15 to £35 according to the value of the house, this hurdle, which (with a few exceptions) remained in position throughout the twenties, was too much for many prospective purchasers otherwise able to afford the commitment. The first attempt to break it down took the form of additional loans from outside sources. Some insurance companies operated collateral security schemes which, in return for a single premium paid by the borrower, indemnified the societies against loss arising from default of a borrowing member. This premium was usually 10 per cent of the amount insured, in other words the difference between 75 per cent of valuation and the full amount of the advance. Guarantees were also offered by the local authorities under the Housing Acts 1923–33, whilst a few building societies would accept an assignment of a life assurance policy of known surrender value, or other securities, in return for a higher than normal advance.

These devices were later overshadowed by the Builders' Pool or Pool Deposit system. Introduced in the London area in the twenties, this had become so widespread by 1939 that it was then thought to account for as much as half the mortgage business of the larger societies.[1] Its development in the thirties was very largely stimulated by the builders' need to widen the market after they had virtually saturated the middle-class demand. Writing in 1934, John Laing estimated that the Pool system enabled about three times as many people to consider house ownership as would have been the case if the 20 or 25 per cent cash deposit were the only method.[2]

Under the Pool system, the cash required from a purchaser was eventually reduced to at most 5 per cent of the society's valuation. This was secured by the builder making cash deposits with the society, usually equal to the amount advanced to borrowers in excess of the society's normal limit, but as competition intensified, builders were able to play off one society against another to obtain the most favourable terms, so that the cash guarantees would be reduced to one third or even one quarter of the 'excess advances'.

A typical example was the arrangement concluded in 1930 between the National Building Society and Keogh and Young Ltd, in respect of the Kingsbury Down Estate. The National undertook to grant 25-year mortgages on the houses to be erected, for which the purchasers would be required to pay £25 in cash against the £795 sale price. For the first ten houses, the builders were to deposit £50 for each sale, £40 for the next ten and £34 for the balance, and they would guarantee the society down to 70 per cent of the purchase price.[3]

It was implicit in the Pool system that it applied only to the cheaper houses. Through it a society was able to obtain almost all the business available on a large estate, for few purchasers had loyalties to a particular society or could afford to pay the whole price in cash. Builders found that the Pool boosted sales, although it locked up a large part of their profit, whilst they were relieving the society of all risk during the period of the guarantee. Some tried to counter the loss of immediate profits by cutting corners and lowering quality, but this could recoil when mortgagors, with their initial stake reduced to a few pounds, were tempted to default as defects began to show through. In other cases, selling prices were increased to meet the extra cost to the builder.

Until building society records became available for research

[1] *The Economist*, 12 February 1939.
[2] J. Laing, *Guarantee Mortgages* (chapter in *House Building 1934-36*, 1934).
[3] From a report in TEG 1 July 1933.

workers it is difficult to form any estimate of the number of mortgage defaulters in the London area, but it seems probable that they were not a significant proportion of borrowers except on very unsatisfactory estates. Laing[1] mentions popular districts occupied by 'showy people who keep cars, and spend freely, but default readily' and cites other districts 'occupied by people of the Communist type' adding darkly, 'it is very dangerous to guarantee mortgages to these'. Lastly he notices some areas where builders had got into financial difficulties because the site, although superficially attractive, was difficult of access. During the fine summer weather, people were beguiled into purchase by clever publicity and salesmanship, only to default later when they found the travelling too onerous. He estimates that a default might cost the builder about £100 in arrears of interest, redecoration and legal and sales costs, plus another £80 or so if legal proceedings were taken.

By means of the Pool and other devices the initial cash deposit was in some cases reduced to as little as 2 or 3 per cent of the sale price, or even abolished altogether in exchange for higher repayments. New Ideal Homesteads and G. T. Crouch were both advertising '£5 total deposit' in 1934, and a year later, New Ideal were happy to make do with 'your endowment or life assurance policy as deposit'. Civil servants, local government officers, school teachers, and others with occupational pension schemes could normally obtain no-deposit terms without difficulty. In other cases, the single premium indemnity already mentioned was adapted to enable advances to be made at valuations which equalled the purchase price plus additions to cover legal and other charges.

Gorged with investment funds far in excess of mortgage requirements, the building societies fought hard for new mortgage business, employing outsiders to tout for mortgage custom, and paying commissions to builders and their salesmen. Advertising expenditure was increased, and provincial societies opened London offices (two within a month of each other in 1931).

In this atmosphere some abuse was inevitable. Collusion between builders and purchasers led some societies to accept valuations at fictitious prices, and when they made their own valuations, they ignored serious defects in the design and construction of houses. In sales literature, builders were understandably tempted to quote the large percentage of the purchase price advanced by the building society as evidence of the soundness and value of their houses,

[1] Laing, op. cit.

taking advantage of the fact that most purchasers were unaware of the cash collateral that supported these boosted loans.

The Borders Case

Although the societies had misgivings about the Pool schemes, and attempts were made from 1931 to 1938 to impose a general code of practice, the competitive atmosphere prevented general agreement. Eventually the situation was tidied up by legislation; the provisions of the 1939 Building Societies Act were so rigidly drawn that Pool schemes of the type common in the thirties were effectively smothered.

This reforming legislation was sparked off by a legal case which sent shockwaves through the whole building society movement. Begun in the Chancery Court in January 1938, it was not concluded until the Appeal Judgements were pronounced in the House of Lords over three years later. Elsy Borders, wife of a London taxi driver and law student, was the subject of an action by the Bradford Third Equitable Building Society for possession of the mortgaged property at Kingsway, West Wickham. She was three months in arrear with her mortgage payments, and it was apparently just another routine case when the writ was issued in the summer of 1937.

With her husband acting as guarantor, Elsy Borders had executed a deed for a 95 per cent mortgage on the £690 semi and £40 garage in October 1934. A few months after the Borders had occupied the house, defects became apparent; the roof leaked, damp entered the bedrooms, and the hot water system was faulty. As a result, there was some hesitation about signing the mortgage deed, and subsequently Mrs Borders had withheld payments. On receiving the writ, she counterclaimed that the mortgage deed was unenforceable because the Society had taken a collateral security from Messrs Morrell (Builders) Ltd, an action which she suggested was illegal under the Building Societies Acts and against the Society's own rules. She claimed return of all the instalments she had paid, together with £500 damages, alleging that the Society had misrepresented the house as being well built, and that she had been persuaded to buy by statements in the builders' brochure. This brochure, around which much of the subsequent legal deliberation centred, was quoted in the court as including the following:

'Incidentally, however, the fact that a leading building society makes a more generous advance over a longer period than to any other estate in Great Britain speaks volumes for the construction of the houses.

All building is carried out under the strictest supervision of the local authorities, and you will be reassured to learn that, before your home has grown even so far as the damp course – the double course of fine slate which ensures the dryness of the house – it has been inspected no less than four times!

BUILDING SOCIETY

Morrell (Builders) Ltd are the only builders in Great Britain who can offer by special arrangement with a leading building society, a 95 per cent mortgage advance over a period of 24 years at 5 per cent interest.

This proves without a shadow of doubt, the amazing value of Morrell houses.'

When judgement was at last given in February 1939 it was greeted with an almost audible sigh of relief by the building societies. The waiting period had been difficult, because they had been left in some doubt as to the security of their collateral in Pool schemes and also exposed to attack by owners of defective or allegedly defective houses who had followed Mrs Borders' example and decided to withhold payments until the faults were made good. The judgement found that the mortgage was enforceable, allowing Mrs Borders no damages, on the grounds that the Society was not responsible for the misrepresentation in the brochure; she was, however, held to have proved that the house was badly built in its roof and foundations.

Mrs Borders appealed, again seeking damages. In the judgement of December 1939 it was held that the Society were aware of the brochure and in the circumstances of the case had rendered themselves responsible for the misrepresentation made by the builders which had induced Mrs Borders to buy the house. The indefatigable lady was accordingly allowed damages. For a second time, the enforceability and validity of the mortgage was decided in favour of the Society.

An appeal was made by the Society to the House of Lords. They then received a judgement in their favour, it being held that they were in no way responsible for the statements in the brochure or for inducing Mrs Borders to believe in their veracity, although the judgement found that the implications in the brochure that the house was well built were untrue.

An era had ended; building societies were never likely to play with this particular kind of fire again.

___

Some examples of costs (from builders' brochures)

Edgware, 1935 (A. W. Curton Ltd)
Semi-detached, three bedrooms, two reception rooms, with garage space, £1,140
Cash Payment: £70
Legal charges: £25
Building Society survey fee: £2 2s
Mortgage: £1 13s 2d per week
Local rates: £16 10s per annum.
Water rate: £2 18s 9d per annum.
Gas: 3s 10d per 1,000 cubic feet
Electricity: Lighting 4½d a unit, Heating 1¼d (contract rate 1d unit winter, ½d a unit summer, plus quarterly charge 17s 8d)
Fares: Three months' season ticket to Charing Cross £3 2 6d.

Edgware, 1938 (John Laing and Son Ltd)
Semi-detached, three bedrooms, two reception rooms, garage space, £870.
Cash payment: £60.
Legal Charges: none.
Building Society Survey Fee: none
Building Society Advance Fee: £1 5s
Mortgage: £1 3s 11d per week
Local and water rates: 5s 10d per week
Gas: 3s 7d per 1,000 cubic feet.
Electricity: Lighting 3¾d per unit, Heating 1⅛d per unit (contract rate, ½d per unit plus quarterly charge).
Fares: Three months' season ticket to Charing Cross £3 2 6d.

Ilford, 1934 (New Ideal Homesteads Ltd)
Terraced (four block), two reception rooms, three bedrooms, £595
Cash Payment: £60 (or £30 with higher repayment)
Legal charges: none
Building Society Survey fee: none

Mortgage: 15s per week (17s 5d with £30 deposit).
Local rates: 4s 11d per week
Water rate: 6d per week
Gas: 8.6d per therm
Electricity: ⅜d per unit plus quarterly charge
Fares: Three months' season ticket to Liverpool Street £3 11s. (or workmen's return ticket 10d daily)

Chapter 12

SELLING
THE SUBURB

Nightingales and Baronial Halls

In the decades either side of World War I a modest amount of newspaper advertising was sufficient to attract to the limited amount of activity the favoured few able to contemplate house ownership. But as conditions eased for both buyer and seller towards the end of the twenties, the speculators were obliged to devote more money and imagination to their sales effort until, in the first half of the thirties, house-hunting became so easy, the inducements so many and various, that it was a popular weekend pastime. For the minimum of trouble and expense, Londoners could compare the purchase terms, amenities and enticements of several hundred housing estates at every part of the outskirts.

Morning and evening papers were of course a most useful publicity medium, and although Howkins thought them 'not generally remunerative from a property selling point of view',[1] local newspaper displays were by no means rare (in the summer of 1939, John Laing and Son were proclaiming the merits of their 8 open estates in 13 local papers as well as in the *Daily Express, News-Chronicle, Homefinder* and *Dalton's Weekly*). The first illustrated announcements of new suburban houses to appear in the *Evening News* were in the issue of 5 July 1905 (the houses were at Goodmayes) and half-page spreads followed that autumn. From May 1908 until the outbreak of war in August 1914, this popular London evening paper carried frequent whole-page features about new developments under the heading *Where to Live*, each consisting of a column or two of 'puff' surrounded by the announcements of builders and estate developers. Occasionally the page was devoted to one district.

Although large advertisements for new houses had been appear-

[1] F. Howkins, *An Introduction to the Development of Private Building Estates and Town Planning*, TEG 1926.

ing sporadically since 1920, it was not until 22 February 1923 that the *Evening News* was able to introduce a regular weekly page of small illustrated announcements entitled *The Homeseeker's Guide*. Similar pages appeared in the London-based dailies about the same time; the *Daily Express*, for example had its *Modern Homes Guide*, which expanded to a Saturday full page from January 1924. Later in the twenties, and through the thirties, both the national dailies and the London evenings carried many full-page and half-page advertisements of the larger firms, coverage of this kind reaching its peak in 1934–6. After that, the big display ads were noticeably fewer, less strident, and often angled towards those who could only just afford to buy.

The boom also stimulated the publication of periodicals entirely devoted to announcements of new housing developments, apart from a small amount of editorial matter on new estates, aspects of house purchase and ownership, and related subjects. By far the most enduring of these was the monthly *Homefinder and Small Property Guide*, produced from 6 October 1931 by a firm which had been compiling local property guides on an annual basis since 1910.

As they felt their inner-area traffic slipping away to the electric tramcar and the motor omnibus, the London-based railway companies began to pay some attention to the promotion of outer suburban business. First in the field was the GNR, whose 'Northern Heights' publicity started early in 1906, backed by a penny booklet, *Where to Live: Illustrated Guide to some of London's Choicest Suburbs*. This contained a great deal of practical information on such matters as housing developments, local rates, schools, fares and train services, and reappeared at intervals over the next ten years or so, evidently with some success, as a GNR official was able to write in 1914 that the company's suburban publications had produced 'a species of regular traffic, which is of the utmost importance from the revenue standpoint'.[1] Other companies soon followed this example, the LNWR with *North Western Country Homes*, the LBSCR with *By Surrey Lanes to Sussex Shores*, the LSWR with *Homes in the South Western Suburbs*, the GER with *Homes by London's Woodland* and *By Forest and Countryside*, and the Metropolitan with *Country Homes*. All these appeared between 1907 and 1914, free of charge or at nominal prices. Both the GWR and GCR published regular gazettes of residential information, *Homes for all – London's Western Borderland*, and *The Homestead*.

[1] H. J. Jewell, article in *Railway News Jubilee Supplement*, 1914.

The latter survived the war, but the Great Western quarterly, which started in January 1912, did not appear after the issue of July 1914.

Perhaps the most famous of all London railway guides to the suburbs was the Metropolitan's *Metro-land*. This name for the company's territory was coined about 1914 when a booklet of this title appeared, mainly devoted to walkers and cyclists. *Country Homes in Metro-land* followed as a companion publication in 1915, replacing the earlier *Country Homes*. From 1919 onwards, *Metro-land* appeared annually, with increasing amounts of space devoted to housing developments. In the autumn of 1926, the Southern Railway brought out a 194-page glossy paper book entitled *The Country at London's Door*, with photographs of new houses, some still under construction, preponderant amongst the many illustrations. The second edition, *Country Homes at London's Door*, ran to 376 pages, and covered the whole of the electrified suburban area, which at that time extended out to Guildford, Dorking, Coulsdon, Orpington and Dartford. Similar books, bearing variations of the title *Southern Homes*, followed until 1939.

In addition to their guides and gazettes, the railway companies occasionally advertised the delights of their suburban areas in the morning and evening newspapers. Underground advertisements in 1927 mentioned specific estates, with the prices of houses, and in that year, the Southern and the Underground carried out a running fight across the pages of the *Evening News*: 'Live on the Underground' . . . 'Live in Kent' . . . 'Live on the Underground' . . . 'Live in Surrey' and so on. The Southern even went into the business of homefinding, the Public Relations and Advertising Department organising itself to dispense information on houses, local rates, season ticket rates, train services etc. A minute of 1934 noted that this venture, 'would be of great assistance in the development of Southern England, it being understood the Company should work in co-operation with and not in competition with Estate Agents'.[1]

Some of the railway residential guides were prepared with the assistance of the Homeland Association, an organisation which also published its own booklets from about 1900 onwards under the title *Where to Live Round London*. These contained railway maps and a considerable amount of information on such important matters as local rates, schools, water supply, subsoils and the death-rates. Estate developers issued brochures, often lavishly produced

[1] BTHR SOU 1/26, 20 December 1934.

on art paper, with numerous photographs, drawings and plans. Some publishers specialising in this field were prepared to supply such brochures to developers free in return for the advertising revenue, the developer undertaking to find a minimum number of advertisers prepared to pay around £3 to £4 a year. As some encouragement, the builder was also to give the advertisers the names of people buying houses, so that they might canvass for orders. In the Edwardian era picture postcards were at the peak of their popularity, and were frequently used for advertising all sorts of products and services, including new housing developments. An example of this type of publicity is illustrated on plate 15.

Standing amidst builder's debris in their serried rows, newly constructed houses were unpromising material for the photographer. Most advertisements and brochures were accordingly illustrated with idealised sketches or heavily retouched photographs which skilfully suggested that the house stood quite along in matured surroundings of judiciously placed trees and shrubs, against a background of windblown clouds and gently rolling hills.

Even during the most feverish moments of the boom, descriptions of the houses remained reasonably factual and restrained. Of course there were occasional bursts of over-enthusiasm such as 'Detached Country Residences' for £925 houses on M. J. Gleeson's 1936 Nonsuch Estate at Cheam, 'Bijou Mansions' at Wembley (Sando, 1926), 'Bijou Baronial Halls' on the Merrylees Estates at Hendon and Mill Hill in 1930, and the 'Laing-built palaces, built of rustic bricks, with avenues of trees, grow more beautiful as the years pass' (Kingsbury, Golders Green and Sudbury Town, 1930). The popularity of the word *bijou* in this context is curious, considering that some dictionaries give one of its meanings as 'little box'.

When talking about the districts in which their houses were sited, the copy writers sometimes allowed their imaginations to become a little overheated: Warminster Road, South Norwood was described in 1926 as a 'Gentlefolks' Residential Area. Healthy and Peaceful', or, two years later, as 'London's smallest Garden City'. George Ball (Ruislip) Ltd gaily collapsed into doggerel to voice the attractions of their particular corner of Metro-land:

'Live in Ruislip where the air's like wine,
It's less than half an hour on the Piccadilly Line.'

Earlier in this book we have seen how the health advantages of

suburban living were frequently stressed in publicity. Rural pleasures were another popular theme. A 1936 advertisement for the
Sunnyside Estate at Whyteleafe, suggested that at Hilbury Road,
you would have 'Devon at your door' for £695 upwards. In 1929
buyers were invited to Brookmans Park to 'live where the nightingales sing', but in 1934 Vincent Estates were claiming that 'the
nightingale is singing at Carshalton'; perhaps it had discovered that
the air is warmer south of the river. An arrangement that seems not
to have been entirely without disadvantages was available in 1937
at the Woodham Estate, West Byfleet, where houses selling at
£500 upwards were 'built round a farm'. For those with tastes a
little less bucolic, George Moss and Sons offered 'a village green,
a beautiful old church, a little moss-grown churchyard, long vistas
of green fields ... you can have your home in the old rectory
garden ...' All this at Northolt, in 1930. At least one speculative
builder was ambitious enough to offer the pleasures of the traditional country life of the aristocracy. For £1,175 to £4,000, a D-C
house at Newberries Park, Radlett, brought, 'the lazy delights of a
country house or the strenuous excitements of country life – Hunt-
ing, Shooting, Beagling and the like ... every phase of the rural life
at Radlett provides the perfect antidote to business worries'.[1]

Among the intelligentsia, *suburb* was of course already a dirty
word. Only the dead and half dead were attracted to such places.
Hopefully, some developers tried to indicate that they had something a little different. Purley Downs Road, Sanderstead in 1935
was thought to be 'away from suburbia', whilst at Kingswood,
those able to afford prices in the range £1,250 to £5,000 could have
a Costain detached house on a 'non-suburbanized estate' (1933).
Only forty houses remained in November 1935 on the six-month-
old Perivale Wood Estate, 'isolated from other estates' and 'rural,
yet only five miles from Marble Arch'. Noel Rees worked very hard
indeed on the text of a leaflet about Petts Wood in 1932, trying to
suggest he had something quite out of the ordinary:

'The war well over and building resumed; the cry went round
"live in the Country", and sleeping villages which surrounded the
metropolis were seized upon and developed. For six months the
term "country home" was justified, then came the change.
Speculative builders with an eye to quick profits had no time
for serious planning. Back came the long barrack-like roads of

[1] Advertisement in HTBG 15 March 1935.

dwellings all cast in the same mould, long ugly fences, boxed-in gardens and lo! the country had vanished for ever – it was nothing but a very *suburban* home.

It was after a long trail of sorrowful headshaking that I came to Petts Wood and, no sooner had I set foot outside the station, when my heart rose within me. Here was something new. Station approaches are not usually the most beautiful things in the world, but at Petts Wood the view from the station steps is perhaps the key to the district. A pleasant green, surrounded on three sides by well-designed, half-timbered rows of shops, sparkling, clean shops, all live and active.

Radiating from these are the "Drives", "Ways" and "Avenues" of Petts Wood, climbing up the hill to the borders of that beautiful land, open and free for all time as a memorial to the man who made our summer evenings longer – William Willett, and away to the back of it lies Chislehurst Common, a fairyland of birch and gorse, all assuring one that Petts Wood is, and must remain, a *country* home.

Birches, hazels, oaks, ash and pine trees have crept away from these common lands and you find them everywhere, little coppices at the corners of the "Drives" and "Avenues"; along the paths, in the gardens, everywhere. At the foot of the hill runs a little brook, spanned by charming little white bridges.

Now walk up Wood Ride, which is the finest example of Petts Wood novelty and charm. Houses of distinctive design, pleasant half-timbering, overhanging bays, sweeping gables, timbered porches, all set well away from the road, bright and sunny in their white dress. No fences, but little low crazy stone walls, where iris and rock plants grow, crazy paths, flower-laden beds, and bright green lawns, while at the back nod the health-laden pines.'

Such effusion is pardonable enough, but elsewhere, strict honesty was not an invariable rule. It was common practice to quote in publicity a very low price to encourage enquiry, whereupon the applicant would be told that all houses at that price had been sold (if indeed there had ever been any). Railway timetables were scrutinised for the fastest trains of the day so that the publicity could be phrased to give the impression that all the trains travelled at that speed. A 1936 advertisement (in the SR Suburban Time-table!) described an estate at Chelsfield as '22 minutes from town', although there was only one train a day covering the journey in that time. In the same book an estate at West Molesey (wrongly described as 'Hampton Court') is said to be '20 minutes from Waterloo', but a glance at the timetable on another page shows a regular service in thirty-three or thirty-four minutes.

By Car, Train and Steamer to the Show House

At the height of the boom, the potential buyer, having read the advertisements, need not travel far to sample the wares. Each year from 1908 the *Daily Mail* held its exuberant Ideal Home Exhibition, which in the thirties always included sample houses erected inside Olympia by the leading London builders. In 1934, 'at the end of a country lane', the visitor was confronted by 'a village of ideal homes . . . ten houses and bungalows of varied design erected by building firms of repute'. Similar specimen houses were shown every winter at the South London Exhibition at the Crystal Palace, and the North London Exhibition at Alexandra Palace. But exhibitions lasted only a few weeks, and to keep their houses before the public eye, some of the big firms established show houses at strategic points in central London. Wimpey had one at their headquarters in the Grove, Hammersmith, from which clients would be taken by car to their 'Surrey Estates' in 1932. Laing's detached three-bedroom show house appeared in 1934 on an island site in front of Kings Cross station. Open from 10 a.m. to 10 p.m. every day, it was an example of a type included in various north London estates, selling at around £775. After undergoing several rearrangements, it ended its days as a Salvation Army canteen for servicemen in World War II. Also in 1934, Davis Estates opened show houses in Vauxhall Bridge Road and Villiers Street; the latter, in the shadow of Charing Cross station, had a small garden. Three years later, Laing had five houses on show at 520 Oxford Street, near Marble Arch. Clapham Junction, easily reached from most parts of inner south London, and a good departure point for the new suburbs on the Southern Electric, was the site of E. and L. Bergs' 'Model Rooms' and of G. T. Crouch's show house, rebuilt there after appearing at the Ideal Home Exhibition (later taken to pieces again, this much-handled house finally settled down on the Purley Park Estate).

Visits to the new estates were made as easy as possible. Free travel to view was widely offered, some builders (Curton of Edgware was one) even providing a private car by appointment at any rendezvous in the London area, weekdays, evenings and weekends. More usual was the issue of vouchers exchangeable for tickets at railway stations. During the thirties New Ideal Homesteads maintained a small bureau near platform 16 on Waterloo station to dispense these vouchers and offer information about their estates. Ever prompt to encourage its subsidiary, Metropolitan Railway Country Estates Ltd, the Metropolitan Railway handed out free First Class tickets to Rayners Lane and other stations, a practice which abruptly ceased when London Transport took over in 1933 (the LPTB also hastily rearranged advertising copy boosting the joys of residence in Metro-land in space booked long in advance by a Metropolitan Railway unaware of its fate).

Once arrived at the suburban station, the prospective buyers would be whisked to the estate by the firms' cars, the speed of travel often being relative to the distance between the railway and the houses. Other variants were tried. During 1934 Costain operated free motor coach trips from East Ham station to their Elm Park Estate, adding for good measure a free painting book for the kiddies. A year later, Costain visitors were regaled with free teas. Teas were also provided on D. G. Howard's West Molesey Estate in 1934 as well as refund of train fares. Later that year, Howard organised a free steamer trip along the Thames to Hampton Court for prospective purchasers, but after three days he was obliged to buy further advertising space to announce that it was overbooked. Only twenty-four years of age, Howard was trying his hand at full-scale estate development after some experience in an estate agent's office. In the Croydon Bankruptcy Court in September 1935, it was reported that he had spent £20,000 on publicising the 320 houses on his Upper Farm Estate, West Molesey. This had been in the expectation of £100 clear profit on each house, but only a hundred had been sold.[1]

In prominent positions near the entrance to almost all estates of any size were found the fully furnished show houses. Surrounded by their hastily assembled gardens, they strove to foster the dream image so sadly lacking in the gaunt half-finished shells that reared up from the mud beyond. Such importance was attached to them that they were always given the utmost priority once work on an estate had started. At Worcester Park in 1935, Wates were so anxious to finish the four show houses on their Station Estate that

[1] ECET 5 October 1935.

work went on all night under floodlights, but when the hammering and thumping aroused the anger of established residents, the local council had the night work stopped. Careful thought was given by some firms to the phasing of new estate construction to achieve the maximum sales impact. Wimpey would endeavour to arrange that the initial heavy construction work was undertaken during the winter, so that the show houses would be ready on a reasonably tidy estate by the early spring.[1]

Furniture and furnishings for show houses were commonly loaned or supplied free of charge by the departmental stores, whose representatives were in attendance alongside those of the builders, to solicit orders. As the show houses were normally open up to 10 p.m. or later every day, including Sundays, it is hardly surprising that there were occasional protests of unfair trading by Traders' Associations. This was also an opportunity for enterprising firms to display new ideas in furnishing. At Edgware in 1934, Roger Malcolm's St Margaret's Estate had the first house in England fully furnished with built-in furniture. With gardens also fully laid out, the extra cost on the basic price of £1,150 was £445, hardly a cheap way of 'saving 75 per cent of the furnishing cost', (chairs and soft furnishings as well as a divan bed still had to be bought).

Boxers, Maharajahs and Free Refrigerators

During the busiest years, the relatively straightforward sales aids so far described were not enough. In the competition for attention in a crowded market place, many, quaint and various were the devices employed by the builders and developers. As the famous had for some time been found willing to give their blessing to chocolates and cosmetics, it was a logical enough step to seek their blandishments for housing estates. So it was that in 1933 Bergs persuaded the radio stars Elsie and Doris Walters and the actor Gordon Harker to speak in praise of their Coombe Estate at New Malden; there was also a letter of commendation from the actress Sybil Thorndike. Two years later, on August Bank Holiday, the film star Noah Beery was to be found leaving the impressions of his hands and feet in the wet concrete at the entrance to W. Greville Collins' Hampton Manor Estate. When he had cleaned up, the prospective customers were able to take tea with him. And in 1935, Jack (Kid) Berg, lightweight champion of Great Britain, was 'personally selling'

[1] TEG 17 September 1938.

houses on the Ruislip Gardens Estate. Striving for even higher things, Gower Builders (London) Ltd advertised one of their estates in 1933 with a leaflet bearing the message 'Visiting Royalty approves of the Spring Park Farm Estate, Shirley'. A close inspection of the accompanying photograph revealed the Maharajah of Alwar leaving a house he had named after himself.

Son et lumière can always be relied upon to attract night crowds. 'FREE! TONIGHT! BRING YOUR FRIENDS TO SEE THE GREAT FIREWORKS AND SEARCHLIGHT DISPLAY AT RUISLIP MANOR' invited George Ball in the *Evening News* of 30 September 1933. Either before or after the excitement, he clearly hoped some might be persuaded to commit themselves to a £450 'Manor Home'. His display was no doubt intended to outdo the great bonfires arranged by E. S. Reid to publicise houses at neighbouring Rayners Lane in 1930–2. Advantage was taken of neon tubes and improved floodlighting techniques when these became generally available in the 1930s. The 'luxury show houses' of the 1935 Tysoe and Harris Cotswold Estate at Park Langley were 'lighted and floodlit after dark', whilst in the same year, the Park Hill Estate at Ilford was lit by neon signs. At Field End Lane, Eastcote, in 1936, Lanes announced that the whole estate would be lit up, 'the largest area floodlit outside London'.

This firm also offered in September 1936 free furnishings to 'all who buy who married or will be married in 1936', which leads us neatly into the free gift department. Offers of furnishings, even furniture, over limited periods were fairly common in the hectic early thirties, when as much as £50 worth might be given away. Larger items were also used as bait. Refrigerators were among the more usual from 1932 onwards, sometimes supplemented by an electric cooker. Modern Houses Ltd, of the Joel Park Estate, Pinner (£895 to £1,500), set up the jackpot in 1935: with each house went an electric refrigerator, washing-machine and cooker, *and* seven electric fires. A year earlier, Peter Deane had given away a 5-valve all-mains superhet. radio, an electric clock and a cooker with his 'entirely labourless' houses at Palmers Green. As there were no less than 21 electric points in these houses, the purchasers were soon to be in a fever of indecision as to where to plug in what. Electric clocks were frequently dispensed, because they combined novelty with low cost, but radios, vacuum cleaners and washing-machines were only rarely used as 'gifts'. Davis Estates hit a new note in 1936, when they offered free telephone installation. At least one builder distributed cash prizes; Canterbuilt of Stoneleigh Hill was prepared to hand over £5 cash in November 1934 to 'any purchaser before Christmas', together with a similar bonus for anyone introducing a purchaser in the same period. Perhaps the most spectacular free gift of all was that advertised as early as 1928 by the Regent Farm Estate, Surbiton: 'A House and a Car for £1,000'. It must be added that the houses, although detached with garage, had but one reception room and two bedrooms. The car was a '4-seater open tourer' of unspecified make. For those still hesitant, the advertisement concluded with a further offer: 'Front Garden Made Up'.

Gardens, dug over, made up, turfed, or otherwise rendered presentable were frequently offered as an extra service even before 1914. It was almost always the *front* garden that received attention, as this rendered the estate more attractive to later arrivals. With similar motives Wimpey, Laing and others organised competitions for the best front gardens whilst there were houses still remaining for sale. At Canons Park in 1935, D-C Estates presented a cash prize of £15 and a challenge cup to the winner of a front garden competition.

Other long-established sales carrots surviving into the thirties were free light fittings and shades, free curtain fittings, free removals and free tickets to town for limited periods. Usually the offer of free removal was prudently restricted to a range of twenty to twenty-five miles, sometimes less than that. A survey of advertisements appearing in the peak years reveals free season tickets for one year offered from Hounslow (1928), Tattenham Corner (1928), Hillingdon (1929), Sudbury Town (1930) and Bexleyheath (1936). In the first and third of these cases the ticket was given only to every third purchaser, in the others only to those purchasing a house during a very limited period. Much rarer was a year's payment of local rates, or one to three years of free maintenance.

There were pleasant minor touches too. Local traders, soliciting custom, would leave free groceries and dairy products at houses newly purchased. On some estates, the sales staff would arrange for larders to be stocked, or would even cook the dinner on the first day.[1]

[1] V. H. Bone, in an interview with the author.

Chapter 13

TRANSPORT
FOR THE SUBURBS

'Henry Oakley: ". . . there is a huge area there, of fifteen to twenty miles, where houses are scarcely to be seen."
Two Officers of the LCC: "They will soon come. Run the trains and they will come." [1]

So extensive was the expansion of London's transport facilities in the first forty years of the century that there is a temptation to over-emphasise and oversimplify the part played by public transport in the growth of the suburbs. Speaking at the end of our period, Patrick Abercrombie saw the London Passenger Transport Board as 'now pioneer, now camp follower' and described its role as 'vigorous if uncertain'. [2] Throughout the years 1901–39 there are many examples in which public transport facilities appear as a causal or permissive factor in residential development, but it is also not difficult to find cases were builders went ahead in a transport desert, confident that services would be quickly provided.

By any measure, the growth of road and rail services around London was impressive. In the first years of the century, as the tramways were electrified, the former horse lines were extended outwards and many new routes provided; with the arrival in 1910 of a reliable vehicle, motorbus services proliferated well beyond the old horse-bus zone. Whilst all this was going on, some of the London railway companies were starting to electrify suburban lines, and in the two decades following World War I, London saw open-air extensions of the tube railways into the outer areas and the electrification of almost all the railways south of the Thames to twenty or more miles from the centre.

[1] Conference on workmen's trains between the LCC and the railway companies, at the Board of Trade, 28 June 1893, (C.7542) (Parliamentary Papers LXXV.823) (Oakley was the general manager of the GNR).
[2] Professor Patrick Abercrombie, *Greater London Plan, 1944*, para. 8.

Much of this activity was piecemeal and unco-ordinated, for despite the clear recommendations of the 1905 Royal Commission on London Traffic and later committees, political jealousies and procrastination, together with a measure of collaboration by the undertakings themselves, delayed the establishment of a central transport authority. When the Transport Board was finally set up in 1933 there followed some large-scale planning and provision, mostly affecting the area north of the river. Even then, co-ordination of housing and transport development remained unsatisfactory, and the Board had no jurisdiction over the main line railway companies' suburban services.

Suburban Tram and Bus
Some indication of the growth of suburban road services in Edwardian London was given at the beginning of this book. Development after 1919 was too extensive and too complicated to allow comprehensive review here, but an impression of it may be gained from the material presented in the appendices.

Sewing threads between the outward stretching fingers of existing radial settlement, electric tramways began the process of dispersal that was to be continued at much accelerated pace by the motorbus. Around 1928 almost every community of any significance in the outskirts of London had achieved some sort of bus service and the builders were losing any remaining reluctance to exploit areas beyond walking distance from railway stations. In such districts as north Romford, north Ilford, Shirley, North Cheam and the higher parts of Coulsdon, a great deal of bus-dependent housing appeared in the late twenties and early thirties.

Trams and motorbuses not only provided the first convenient means of moving from one suburb to another across the radial routes, but linked the suburbs with the older industrial zones and retail centres. They played an important role in consolidating the uneven mix of factories and housing estates that appeared in parts of outer west and north-west London and in connecting the docks and riverside industries with new housing in the outer east and south-east districts, thus determining to some extent the type of properties found in those areas. The importance of road transport services to a suburban industrial zone was well illustrated by North Acton where there were 180 factories with a total of 34,000 employees by 1938; in that year, traffic flow was almost entirely confined to peak hours, and apart from a few cyclists, was carried exclusively by motorbuses and trolleybuses linking the factories with nearby residential areas.[1]

In middle-class suburbs the electric tram was opposed as an agent of working-class dispersal and also because its overhead wires were considered unsightly. 'Harrow is unspoilt by trams' was a boast of 1909,[2] echoing earlier opposition in that district. In 1900 the Middlesex County Council had proposed tramways and the local newspaper at once sensed a threat: 'Harrow is being spoiled rapidly enough without creating facilities for undesirable residents to come in and further increase the number of inhabitants to the acre. There are over many now for a country place'.[3]

Opposition of this sort has perhaps tended to obscure the part played by the electric tramcar in succouring the growth of suburban villas. Most of the new areas were served by the private companies, a fact which may have diluted the social prejudice against the tramcar; certainly the brightly painted and frequently cushioned vehicles operated by private enterprise managed to appear almost petit-bourgeois in contrast to the cloth cap, shag and spit image created by those operated by the LCC and the east London municipalities. It was the branches and linking lines that created the heartland of tramway suburbia, not the radial routes from central London, and the political geography was such that the private undertakings had mostly the former type of service. Thus the cars of the London United in the west and south-west, those of the South Metropolitan in the south, and the Metropolitan in the north and north-west, undoubtedly assisted the spread of such favoured areas as Surbiton, New Malden and Raynes Park, Sutton, Carshalton and Wallington, and Palmers Green, Winchmore Hill, Friern Barnet, Whetstone and Finchley. In most of these districts new houses appeared in the years 1900–14 at a rate which could not be explained by the timing and location of railway service improvements.

In areas such as those mentioned, the electric tramcar became a prominent feature of suburban life. Children travelled on it to reach the more widely dispersed secondary schools; housewives used it to search for lower prices in the older retail centres; and at week-ends the tram offered a means of escape to the London countryside. In 1907 Albert Emil Davies (later a Labour member of the LCC) and Ernest Gower wrote a booklet entitled *Tramway Trips and*

[1] Evidence of the LPTB to the RCGDIP 1938, Part III, para. 9.
[2] EN 16 July 1909.   [3] *Harrow Gazette*, 17 March 1900.

Rambles, which described rides on 23 tram routes, mostly through the outskirts of London, and 40 walks between tramways. On Tram Ride No. 3, from Shepherds Bush to Uxbridge, twelve-and-a-half miles in an hour twenty minutes, fare 5d, the authors noted building operations in 'full swing' between Southall High Street and the canal bridge, but it was still possible for them to indicate country walks from Southall to Hanwell, Hayes and Hounslow. The habit of tramway pleasure trips at weekends lasted into the twenties, and it was the suburban tram as well as the suburban bus and train which introduced many Londoners to that pleasant Sunday countryside soon to disappear under the tide of bricks and mortar.

Some very long country motorbus routes had been established by 1913. That summer a General advertisement[1] showed daily services from Golders Green to St Albans, from Victoria to Epping Forest and to Sidcup, from Shoreditch Church to Farnborough, Kent, and from Hounslow West Underground to Windsor. Shorter services were operating between Kingston and Esher and between Hounslow West and Staines. On Sundays, it was possible to ride on a motorbus out to Cockfosters (from Victoria), to Chingford (from Elephant & Castle), to the remote Essex village of Lambourne End, just outside the Metropolitan Police District (from North Woolwich), to Chigwell Row (from the Bank), to Sidcup (from Oxford Circus), to Epsom and to Hampton Court (from Charing Cross) and to Whyteleafe (from Stockwell). Some of these services also operated on certain other days of the week and almost all were opening up what were to become daily routes. Equally important, they were inculcating many youngsters with the attractions of living at the edge of the country. Couples cuddling in the back upstairs seat of the Sunday bus, legs cosy beneath the weatherproof cover, would survey the semi-rural landscape and dream of settling down.

As early as 1915, a regular if infrequent new bus service gave some point to the contemporary offer of 20 ft. by 200 ft. plots for £10 at hitherto inaccessible Biggin Hill, Kent ('LGOC bus 136 passes through the estate to Bromley station'[2]). It was stuff to stir the imagination of any Cockney soldier reading it in the Flanders mud. Here in truth was evidence that the motorbus was widening the choice of residential location in the most dramatic fashion.

The war ended, the motorbus went almost everywhere, Labour and running costs were low and there was virtually no competition from private cars. The ready availability of the bus was largely

[1] EN 11 July 1913.   [2] EN 5 March 1915.

responsible for the formation of the great profusion of small activity nodes around outer London. A typical cross-suburban route was the 140, from Mill Hill to Hayes, Middlesex, which had started life in 1932 as a fifteen-minute service from Colindale to Northolt via Kingsbury, Harrow and South Harrow. By 1939 it was working from Mill Hill via Queensbury station and then over its former route, extended at the south end to Northolt, Yeading and Hayes, with a five- to seven-minute frequency on the Mill Hill–Queensbury section. In May that year, London Transport announced that the Saturday frequency from Mill Hill to Queensbury would be improved to three-and-a-half minutes, from Mill Hill to Northolt to seven-and-a-half minutes, and from Mill Hill to Hayes, to fifteen minutes, 'to meet industrial and shopping movement all along the route'. As car ownership spread, bus services of this type gradually became uneconomic, although the problem did not reach serious proportions until the late 1950s.

With a near-monopoly in central London, the General were willing enough to establish new services in the developing outer districts, trusting that they would at least cover their running costs within a year or so. But in 1923, when the profitable base was threatened by 'pirate' buses (many of them operated by ex-servicemen), the LGOC began to make warning noises: the services in the outer suburbs could not be maintained 'if the main routes of heavy traffic are to be impoverished'.[1] Poor patronage of such services as Forest Hill–Chislehurst, Woolwich–Dartford, and Kingston–Windsor was said to be a matter of special concern, as these were operated by single-deckers with very small seating capacity. Later in the same year another announcement revealed that of the 155 services worked throughout London, 34 were making no contribution to profits and 14 were earning less than working expenses. An example of the latter was route 110, Golders Green–Finsbury Park (started in April 1922) whose single-deck B-type buses carried a full load only at weekends.[2] But as the worst of the opposition in the central area was overcome, the fuss died, and new services continued to be established in the developing suburbs on a generous scale. Few of the small firms tried their hand in the new districts, and where they did, it was to take advantage of the absence of the major operators, a venture not always attended with success. Nancy Clark recalls a small brown single-decker which appeared on the

[1] LGOC Guide, July 1923.
[2] LGOC Guide, October 1923.

Hadley Wood–Barnet run in the early twenties, only to vanish without trace after a very short time.[1] Although most of the enduring suburban services before 1933 were provided by the General, other operators were prominent in the south-eastern sector of Greater London and along the main radial roads, especially those on which the co-ordination policy of the Underground group required the passenger to change between General bus and Underground railway (e.g. Southgate to central London and Finchley to the West End). Services of this type were built up from the mid-twenties and with the general adoption of pneumatic tyres towards the end of that decade raising maximum speeds from 12 to rather more than 30 miles per hour, became attractive to the through suburban passenger because they offered superior comfort at similar or only slightly longer journey times.

Builders' Buses

The ready availability of cheap land on the fringes of London after 1919 tempted many developers to exploit areas devoid of regular public transport. Once work had begun on such an estate, unremitting efforts would be made to persuade a bus operator to divert or extend an existing route. If there were other houses going up in the same area this was more likely to be successful, but if the estate was isolated, the developer could be driven to setting up his own transport service as an alternative to bankruptcy, or at any rate unacceptably low sales. There were several examples of this, and at least one of a builder maintaining a service after a regular operator had withdrawn, disappointed at the lack of revenue.

Transport services sponsored by builders were of course not unknown before 1914, and the horse-bus to Cranbrook Park has been mentioned. As early as 1905 we find the Polytechnic Estate Ltd providing a motorbus between their Cannons Hill Estate (near the present Wimbledon Chase station) and Wimbledon station.[2] The first post-war example which can be traced was at Orpington, where residents on the Grangewood Estate in 1924 were 'conveyed to and from the station by estate cars morning and evening'.[3] Alas, this luxurious facility was withdrawn once all the houses had been sold. Costains' Selsdon estate, started in 1925, was two hilly miles from South Croydon station. Until the General were finally persuaded to extend their route 54 in 1928, this firm ran their own

[1] Nancy Clark, op. cit.   [2] EN 6 March 1905.   [3] EN 19 December 1924.

small single-decker, adorned with the message 'Selsdon Garden Village'. When, in 1930, the General decided to withdraw their route 164, connection between Messrs Harwood's houses at Longdown Lane (on the outskirts of Epsom) and the Waterloo line at Ewell West station was maintained by a bus operated for the builders, with fares on a season ticket basis.

Morells' Coney Hall Estate was a generous one-and-a-half miles south of Hayes station. In January 1934 the firm were advertising what they were pleased to call a 'Victory Super-Bus' between the station and the estate. Five months later this had been rechristened 'Morrells' Free Luxury Coach' and was working every ten minutes between 7.30 a.m. and 10 p.m.[1] This service was of course available to visitors and potential purchasers as well as to residents, but it was the latter who were to be most upset when it was withdrawn upon completion of the estate. London Transport refused to step into the breach, not least because some of the roads were still unmade.

Reference has been made earlier to the New Addington Estate of the First National Housing Trust. Far more remote from civilisation than anything mentioned so far, this was over three miles from the station at South Croydon. During 1938 and 1939 a bus service was operated on behalf of the Trust between Featherbed Lane and Croydon by A. Bennett, a Shirley private hire firm. On 5 July 1939 this was replaced by a new London Transport service, 130 (Croydon–New Addington).

T. F. Nash Ltd had begun their Havering Park Estate at Collier Row, about two-and-a-half miles north of Romford station, in 1937. In February 1939, after about 2,000 of the planned 9,000 houses had been completed, the firm announced that they were so tired of London Transport's delay in providing a service that they had purchased their own 32-seater bus. This ran between 6.30 a.m. and 10 a.m. and between 3.30 p.m. and 9 p.m., working round the estate every fifteen minutes, picking up passengers as required and conveying them to and from the existing LPTB bus route. As the estate was within the London Transport area, the Board posted officials to ensure that no tickets were sold.[2]

A rather different type of sponsored bus service, not unrelated to suburban expansion, was a fare-stage service between Kingston and Ashford (Middlesex) via Lower Sunbury, started in early July 1931 by Bentalls, the well-known Kingston-on-Thames departmental

[1] EN 10 January 1934.   [2] HF 18 February 1939.

store. As the main objective was to encourage former customers who had moved away from the store's catchment area to return to Kingston for their shopping, no buses were provided on Wednesday afternoons or Sundays. This operation had to cease in December 1933 with the arrival of the London Transport era.

Cheapest by Tram

Builders' buses might sometimes be free, but London's electric tramcars were the vehicles that provided the best of all fare bargains, covering as they did very long distances at little more than nominal fares. Even after 1919, the tramway remained the cheapest form of transport in London, for although the LCC workmen's fares were increased to 2d return for four sections (4·8 miles), 4d for eight sections, and a maximum of 6d return for single distances over 9·6 miles, they could not be bettered on most alternative railway routes. Workmen's fares on the other London tramways were generally maintained at around a ½d a mile during the 1920s. After the formation of the LPTB in 1933, the workmen's return fares on tramways other than the old LCC lines, and on the trolleybuses which replaced them, were at half the ordinary fare for the single journey. On the former LCC system, the corresponding fare was 1d return where the single was 2d, 2d where the single was 3d or less, and 3d where it was 5d or less. Ordinary fares on tramcars and trolleybuses after 1933 were 1d for 1·2 miles, with a lower rate for longer rides. There were also returns at less than double the single fare, supplemented by special very cheap 'midday returns' on many important routes, (a facility carried over from the LCC regime). On buses running alongside tramcars, the ordinary fares were the same, but with no cheap facilities; elsewhere, the bus rate was generally 1d a mile.

Railway workmen's fares were increased by an average of 100 per cent from September 1920, and in 1927 were stabilised at rates between ¼d and 1d a mile according to distance with a minimum of 2d. At the same time, the ordinary Third Class (present Second Class) fare became 1½d a mile. Comparative workmen's, ordinary and season ticket rates are given in a note.[1]

[1] For a single journey of *one mile*, the workmen's return rate was 2d, the Third Class return 3d, the Third Class quarterly season rate, 3·08d; *two miles* 3d, 6d, 4·24d; *five miles*, 6d, 1s 3d, 6·92d; *ten miles*, 9·5d, 2s 6d, 10·76d; *twenty miles* 1s 2·5d, 5s, 1s 4·54d. (All fare information is taken from *London Housing* (LCC, 1937) and the LPTB evidence to RCGDIP, 15 February 1938).

Apart from the Metropolitan Railway, which charged the main line fares, the maximum ordinary single rate on the Underground lines was 1d a mile, as on the buses, tapering after four miles to give ten miles for 7d and twenty miles for a shilling, with appropriate intermediate stages. Workmen's rate was the ordinary single fare for the return journey (minimum 3d) and season ticket rates were below those of the main lines, giving for example a return rate of 8·8d over ten single miles, and 1s 0·7d over twenty single miles. There were also some special facilities, such as the cheap midday fares on the Morden line, originally introduced to compete with the LCC trams along the same route.

White-collar workers from new areas such as Edgware and Morden took workmen's tickets in large numbers, overcrowding the last workmen's trains, then waiting about in the central London stations and streets until their offices opened at just before 9 a.m.[1]

As the 1930s came to a close, the working expenses of the London railways were rising against a falling traffic, a pattern to become familiar in later years. To meet the situation, LPTB fares were adjusted on 11 June 1939. Whilst the penny a mile ordinary rate for the Underground was retained, some substandard fares were increased, and some of the cheap road fares inherited from the LCC were withdrawn or increased.

The Magic Half-Mile

Although few new railways were opened in the London area after 1919, almost 70 new stations were provided. Most of the southern suburban lines were electrified, and north of the Thames, Underground trains were projected over a number of steam suburban lines.[2] Almost everywhere, train services were improved significantly to cope with the increased traffic brought to the existing lines.

In recognition of the contribution that new railway works made towards the relief of unemployment, government credit was made available to the railway companies and the LPTB under various statutes,[3] enabling capital to be raised at very low rates of interest, or even granting interest. Almost all the new lines built in the London area between 1919 and 1939 enjoyed this assistance. An-

[1] Frank Pick to RCGDIP 1938 (Q.3172).
[2] The railway developments of the period are summarised in Appendix 4.
[3] Trade Facilities Acts, 1921-6; Development (Loan Guarantees and Grants) Act, 1929; London Passenger Transport (Finance) Act, 1935; London Transport Public Act, 1935; Railways (Agreement) Act, 1935.

other aid, with similar objective, was the remission of Passenger Duty on First and Second Class fares. This was granted in 1929 on condition that the railways spent the capitalised value of the duty on improvement schemes (the Southern used theirs to electrify the Brighton line).

It is particularly interesting to note that in the debate on the Railways (Agreement) Bill, 1935, which was to facilitate the construction of several new lines, including the Southern's suburban Chessington branch, the Chancellor of the Exchequer made the point that the peak expenditure on the new works stimulated by the bill and by the contemporary LPTB legislation would probably coincide with the tailing off of the house building boom. This, he observed, made the railway assistance schemes 'not only wise, but timely'.[1]

Some of the new lines preceded the major residential construction (Hendon–Edgware; South Wimbledon–Morden; Wembley Park–Stanmore; Arnos Grove–Cockfosters), others proceeded simultaneously (Morden–Sutton; Motspur Park–Tolworth), and in a few cases the railway arrived after it had solidified (Golders Green–Hendon; Leytonstone–Newbury Park). Openings of new stations and improvements such as widening, resignalling and electrification can be similarly grouped.

As a large proportion of the new house owners required good transport facilities to their employment in central London, railways remained of first importance in the outer suburban zone. When choosing estate sites, many developers gave priority to their convenience in relation to railway facilities. 'Station on the Estate' was a favourite phrase for house publicity, even if truth was sometimes strained. Wates claimed in 1936 that 'every estate is within a short distance of a Southern Electric station with fast trains to town every few minutes'[2] and no doubt reaped great benefit from such foresight. Hugh Davies advertised his Osidge Estate, near Southgate station, with a paraphrase of a pop song: 'Home James, and don't spare the horses, it's a home on the Tube for me'.[3]

But not everyone could be on top of the station, and it was then necessary to be a little more subtle. A brochure for Gower Builders' Shirley Park Farm Estate advised in August 1933: 'East Croydon station, which serves the estate, is but 17 minutes from Charing Cross, and it should be noted that the trains on this line are especi-

---

[1] Hansard, House of Commons, 13 December 1935.
[2] Advertisement in HF January 1936.   [3] HF March 1935.

ally comfortable.' This last phrase referred to the new electric trains of the Brighton service, but alas, the 'especially comfortable' seats were likely to be few and far between at East Croydon in the mornings. If he did manage one, the Shirley man might think it compensated somewhat for the long bus ride he had to take to reach the station, not to mention the change of train necessary to reach Charing Cross.

As in the years before 1914, the predominance of commuters in the population of many of the new suburbs ensured that any promise of new railway facilities would cause land values to rise rapidly and substantially. Frank Howkins wrote in 1926:

'The opening of stations with a reasonable service of trains will cause an almost sudden jump in values of adjoining land. The distance this influence extends will depend upon the direction of existing roads and the topography of the district. As a rule, a circle drawn with a radius of half-a-mile from the station will be the area most affected, as a ten minutes walk to and from the station does not call for excessive exercise or entail expense in further fares.[1]'

Developers were never slow to underline this point as a means of awakening interest in their wares. 'Purchase now and secure the benefit of increasing values' counselled the Sunnymeads Estate Company in July 1926 after the SR had agreed to erect a station to serve their Riverside Estate. At Theydon Bois in 1935, a Mr Soper was unrestrained in his excitement: 'Buy now . . . and let electrification insure against depreciation!' And, occasionally, the licking of lips could almost be heard: 'Later, when the Tube is working, prices will increase. . . .' (East Barnet, 1931.)

At the Annual General Meeting of the SR in 1927, Sir Robert Perks called attention to the 'great increment in the value of the land, which goes into the pockets of vigilant people at our expense', and ten years later, Frank Pick, of London Transport was complaining: 'There are very gross cases happening now, On all our proposed extensions, things are happening today which are little short of disgraceful'.[2] This attitude arose because railway companies in general were given statutory powers to buy and retain

---

[1] F. Howkins, *An Introduction to the Development of Private Building Estates and Town Planning*, EG, 1926.
[2] RCGDIP, 2 March 1938 (Q.3476).

only such land as they required 'for the purposes of the under-taking',[1] and were obliged by parliament to dispose of any lands found to be surplus by selling back to the original owners (or, in their absence, neighbouring owners). Thus, unless they obtained powers *ad hoc*, the railways were debarred from taking any share in the increments they created. It was suggested from time to time that railway undertakings might be given powers to develop land to recover some of the cost of constructing new suburban lines; in 1905 the Royal Commission on London Traffic had recommended that railway companies 'under proper safeguards' might be allowed to buy land likely to be increased in value by the opening of such lines,[2] but in common with most of this Commission's proposals, this seed fell upon stony ground. The idea came up for the last time in London Transport's evidence to the 1938 Barlow Commission, when Frank Pick bravely proposed that instead of throwing the burden on the bus and tramway system, it should be possible for the LPTB to subsidise unprofitable new railways by dealings in land.[3]

Yet even at their own stations, the transport undertakings allowed the benefits of development to slip through their hands. When 9 shops and 27 flats were built over Hendon Central station in 1927, the Underground Company was content to accept a 99-year lease and a ground rent of £350, but in 1938 this property changed hands for £38,000, its annual rent roll then almost £4,000, destined to rise to £4,220 by 1944.

Metro-land

Only one railway undertaking managed to follow a positive land policy, largely as a consequence of a special situation.[4] In 1904, Robert Perks explained to the Royal Commission on London Traffic that this company possessed an unusually large amount of surplus land alongside existing and authorised lines, much of it 'forced upon them by parliamentary opponents'.[5] Under an Act of

[1] Land Clauses Act, 1845; Railway Clauses Consolidation Act, 1845.
[2] RCLT 1905, Vol. I, para. 216.
[3] RCGDIP 1938 Q.3484–5.
[4] Others dabbled. The SR took some interest in the All Hallows Estate Company who proposed to develop a seaside and residential community on the Thames Estuary, agreeing to contribute £50,000 and a director in 1934. (BTHR SOU 1/4).
[5] Evidence of R. W. Perks, M.P. to RCLT, 17 March 1904, Q.19552.

1874,[1] the Metropolitan enjoyed the unique distinction amongst railway companies of being able to grant building licences and sell ground rents in respect of its lands in the City of London, a situation which led to a mixture of land and railway revenues, culminating in a great financial muddle. In an endeavour to sort things out, the Company's ordinary stock was divided to separate the two types of income, and £2·64m. of the 'Surplus Lands' stock, representing a valuation of the properties, was issued to all proprietors of the ordinary stock registered at 30 June 1887 in the proportion of £1 of new stock for every £2 of Metropolitan Railway Consolidated Stock held. These manoeuvres duly received statutory endorsement[2] and a Metropolitan Railway Surplus Lands Committee (three members appointed by the holders of the new stock, plus two of the railway's directors) was formed to control and manage the estates, the freehold remaining vested in the railway company. As opportunity occurred, some of the land was sold off, but new property was purchased and developed with those lands retained. In the years immediately before 1914, attention was turning to suburban residential development, and two estates were begun on 'surplus lands' alongside the railway at Pinner.

Robert H. Selbie, who came on to this scene as secretary of the company in 1903, becoming general manager five years later, was increasingly dissatisfied because the Metropolitan was not getting a proper benefit from the undeveloped lands it served and in some cases owned. Late in 1912 he suggested the formation of a separate company, in which the Metropolitan would take a financial and controlling interest, to develop estates adjacent to the railway. His memorandum to the board stressed that the districts served by the Metropolitan were 'daily growing in popularity and the experience of some at any rate of the principal house and estate agents is that they cannot supply the demand for houses at rentals between £40 and £100 p.a.' The board approved in principle, but further action was deferred by the outbreak of World War I.[3]

In November 1918, Selbie was pushing the board again:

> . . . in view of the large demand there will be for houses as soon as Peace is declared and the Forces are demobilised, and also in view of the advertisement the districts served have received

---

[1] Metropolitan Inner Circle Completion Act, 1874, sec. 64–5.
[2] Metropolitan Railway Acts, 1885 and 1887.
[3] BTHR MET 1/26, 1/27, 10/322.

13. Modernism pushes through Berg romantic styles at Avondale Avenue, Hinchley Wood (built c. 1935). (Photo: Alan A. Jackson.)

Modernism for £395: Howard Houses at West Molesey, built 1934. (Photo: Alan A. Jackson.)

Compromise Modernism: Hollywood Houses, Hillside Gardens, Edgware. The house at the right was the 1935 show house, price £995; the window above the front door is not the original one. (Photo: Alan A. Jackson.)

14. Edgware interior, 1935; dining-room of a Curton house, Edgwarebury Lane Estate. (From sales brochure, A. W. Curton Ltd.)

Edgware interior, 1935; sitting-room of a Curton house, Edgwarebury
Lane Estate. (From sales brochure, A. W. Curton Ltd.)

during the War, I am of the opinion that the scheme should be taken in hand forthwith.[1]

Noting 'the dearth of middle-class residences, especially in the outer suburbs of London', the board agreed to act, and in January 1919 approved proposals for the incorporation of a separate company, to be known as the Metropolitan Country Estates Ltd, with a share capital of £150,000 (later increased to £200,000), of which the railway company would contribute a large proportion, and with voting rights carefully arranged to secure absolute control by the parent.[2] Two estates, the Cedars at Rickmansworth (454 acres, £40,000) and the Chalk Hill at Wembley Park (123 acres, £22,500) were at once purchased through a syndicate, for transfer to the new company. A third, of 40 acres, at Neasden, on railway land, together with an additional 10¾ acres of railway land to enlarge Chalk Hill were also sold to the new company for £11,683. All this by way of a beginning.[3]

Up to this point everybody concerned, not excluding the usually competent Selbie, appears to have overlooked the fact that although the scheme to some extent followed naturally from the earlier Surplus Lands activities, it greatly extended the railway's scope and freedom of action in this direction, in clear contradiction to the view traditionally taken by parliament. At the last moment, when the prospectus was submitted to counsel for final approval, it was deemed wise to seek an opinion on this question from the Hon. Frank Russell K.C. This luminary suggested that although the railway company would not technically or legally be holding land, the scheme had the effect of enabling the company to purchase and hold land without any statutory authority, and if the arrangement were in any way attacked, the Court might hold it to be invalid on the grounds that it was against public policy.[4] Although the difficulty might be overcome by special legislation, that could well have proved insuperably controversial. In the event, it was decided that the railway company would take no direct financial interest in the Estates Company, but would enter into an agreement which would allow the use of the railway's name in the new company's title, and provide for all possible assistance through the railway's organisation in the development of the estates to be purchased. In return, the railway company was to have the right to nominate the chairman

[1] BTHR MET 1/34.　　[2] BTHR MET 1/28.　　[3] BTHR MET 10/52.
[4] BTHR MET 10/322 (22 May 1919).

and two other directors of the new company over a period of ten years.[1]

When the prospectus appeared in June 1919, it offered the stockholders of the railway and the Surplus Lands Committee 'preferential consideration'.[2] Selbie was made a director, and all but one of his colleagues on the new board, including the chairman, were also directors of the Metropolitan Railway. As promised, the railway company duly gave its creature every assistance, including offices at Baker Street station, the full-time services of Henry Gibson, the Surplus Lands Committee's surveyor and valuer, and the part-time use of other railway staff, as well as making available its publicity and purchasing organisation. These arrangements ensured that the Metropolitan could direct and control the pattern of investment and development to bring the optimum traffic benefits (as we shall see, the new company, with only one exception, confined its activities to middle- and high-value housing developments). It was in all a very cosy contrivance, endowed even with probity and respectability. As Selbie smugly wrote later, 'Railway companies are trusted and not open to the suspicion that often attaches to the speculative builder and estate developer'.[3]

Over the next dozen years,[4] the Estates Company developed some 10 estates alongside the main line and the Uxbridge branch, peopling the territory which the railway claimed as its own *Metroland*. Although in the early days, the MRCE erected some houses on its own account, the usual pattern was to lay out an estate and then sell off sections to builders, or, on the more expensive sites, sell plots to individual purchasers wishing to have a house erected to their own choice of design. A 1923 pamphlet also offered the alternative of a house or bungalow built on a selected plot for a fixed sum including the cost of land and all fees (if desired, the payment could be made by depositing a minimum of £200 and repaying the balance quarterly over a maximum of fifteen years with interest at 6 per cent). At Neasden, Rickmansworth and elsewhere, the MRCE erected shops to serve its estates. The company also arranged finance and mortgages, and, in co-operation with its parent, free travel for intending purchasers. It all went quite swimmingly, set off to a good start by the publication in 1920 of a vocal

[1] BTHR MET 1/28, 1/35.   [2] BTHR MET 10/52.
[3] Railways and Land Development', *Modern Transport*, 11 June 1921.
[4] The original agreement between the railway and the estate companies was extended for a further ten years in 1929, but the MRCE assumed a quite separate and independent existence upon the formation of the LPTB in 1933.

one-step entitled *My Little Metro-Land Home* (words by Boyle Lawrence, music by Henry Thraile).[1]

Nearest to London was the 40-acre Kingsbury Garden Village, on railway land at Neasden, the only one of the estates catering for low incomes. About 40 houses built by the company were ready in the early part of 1921, and within eight years the estate was virtually sold off. Immediately to the north of the Garden Village, served by Wembley Park station, was the Chalk Hill Estate, where roads had been laid, and plots of a ¼-acre upwards were on offer by 1921. The Metropolitan put in a siding for the delivery of building materials, as it had done at Neasden.[2] Ten years later, this farm land, which had been acquired at £183 an acre, was selling at the equivalent of £700, but by that time very few of the ¼-acre plots remained.

To the south of the line at Wembley Park lay the domain of the Wembley Park Estate Company, mortgagors of the Metropolitan Railway,[3] where a beginning had been made in the Edwardian years. A very small number of detached three-bedroom houses were available for £1,250 in 1921, but development after that was rapid, leaving the Metropolitan Railway cause to regret their agreement to pay the Estate Company a bonus of 25 per cent of any increase in traffic revenue at Wembley Park station (they were obliged to fork out the maximum payment of £700 each year from 1919 until the agreement finally expired in 1927).[4]

Further down the line, at Pinner station, were the Surplus Land Committee's Cecil Park and Grange Estates, already mentioned, to the south and north of the line respectively, on which detached houses in the bracket £1,300–£1,600 were still being advertised as late as 1931. But the largest of all the developments was the Cedars Estate, on both sides of the line between Rickmansworth and Chorley Wood stations. The northern section was originally intended for 'more pretentious' houses on plots of at least 1 acre, but sights were lowered as time passed. A 1921 account reported 3,500 yards of road laid out, with names such as *The Clumps* setting the tone. Already 30 houses had been erected by the MRCE and several plots of 1–6 acres sold. With the extension of electric service to

[1] Published by the Herman Darewksi Music Publishing Co.
[2] BTHR MET 1/28, 1/35.
[3] The mortgage, for £35,000, dated from 24 November 1898 and was discharged when the Wembley Park Estate Co. sold the bulk of its unrealised land (126 acres) to the British Empire Exhibition Assets Co. in 1922. (BTHR MET 1/28).
[4] BTHR MET 10/685.

Rickmansworth in 1925, the Cedars Estate was provided with 100 trains a day, some covering the seventeen-and-a-half miles to Baker Street in twenty-five minutes. By 1928, 114¼ acres had been sold, but 456 remained on the company's books.[1]

Furthest flung of all was the 78-acre Weller Estate at Amersham, not purchased until 1930. Planned to take 535 houses and 51 shops, this was both sides of the line around the station. Evidently a little apprehensive of the scheme's success, the MRCE sought a subsidy from the railway of £10-£15 for each house or shop built. Taking into account the difficulty arising from joint ownership of this part of the line with the LNER, and some doubts about the validity of the Wembley Park precedent, the board rejected the proposal in July 1930.[2]

MRCE schemes for the Uxbridge branch evolved in the late twenties. These were: Hillingdon Mount, Eastcote Hill, Manor Farm (Eastcote Road, Ruislip), Elm Grove (Ruislip), and the 213-acre Harrow Garden Village around Rayners Lane station. Housing development on the latter was undertaken by E. S. Reid, a former Deputy Engineer to the Harrow Council. Starting on the north side of the line in 1929, Reid found the country roads breaking up under the loads of building materials, so he paid for a siding to allow delivery of the heavier items by rail.

These various activities of the Metropolitan Railway's offspring, combining as they did to form a powerful influence on the nature of suburban growth along the line, encountered no serious opposition, either in parliament or elsewhere. Despite this they were not copied by the Underground or the main-line companies, perhaps because it was realised that any significant extension of this sort of railway enterprise would arouse a powerful and probably successful lobby among those who stood to gain from railway improvements.

Encouraging the Railways
Landowners and developers had occasionally encouraged suburban railway extensions by donating land or selling it well below the market price. In 1912, for example, Sir Audley Neeld, Sir Theodore Brinckmann and the Maple Trustees gave parcels of land for the Underground's Edgware extension. But such gestures, in common with full-scale promotion of suburban railways by landowners, belonged more to the nineteenth century than the

[1] BTHR MET 10/756.   [2] BTHR MET 10/685, 10/702.

twentieth. The developers of the twenties and thirties went no further than gifts of land for new railway stations or enlargements of existing stations, or cash subsidies of one kind or another.

This sort of thing had of course started much earlier, and some reference has already been made to Cameron Corbett's assistance with station construction in the Ilford area. He also contributed to station improvements at Hither Green for the convenience of residents of his St German's Estate (south-west of the station and dating from the late 1890s). To the east of Hither Green was the 334-acre Eltham Park Estate, where Corbett started building in 1900. For this he made a contribution towards 'superior passenger accommodation', and the result was Shooters Hill and Eltham Park station, opened by the SECR on 1 July 1908. Corbett's houses were substantial, many of them with servants' annexes, and the new station, with its long canopies on both platforms, and its covered access ramps, did not disgrace them. It was sited less than half a mile to the east of Well Hall station, which the railway company, ever anxious to turn the odd penny, had planned to close until they discovered they were under a statutory obligation to keep it open and so did not rate their chances of overcoming the opposition very highly. Another Edwardian station which owed its existence to the agitation and assistance of developers was Dollis Hill, on the Metropolitan, between Willesden Green and Neasden. Opened in 1909, it served the flats of Ben Andrews and the houses of the Dudding Park Estate Company, south and north of the line respectively.

Almost all the new stations opened in the London suburban area after 1920 had some form of subsidy from interested developers. Riddlesdown, West Weybridge (now Byfleet and New Haw), and Sunnymeads, all opened in 1927, Petts Wood, 1928, and Hinchley Wood and Whitton, 1930, were in this category, as were Woodmansterne, Stoneleigh and Belmont Halt (Harrow) in 1932, Berrylands and Northwood Hills in 1933, and Hersham in 1936. All these stations were soon very busy: by 1934 Petts Wood was issuing 320,000 tickets a year together with 13,000 seasons, and £3,065 was spent on improvements as early as 1931.[1] Whitton and Stoneleigh also required substantial enlargement to meet increased traffic before 1939.

Around 1930, the SR was able to provide a serviceable if plain island platform station for between £7,000 and £8,000, a sum which developers' contributions could usefully reduce. At Wood-

[1] BTHR SOU 1/25.

mansterne, for example, the building cost was £7,000, the land was conveyed free, and the various offerings totalled £1,500.[1] The £7,650 station at Hinchley Wood, on an awkward site, was subsidised by Percy Fisher (the landowner), who provided the necessary plots together with £2,500, as well as purchasing £500 of SR stock to be forfeited if 150 houses had not been built within three years (he didn't lose it). Land for a goods yard (never built) was transferred at the low price of £420 an acre.[2] No less than seven firms helped in the erection of Berrylands station, near Surbiton, meeting over 90 per cent of its £6,275 cost.[3] After a couple of false starts, the SR received £5,000 of the £9,900 they wanted for a new station at Hersham, between Esher and Walton on Thames. The guarantors deposited £15,000, to be refunded with 4 per cent interest when 500 houses were ready for occupation, or the revenue from the new station exceeded £1,000 a year.[4]

At Hillingdon, opened in 1923, the Metropolitan Railway made it a condition that land would be donated for a goods yard.[5] Farther east, the same company required the builder-sponsors to guarantee Northwood Hills against all loss for five years, but the loadings after the station opened in 1933 were so satisfactory that the guarantee was annulled. A prize offered for the most suitable name was won by a North Harrow woman who explained that she had combined three local features, Pinner Hill, Haste Hill and Hogs Back.[6]

Elm Park (1935) arose from an agreement between Richard Costain and Sons and the LMSR. The builders had completed 500 of a planned 700 houses by the time the station was ready. Albany Park (1935) and Falconwood (1936) were sponsored by New Ideal Homesteads, who handed over lump sums and gave land to the SR, as well as suggesting the names. This firm parted with further cash and land in return for additional facilities provided on the up-side at Albany Park in 1939.[7] Contributions were also gratefully received from builders and the local authority towards the cost of a footbridge which gave access to the newly developing down side of the line at Coulsdon North in 1929.[8]

---

[1] BTHR SOU 1/18.   [2] BTHR SOU 1/18, 1/25.
[3] BTHR SOU 1/18.   [4] BTHR SOU 1/26.
[5] BTHR MET 10/327. The gift enabled the railway to transfer to the MRCE, for the development of the Hillingdon Mount Estate, a 7½-acre site on the opposite side of the line, which had been purchased earlier. This transfer was effected in 1926 at a profit of £105.
[6] W. A. G. Kemp, *The Story of Northwood and Northwood Hills, Middlesex* (Kemp, 1955).
[7] BTHR SOU 1/19, 1/21, 1/26, 1/81.   [8] BTHR SOU 1/25.

At Lullingstone, between Swanley and Eynsford stations, the Kemptown Brewery Co. bought 5,500 acres of the Castle Estate from Sir Oliver Hart Dyke in 1933, the first change of ownership of this land for 500 years. As it was intended to develop the site for building, the brewery offered the SR £5,000 towards a £15,500 two-platform station and goods yard, giving land for this and for access roads.[1] Although the SR built the station, development had not started before the outbreak of war. Afterwards, the area fell within the Metropolitan Green Belt, so the station buildings, which had stood isolated amidst the splendid Kentish countryside, were eventually demolished in the 1950s.

Examples of public authorities encouraging or influencing the provision of suburban railway facilities are more difficult to find. After the muddle about transport provision for Becontree, a wiser LCC consulted with the Underground Company on the siting of the large estates eventually built at Watling (Edgware) and St Helier (Morden), and there can be little doubt that the prospect of these important developments much strengthened the case for starting work on the tube railway extensions to both places. At St Helier, the LCC also gave land to the SR for the new Wimbledon and Sutton Railway's right of way through the estate, including enough for a station and goods yard.

Many and various were the repercussions of the suburban building boom on the railways. Additional berthing facilities had to be provided for passenger trains, and in one case, the enormous growth of suburban traffic required the construction of improved approaches to a London terminus (the Wimbledon flyover, completed by Wimpey in 1936, together with associated track rearrangements and resignalling, cost around £500,000). Existing goods yards, swamped with inwards mineral and coal traffic, had to be enlarged; between 1932 and 1938, the SR spent sums ranging from £1,300 to £3,000 on improvements to freight facilities at Welling, Sidcup, Eltham Well Hall, Bexleyheath, St Mary Cray, Worcester Park, and Orpington, all new suburban districts.[2] At Rayners Lane, in the thirties, the Metropolitan built an entirely new goods and coal yard. Special sidings and accommodation for builders were provided at Rayners Lane, Kenton and elsewhere. The Southern noticed a fall in the building material traffic before the end of 1935; at the annual meeting early in the following year, the chairman

[1] BTHR SOU 1/26.
[2] BTHR SOU 1/26.

mentioned a 'diminution of over 200,000 tons in the quantities of housebuilding and roadmaking materials conveyed'.

A number of older stations, particularly on the SR, were modernised and enlarged to accommodate the extra passenger traffic. At Hayes (Kent) in 1934–5, the station was rebuilt at a cost of some £14,000, the scheme including shops, each expected to yield rentals of around £75 a year. A similar project at Bromley South, in conjunction with the widening of the main road, was approved in 1937 at a cost of almost £33,000. During 1937 an £18,000 reconstruction was completed at Raynes Park, with ten shops costing a further £4,600 expected to reap £500 a year. The Victorian suburb of Surbiton had continued to grow southwards in the twenties and thirties, and the increased traffic justified a £150,000 station rebuilding which was finished in 1938. At Worcester Park, where suburban settlement had first appeared in the middle of the nineteenth century, the area around the station was flooded with new housing after 1925. Between 1935 and 1939 the facilities here were improved at a cost of almost £14,000. In 1935 Guildford received a lengthy footbridge with lock-up shop and passimeter ticket office to meet the needs of developments west of the line stimulated by the electrification ten years earlier and to be further boosted by the main-line electric services then being prepared. By the end of 1930 the very rapid growth of the area served by the Bexleyheath line had rendered the original stations inadequate. Enlargements and improvements were carried out during 1931 and 1932 at Eltham Well Hall, Welling, Bexleyheath and Barnehurst at a total cost of almost £22,500.[1] Even the impecunious LMSR was obliged to recognise suburban pressures, with new stations at South Kenton, Elm Park and Belmont and in 1935 reconstruction on the up-side at Mill Hill to provide a booking-hall and waiting rooms.

As well as assisting with new stations, developers gave land for the enlargement of existing facilities. Morrells provided a plot for the extension of Chelsfield Goods Yard in 1934, and O'Sullivan (Kenley) Ltd, builders of 'Orpington Garden Village', conveyed land free of charge for the enlargement of nearby St Mary Cray station in the same year.[2]

An Electric Suburbia
Almost all the new stations just mentioned, indeed over a third of

[1] BTHR SOU 1/18, 1/19, 1/20, 1/25, 1/26.   [2] BTHR SOU 1/19, 1/26.

the additional stations opened in the London area after 1919, were on the Southern Railway. This company actively pursued the development of passenger traffic, continuing the electrification of suburban lines started by its predecessor companies with such vigour that by the end of 1931 it had covered virtually the whole of its suburban area, having converted 293 route miles (800 track miles) at a cost of £11·8m. (£6·25m. charged to capital).[1] Besides bringing many benefits to the operator, the electric services offered the passenger more frequent and faster trains at regular intervals throughout the day, dispensing with the need to consult timetables; over the whole SR suburban system in 1932 there were five electric trains for every two run before.[2]

It could not have been done otherwise, but the system and method adopted were the cheapest in terms of initial capital cost: traction supply through unprotected conductor rails; the minimum of resignalling, especially in the outer area; and, until 1939 in the suburban zone, the use of converted steam railway coaches. Such economy brought with it several disadvantages: the current supply was vulnerable to winter conditions, particularly when rain or snow arrived as temperatures were falling through freezing point; the retention of the dual class accommodation in the old rolling stock, with First Class accommodation often disproportionate to demand, led to rush-hour overcrowding (a typical eight-car train had almost one-fifth of its seats pre-empted for First Class passengers); and, finally, the retention of manual signalling in the suburban areas could cause disruption of the intensive service during conditions of bad visibility. But these blemishes could not blunt the tremendous impact of the electrification programme, which combined with the housing boom to produce impressive traffic increases at many suburban stations. Between 1925 and 1934, tickets issued at Beckenham Junction increased from 277,338 to 394,808, seasons from 5,345 to 14,680. At Ravensbourne the increases in the same period were 9,151 to 24,887 and 145 to 822; at Orpington 272,060 to 403,451 and 2,677 to 13,378; and at Grove Park, where 71,133

---

[1] Sir Herbert Walker, general manager, SR, at the Annual Dinner of the British Electrical and Allied Manufacturer's Association, 18 May 1933.
[2] For example, Coulsdon North to London Bridge, journey time reduced from 41 to 26½ minutes, Caterham to London Bridge from 45½ to 34½ minutes, Bexleyheath to Charing Cross from 51 to 34 minutes. Frequencies outside rush hours were increased generally to every 15 or 20 minutes in the outer areas, every 5 or 10 in the inner zone, Thus, after electrification, Caterham had fifty-four trains a day each way instead of twenty-six.

tickets were issued in 1924, 917,585 ordinary tickets and 12,041 seasons were sold in 1934, an increase partly related to the LCC estate at Downham.[1] The Hayes Branch, sponsored in anticipation of building development in 1879, and opened in 1882, remained very quiet until about eighteen months after its electrification in 1925; by 1934 gross receipts had increased almost twelvefold.[2] In 1925, with steam working, the three south-east suburban stations of Welling, Bexleyheath and Sidcup ($11\frac{1}{2}$, $12\frac{3}{4}$ and 12 miles from Charing Cross) dealt with 1,097,400 passengers and sold 8,690 seasons; ten years later, with electric service in operation since 1926, the corresponding figures were 4,753,600 and 57,600.[3]

Traffic figures for the SR London termini well illustrated the powerful influence of an efficient and regular electric service through areas of cheap building land on the fringes of the metropolis. A 1926 census showed 13,446 passengers arriving at Charing Cross between 7 and 10 a.m. on a typical day; by 1935 the number had grown to 31,723 and three years later, 37,095. Corresponding figures at Waterloo were 36,415 in 1933 and 47,051 in 1938, whilst at London Bridge, the figures in these two years were 49,001 and 60,034.[4] Train services were built up to match the traffic. In 1924, the Bexleyheath line was served between 5 p.m. and 6 p.m. by two steam trains (both from Cannon Street); in 1926 there were three electrics in this evening hour, offering 1,956 seats, two trains from Cannon Street and one from Charing Cross; but by 1939, there were eight trains from London at this time, a total of 5,216 seats.

The company found it all very satisfactory. As early as 1928, the general manager, Sir Herbert Walker, was telling the Railway Students' Association that the suburban traffic receipts had continued to increase despite the general business depression, the traffic daily becoming of increasing importance in the financial results of the company. He went on to explain that no less than a quarter of the passenger receipts and nearly one fifth of the total

[1] *SR Magazine,* 1935.

[2]

		Tickets issued	Season tickets issued
Eden Park	1925	8,358	61
	1934	75,841	4,188
West Wickham	1925	46,985	336
	1934	251,024	18,711
Hayes	1925	21,856	159
	1934	177,424	5,831

(*Railway Magazine,* January 1936).

[3] E. C. Cox, in a paper to the Institute of Transport, November 1936.

[4] BTHR SOU 1/3, 1/84, 1/89.

income were derived from the electrically-operated suburban services.[1] In his 1933 speech to the British Electrical and Allied Manufacturers' Association, after the virtual completion of suburban area electrification, Walker gave more detail. Working expenses of the electric services (wages, uniforms, current, maintenance, and renewals) were approximately 1s 3d a mile or about half the cost of steam working, but as a little over 8 million steam working miles had been replaced with 20·6m. electric train miles, there was an increase in working the electric service of £206,140 a year. In the first complete year of suburban electrification (1932) these lines had attracted 215·7m. passengers compared with a total of 137.9m. in their last years of steam working, an increase of 56·42 per cent. This represented an addition to revenue of £1·11m. after deducting the increased working cost just mentioned; in relation to the capital charge of electrification it showed a return of 17½ per cent. To some extent these excellent results were attributable to the Southern's ability to keep freight working off the tracks in the daytime and to a high uniform load throughout the day. The excellent rate of return more than held up; by 1938, Walker was able to boast that the electrification policy had 'proved a goldmine' because of the extensive suburban development south of the Thames, 'for which it was largely responsible'. Although the electrified rails now extended far beyond Greater London, no electrification had been undertaken unless estimated to produce a net return of considerably more than 4 per cent of the capital cost, taking into account the extra expense of electric working. In fact suburban electrification had by this time yielded a 27 per cent return on capital and 16 per cent on total expenditure.[2]

So successful was the marriage of the Southern and the speculative builder that some parts of the system were beginning to show signs of strain by 1938, indicating that further capital expenditure would eventually be required. Commenting at this time, the Evening News noted that on the south-eastern lines, compartments designed to seat ten were often loaded up to double that number. New rolling stock of larger capacity (twelve seats to a compartment) was proposed in 1939, but did not appear in quantity until after the end of the war.

In addition to its electrification programme, the SR built two new railways in the London suburban area. The Wimbledon to Sutton line, opened in 1929–30, was the realisation of a pre-1914

[1] Railway Magazine, December 1928.   [2] Railway Gazette, 1 April 1938.

scheme taken over from the Metropolitan District Railway.[1] It provided a useful facility for the western margin of the LCC estate at St Helier, and shared with the Underground (who took by far the largest bite) the traffic originating from the great sea of private enterprise housing which covered the woods and fields between Morden and Epsom in the late twenties and the thirties. The second line was a suburban speculation promoted in 1930 in the expectation of government assistance. Forming a loop with the Raynes Park–Leatherhead line, the new railway was to run from Motspur Park through Tolworth and Chessington to Leatherhead. Work did not begin until 1936 after the scheme had been approved under the Railways (Agreement) Act, a measure which enabled the capital to be raised at a very low rate of interest guaranteed by the Treasury. When the outbreak of war stopped work in 1939, only the first four miles, from Motspur Park to Chessington South goods yard, had been completed. Originally the cost of the full seven-and-a-quarter miles had been estimated at a little under £700,000, for which the SR chairman thought they would get 'a very valuable railway', hopefully profitable because it would be 'outside the effective bus area for people coming into London'.[2] But with no less than 8 bridges and a 140 ft. viaduct in its first four miles through corrosive, heavy clay, this line proved difficult and expensive to construct. And much of the land had to be bought at development prices from builders about to cover it (in one instance over £7,000 was paid after arbitration for little more than 2 acres[3].)

After a bitter clash in 1923 over the Wimbledon and Sutton line, and a proposed tube extension from Clapham to Sutton via Morden, the Underground Company left the Southern's territory alone.[4] The arrangement reached in that year provided that the tube would terminate at Morden without connection to the Wimbledon–Sutton line, which was to be built by the SR. The tube line to Morden opened in 1926, its terminus skilfully fed by buses, bringing traffic from all directions, including much that had formerly gone via the Southern.[5] Some half-a-million passengers a week were passing over the new line by the beginning of 1927 and its success, enhanced by

[1] For a full account see Alan A. Jackson, 'The Wimbledon and Sutton Railway', *Railway Magazine*, December 1966.
[2] At the Special General Meeting, 27 February, 1930.
[3] BTHR SOU 1/20.
[4] *See* Alan A. Jackson, op. cit.
[5] At the SR Annual General Meeting in 1928, the chairman claimed that the tube extension had abstracted four million SR passengers.

substandard fares, quickly became an embarrassment. Trains were so well loaded with terminal traffic that passengers using the intermediate stations found it difficult to travel. Ten years after opening this had become the most heavily-used of all the tube lines at peak hours, with 13,500 passengers northbound through Oval station between 7.30 a.m. and 8 a.m.[1] Workmen's-ticket traffic was very heavy, and when overnight purchase of these tickets was refused in 1937 in an attempt to reduce overloading of the final workmen's train, enormous queues formed at the Morden booking office each morning. In 1938, the workmen's tickets issued at this station totalled 7,300 daily, constituting 55 per cent of the outward traffic up to 10 a.m.[2] In vain did the seven local authorities concerned press for construction of a relief line and extension southwards to Epsom and Mitcham. When they pointed out that the population of the combined area had risen from 248,000 to 378,000 between 1931 and 1937 and was likely to reach 500,000 by 1948, the LPTB replied that this additional traffic was not considered anything like enough to justify the heavy capital expenditure required.[3]

New Railways for Northern Suburbs

North of the river, the most significant expansion of railway facilities was the projection of tube trains to the outer limits of north and north-west London, either over new lines: Wood Lane–Ealing (1920), Golders Green–Edgware (1923/4), Finsbury Park–Cockfosters (1932/3); or alongside or over existing steam and electric railways: Queens Park–Watford Junction (1915/17), Hammersmith–Uxbridge (1932/3), Acton Town–Hounslow West (1932/3) and Archway–High Barnet and Mill Hill East (1939/41).[4]

For its part, the Metropolitan Railway undertook the construction of two new electric lines: Rickmansworth–Watford (in conjunction with the LNER, 1925) and Wembley Park–Stanmore (1932). The first was a carry-over from pre-1914 inter-company rivalry,[5] the second, like the Chessington line, was a speculative development framed to catch a government financial guarantee.

[1] LPTB Annual Report, 1936.
[2] LPTB evidence to RCGDIP, 1938, Part III para. 9.
[3] TEG 22 January 1938.
[4] For a full account of tube railway development in the suburban area see Alan A. Jackson and D. F. Croome, *Rails Through The Clay* (Allen and Unwin, 1964).
[5] For a full account see Alan A. Jackson, 'The Metropolitan Railway at Watford', *Railway Magazine*, December 1961.

The Edgware, Cockfosters and Stanmore extensions, and the tube routes to Uxbridge and Hounslow (shared with Metropolitan and Metropolitan District trains), traversed areas that were very quickly covered with private enterprise housing, much of it of middle and low value, and of course the Edgware line also served the big LCC estate at Watling. Substandard fares, sharply tapering towards the outer termini, were adopted on the Edgware and Cockfosters lines in an attempt to clothe them with housing. A complicated network of feeder bus services, operated by the associated General, and providing attractive through-fare facilities, was arranged to coincide with the opening of both these lines; on the Cockfosters route there were also through fares over the diverging tram line towards Enfield. In this way some traffic was abstracted from the old steam suburban lines of the LNER and LMSR out of Liverpool Street, Kings Cross and St Pancras; these were easy game, providing some sustenance until new business was built up.

Traffic on the Edgware line was initially disappointing, a reflection of the sluggish start of development around the terminus (studied in Chapter 14), but by the early thirties it was at such a high level that additional facilities were required. A count of the passengers using stations north of Brent (inclusive) in one month of 1924 found 413,000, but in November 1929 the corresponding figure was 2 millions.[1]

On the Cockfosters line there was a similar slow start. In February 1934, Arnos Grove station was said to be producing only 500,000 passengers a year, and an official writer claimed that local features (a mental hospital, a sewage farm and a cemetery) were hampering 'high class' development. Some 750 houses were due for completion that summer around Southgate station, but at Enfield West (now Oakwood), the rural surroundings 'reacted against rapid development of traffic'. Bus and train services, the same writer noted, would here be 'much in advance of requirements' for some time to come, for there was no apparent tendency for private firms or local authorities to build housing estates and the main use of the line was at weekends and holidays.[2] Yet within little more than three years the situation at these three stations had changed out of all recognition, with houses in all directions except to the east and north of the terminal mile. In May 1935, Sir Philip Sassoon had no difficulty in disposing of the 75-acre West Pole

[1] GGG 14 January 1927, *Daily Mail*, 10 December 1929.
[2] *Pennyfare*, February 1934.

Farm (just south of Cockfosters station) at a price of almost £1,600 an acre.[1]

The Metropolitan's Stanmore branch was a good deal less successful than these Underground extensions, penetrating as it did the Edgware tube territory or its established feeder-bus zone and suffering the handicap of a roundabout route to the City and (until 1939) main-line fare scales. Its one bright spot was the development of an extensive new suburb called Queensbury on the site of the Stag Lane aerodrome which had closed in October 1933. An 80 ft.-wide central boulevard was built to link the station, shopping centre and cinema with Stag Lane, and in the five years to 1938 Laing and other firms covered the area immediately east of the new railway with thousands of semis, mostly priced at £600 to £800. Unusually for suburban development before 1939, two factory zones were established by Laing, one west of the railway at Queensbury station, another around Castle Road on the east side of the new suburb and close to the World War I factories along the Edgware Road. But these pockets of industry were to be a further factor in stunting the traffic growth of the radial electric railway.

Nor was the Metropolitan's joint venture into Watford with the LNER any more fortunate. It proved extremely expensive to build; it tapped the same territory as existing LMSR branches (both electrified by 1927); and it suffered from a poorly sited terminus on the western outskirts of Watford. Rather more worthwhile was the Metropolitan's electrification of its main line between Harrow and Rickmansworth in 1925 followed by the quadrupling of tracks between Wembley and Harrow seven years later.

The only other suburban railway improvement remaining to be mentioned is the electrification and quadrupling of the LMSR line between Barking and Upminster in 1932, a scheme which included the projection of District Underground trains from central London to Upminster and new stations at Upney, Becontree, and Dagenham Heathway. This served the LCC town of Becontree, and also, within a few years, an accretion of low cost private enterprise housing at Elm Park, Hornchurch and east and south of Upminster, for which further new stations were eventually opened at Elm Park and Upminster Bridge.

All suburban extensions of the Underground built after 1929 were undertaken with capital raised at very low rates of interest (usually 2½ per cent) on government guarantee of principal and

[1] HTBG 31 May 1935.

interest, or government grants of interest for limited periods, under legislation directed towards the relief of unemployment. There was no difficulty in attracting capital in such circumstances; when the Treasury-backed London Electric Finance Corporation Ltd made an offer on 17 July 1935 of £32m. 2½ per cent guaranteed debenture stock, 1950–55, at £97 per cent, it was greatly oversubscribed, and this was typical.

In promoting suburban extensions of the Underground, the undertaking's spokesmen were fond of pointing out that the lines would be increasingly used as the capital's population moved outwards, and that they provided at relatively low cost a heavier loading throughout the length of the original capital-intensive tunnel sections, which were not being used to full capacity. Thus, it was argued, the full benefit of the initial capital investment would be secured.[1] Pursuing this somewhat twisted reasoning, the Underground company, and its successor, the LPTB, propounded the doctrine that the prosperity of the undertaking as a whole could only be maintained by a policy of continual expansion, by which was meant simultaneous outward growth of London and the railway system.

Underground railway extensions in the open air were not cheap. For the sake of operational simplicity, the elaborate and costly signalling and safety arrangements required for the operation of an intensive train service in tunnels were perpetuated on the outer sections, so that these lines, with their specialised rolling stock, were a good deal more expensive than the Southern's 'make do and mend' electrified routes. Even so, the contrast in cost between tunnel and open lines on the Underground was considerable; in their 1938 evidence to the Barlow Commission, the LPTB gave the figures for one mile, without rolling stock, as £675,000 and £275,000.[2]

Occasional insights into the economics of suburban extensions of the Underground were offered by Lord Ashfield and his deputy, Frank Pick, though they were not always consistent. Speaking at the London School of Economics in 1934, Ashfield appeared discontented, bemoaning the fact that his Underground railways could pay only 1 per cent on the non prior charge capital and that the average return on the whole capital was a mere 3¼ per cent, with

---

[1] e.g. Lord Ashfield (chairman of the Underground Co.) to the parliamentary committee on the Morden extension bill, 1923.
[2] RCGDIP 1938, LPTB evidence, Part III, para. 10.

no provision for redemption. He criticised the low density of London's suburban development, pointing out that twelve houses to the acre was insufficient to make his railways remunerative because this provided only 24,000 people within the half-mile catchment area, say 3 million passengers a year per station. His contention was that at least another million passengers per station per year were needed to support a railway with stations a minimum of ¾ mile apart.

But this was not the whole story. As the Underground Company had effective administrative control over the major bus operator after 1912 and over all the private tramway companies after 1915, useful extensions of suburban station catchment areas could be organised by providing road transport feeders and manipulating the fares. It was because they could not follow suit (and indeed suffered at some points severe loss of traffic as a result of station-feeding) that the Metropolitan and Southern worked so hard to expand their long-distance commuter traffic; and the former company, with less scope to build up an outer zone, had that much stronger incentive to exploit its territory in the rather special way already described.

London Transport returned once again to the old theme when about to embark in 1936 on a large number of new railway facilities included in the government-sponsored 1935–40 London Railways Development Plan. Because the railways in the central zone were losing traffic as a result of the outward spread of the population, 'the policy of extending the Underground railways is the inevitable concomitant'.[1] But the new railways proposed in the development plan would require a population increase of at least 600,000 in those outer areas they served if they were to be remunerative, so: 'the Board have a special interest in the redistribution and expansion of the population of London and are deeply concerned in the continuance of the present movement which is of great social value in enabling housing to be modernised and the standard of living raised'.[2]

And, in 1938, in the context of a second new works programme vaguely adumbrated, the LPTB suggested this would need another 500,000 to 750,000 migrants in the 12- to 15-mile zone around London.[3]

Although much of the new Underground railways' traffic was in workmen's tickets or other substandard fares (this was part of the

[1] LPTB Annual Report 1935–6.   [2] Ibid.
[3] RCGDIP 1938, LPTB evidence, Part III, para. 10.

financial problem) some of the accretions were as impressive as those on the SR. At Rayner's Lane, the number of passengers increased from 22,000 in 1930 to 4 millions in 1937, a period which saw the addition of Piccadilly Line tube trains to those of the Metropolitan and District Lines and the appearance of hundreds of new cheap and medium-priced houses north and south of the line at this point, many on the MRCE Harrow Garden Village development mentioned earlier.[1] At nearby Ruislip Manor, the same factors caused an increase in annual traffic from 17,000 in 1931 to 1,300,000 in 1937, by which time there was hardly a vacant plot remaining within the half-mile radius.[2] Some figures for the tube extensions have already been given.

During the twenties and thirties Londoners made more use of their public transport than ever before. This reflected the increasing prosperity of the area and the rise in real incomes as much as the many improvements in the services. Passenger journeys originating in the Greater London area (trams, buses, and Underground and suburban railways) rose from 1,800 m. in 1911 to 4,000 m. in 1935, a growth of 120 per cent in a period when population increased by 19 per cent.[3] But after this the pace slowed; journeys per head by bus, tram and local train in the London Transport area in the year ending 30 June were 432 in 1934 and 444 in 1939;[4] the shadow of the future lay across the pages of the LPTB Annual Reports as early as 1936, the year when the increasing use of private cars first received a mention.

A few Jewels in the Dross

Those prejudiced against suburbs will often admit that their attitude is in part conditioned by the general lack-lustre appearance of these areas; indeed many are prepared to write off all the houses and other small buildings of the period as a complete architectural disaster. Others, more perceptive, can find some of the speculative builders' cottagey designs quite agreeable, given a setting softened by time and nature and an evening or autumnal light. But for architectural distinction in the suburban environment, it is necessary to seek out certain railway stations (and a few churches).

At one time railway companies would give a new suburb little more than wooden platforms and a simple wooden or corrugated

[1] *Railway Gazette*, 7 October, 1938.   [2] *Railway Magazine*, August 1938.
[3] LPTB Annual Report, 1935–6.   [4] LPTB Annual Reports, 1935–1939.

iron shelter whilst they waited to see how traffic would develop; or they would erect their standard roadside station, pleasant enough, perhaps, but lacking special merit. In the neo-Georgian period there came a change of heart. Just before 1914, the LNWR provided some acceptable buildings for the new suburban line to Watford, and after the war, the Underground, patron of good design in several fields, took the lead. Others followed, with the Southern lagging in the rear until about 1936.

For the Edgware extension, S. A. Heaps designed stations in matching neo-Palladian styles, with airy ticket halls and well-mannered exteriors harmoniously clothed with a mixture of red and purple sand-faced bricks, Portland stone and tiles. As focal points for the new areas they served, they set an example of dignified good taste, but they were not imaginative or original enough for Frank Pick, who exercised the Underground's design patronage. When the Morden extension was being planned, Pick sought out Dr Charles Holden, who supplied some stridently angular, boldly modernistic buildings in Portland stone. They looked good under floodlights, but were rather garish, even harsh, in daylight.

Pick, still searching for what he had in mind, accompanied Holden on a study tour of north-west Europe in 1930, returning much impressed by the large public buildings with unrelieved brick elevations which were then coming from the Scandinavian and Dutch architects. Quite soon afterwards, Holden designed a fine station to replace the crude shack erected at Sudbury Town in 1903. Precursor of a whole series, this building was a masterpiece of clean, undemonstrative styling in brick, concrete and glass, modernistic in conception without being harsh. Some of the subsequent designs were the work of Holden, his pupils and associates, whilst others came from the drawing boards of R. H. Uren, S. A. Heaps, L. A. Bucknell or James, Bywaters and Pearce. There were many semblances of pattern and form, notably in the high curtain walls of the ticket halls, vertical masses of steel-framed cathedral glass windows amid unrelieved brown bricks left bare inside and out. Detailing of such items as station name displays, lamps, advertisement panels and doors was suggested by Holden, who made much use of bronze. But each station was distinctive, and some were very much better than others; in the first rank were Arnos Grove (Holden, 1932), Oakwood (Holden, with James, Bywaters and Pearce, 1933), and Rayners Lane (Holden and Uren, 1938). All stood out boldly and impressively from their often undistinguished surroundings.[1]

Holden took great trouble to ease passenger flow, beginning with a wide inviting entrance, level with the pavement, as easy to step into as a shop. Inside, wall corners were rounded and stair design perfected, evolving to a smooth, good-natured whole which matched the success of the external impact. At this time it was still unusual for architects to be allowed to treat a railway station as a unit; interiors and platform structures were traditionally the province of the civil engineer's department. Holden and his colleagues, with the support of Frank Pick, overcame this, producing buildings fully integrated from street entrance to platform edge.

The Underground's patronage of the best in contemporary architecture was not received everywhere with acclamation. Fearing, with good reason, that they would get something like Arnos Grove or Rayners Lane, the residents of Pinner, whose village street had been all but engulfed by the new suburbia, petitioned the LPTB in the summer of 1939 that the new station 'should conform to the medieval character of the village'. It is not clear whether they supplied the Board with an illustration of their conception of a fifteenth-century railway station.

Perhaps the preservationists of Pinner would have been more content with something in the elegant and prosperous-seeming domestic style favoured by the Metropolitan's architect, C. W. Clark, in his designs for the Stanmore and Watford branches.

For the Barking to Upminster electrification and widening of 1932, LMSR architects supplied neat and sober brick-faced stations which showed some evidence of attention to the design and appearance of the interiors and the platform structures. A year later, at South Kenton, the company seemed quite adventurous with a design that was perhaps intended as a prototype for suburban stations. A mélange of cream and green paint and chromium plate, this station had specially detailed doors and furniture with a curved-windowed waiting-room which gave a fine view of the line. A clergyman was moved to write to the Railway Magazine: '. . . in the originality of thought and artistic ideals displayed in its design there is an indication that the railways will one day regain the poetry and romance of which standardisation has tended to rob them'. Alas,

[1] In 1970, Sudbury Town, Arnos Grove, and Southgate earned a place in the government list of buildings of historical and architectural interest.

it has not worn well. No tragedy perhaps that an LMSR obsessed with micro-economics decided to build no more like it.

In tune with its methods of electrification, the Southern's new stations for the suburbs of the twenties and thirties were mostly low-cost affairs with the bare minimum of facilities. Usually they consisted of a simple island platform supporting a small waiting-room, lavatories, staff room and ticket office, connected to the road-way by stairs, footbridge or subway according to site layout. There were no street buildings. In this pattern were Motspur Park (1925), South Merton, Morden South and Sutton Common (all 1929–30), Hinchley Wood (1930), Woodmansterne (1932) and Stoneleigh (1932). Where a roadside building was included, this was frequently no more than a simple box, perhaps containing a shop or two. Some were very crude cement-faced structures (West Sutton, St Helier (both 1930)), but others were more pleasingly finished with facing bricks (Albany Park (1935), Falconwood (1936)). There was little evidence in any of them of an architect's touch.

Wimbledon Chase, opened in 1929, clearly *was* the work of an architect, although the style it established was not adopted for other suburban stations on the Southern for several years. All gentle curves, it grouped shops and entrance hall into a long, flat-roofed single-storey building faced with glazed blocks. A wide, welcoming entrance bore the message on the raised facade above in bold letters: SOUTHERN RAILWAY. It was a good try, but it sat somewhat awkwardly in the angle of the street and the embank-ment, and its island platform, to which it was linked by a stark parcels and luggage lift tower, was straightforward utilitarian from the civil engineer's drawing office, having no obvious relationship to the rest. A similar design, rather more carefully executed, was used for the four stations of the new Chessington line of 1938–9. Here the luggage lift towers were tidily grouped with the stairways and street building, and although the overall appearance was not properly assessed (the platform buildings presented hideous backs to the outside world) at least some attempt was made to integrate all the units of the station. Internally, the platforms, protected by graceful 'Chisarc' cantilevered reinforced concrete canopies lit by porthole glasses and neon tubes, expressed a modernity which con-trasted strongly with the Edwardian outlines of the trains. Two of these stations were executed in reinforced concrete throughout, the other two having roadside buildings in brick, but all were to the same basic plan, with slight modification at Chessington South, where the tracks were below street level. Whilst they were undoubtedly a great advance on the earlier small suburban stations of the SR, making a modest contribution to the appearance of the new suburbs they served, these stations were far less successful than Holden's treatment of similar embankment sites. At South Harrow, for example, in 1935, the several components were handled felicitously, combining to radiate a quiet, confident dignity not perceptible at Maiden Manor, Tolworth or Chessington North.

Chapter 14

NEO-GEORGIAN CASE STUDIES: (1) EDGWARE, THE UNDERGROUND SUBURB

Eight miles from Marble Arch, along Roman Watling Street, northbound coaches and wagons made their first halt for refreshment and change of horses at the village of Edgware, a mile-long string of inns and shops and tile-roofed brick and timber cottages. On the west side of the village, between the main road and Stanmore, was Canons Park, site of the Palace of Canons.[1] Eastwards, a lane straggled between hayfields and pasturelands to Mill Hill, crossing four streams in its first mile. The 2,000 or so acres on this side, as far as Deans Brook in the east and the Hertfordshire boundary in the north, formed Edgware parish; 1,500 acres on the west side of the main road, north and south of the Edgware brook, comprised the parish of Little Stanmore. In 1901, the census enumerators found 868 people in the first parish, and just over a thousand in the second, virtually all of them concentrated in the village of Edgware. Apart from succour of the through traffic, their main task was production of hay for the London horses, in fields 'manured by dung and other matter brought from the Wen'.[2]

Ever since the railways had emptied the main roads of most of their through traffic, Edgware had stagnated, coming to life only at holiday times when the hayfields and the numerous inns proved an attraction for Londoners. The branch railway serving the village was a poor thing, wandering circuitously towards the GNR main line at Finsbury Park, via Finchley, single line to the latter point, without a crossing place, and worked 'one engine in steam'. At the

[1] Residence of James Brydges, the first Duke of Chandos, demolished in 1747 and replaced by a smaller and less splendid mansion.
[2] William Cobbett, *Rural Rides*, Vol. I.

beginning of the century, the little terminus in Station Road (then Church Lane) saw about twenty-three departures and arrivals daily; a journey to Kings Cross, usually involving at least one change of carriage, would take from forty to forty-five minutes. There was little change in this service during the subsequent forty years. A horse-bus was the only other form of public transport, linking the village with Hendon six times daily, supplemented between 1901 and 1904 by an LGOC horse-bus which ran from the south end of the village to Cricklewood.

The Beginnings of a Suburb
London's outward advance was signalled by the opening on 3 December 1904 of the Metropolitan Electric Tramway company's line along the main road from Cricklewood to a point just north of the crossroads at the centre of the village. The construction of this tramway, and its subsequent extension to Stanmore Corner (31 October 1907) entailed a widening of the road through Edgware, the first of many violent physical changes to come in the first quarter of the new century. The tramway was intended to link up with lines coming south from Watford via Stanmore, but in February 1906, 'a surprise to many in court', the Light Railway Commissioners found insufficient evidence of public need for further extension beyond what the Company were to call Canons Park.[1] Such public need as did exist was soon to be met by motor-buses rather than electric trams – a daily twenty-minute service between Kilburn and Watford via Edgware was started by the General in July 1913.

But neither bus nor tram provided direct connection between Edgware and central London. A journey to Cricklewood would take more than thirty minutes, and there a change had to be made for another half-hour's ride to Marble Arch.

Railway promoters had not overlooked Edgware's possibilities for suburban development. In 1901 the villagers learned of plans for an electric railway to connect with the proposed tube line from Charing Cross to Hampstead, and a year later there was a proposal to extend this electric railway from Edgware to Watford. All three lines were eventually authorised by parliament, but there were several subsequent changes of plan and fresh legislation, the Edgware–Watford scheme finally lapsing in 1911. Although much of

[1] HFT 2 March 1906.

the land was bought, no construction work had been started on the Edgware tube extension at the time of the outbreak of World War I.[1]

These transport plans and achievements stimulated the very first stirrings of suburban activity in the village. Some plots on the Manor Park Estate (east of the main road and north of Church Lane) were auctioned in 1903 and another 79 acres of this estate came into the market eight years later. A terrace or two of solid-looking villas in contemporary London style duly appeared, and Manor Park Crescent, with the new London and County Bank and adjacent small parade of shops on the main road corner, at the first tram terminus, imparted a definite metropolitan stamp on the decaying coaching village. Bank Parade Tea Rooms offered 'Teas at Popular Prices' for weekend tramway excursionists. A more precarious enterprise was Mr Flowerdew's Hale Brook Estate, 6 pairs of substantial semis on the east side of Edgwarebury Lane, together with another 8 pairs on the north side of Hale Lane. Destined to stand for many years in stark isolation amid the tree-girded meadows, they were advertised in May 1906 at £490 leasehold, four bedrooms, 300 ft. gardens and 'room for motor'.

To the west, Sir Arthur Philip du Cros started to sell off Canons Park in 1905, the northern section for an eighteen-hole golf course, and a piece in the south for the Whitchurch Gardens Estate, where semis were going up around a bowling green and tennis courts in 1911. Apart from a few new houses and cottages in Church Lane, near the GNR station, we have now noticed the sum of Edgware's Edwardian development. In the first twenty years of the century the population increase of both parishes was barely 1,600.

A Pioneer Rewarded

In 1910 an ambitious young estate agent had looked over the Edgware area, deciding to set up his brother in a small office opposite the High Street smithy. Until this time, George Cross had confined his activities to hotels, shops, offices and flats in central London, but much impressed by Owers' exploits at Golders Green, he dearly wanted to speculate in suburban development. He was aware of the electric railway proposals, but could hardly have been prepared for the long delay in their execution. Of course his brother

[1] For a full account of the several proposals for new railways at Edgware, see Alan A. Jackson, 'Beyond Edgware', *The Railway Magazine*, February, 1967.

did little or no business, and Cross concluded he had 'backed a loser'.[1]

The London Tube boom was over. As the heavily capitalised lines were increasingly subjected to competition by the motorbus, financial returns were miserably low, so that it became virtually impossible for the Underground Company to attract capital for further extensions at an acceptable rate of interest. Thus the Edgware line remained unbuilt, even in the form of the electric light-railway subsequently proposed as a cheaper alternative. But the immediate post-war economic conditions revived its prospects. The Trade Facilities Act of 1921 offered a Treasury guarantee of interest and capital for any approved works that would relieve unemployment, and work on the tube extension from Golders Green started in 1922 as part of a wider programme devised by the Underground Company to meet the requirements of the Act. Three years earlier, George Cross, whose London hotels had done well in the war years, again turned to Edgware. His brother suggested the 5-acre Portsdown Estate which had a 700 ft. frontage to Church Lane opposite the site of the electric railway terminus. Cross turned it down, thinking it too small, and the house and land were bought by an old lady as a home, for £4,000. Within two years, she was under siege. She had no particular wish to move, nor any need for cash, and resisted many offers at substantial increments over the price she had paid. Eventually she was moved out by a bid of £29,000.

By Tube to the Best Sites

Meanwhile, on 1 October 1919, Cross had purchased the 54-acre Edgware Manor Estate, paying £175 an acre, going on to buy more until he had a total of 70 acres south of Hale Lane from the GNR station eastwards to Deans Brook. This was poor quality farmland, rather wet, and rented out for grazing at £1 10s per acre a year. Cross put some pigs on some of it, feeding them with swill from his London hotels. Then 'the not quite unexpected happened'[2] and he received notice to treat for the section of his land required for the railway station and approaches. Although he could have taken an immediate increment of £35,000 for the total holding, he was determined to develop it himself, 'moulding that important slice of the suburbs of London in any way I pleased, planning the roads where I wished, naming them as I fancied'.[3] Retaining the Con-

[1] George Cross, *Suffolk Punch*, 1939.   [2] Cross, op. cit.   [3] Ibid.

sultant Surveyor to the Hendon Rural District Council as his adviser, he quickly had the land drained preparatory to laying out the first roads (Penshurst Gardens and Heather Walk).

On the land he had been compelled to sell, J. Parkinson and Son erected a £17,000 station of pleasing proportions designed by S. A. Heaps, the Underground Company's architect. Described as 'Italian in style', it had high-pitched tiled roofs over a booking hall set between wings extending towards the road. The eastern one contained shops, the other a bus waiting shelter, and the whole was ornamented with miniature doric columns. Heaps later expressed the hope that the effect would be 'sufficiently dignified to command respect and sufficiently appealing to promote affection', but would have preferred the building to have abutted on to an open square rather than a bend in the road. With land selling at ten times its agricultural value, a proper setting was out of the question.[1]

Before the railway was opened to the public on 18 August 1924 there was an official ceremony to which local personalities were invited, including George Cross. The man from the *Golders Green Gazette* found free cigars, 'titbits and champagne in a tent' and 'a very pleasant little string quartet'. J. P. Thomas, the Underground's Operating Manager, beguiled the press with tales of future extensions to Elstree, Watford, Totteridge and Stanmore, and promised that the trains would be so frequent that Edgware residents would be independent of timetables. At first the service was every eight minutes to Moorgate at rush hours, passengers for the West End changing at Golders Green, with a ten-minute service to West End stations at other times. Edgware's inhabitants could now reach Charing Cross in thirty-five minutes compared with fifty-eight before.

Road public transport had remained much as described earlier, apart from an hourly single-deck bus to Golders Green and South Harrow introduced in July 1922. With the opening of the electric railway, half-hourly feeder bus services were inaugurated from the quadrangle outside the Edgware station to Pinner Green, to South Harrow and to Watford. A garage was erected alongside the new station to accommodate the twenty buses needed to operate these three services.

At first Cross found little interest was shown in his Manor Estate building plots and he was obliged to erect a few houses at his own expense to encourage others. Semis with three bedrooms, these

[1] *TOT Staff Magazine*, February 1927.

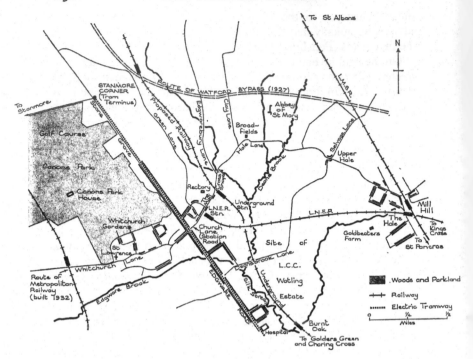

V Edgware, 1924

were advertised in November 1924 at £1,100. More success attended Premier Parade, the 8 shops he erected in Hale Lane alongside the new station. All but one, together with an adjacent plot for Sainsbury's, were sold before building was completed. Another 12 shops were added soon afterwards and a plot at the corner of Hale Lane and Penshurst Gardens was bought for a National Provincial Bank branch (opened in 1925).

By the beginning of 1925, under the stimulus of the new railway in full operation, most of the Edgware Manor plots were sold, either for individual houses or for sectional development by speculative builders. At least one of the latter was still trying to dispose of his houses as late as the summer of 1932, but Cross had no complaints. He managed to clear a net profit of around £56,000 from this land, which had not required any capital beyond the £12,050 purchase price.[1]

[1] Full financial details are given in Cross, op. cit.

Another large Edgware estate of just under 274 acres came into the market in September 1924 just a month after the opening of the railway. Broadfields Manor was described as, 'Many acres of pleasantly timbered undulating pastureland ... free from the presence of factories and other forms of development which ruin so many residential districts . . .'.[1] It failed to go as one lot, and when split up some of the northern sections remote from the station did not attract buyers. Hyman Kerman took 25 acres east of Broadfields Avenue and north of Hale Lane at £960 an acre to be resold a year later at a substantial increment. This was land which would have been difficult to move at £150 an acre five years previously.

Owers and Death were keeping a close eye on things from their headquarters at Golders Green and Cross and his brother were also subject to some competition from Walter Leslie Raymond, an estate agent, surveyor and auctioneer from Hampstead and Golders Green, who opened a base at Edgware in July 1924, a few weeks before the railway started. Raymond was involved in the purchase of the Portsdown Estate already mentioned and in its subsequent development. His first venture was The Mall, a 'semi-Georgian' parade of 29 shops and flats designed by Welch and Hollis, completed in 1927. Opposite the new station, it was set back to widen the lane to a distance of 90 feet between frontages. An interesting feature was the provision made in the construction of nos. 30 and 31 for the passage of a double line of railway underneath should an extension north-westwards be required at some future date. Raymond set up permanent offices in nos. 24 and 25, almost exactly opposite the station, in August 1928. The balance of the Portsdown Estate was to accommodate the new post office and yard (1930), the Ritz Cinema and car park (1932) and The Old Rectory Garden Estate of 26 houses (1932).

With appetite whetted by the success of his first suburban venture, George Cross secured 85 acres of Canons Park in 1926 from the Pards Estate,[2] paying just under £566 an acre. Anxious to preserve a little of the atmosphere of the old parklands, Cross entrusted planning to A. J. Butcher, ARIBA, who preserved some of the trees and split the site up into units of 30 feet frontage to curving roads.[3] Publicity appearing in the autumn of 1927 mentioned garaged houses of three to six bedrooms, semis and detached,

[1] From a sales catalogue in Hendon Reference Library local collection.
[2] The Pards Estate was a trust formed by Sir Arthur du Cros in 1919.
[3] GGG 8 October 1926.

at prices from £1,425 to £3,500. Cross invested in excess of his outlay on land, building roads, financing builders and erecting 'encouragement' houses on his own account; he also had to meet an expensive damages action brought by a neighbouring landowner. And there were few customers for suburban houses at the end of the twenties who could afford the prices on this estate. Not surprisingly, the results of Canons Park were a good deal less satisfying than the earlier venture, showing a profit of only 6 per cent before tax. Cross blamed the high price of the land and the unforeseen factors which extended the pay-off period well beyond the desirable five-year maximum.[1] He also had minor troubles. In 1929 a row blew up with the RDC, who installed street lamps only to discover that a janitor had been placed at the entrance to the estate to refuse admission to all except those with business there, so making it private. Cross navigated this problem by explaining that the guardian was a necessary precaution; cockney trippers at weekends had proved a great nuisance, leaving litter, taking picnics around the lakes, even bathing in the nude.[2]

During 1928 the rest of Canons Park was sold by the Pards Estate to Canons Ltd and to the council (who took some land on the west side for a park). The mansion and its immediate surrounds were bought a year later by the North London Collegiate School for Girls to accommodate the Junior School; by 1940 the remainder of the school had moved here from Sandall Road, Camden Town.

Two years after the opening of the Underground station, as well as the developments already noted, building was proceeding along Edgwarebury Lane under Jarvis and Streather and there were houses for sale in the so-called Edgware Garden City (between the church and the LNER station), also in Elmer Gardens, off the High Street in the southern part of the village. Whitchurch Gardens, started before 1914, was nearly completed, and John Hogan had started to erect houses along Whitchurch Lane. Owers was advertising twenty houses which had appeared on the Broadfields Manor Estate in the summer of 1925 and Leslie Raymond had some to sell in the nearby Drive and Rise. Almost all this property was priced over £1,000, some of it as high as £1,450 and £1,595. Streather's houses in Edgwarebury Lane, with four bedrooms, two reception rooms, 'lounge hall', kitchen, scullery and garage were advertised in 1926 at £1,450.

[1] Cross, op. cit.
[2] EG 4 October 1929.

Disappointments

That summer, the *Golders Green Gazette* had spoken of progress to date in rosy terms:

> 'Within the last two or three years, a considerable change has taken place, and a beautiful garden suburb has sprung up. Handsome shops are already erected, and good wide roads have been constructed, or are in course of construction . . . Edgware rests on a hillside facing south, protected from north winds, and catching every gleam of sunshine. . . .'[1]

But there were others who did not see New Edgware as the New Jerusalem. In his first annual report (for 1927) Major B. J. Temple, the chairman of the Edgware Ratepayers' Association, painted a rather different picture:

> 'Your Committee have long viewed with grave concern the indiscriminate expansion of inartistic building enterprise. Various commercially minded builders and building speculators are gradually but surely obliterating the rural delights which gave Edgware its chief charm. Instead of a beautiful village, we may, ere long, be gazing on an ugly township.'

Passing over the odd thought that there might be building speculators not commercially minded, we can see the Major's point. He went on to say that although a Town Planning Scheme existed, it appeared to be framed not by artists and architects, but by land development exploiters: 'Aesthetic purposes can nowhere be seen in the plans'. Turning to Canons Park, he had this to say: 'A Town Planning Scheme which could devise no use for that glorious estate other than conversion into a close colony of suburban villas cannot be said to have been inspired by lofty imagination'. So much for the efforts of Mr Butcher.

But for some people, the obliteration of Edgware's rural charm was not proceeding fast enough. At the Annual General Meeting of the Underground Company in February 1927, Lord Ashfield, the chairman, complained that the Edgware extension had shown only 14 per cent traffic growth in its second full year, a much slower rate than had been expected:

> 'We have sought to account for the retardation in growth, though not very successfully, unless it is that land speculation at the

[1] GGG 9 July 1926.

Edgware terminal has forced up prices to a level which restricts purchasers. This is an evil which besets all railway enterprise, and suggests as a remedy some means by which the increment in the value of the land could be appropriated to pay some share of the enormous costs attending the construction of Underground Railways in Greater London.'

Whether the speculators would have been so ready to embark on the development of new areas if they had been obliged to pay part of their gains over to Lord Ashfield is an open question, but the assessment of the Edgware situation was accurate enough. Land values had increased by between 30 and 40 per cent in 1925 alone[1] and some parcels had changed hands several times, each time with an increment. As a result, most of the Edgware builders tried to provide a showy, spacious-seeming house which they hoped would in the customer's eye justify the high prices they were obliged to set to secure a reasonable margin. The *Golders Green Gazette*, in reporting Lord Ashfield's remarks, cautiously commented that they pointed towards 'obstruction for the purposes of profiteering' and would be harmful to Edgware.

Perhaps to restore what is nowadays known as the 'image', but also to inject some adrenalin into the sluggish market, estate agents and builders came together in July 1927 to form an Edgware Publicity Association, with the declared object of boosting the district 'to the skies'. On the committee we find the Cross brothers, Raymond's partner, Harold Crump, and the builder Reginald Streather, son of Edward, builder of much of Golders Green. By November, the Association's fiery slogans, *Edgware – Live There* and *Live Where ? – Edgware* were featuring in newspaper insertions and posters displayed on railway stations. Bravely, the *Golders Green Gazette* remarked that only two of the twelve members of the committee followed the advice they dispensed. From time to time the EPA managed puff pieces in the local and national press which always suggested that a great property boom was just about to erupt at Edgware. This story had been circulated even before the formation of the EPA; in the autumn of 1926 the *Daily Express* carried a prophecy that the following spring would see a building boom at Edgware 'exceeding anything known in this country, even Golders Green, and more on a parallel with the land rush at Miami without the risk of loss or hurricanes'. In August 1928, the new *Edgware*

[1] Ernest Owers, quoted in GGG, 16 October 1925.

15. Houses advertised by picture postcard, Merton c. 1909. (Photo: Clark & Mann.)

The Rural-Romantic dream: Cover of *Metro-land*, 1925 edition.

NORTH HARROW ESTATES

SEMI-DETACHED Brick-Built Villas within 3 minutes of North Harrow, 5 minutes West Harrow Stations. Train journey about 16 minutes Baker Street or Marylebone.

3 Bedroom Houses from **£750** Leasehold.
£920 Freehold.

3 Bedroom Houses, Large Type **£850** Leasehold.
£1,040 Freehold.

4 Bedroom Houses **£950** to **£1,450**.
Repayments as Rent arranged.

ADVANCES are being granted on this property by The Middlesex County Council under The Housing Acts, 1890—1924.

Electric Light.   Large Gardens.
Rates 8/- in the £ per year.
Pinner Parish.   Facilities for Garage.

A. CUTLER, *Builder*,
Estate Office, Pinner Road, North Harrow.
Phone—Harrow 139.
Hundreds have been satisfied.

SAY YOU SAW IT IN "METRO-LAND."
102

Metro-land advertisement, 1925 edition.

16. Southall-on-electric-tramway, scene at the Broadway c. 1909. (From a commercial postcard by John King.)

Sunday country buses at Golders Green station, summer 1913. *Left:* ex-MET Daimler on route 109 (Hatfield); *right:* B-type on route 84 (St Albans). (Source unknown.)

Gazette unexpectedly announced: 'Edgware's Day has arrived! The boom has burst on Edgware with the recent spell of fine weather'. But in the next issue, Leslie Raymond was rather more circumspect, informing the newspaper that he preferred 'increasing momentum of business' to 'boom'.

Signs of Progress

In fact things were beginning to move a little faster as the twenties came to an end. Church Lane, renamed Station Road, with its continuation, Hale Lane, was widened to 90 feet between frontages in 1929–31, and the shopping section was equipped with one of the most advanced street-lighting systems to be found around London at that time. The new shops (to which Cross and Cowen added The Quadrant, on the west side, in 1928) now took a firm grip on Edgware's trading, causing the main road, with its redundant inns, to fall farther into decline. A branch of the Midland Bank opened in the Mall in January 1929, the third bank in Edgware and the second in the new centre. Cutting across the northern part of Edgware parish and creating over four miles of cheap housing frontage in the district was the raw wound of the Watford Bypass road, opened in 1927, and used from October 1929 by the first Green Line coach service, route 'V', (later 'T'), Watford to Golders Green station. In December 1929, the *Edgware Gazette* was murmuring reassuringly 'more progress has been made this year than in the previous three years'.

Between 1927 and 1930, builders were busy along Hale Lane and Edgwarebury Lane. On the west side of the latter, Arthur William Curton, son of a District Railway official, was beginning to make his own corner of New Edgware after completing his first venture at Burnt Oak. Commendably occupying one of his own houses at 71 Edgwarebury Lane, Curton was soon to become a prominent figure in the new suburb; council member, and later alderman and mayor of Hendon, he was active in many Edgware organisations. All priced over £1,000, his 'uniquely designed Tudor Houses', with their half-timbered gables, oak-panelled rooms, lounge halls and 'marble bathrooms' had from two to four main rooms downstairs and from three to six bedrooms. Streather was busy in Hale Lane and Farm Road at this time, whilst on Cross' Edgware Manor Estate, the last spaces were being taken. On the Broadfields Manor Estate, C. B. Heygate ('Builder and Owner') was filling Hillcrest

Road, High View Avenue and High View Gardens with his high-gabled, prominently bay-windowed houses, almost all of them priced over £1,000.

West of the main road, both Whitchurch Lane and George Cross' Canons Park were filling up. Further south, opposite Deansbrook Lane, builders were at work either side of Bacon Lane, and the rectangular Canada Park Estate facing the Red Hill Hospital, was begun in 1930.

There were few houses to be had for less than £1,000. In Farm Road, for £875 Streather could only provide comparatively small rooms in a semi with garage space. Such lower priced houses as there were mostly appeared on the western side, as on the Berridge Estate (Bacon Lane and Camrose Avenue), which offered three-bedroom semis for £695 in 1929.

A further piece of publicity puff appeared in the *Daily Mail* late in 1929. This revealed that 'nearly 20 estates' had been started that year, one builder having sold 120 houses. There were more solid indicators of progress. The number of passengers using Edgware tube station had grown from 75,000 a month in 1924 to 233,000, whilst the buses at the station were carrying 6,000 passengers daily, six times the 1924 figure. The 1929 estimate of the population of the two Edgware parishes was over 8,000, rather more than double that of 1921.

But there was still much dissatisfaction at the rate of growth. Too many of the people involved in New Edgware had lived through the great Golders Green boom and felt frustrated because history was not repeating itself in what they had seen as a parallel situation. It was thought that some catalyst was needed to set off the explosion, although no one quite knew what it might be. Early in 1930, Harold Crump decided to revive the Publicity Association, gaining modest financial support from the builders Curton, Streather and Hogan, the estate agents George and Frank Cross, and Leslie Raymond, and the draper Stanley J. Lee of the Mall.

Meanwhile Lord Ashfield was doing what he could, building up the bus and train services, often in advance of the traffic on offer. In 1927 the South Harrow–Edgware station bus was projected alone Hale Lane to Mill Hill (*Green Man*) every fifteen minutes, serving Upper Hale, a new district on the margins of Edgware and Mill Hill, and at the end of the year a new service was started between Edgware station and Boreham Wood via the Watford By-pass. Green Line coach services between Watford and central

London via Edgware began in 1930. Operators outside the Underground combine did not neglect the new suburb. November 1928 saw the start of a Birch Brothers bus service between Edgware and Hendon Central station via Hale Lane and the Bypass, operated by pneumatic-tyred 'Pullman' single-deckers with thirty seats. In 1931 the Premier Bus Company were working from Edgware (*The Boot*) to Marble Arch, Charing Cross and Old Ford, in East London.

On the Underground, all trains on the Edgware line were diverted to run via Charing Cross on weekdays during 1925 (and on Sundays from 19 June 1927). That year weekly seasons were introduced and the last train to Edgware was put forward to 12.1 a.m. from Leicester Square. A fast train introduced on 13 June 1927 left Edgware at 8.58 a.m., running non-stop to Golders Green, missing two stations after that, and reaching Charing Cross at 9.28, with a similar return working in the evening. Primarily for the benefit of *hoi polloi* of the LCC estate using Burnt Oak station, the first departure from Edgware was made at 5.25 a.m. after 24 September 1928. At the other end of the day, the last West End departure was adjusted to allow Edgware revellers to stay in town until 12.34 a.m. from November 1930.

By 1931, the train service from the terminus was available between 5.17 a.m. and 11.53 p.m. (8 a.m. to 11.5 p.m. on Sundays) and trains arrived and left Edgware every two to three minutes in the rush hours and every five minutes at other times (five to seven minutes on Sundays). The cheap return fares and excellent late night facilities evidently attracted some theatre traffic. Reporting a derailment at Edgware in May 1934, the local paper mentions 'ladies in evening dress and their silk-hatted escorts' waiting on the platform at the time it occurred.[1] Such people were also served by the taxi rank established outside the station in January 1930.

A New Hope

As the thirties dawned, there was excited talk among the newspapermen and gossips of a cinema and of further extension of the Underground towards Elstree and Watford.

It was the cinema which was to become the focus of the developers' hopes, a talisman for the boom they still expected to accelerate the now steadily strengthening growth. Schemes for a cinema had first been mooted early in 1929, but definite news of the sale of the

[1] HTBG 18 May 1934.

central site at the corner of The Mall and Manor Park Crescent did not break until April 1931. In the following September, the *Edgware Gazette* announced somewhat dramatically that the new building would 'complete Edgware as a township . . . establish Edgware as the pivotal centre of a large and increasing district', adding that 'local residents are paying daily visits to the site', as if it were some kind of shrine.

These visits were to watch construction work, which started in August, proceeding rapidly until on 2 May 1932, the 2,120 seat Ritz was opened to the public. The occasion was marked by a special supplement to the *Edgware Gazette* which extolled the amenities of New Edgware and enthused over W. J. King's picture palace:

> 'a worthy architectural contribution to a suburb of noteworthy new buildings . . . built on Romanesque lines in simple bold stone courses . . . whilst conveying the impression of solidity, lacks nothing in beauty of outline and facade . . . at night the central section will be a beacon, blazing in magnificence across miles of country.'

The writer then took his readers inside the building, up the marble steps, past plaster frieze panels depicting dancers, into the auditorium, with its elaborate murals and castellated walls 'from which romance peeps' and its ceiling glowing 'with the effulgence of an Eastern Dawn'. Clearly Edgware would never be the same again. In truth the fashionable 'atmospheric' décor, with its attempts to portray distant hills and valleys, cascades and wooded country, punctuated by four 'statuary subjects', The Ram, The Knight, Cupid and Youth had a somewhat amateurish appearance. In the tea lounge, modest suburban mums were confronted with what *Cinema Construction* described as delicate carvings of nude figures 'lost in a silvery mist and light floral garlands, giving a cool and restful impression'.

This outwardly rather ugly building, which was to have been called The Citadel, and had been designed to look like one, contained 10 shops, which Raymond promptly offered on leases up to 21 years at £145 a year. The whole structure rested on wet ground, so that for some years the pit containing the Compton electric organ was apt to flood after heavy rain, an event not calculated to improve the Eastern Dawn.

Like many other things in this early Edgware, the Ritz did not at first live up to expectations. Five months after opening, the free-holders, British Associated Cinemas, were successful in their appeal for a reduction in its rateable value. Takings were said to be rather less than £26,000 a year against an estimated £36,000, and not enough to cover costs; the area was not yet fully developed, it was pleaded, and a 'family trait' for the cinema had yet to be established there.[1]

Nearer the old village, on the opposite side of the road to the Ritz, a large public house, The Railway Hotel, was completed in 'beautiful Tudor style' in 1931. Replacing an old house of the same name, it was typical of many provided for the new suburbs, a close cousin to the Stoneleigh Hotel mentioned in the next chapter. A contemporary critic thought this £30,000 building 'a technically perfect example of revived timber-framed construction and up to the high standard of Messrs Liberty and Co.'s building of a similar type in Great Marlborough Street, but far too mannered for A.D. 1932'.[2]

From Parish to Borough

1931 census returns established that the two parishes had a population of almost 13,000, nearly four times the 1921 figure. The increase was distributed more or less equally, Little Stanmore registering 6,918 against 2,015 in 1921, and Edgware 5,353 against 1,516. At this time local government was still by parish councils and the Hendon RDC, which also covered Great Stanmore, Pinner and Harrow Weald. Since the middle twenties there had been mounting criticism of the inadequacy of local services, particularly of road cleansing and the inefficiency of the part-time fire brigade. Then came the news that Hendon UDC, not without ulterior motive, was preparing to annex the eastern part of Edgware.

This move was achieved in April 1931, the old Edgware parish becoming a ward of the Hendon UDC, filling three of the thirty-three council seats. Little Stanmore slumbered on a little longer, assuming control of the former joint fire brigade, which was soon to suffer the indignity of having its own station burnt to the ground. Eventually, on 1 April 1934, this western section of Edgware was incorporated into the Harrow UDC, and the Hendon RDC disappeared. With its already large empire now swollen to 125,000

---

[1] TEG 24 September 1932.
[2] Basil Oliver, *The Modern Public House*, 1934.

subjects, Hendon council had little difficulty in achieving the desired borough status from 27 September 1932 (in common with a number of other outer London authorities in the thirties, Hendon sought this change partly as a deterrent to LCC expansion). The three Conservatives elected for the Edgware seats were ousted in the 1932 elections by a team of Independents headed by the builder A. W. Curton. Curton was re-elected in 1935 under the description 'Anti-Socialist Independent' and the slogan *Apathy is my Chief Opponent and your Worst Enemy*, securing 1,600 of the 1,779 votes cast by an electorate of 4,365 (his Labour opponent, a clerk living in Hale Lane, secured the remainder). At the last election before the war Curton obtained 1,861 votes to Labour's 547.

Curton was not the only developer involved in the government of Edgware. George Cross's estate agent brother Frank sat on the Edgware Parish Council from 1922 until its demise in 1931, becoming chairman in 1928. He went on to represent Little Stanmore on the RDC (to which he had first been elected in 1921) but when elections were held in 1934 for the enlarged Harrow UDC, he was defeated by the Ratepayers' Association candidate.

It was in the thirties, especially in the second half of the decade, that the growth of Edgware at last accelerated to meet the expectations of the now somewhat chastened pioneers. From a 1931 population of 5,353, Edgware parish alone expanded to 9,187 in mid-1935 and 17,523 in 1939.

Building after 1930 was marked by two features: the rapid development of the area west of the old village which followed the opening of the Metropolitan's Stanmore railway and subsequent improvements to the bus services; and the slightly larger number of modestly-priced houses that became available with the arrival of the big firms, Laing, Taylor Woodrow, and Wimpey.

The new electric railway left the Metropolitan main line at Wembley Park, running along the western side of Canons Park, with a station of that name in Whitchurch Lane to serve the western part of Edgware. This line opened on 10 December 1932, providing through trains to London only in the rush hours, the fastest taking twenty-two minutes to reach Baker Street, where a change was necessary to get to the West End or City business areas. Because the route was circuitous and fares were at main-line levels (Canons Park to Charing Cross 1s 2d single in contrast to 7d single, 9d return on the tube) traffic developed only slowly. Frequent bus services along Whitchurch Lane and from Stanmore, with through road-rail season ticket facilities, sucked much of the potential traffic into the tube station a mile or so to the east.

Although Edgware houses were in general still far from cheap, Streather and Hogan had some for sale at £695 in 1932, and a year later there were 'country houses in miniature' on Canons Park land at Whitchurch Lane, offering three bedrooms, a cloakroom, box-room and garage space, all for £750. At Camrose Avenue, just to the south of these, Hartley Estates erected three-bedroom 'suntrap' houses to sell at £595 in 1935.

But it was the big firms that did most to break down the price barrier in Edgware. Laing started a large new estate on the west side of the new Canons Park station in 1933, with prices from £610 upwards, and another, north of the Watford Bypass, between Edgwarebury Lane and Broadfields Avenue, in 1936, where the cheapest houses were £815. This second development did, however, contain a fairly high proportion of more expensive detached houses with prices up to £1,625, probably because the town plan imposed a density of only eight per acre. Taylor Woodrow's nearby Broadfields Park Estate (east of Broadfields Avenue), with its three-bedroom semis selling at £735 to £925, dated from 1935. Further east again, Hilbery Chaplin's Fairview Estate of 1936 also offered houses at less than £1,000, as did George Reed and Son's Golf Course Estate of 1934-9, just north of Apex Corner. On Wimpey's 1937 Mote Mount Estate, east of the Barnet Bypass, at the northern margins of Mill Hill, but still in the Edgware Underground catchment area, prices were £895 to £1,250.

Curton continued to build his rather expensive Tudor types, filling up the area west of Edgwarebury Lane and south of the Bypass, and completing his 700th house in 1937 (his semis sold at £1,115 to £1,785 and there were detached versions on exactly the same plans for £1,200 to £1,885). When the Edgware Golf Course on the north side of Canons Park was sold for building in 1937, Curton took most of it for an estate of 500 high-cost houses (£1,250–£2,500) of up to six bedrooms, settling his daughter in one of them after her marriage in 1938. The other developer on this land was D-C Houses, selling at £795 to £1,250. Roger Malcolm Ltd, who were associated with Leslie Raymond and had completed earlier estates at Old Rectory Garden (1932), Mill Ridge (1933-4) and St Margaret's Road (1934), mainly semis all over £1,000, were now building modernistic 'suntrap' semis with coloured 'wet-look' tiles in Broadfields Avenue, for sale at £1,300 upwards. Around the edges of Curton's territory, in Green Lane and at the top of Hillside Gardens, 'Hollywood Homes with Canadian and American features' were constructed by Tijou and Mills from 1934 onwards. Mills was a Canadian, which explains why these semis contained such mysteries as 'Canadian Ironing Boards' and 'Ultra Modern Basements'; the centrally-heated Anglo-American was appropriately the more expensive at £1,125, the Canadian version a mere £975. In the first half of the thirties, some slightly cheaper houses (£800 upwards) were to be found around Farm Lane and Deans Lane, where Streather, W. F. Thorpe and others were building semis.

With the new district now well established and Station Road the undisputed main shopping centre for the hundreds of houses east of the old village, land values around the two stations reached new heights. Late in 1932 a plot with 170 ft. frontage and a depth of 100 ft. next to the LNER station brought the railway company £7,000.[1] George Cross bought it without hesitation from the purchaser for £9,000, erecting shops which he was able to let before completion to Woolworths, Times Furnishing and Meakers, achieving a rent roll of just under £3,000 a year for a total outlay of less than £25,000.[2] Six years later, his brother Frank managed to extract almost £14,000 from the LPTB when they needed his three-storey, 16 ft.-frontage office building to make an entrance to their new bus garage.[3]

Services and Amenities Follow Behind

From around 1930, services and amenities began to catch up with the increasing pace of Edgware's development, though there were serious gaps (many of the earlier estate roads remained unmade until the middle thirties).

In March that year, noting that the last delivery of the day left the Edgware Post Office at 3.30 p.m., the local newspaper commented that this was 'obviously not good enough for a large and rapidly growing area'. But when a new Crown Office opened in Manor Park Crescent on 29 September, the service was truly commendable. The new postal and sorting office was open every weekday from 8 a.m. to 7.30 p.m. (to 8 p.m. from mid-1933) and on Sundays from 9 a.m. to 10.30 a.m. Serving a district roughly corresponding to the two Edgware parishes but also including the LCC

[1] TEG 10 February 1932.   [2] Cross, op. cit.   [3] TEG 23 April 1938.

Watling Estate, it provided seven daily collections and three deliveries for the 38,000 items handled daily. The staff comprised thirteen clerks, forty-two postmen, a head postman, an inspector and four telegraph boys (three years before for 8,000 daily items, the staff had been four clerks, thirteen postmen (five part-time) and two boys). New pillar-boxes were provided every year in the growing area, seven in 1931 alone. During 1934 an evening delivery at 7 p.m. was started, ensuring that letters posted in central London for Edgware between 2 p.m. and 3 p.m. would be delivered the same day; a second Sunday collection was introduced at the same time. When Edgware and Stanmore became a separate unit of the Harrow postal district in 1935, a head postmaster was installed at the Edgware Crown Office to overlook a staff now grown to sixty-three postmen, two head postmen, one inspector and nineteen clerks.

Edgware's first telephone exchange, in a house in Station Road, dated from the early 1900s. By 1927, the staff handling its 411 lines were under considerable pressure, so much so that as much as twenty-five minutes might be needed to make a local call. The new exchange in the High Street, opened in March 1928, became automatic in the following year, by which time there were 1,300 subscribers.

Part of the 1865 Hendon Poor Law Institution at Red Hill (in the main road south of the village) was converted in 1927 to a 175-bed general hospital, serving the LCC estate and the demands of the growing area on both sides of the village. By 1933 the hospital was under considerable strain, with 4,000 in-patient treatments a year and some 19,000 out-patient attendances. Between 1930 and 1938 the population of the sixty-three square miles served by this hospital grew from 185,000 to 500,000. To meet this, a large extension was completed by the Middlesex County Council in 1938–9, comprising a reception and operating block, a 60-bed maternity unit, a 294-bed medical block, a nurses' home and doctors' hostel, a chest clinic and space for 72 more beds around the 1927 block.

When the Hendon UDC opened its second fire station at Hartley Lane, Mill Hill, in October 1929, with two engines and adjacent cottages for the men, the service was made available to the Edgware parish in advance of annexation. After increasing the establishment at Mill Hill from 8 to 18 men in 1934, the Hendon Council relied on a total of 4 dual-purpose fire engines and 31 men to serve a population which was to grow from 134,160 in mid-1935 to 140,650 in mid-1936 and 145,100 in mid-1938. The inadequacies of the service were revealed at a public enquiry following a fire at Golders Green in 1938. After this, the establishment at the two fire stations was increased by a further 5 men and wages were raised to London rates.

The whole of the two parishes had been within the Metropolitan Police District since its formation early in the nineteenth century, but the police establishment continued through the 1920s at the level appropriate to a large country village. When at last, in 1931, some 20 more men were added, the force was still inadequate to cover a large area which included Mill Hill, Burnt Oak and Kingsbury as well as Edgware itself. In April 1932, shortly before the opening of the new police station, the *Edgware Gazette*, reporting a series of housebreakings on the LCC estate, noted that a policeman was a rare sight in that district of 20,000 inhabitants. Radio-equipped cars began to operate around Edgware about 1934, bringing an increase in mobility and flexibility which went a long way towards relieving the strain thrown on the police by suburban expansion. Similar benefits flowed from the police telephone call boxes installed in the Hendon area during 1935.

The village school of 1895, enlarged in 1912 to take another hundred children, had 350 pupils by 1922. At the end of the twenties, room had to be found for almost 900, and in April 1931 some juniors and infants were moved to a temporary wooden school on a 6½-acre site just south of Whitchurch Lane. This land was used for the 560-place Camrose Senior School, designed by W. T. Curtis and opened in December 1932. At the end of 1935, Edgware Ratepayers' Association was pressing hard for better facilities at the village school and a new secondary school for the area. The former was eventually replaced by a 450-place junior and infants school opened on an adjacent site in September 1938, whilst the needs of the new district around the Watford Bypass were met in 1937 by classes held in the new St Andrew's Church Hall. A council school for these children was begun at the north end of Broadfields Avenue in 1938, but completion was delayed by the outbreak of war.

Many of those who faced the world from a home priced at £1,000 or more sought something a little closer to their middle-class aspirations, a need met by the private school for 5- to 16-year-old boys established in a house in Glendale Avenue in January 1931.

With the artless cachet *Camford* and the fine slogan *Boys only*, *under Masters only*, this school moved to larger premises in Hale Lane a little later. Girls of all ages, and boys to the relatively harmless age of 9, were received at the Broadfields Private School, opened in Broadfields Avenue on 2 May 1932 'in view of the lack of educational facilities in this rapidly expanding suburb'. Broadfields was accommodated in two Streather detached houses whose combined gardens served as a quarter-acre playing-field. The interiors of the houses were 'tastefully decorated in brown and cream', presumably to match the girls in their dark brown uniforms. Also in a new house was Parkside, a preparatory school in Green Lane, on the Curton estate. At Stonegrove, on the northern outskirts of the old village, was the Mornington School of Commerce, offering individual training to boys and girls from thirteen for careers in commerce or the civil service.

Spiritual provision for the rapidly growing population was unremarkable. Until 1937 Anglicans had only the medieval parish churches of St Lawrence, Whitchurch, and St Margaret, Edgware (the latter with some enlargement, completed in 1928). A combined church and social hall, together with curate's house, was opened on the Broadfields Estate, north of the Watford Bypass, in February 1937, at a total cost, including land, of £5,218 (all met by donations, though funding was eased by a single contribution of £4,000). The exterior of St Andrews was executed in rustic Flettons, its interior in shades of light stone, pale blue, and aluminium. There was a stage at one end, and an altar, with folding screen, at the other. Roman Catholics worshipped at St Anthony of Padua, Garratt Road, which dated from 1913 and was doubled in size to seat 300 in 1931. A small Wesleyan Methodist chapel was opened nearby in 1926. The St James Presbyterian Church Hall at the corner of Heather Walk and Hale Lane, with its 250 seats, came into use in April 1933. Baptists started on the Harrow side of Edgware with a 'Pioneer Mission' held in a tent during the summer of 1934, proceeding to their Gothic style church and school hall in Camrose Avenue early in 1936.

Some space for open-air recreation was salvaged from the flood of building. The original (1931) recreation ground near the Underground station, more used than any of the others, gave way in 1938–9 to the new bus garage. A large area north of the Watford Bypass and west of Edgwarebury Lane was secured for public use in 1929 and the Stonegrove recreation ground was added in 1934.

Fields and woodlands were still readily accessible in the north, and during the thirties, each Easter, Whitsun and August bank holiday saw an invasion of ramblers and picnickers, 'men and women above middle age, young flappers in shorts, and hundreds of children', arriving by tube train and carrying their food in 'attaché cases, haversacks and paper parcels'. Many were bound for the Aldenham Reservoir, a favourite spot for picnics, bathing and sailing. In the late evening they queued three deep in the station yard for trains home.

Getting Together

Among the first of the social organisations to be formed in Edgware was the Literary Society, founded in 1926 and still very active in 1939. Meetings, held in private houses, took the form of discussions, readings and debates, but for more important functions the Society used the Mornington School of Commerce. An amateur dramatic group came out of it in 1927, the leading light a lady resident in Heather Walk, the first president Frank Cross. In the early thirties, after moving from its original home in the Stanmore Institute to the more spacious Express Dairy Hall next to the Underground terminus, the Society was mounting about three plays each season. This new hall was shared with the Operatic Society, formed in 1929 by a lady who ran a school of music and dancing in her Edgware house. Completed in 1929 above the Dairy's shop, and enlarged in 1932, the hall was in great demand for social functions and meetings. Regular Saturday night dances were held there from June 1935. Three tennis clubs were operating in Edgware by this time, at The Drive (hard courts), at Whitchurch Gardens, and at Penshurst Gardens.

Founded in 1927 by the rector of Edgware and A. E. Watling, the Edgware Ratepayers' Association was an organisation much more active at some periods than at others. An early achievement was the defeat of a scheme by Cynodrome Ltd to open a greyhound-racing track between the two stations. The firm had purchased the 4-acre site in 1925 and intended to put up stands for 3,000 spectators. A third of the population petitioned against it, the RDC refused planning permission, and the Ministry of Health upheld the decision on appeal early in 1928. Another success, in 1933, was Hendon Council's agreement to the ERA's request that grass verges be laid wherever possible when roads were being made up.

The Association also successfully opposed the efforts of developers in 1935 to have the town plan varied to permit construction of houses at twelve instead of eight to the acre on the Broadfields Estate north of the Watford Bypass. In the early thirties member-ship fell to about 100, but a fresh injection of enthusiasm brought the total to almost 600 by the end of 1934 and to 1,430 four years later. When a Rotary Club was formed in March 1930, Leslie Raymond and A. W. Curton became the president and vice president. Curton also held office for many years as vice president of the Ratepayers' Association.

From July 1927, the district had its own newspaper, the *Edgware Gazette*. This was an edition of the *Golders Green Gazette*, itself dating only from November 1923. The new paper was at first published from the parent office, but an editorial office was opened in Station Road in October 1928. The much older, rather more staid *Hendon and Finchley Times* (later *Hendon Times and Borough Guardian*) also gave generous space to Edgware news.

The Arrival of the Jews
When considering the development of Golders Green, we noticed the tendency of middle-class Jews to settle in the north-western suburbs. This limited radial movement went on to Finchley and Hendon in the 1910s and 1920s, and it was not long before the new suburb at Edgware began to attract its first Jewish residents. In June 1929 an advertisement in the *Jewish Chronicle* suggested that the Jews in the district should come together to form a congrega-tion, and on the High Festivals that year, about fifty attended services in St Lawrence's church hall, Whitchurch Lane. Within twelve months, a Hebrew Congregation had been formed and the High Festival attendance had more than doubled.

In mid-1931 we find the local paper estimating that there were some 120 Jewish families in the district, perhaps 400 to 500 people in all, a figure which the journalist found 'fairly huge for a district so recently sprung into prominence'. If we accept these figures, and assume that the majority of the Jewish families were living east of the main road, within easy walking distance of the Underground station, it would seem that at this time some 10 per cent of the new residents of Edgware were Jewish.

Over 200 attended the High Festivals of 1933, and the Hebrew classes were then regularly attracting about forty children. Towards the end of that year, a building fund was started for a synagogue, encouraged by a gift of one third of an acre on the Watford Bypass from F. Howkins, the Golders Green estate agent. The £3,000 United Synagogue, designed by Mr Eprile, was consecrated on 2 September 1934, when Dr Hertz, the Chief Rabbi, said that it was gratifying to see that as the Jews dispersed from the East End 'and struck forth into the new and healthy suburbs' they did not forget their Judaism or their Yiddish life. Seven classrooms and a community hall were added in 1939 at a cost of £5,400. An audience of 700 attended a 1939 lecture in the Express Dairy Hall on 'The Jew in Europe and the Refugee Problem', organised in co-operation with Edgware's Christian churches. Addressing this meeting, Councillor Gilpin remarked upon Edgware's growing Jewish population and claimed that in no other district around London did Jew and Gentile live together so amicably.

Edgware at the end of the Thirties

In the last summer of peace, houses were still going up around the outskirts of Edgware, especially to the north, beyond the Watford Bypass, where Laing had plans to advance over the meadows towards Edgwarebury and Elstree. Close by, railway engineers had just started to construct the three-mile tube extension to Bushey Heath, with its intermediate stations at Brockley Hill (on the Bypass, near Edgwarebury Lane) and Elstree South (at the foot of Elstree Hill).[1] Much of the land required for this railway had been in the hands of the undertaking for many years, including a strip between the Bypass and Edgware station, which had been kept clear of housing to avoid any repetition of the expensive mistake at Golders Green. Although avowedly required to reach the only suitable site for the 553-car depot and the maintenance works needed to service the several Northern Line extensions included in the 1935 London Railway Development Plan, the new line would pass through an area which, within the borough of Hendon alone had room for another 7,000 houses, mostly at six and eight to the acre, an additional population of about 30,000.[2] A basis for this further expansion already existed; Laing, Taylor Woodrow and

[1] This extension had been authorised in 1937 and was to have been completed in 1941. Construction was suspended early in the war and never resumed. Work at Edgware station had started in 1937, and on the extension itself in June 1939. (See Alan A. Jackson, *The Railway Magazine*, February 1967, op. cit.)
[2] HTBG 29 January 1937.

others had firmly established a new district north of the Bypass; developments in the eastern parts of Stanmore and at Boreham Wood had justified conversion of the Edgware-Boreham Wood bus service to double-deck operation in the autumn of 1937; and to cope with increased traffic from North Edgware, this bus was diverted to provide a second service along Edgwarebury Lane when the former Edgware–Canons Park tramway was converted to trolleybus operation in 1938.

Some considerable anxiety existed in Edgware about this tube railway extension, which it was erroneously thought would further increase the already serious peak-hour overcrowding between Edgware station and central London. Figures had already been given to illustrate Edgware's rapid growth after 1935. Most earning adults travelled daily to London for about £1 a month (quarterly season rate), and by 1936 the railway between Edgware and Golders Green was carrying 24 million passengers a year, most of them in the rush hours. As early as 1929, the users of Golders Green station had protested at the lack of room left for them after heavy uptake at the outer stations, and although the remaining six-car trains were soon afterwards lengthened to seven cars, this was not enough. To accommodate the increase in trains terminating at and starting from Edgware, five more sidings and a third platform were built at the terminus in 1932. With this improvement, Edgware could turn around forty trains an hour, the absolute maximum that the signalling of the line could absorb. By 1936, despite these measures, the Edgware–Morden line was indisputably the busiest of all London's Underground railways and there was no sign of house construction abating at either end. Overcrowding of rush-hour trains led not only to discomfort, but to frustration when loading delays caused trains to be turned short of their advertised destination in order to restore the timetable. The row rose to a crescendo in 1937 when the various troubles of the line's passengers were well aired in the press. In the House of Commons a Labour M.P. called the conditions 'discreditable and disgraceful', spicing his remarks with the comment that young girls and men were pushed up together in such a fashion that 'even the question of decency arises'. Max Miller made a joke about it, but the pun required him to move the scene to the Piccadilly Line.

More seriously, a respected and conservative technical periodical, the *Railway Gazette*, was moved to remark upon 'the obvious inability' of the line to accommodate the increasing number of rush-hour passengers, adding somewhat ruefully that the results of the Underground's enterprise in extending into virgin territory had been to afford huge profits to land speculators and later to bring severe criticism upon its own head.

As an interim measure, some improvements were made to the line's power supply and to the rolling stock to permit acceleration of the service and insertion of additional rush hour trains (a number of them lengthened to nine cars, with special arrangements at the stations). Subsequently the opening of tube service through Highgate to Finchley and beyond reduced the pressure on Golders Green, and further relief came with the arrival of roomier rolling stock in 1938-9 and equalisation of fares between the Metropolitan and Underground lines in June 1939.

At the end of the thirties, the hopes of Edgware's pioneer developers had at last been fulfilled and there were confident expectations of further profits with the northward advance of the Underground to Bushey Heath. Well-pleased with their comfortable houses, the new residents were now finding travel to town a little easier, and Edgware seemed far enough away to offer some security from the German bombers that threatened. The new suburb was settling snugly in its shallow bowl, sheltered on three sides by the Stanmore-Mill Hill ridge, and appropriately oriented towards the city which had brought it to life.

Chapter 15

NEO-GEORGIAN CASE STUDIES: (2) SOUTHERN ELECTRIC STONELEIGH

A Sort of Fourth Estate

The slightly undulating clay farmlands south of the village of Malden, bordered on the west and south by the little Hogsmill river, and on the east by the Ewell–London road, attracted suburban development of a sort long before 1914. As early as 1865 the Landed Estates Company had purchased the mansion and grounds of Worcester Park, laying out The Avenue, which ran south-west from the station provided four years later with the opening of the Wimbledon and Epsom railway. The small middle-class community which occupied this estate was complemented by another, of labourers and servants, on the opposite side of the railway, a settlement encouraged by the 6d workman's return to Waterloo and cottage rents as low as 7s a week. H. G. Wells, who lived in the Avenue in the 1890s, put Worcester Park into his novel *Ann Veronica*, published in 1909. In this he mentioned the appearance of a new group of houses east of the railway in the early 1900s, following on after the Avenue, the Pavement (the shops serving the Avenue) and the workers' cottages, as a 'sort of fourth estate of little red and white rough-cast villas with meretricious gables and very brassy window blinds'. This was in fact the first wave of the great flood that was to wash southwards either side of the railway in the twenties and thirties.

At the time Wells' novel appeared, the ground was already prepared. The extensive Stoneleigh Estate, consisting of three farms (Worcester Park, Sparrow and Cold Harbour) was being offered for building purposes. It stretched eastwards from the Avenue settlement, across the railway as far as the London Road, and southwards to the Kingston Road and the outskirts of Ewell village.

Little interest was shown, and by 1909 only Park Avenue, at the extreme southern tip, had been laid out for building. A year or two later, Stoneleigh Drive (now Lynwood Road) was projected south-wards from Worcester Park station, alongside the railway. Plots in Park Avenue were auctioned from time to time, with an unenthusiastic response no doubt related to its distance from any public transport. At the end of the twenties there were still only about two dozen houses in this road, most of them dating from after 1920, together with a few more on estate land along the London Road, opposite Nonsuch Park. In its more convenient location, Stoneleigh Drive did rather better, but a quarter of a mile or so from Worcester Park station it petered out. In 1929 the fields and copses of the extensive Stoneleigh Estate looked much as they had done twenty years earlier.

Speculation Electrified
During the summer of 1925 the railway from Wimbledon through Worcester Park to Epsom had been electrified, receiving the usual Southern Electric regular interval service of three trains an hour throughout the day. At the same time, a new station, Motspur Park, had been opened to serve the suburban growth which was creeping south-westwards under nourishment from the railway and the Wimbledon-Kingston electric tramway.[1]

As this growth began to consolidate, and as Ewell Court and various other sites around the pretty village of Ewell received their first spattering of red tiles and pebbledash, the Stoneleigh Estate Company bestirred itself. Certain arrangements, to be mentioned in a moment, were set on foot in the summer of 1930, and on 1 August the following year, under the headline 'A New Suburb', the *Estates Gazette* announced that Sparrow and Worcester Park farms had been sold. The whole area of about 350 acres was covered by an Interim Development Order of Epsom RDC which provided for 24 acres of open space, some 3,000 houses (density lowest in the zone most distant from London) and an appropriate number of shops to serve them. During 1930 the RDC had instructed its engineers to prepare a drainage scheme for the area, but building work was to begin before the sewers were completed in 1933.

[1] The station called Motspur Park was opened on 12 July 1925. Its name was derived from a nearby farm, embellished with 'Park' by villa builders at the turn of the century.

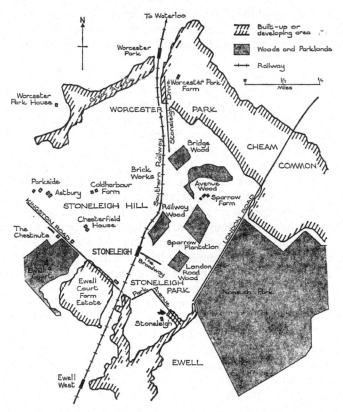

VI Stoneleigh, 1932

Little time was lost in realising the increment on what was now a most attractive proposition, and 353 acres in 'numerous convenient lots' were offered at the London Auction Mart on 22 September 1931.[1] Some sites went at over £400 an acre, but the most desirable section of about 200 acres, in the south-eastern corner, was to be developed as an entity by Messrs Atkinson and Marler. These agents first advertised frontages for sale to builders in January 1932, but construction of roads and main services on what was now called the Stonleigh Park Estate did not start until late that summer. By August 1933 the last of the building plots had been sold.[2]

A major ingredient in the successful disposal of Stoneleigh,

[1] TEG 5 September 1931. [2] TEG 2 January 1932; 5 August 1933.

coming on top of the Development Order and the drainage scheme, was the new railway station serving the Stoneleigh Park Estate. Negotiations for this had begun in June 1930 between the Southern Railway and the Stoneleigh Estate Company, but the agreement finally made in July 1931 was between the railway and the trustees of the late J. J. Stone. Under this, the landowners were to contribute £3,000 of the £7,550 cost, convey free of charge two pieces of land and provide access from the London and Kingston roads. In earnest of their intentions, Stone's trustees deposited a certificate for £1,000 of SR 5 per cent debenture stock. Situated close to the twelfth mile post from Waterloo at the point where the line from Worcester Park emerged from a cutting on to an embankment across the Hogsmill valley, this station, with its 520-foot island platform, was opened on 17 July 1932 before any serious work had begun in the surrounding fields. Naming had presented something of a problem; North Ewell, Court Farm and Nonsuch were considered and rejected, Stoneleigh Park was then adopted, but the second word was dropped before the opening to break the sequence of three Park stations already existing on this line.[1]

The new station was to become the natural focus of the suburb it was to serve, its catchment area embracing the whole of the Stoneleigh Park Estate east of the line, the district around Cold Harbour Farm on the west side (later to become the Stoneleigh Hill Estate), and all the new housing appearing along the Kingston Road and between that road and the Hogsmill (Ruxley Farm and Ewell Court). Within five years of its opening, all the pasture and woodland lying inside one mile's radius of its platforms had disappeared beneath bricks and concrete.

Stoneleigh Park

Work at the northern end of the Stoneleigh Estate began in the summer of 1932 when the trees of Bridge, Avenue and Railway Woods were felled to make way for new roads coming south from Worcester Park on the eastern side of the railway. Early in August, John Cronk had 64 houses completed alongside the railway in blocks of four, each house 18 feet wide by 25 feet deep, with three bedrooms and two reception rooms, selling at £525 freehold.

To the south, Atkinson and Marler's Stoneleigh Park Estate was started, under the direction of the firm's senior partner, G. L. C.

[1] BTHR SOU 1/18, 1/20, 1/25, CT 24 January 1931.

Paine. By October a beginning had been made with the Broadway, an 80-feet wide shopping street running east from the new station. Soon afterwards, residential roads were pasted over the meadows to the south, furnished with decorative arches at the points where they emerged on to the London and Kingston roads.[1] The narrow concrete estate roads, hemmed by minimal grass verges and tarmac or gravel footways, followed a somewhat erratic pattern; those north of the Broadway, coming a little later, formed a grid parallel to the railway.

The first houses appeared in Briarwood, Calverley and Kenilworth Roads south-east of the station, and in Rosedale Road to the east, during the spring of 1933. In September, Beric Ltd had semis in Woodstone Avenue at £765, £785 and £805, and a little later, two other firms were offering semis in Bradstock and Waverley Roads for £795, whilst a fourth was erecting semis with garage space at £775 and bungalows at £700. Many of these early houses were of the chalet type, with the main entrance facing that of the house adjoining. Activity was intense from the summer onwards, so that by the beginning of December 1933 over 725 houses and bungalows had been finished, with a further 232 in construction. Two years afterwards, a resident recalled his impressions on purchasing a house at this time:

'Immigrants in a strange land surrounded by shells of houses dotted here and there, stark ribbons of concrete where homes would one day be, heaps of bricks, timber and the miscellany of builders are to be seen everywhere, and bustling workmen darting about their varied jobs. A casual survey of the scene under the merciless rays of the hot summer sun of 1933 came as a rude reminder of those far-off days in Flanders. . . .'[2]

When this was written in the autumn of 1935, the Stoneleigh Park Estate was virtually complete, and the Epsom Council had taken over the last few roads for lighting, repair and cleansing.

Stoneleigh Hill and Ewell Court

Immediately west of the station was the area which became known as the Stoneleigh Hill Estate. This was developed by Atkinson and

[1] These arches were in need of repair after little more than four years. Epsom Council decided to meet the cost, deeming their retention desirable 'in the interests of the amenities'. They still stand.
[2] *The Resident* (SRA), November 1935.

Marler in similar fashion, with roads and services laid out before groups of plots were sold off to various builders. As a first step, the Stoneleigh Hill Estate Company was registered in June 1933, and six months later, work was sufficiently advanced to allow an invitation to 'progressive builders' to take frontages at £5 a foot upwards to appear in the *Estates Gazette*. Meanwhile, Messrs Berg and Dale, who had made an earlier start with the 'Station Estate' abutting the western side of the railway, were able to offer £795 semis at the beginning of November.

A uniform density of eight to the acre, combined with the slightly elevated situation, brought a nuance of superiority to this side of the railway, where prices tended in general to be a little higher. Apart from Mavis Avenue, where the semis of Cuddington Estates Ltd sold at £650–695 in 1937–8, Stoneleigh Hill houses cost anything from £725 to £1,150, with the majority in the £800–900 range. About twenty different builders were busy on the hill between 1934 and 1938, but a rather larger number of different styles and designs can be identified; most types of 'estate' construction are found, from the conventional 1930s semis to chalets and 'hallway to hallway' semis with integral garages, and there are also a few detached houses and some bungalows. With the exception of Wimpey's share of Walsingham Gardens, all were erected by quite small building firms attracted by the readymade sites. Typical of these was Sam Nove, offering 'Novean Homes' to 'families of good breeding who wish to acquire a house to be proud of at a cost of less than £1 a week' (Ravensfield Gardens, 1934). Competition was keen; bait held out on the hill included refrigerators and cash rewards to anyone introducing a sale. Although not all the houses were occupied, most of the construction was completed by 1938, when Epsom Council took over the remaining roads and provided them with street lighting.

South of the main Kingston Road, beyond the boundary of the Stoneleigh Estate, but within the area served by the station, was the extensive Ewell Court Estate, covered by Wimpey, J. J. Hodgson and others between 1932 and 1937. An advertisement for the Hammersmith firm's houses, painted on a wall, can still be discerned from the platform at Stoneleigh station, its message a memorial to the progress of inflation: 'You can buy a Wimpey Detached House for £728 freehold – 17/5 weekly 12 minutes from here'. To the north of Ewell Court, also on the east bank of the Hogsmill river, was the Ruxley Estate, mostly bungalows, developed by Atkinson and Marler between 1936 and 1939. On the Stoneleigh flanks of the Kingston Road, towards Tolworth, another major builder, Davis Estates, covered the extensive grounds of the Victorian mansion of Parkside in 1934–37, and between there and Worcester Park Road, the Tolworth Hall Estate appeared in 1934–38. Davis unsuccessfully appealed to the Ministry of Health under the 1932 Town Planning Act to be allowed to build at Parkside to a density higher than the six to the acre stipulated in the covenant. This defeat led to a pleasantly spacious little estate, its impact softened by preservation of many of the original trees.

Not all the residents of the Kingston Road area used Stoneleigh station. They enjoyed a frequent bus service to Epsom, Surbiton and Kingston, and, after the opening of the railway from Motspur Park in 1938, many living on the western fringes found Tolworth station more accessible. A further divisive influence was the Ewell Court Residents' Association, whose relationships with the Stoneleigh Association were not always harmonious.

Creating a Centre

Early attention was given to forming a shopping centre along the Broadway at Stoneleigh station. A block of 18 shops and flats on the south side between Kenilworth and Dell Roads had almost all been let by November 1933. Its 'Tudor Elevation' was the work of J. H. Coleman, AIAA, who also prepared sixteen house designs for the Stoneleigh Park Estate. A shop, with six-roomed flat above and storeplace at the rear could be rented at £175 a year. The second block, immediately west of the first, with fifteen units behind a frontage in debased classical style, was ready in 1934. This imposed a distinctly urban stamp on the new district, arousing some concern, and when a third smaller block in the earlier cottage style appeared west of the railway in the same year, the hope was expressed that enough was enough:

'It has been questioned in many directions as to whether it was a wise plan to place large blocks of shops in the midst of a purely residential district which, from all points of view, is a dead end. This doubt was accentuated by the addition of a second block with massive elevation totally out of keeping with the surroundings and adding an unwanted touch of suburbia.'[1]

[1] Ibid., December 1935.

Indeed. More will be heard of this disillusion later; it really is a tribute to the developer's skilful publicity in the early days of Stoneleigh.

A sub post office, shared with a confectioners', was opened in the first block in 1933, a Midland bank branch joining it next door on 12 March 1934, its mini Corinthian columns rather lost in the Tudor Elevations. When the nearby Cake Shop opened in June that year, the tiny tea room at the back quickly became Stoneleigh's first social centre. Here were held the fortnightly whist drives organised by the Resident's Association; here, amid tea and buns, the Stoneleigh and Ewell Motor Club held its first meeting in March 1935.

Undeterred by the romantics who saw their illusions fading fast, Atkinson and Marler arranged for the erection in 1937 of a further block of shops on the north side of the Broadway. A year later the four blocks were occupied by a total of 38 tradesmen, including no less than 8 grocers. Above the premises of the South Suburban Co-operative Society two dentists were busily drilling and pulling. The last year of the thirties saw the construction of a fifth range of shops at the eastern end of the Broadway, on the north side, in the same classical style as the 1934 block it faced. This attracted Woolworths, Stoneleigh's first multiple.

A second shopping complex grew up at the junction of Stoneleigh Park Road and the Kingston Road on the western side of the railway, continuing on both sides of the main road towards Tolworth. Completed between 1933 and 1935 this had 46 shops open for trading in 1938. Considered at the time slightly less select than the Broadway its facilities included a fried fish shop, a Canine Surgery and a branch of Barclays Bank.

The role of the Broadway as Stoneleigh's focal point was confirmed in March 1934 when the Epsom magistrates allowed a provisional licence for a public house, to be built on the south side against the railway line. In support of their application, Truman, Hanbury and Buxton, the brewers, outlined the rapid development of the district, claiming that there were already 2,080 houses within half a mile of the station. They illustrated their case with a selection of aerial photographs taken at various stages in the construction of the suburb, photographs which caused Mr Tudor Rees to comment that they were 'very pathetic comparisons of beauty'. The £20,000 Stoneleigh Hotel, on its 1-acre site, was ready on 4 November 1935. Built in the fashionable mock Tudor style it was a *superpub* to match the supercinema also promised. Apart from the usual bars and off licence, it included a restaurant, a billiard room, and a large hall for meetings, receptions and dances. This room, which comfortably accommodated about 150, provided a much needed social centre, although before long it was too small for some functions. One native of the area has recalled to the author that the opening of the Hotel, with its hall and its dancing lessons, provided a rendezvous at which the young people of Ewell village could exploit the great crowd of new partners of the opposite sex brought to them by the advent of Stoneleigh.

Stoneleigh could not raise its head as a suburb until it possessed its own cinema. The 1934 Worcester Park Odeon and the 1937 Granada at North Cheam, with its 2,000 seats were not enough. A builder named Lavender had been hopefully nursing a plot opposite the Stoneleigh hotel, but could not attract a buyer, probably because it was too small; at any rate, he was overtaken by Mrs Thompson, proprietress of Epsom's Court Cinema, who with J. Gardner, negotiated the purchase of a plot in Kingston Road next to the railway bridge and shopping centre. After some old wooden farm cottages had been demolished there quickly appeared the large Rembrandt cinema, which was ready for opening in October 1938. Designed by E. Norman Bailey, with elevations of pale cream artificial stone broken up by the large plate-glass windows of the first floor café, this building had a capacious foyer with period fireplace and matching furniture, and a rose pink auditorium filled with 1,500 seats. Stoneleigh was complete.

Church and School
Facilities for education and Christian worship had already been established. First in the field with the latter were Baptists, whose hall in Chadacre Road, Stoneleigh Park was opened in September 1935. Methodists began by worshipping in each other's houses, moving into the hall of Stoneleigh West School when this was available in 1937. Proposals for a dual-purpose church and social hall in Stoneleigh Crescent met with objections from neighbouring residents, presumably because they did not want the traffic it would bring to a quiet road. They petitioned the Epsom Council, but a counter petition outnumbered theirs and the £6,000 building was completed early in February 1938.[1] Both Baptists and

[1] Information from the Rev. Cecil H. Smith, Stoneleigh Methodist Church.

Methodists prudently acquired enough land for the churches they hoped to have later, but neither of these was completed until after World War II.

A small red-brick hall in Dell Lane behind the Broadway shops served the needs of the first Anglicans from July 1936. Its dedication to St John the Baptist was carried over to the church, which was opened in May 1939. A plain red-brick building, with 300 seats, designed by Professor A. B. Knapp-Fisher, this was situated on the west side of the railway, right against the station. Its stumpy tower was not finished until after the war.

Roman Catholics received their 200-seat church (St Clement, Kingston Road) in 1937 and the 300-seat Congregational church in London Road was opened in the same year.

Two large schools were quickly provided by the Surrey County Council. A temporary Junior Mixed was opened in Sparrow Farm Road in January 1934, and the Stoneleigh East Council School, the permanent structure, with room for 384 children, followed on the 5-acre site on 27 October. On the other side of the railway, Stoneleigh West School, catering for infants, junior girls and senior boys and girls, also dated from 1937. Situated at the northern end of Newbury Gardens, it had 8½ acres of playing fields, a cookery classroom, a science laboratory and a medical room; the junior department was staffed by a headmistress and seven teachers, the senior by a headmaster and ten others. Those who preferred the special blessings of private education were invited to send their boys to Ewell Castle and their girls to Bourne Hall, where for a fee of 5-guineas a term they would be taught from junior level to university entry. A kindergarten and preparatory school, appropriately named 'The Tudor' was started in a house in Seaforth Gardens early in 1937 by a lady with B.A.(Hons).

Barricaded about by the close ranks of the spec. builders' houses, a precious 25 acres of Sparrow Farm were preserved for posterity as Cuddington Recreation Ground. Although some of the original trees remained, together with a stream, this land inevitably assumed a rather sad and trapped appearance, neither country field nor town park. A much more valuable and extensive open space available to Stoneleigh residents on this side of the railway was Nonsuch Park, fronting the Ewell–London Road. This was rescued from the threat of building development in 1937 by the combined efforts of local residents, the Epsom and Sutton councils and the Surrey and London County Councils, the latter purchasing it with Green Belt funds. West of the railway, Epsom Council secured the 15-acre Auriol Park (at the top of Stoneleigh Hill) in 1937.

Organising the Residents

At the start, Stoneleigh was wholly within the boundary of the Epsom RDC, a fact which undoubtedly eased its rapid conversion from farmlands to suburb. When the RDC disappeared under the 1933 Surrey Review Order, the larger part of the new district went to the Epsom UDC (later the Borough of Epsom and Ewell), whilst the balance, north of Sparrow Farm Road, was allocated to the Sutton and Cheam UDC. Despite the fact that the road layout had already been fixed, the boundary between these two authorities followed the farm hedgerows, a little piece of myopic bumbledom soon to create several problems, including different rateable values for adjacent houses of exactly similar type.

This new boundary very broadly coincided with that of the Stoneleigh Park Estate, leaving to Sutton and Cheam the slightly cheaper, more densely spaced housing immediately to the north. West of the railway there was no similar political division, but the existence of the Worcester Park Brickworks, together with the large area taken for new schools at the summit of Stoneleigh Hill created a no-man's-land almost exactly at the watershed between Stoneleigh and Worcester Park stations. And, to the south and west, the Hogsmill river, the old village of Ewell, and Nonsuch Park combined to form an effective barrier which corresponded more or less precisely with the limits of the southern catchment area of Stoneleigh station. Not many of the new London suburbs enjoyed such clearly defined geographical identity. It was to be one factor in Stoneleigh's relatively smooth progress towards social cohesion; another, more important, was the dynamic residents' association.

In March 1933 the first organisation of this kind was formed with the support of the builder John G. Cronk, who took the chair at the initial meeting. Almost immediately the Stoneleigh Park Residents' Association had a row on its hands.

Those who lived at the Worcester Park end of Stoneleigh Drive (now Lynwood Drive), not at all pleased to find themselves in the same road as Cronk's terraces of small houses, issued a summons against the Sutton and Cheam Council regarding the naming of the continuation road. An extended correspondence published in the local press stirred the pot; the grievance was simply that the older houses had cost their owners £1,000 and £1,250 (in more expensive times) and their rateable values were £38 or more, whilst Cronk's four-blocks sold at a mere £525 with a rateable value of only £28. This was thought certain to bring down the value of the earlier houses, especially if they were included in the same road. As all Englishmen know, to rename a thing is to make it something quite different, so the Council wisely compromised by calling the new section Stoneleigh Avenue, a decision upheld by the magistrates. Dissatisfied, the aggrieved parties eventually secured the further change which made their part Lynwood Avenue, thus comfortably severing all connection with the newcomers.

Meanwhile, the Residents' Association membership had increased from 120 to over 600 and the new administrative boundaries were forcing a regrouping. This came in October 1933 with the formation of a Stoneleigh Residents' Association and Social Club to take care of that part of the new suburb within the Epsom Council area. A vigorous group, soon to dominate the scene, it was backed by Howard Browne, proprietor of the short-lived *Epsom and Ewell Times*, whose first issue appeared in the same month. A doctor living in Glenwood Road accepted the chairmanship, the secretary was a surveyor in the employ of Atkinson and Marler, and the treasurer was the Broadway newsagent, C. J. Uncles. Browne gave the new body plenty of space in his newspaper, which was published at Worcester Park and later renamed the *Stoneleigh Times and Epsom Courier and Ewell Times*.

After a short time, the SRA was reorganised, taking a form more representative of the residents. Active members and officers then included bank and local government officials, civil servants and chartered secretaries drawn from the new community, and such was the effort devoted to its work that the membership, which stood at 600 at the beginning of 1936 reached 900 in the following year and about 1,400 by mid-1939, when it was claimed as the largest organisation of its kind in Surrey. With the backing of the SRA, one of the vice-chairmen, a junior civil servant named A. J. Smith, was elected for the North Ward in the council elections of 1935.

By the end of 1936, this ward, which included the whole of the Epsom part of Stoneleigh, constituted almost a quarter of the total electorate of Epsom and Ewell, but was represented by only three councillors. In that year, new ward boundaries were drawn: a

VII Stoneleigh, 1939

Stoneleigh ward covering the Stoneleigh Park Estate; a Cuddington
ward for most of the area west of the railway, and a Ewell Court
ward for the remainder of Stoneleigh south of the Kingston road.
When the first elections were held for the new Epsom and Ewell
Borough Council in 1937, all three of the SRA candidates for the
Stoneleigh ward were successful and similar victories were gained
in the Cuddington ward, with the co-operation of the Cuddington
Residents' Association. A year later, residents' association candidates in all three Stoneleigh wards secured election, each with over
a thousand votes, the highest individual totals in the whole
borough.

Social activities organised by the SRA included whist drives,
dances, cricket, children's parties and keep-fit classes. The association also nurtured the Stoneleigh Orchestra (1934), a motoring
club (1935), the Stoneleigh Cricket Club (1935), a snooker club

(1936), a choral society (1936), and the Stoneleigh Wheelers, a cycling club (1937). Tennis, always popular in pre-war suburban London, flourished under independent auspices; a hard-court club established in 1934 moved four years later to a site at the corner of Seaforth and Amberley Gardens where the four courts were served by a pavilion shared with the Stoneleigh Dance Club. In 1939, the SDC, in intervals between the main business, was enjoying the pavilion's 'bar-lounge', which was enlivened by 'music from the radiogram'.

By far the most important task of the SRA, well publicised in Browne's newspaper and the Association's own sheet, *The Resident*,[1] was the constant struggle to improve the amenities of the new district. Such matters as street services, lighting, trading from private houses, a branch library, stamp machines, postboxes, telephone boxes and a new footpath under the railway to strengthen the link between the two sides[2] were taken by the SRA in its stride, leaving plenty of energy over for the subject of railway accommodation, a topic which provided enough business to justify a subcommittee.

The Battle with Waterloo

Between 1934 and 1939 the SRA carried on almost continuous skirmishing with the Southern Railway Company, reinforced on its northern flank by the two residents' associations covering the Worcester Park area. In July 1934, the SRA was already complaining of 'gross overcrowding' on trains leaving Stoneleigh station between 7.23 a.m. and 8.45 a.m., and on the down trains from Waterloo between 5.25 p.m. and 6.25 p.m. Inward, the crush began at Worcester Park, beyond which point five standing was the rule in the Third Class compartments. A major grumble was the inclusion in all trains of little-used First Class accommodation, another the inconsistent amounts of Third Class seating available. For example, in June 1934 on the same eight-car train on different days there were 78, 60, 65 and 78 First Class seats, whilst Third Class seats numbered 540, 470, 480, and 540. A count by the SRA in 1935 showed that only about 2 per cent of Stoneleigh passengers bought First Class tickets, and on the busiest trains the First Class passengers

---

[1] Published monthly from October 1935 at 2d a copy.
[2] Provided by the efforts of the SRA, but subsequently maintained by the council.

averaged only three per compartment. No doubt they would have argued that this was what they paid for.

Additional rush-hour trains were eventually provided to relieve the mounting traffic from Stoneleigh and Worcester Park, notably after installation of colour light signalling between Raynes Park and Waterloo and the 1936 flyover at Wimbledon had given the required extra line capacity. Monday to Friday up trains between 8 a.m. and 9 a.m. from Stoneleigh were increased from four in 1932 to five in 1934 and finally seven in July 1936, and there were corresponding additions to the down service in the evening. After July 1936 some trains ran fast between Motspur Park and Waterloo, which was reached in twenty-three minutes from Stoneleigh; in 1938 some rush-hour trains took only twenty-one minutes.

But the SRA was not content with the 1936 improvements. The retention of First Class accommodation still rankled. One day in April 1937, representatives of the Association established that the 8.7 a.m. from Stoneleigh had only fifteen First Class passengers spread over six compartments at the rear when it left Wimbledon, whilst Third Class passengers to equal number were squeezing themselves into one compartment elsewhere on the train. This conjures up a picture of the intrepid observers, notebooks in hand, clambering along the footboards as the train rushed towards Waterloo, devotedly totting up heads at peril of a messy death. But of course it was not like that, nor was the report entirely fair in its implication that every Third Class compartment on the train was equally overcrowded. No doubt, as ever, the train was unequally loaded, well-packed towards the front by those who from sheer obstinacy, or blind habit, gave absolute priority to getting as close as possible to the exits at the terminus.

Further relief for Stoneleigh's commuters came with the opening of the new railway to Chessington in 1938–9, after which many passengers used Malden Manor station instead of Worcester Park, whilst some in the far west of Stoneleigh made their way to Tolworth. Later, with the arrival of new and roomier rolling stock and the abolition of suburban First Class facilities in 1940, travelling on this line became much more tolerable.

The rapid growth of traffic at Stoneleigh soon overtaxed the single island platform, served by its narrow open footbridge. A count made in 1935 by the SRA found 1,500 passengers leaving for London on the seven trains between 7.20 a.m. and 8.40 a.m., 350 of them on one train (the 8.40). In the evening rush, when the staircase and bridge slowed down the clearance of the platform, getting *into* the station required a strong physique and much determination. An SRA campaign for a larger station eventually met with some success; after making minor improvements in 1936, the SR rebuilt the bridge, moving it to the south end of the platform so that a full-width staircase could be provided. The new covered bridge was big enough to accommodate a booking office and waiting space opposite a ticket barrier at the top of the stairs. Although there was no right of way, the public were allowed to cross the bridge whilst the station was open for traffic. Just before this work was finished in 1939, with the suburb virtually completed, the number of people using the station daily was well over 3,000.

One benefit of residence in the southern suburbs was a generous provision of cheap through trains to seaside resorts during the summer. At Whitsun 1935, Stoneleigh had through trains to Brighton (4s 3d return) and to Bognor (4s 6d), whilst in June 1937 a Sunday through train to Littlehampton offered a return trip for only 4s. These excursions, which also ran on Thursdays, called at all stations from Raynes Park to Epsom to pick up the bucket-and-spade traffic. Other specials serving Stoneleigh included trains which ran direct to the Army displays at Aldershot at a fare of 4s 9d return, including admission to the Tattoo.

As we have seen, this was very much a railway suburb, the double track forming its spine, the station its heart. But the line also split the community into two parts linked by only two footways. This feature, together with roads rendered unsuitable for bus operation by their layout and restricted width, confined public road transport to the main roads at the periphery. To the east, the London Road had General route 70 (Morden Underground–Epsom–Dorking) and every fifteen minutes, a Green Line coach, operating between Oxford Circus and Dorking. Through road/rail season tickets were issued to London Underground stations via service 70 and Morden station, and a fare stage was established at Nonsuch Park gates in 1935 after representations by the SRA. Along the Kingston Road, to the west, there were bus services to Tolworth, Surbiton and Kingston in one direction and Epsom and Redhill in the other.

Intention and Reality
Atkinson and Marler's 1932 publicity brochure for Stoneleigh

18. Southern suburban design: Chessington North (opened 1939).

Underground suburban design (1): South Harrow (opened 1935). (Photo: London Transport (1936).)

Underground suburban design (2): Elegance at Arnos Grove. Dr Charles Holden's station of 1932. (Photo: London Transport.)

17. The Metropolitan colonises Ickenham. No commuters could be found when this photograph was taken at the newly opened halt in 1905. (Source unknown.)

Builders' station: Shooters Hill and Eltham Park, ready for opening in 1908. (From a commercial postcard.)

Park had promised houses 'dignified and individualistic to gaze upon', set in idyllic surroundings where:

'the green grass is not banished from the sidewalks; where in spring the trill of the lark may accompany the worker as he walks to the station; where the air is clean and fresh and nature's own lifegiving decoction. ... It is at such places as Stoneleigh Park that the ideal of individuality is so intensely realised. A street in a town is just like any other street, and a house just like any other house. But at Stoneleigh every street and house is distinctive ... the creators of the place ... have taken pains to see that there should be no mass, impersonal effects, but that every latitude should be given for character and personality to spread themselves.'

To the extent that an exceptionally large number of building firms contributed to Stoneleigh, giving it a considerable variety of conventional house designs, these promises were realised. But the unsure handling of the road layout, the failure to make imaginative use of the undulating site, with its views towards Epsom Downs, the almost complete destruction of existing timber and boscage, the regular building lines, and the ponderous shopping parades, gave the new district a townscape virtually indistinguishable from any other London suburb of the period. If anyone had thought it might be otherwise, they were quickly disappointed. Expressions of disillusion appeared in the local press as early as 1935:

'These people have been lured here by tempting advertisements about living in the country. By coming here in thousands they have defeated their own object – the country has disappeared – a new suburb has been built, and the true gainers are the builders, estate agents and the multiple-shop owners.'

A year later, another correspondent was complaining that instead of the promised new model self-contained town, 'our hoped-for Utopia has become a dull, soulless dormitory for London workers'.

At this time professional consciences were stirring, beginning to realise the great ugliness of the unrestricted, unplanned growth of London and voicing misgivings; Stoneleigh, which seemed a fair example, was chosen in June 1934 by the *Architects' Journal*. Two aerial photographs, one taken in October 1932 before any houses had been built and another in February 1934, were dramatically brought together to illustrate the effect of speculative building on London's countryside:

'a kind of development in which neither the seclusion of rural nor the convenience of urban living are provided, and the maximum amount of desirable countryside is spoilt, both for the dweller in it, and the townsman desiring access to it. Existing trees, it appears have not even been preserved in the surviving open spaces where preservation could only have been a question of forethought.'

Atkinson and Marler bravely fought back with some rather pathetic little snapshots of their occasional efforts to spare trees, arguing that the second of the aerial photographs was taken in winter when trees did not show up well from above.

Stoneleigh's faults, already sketched, are fairly characteristic of London suburban development of the twenties and thirties, but its road layout was especially perverse. The obvious and logical road crossing at the station which would have given the suburb greater unity and welded together the main shopping and social centre, was ignored by developers anxious to secure profit from the land right up to the fences each side of the line. On the east, only about a third of the roads had anything like direct access to the centre and the station, whilst on the west, straightforward approach to the centre or to the main Kingston–Epsom road was quite impossible from the majority of the houses.

Yet, despite all its blemishes, Stoneleigh has evolved to a not unattractive, restful, maturity. Mercifully preserved from the worst excesses of modern motor traffic by its quaint road layout, it has not quite lost its rurality. Here and there, some of the old farmland trees can be seen, and in high summer, the quarter-mile cutting north of the station is crowded with wild flowers; viewed from the low angle of a railway compartment, the trees and bushes of these banks, residue of Railway Wood and the copses of Coldharbour Farm, obscure everything that man has placed here since 1932.

Chapter 16

NEO-GEORGIAN CASE STUDIES: (3) THE LCC COTTAGE ESTATES

Becontree: A Town without Work or Transport

By far the largest of all the estates developed by the London County Council was that known as Becontree, a name chosen as a compromise for a site which spread over the boundaries of three local authorities (Ilford, Barking and Dagenham). In size, if not in amenities, social life and sources of employment, this was indeed a town (the 1931 census found it already larger than Darlington or Bath), covering some four square miles of flat and fertile market-gardening land between the Thames and Chadwell Heath. By the end of the thirties, its population had reached about 116,000, accommodated in 25,769 dwellings, most of them three- to five-room cottages.

At its northernmost point, Becontree came within a few hundred yards of Chadwell Heath station on the LNER line from Liverpool Street to Ipswich; the Fenchurch Street–Southend railway passed through the southern section without a station; below this, the main highway from Barking to Rainham, Ripple Road, ran across; and along the southern edge was the Barking to Tilbury railway, with a station at Dagenham Dock about half a mile from the south-east corner of the estate. The plan provided for ring roads through the outermost sections, and at the centre an inverted Y of through roads to connect the existing railway stations; the trunk of this Y (Valence Avenue, running south from Chadwell Heath) and the branch towards Barking were each to be 100 feet wide with median strips suitable for a double-track electric tramway. Other through roads were to be 60 feet and Ripple Road would be widened to 80 feet. South of Longbridge Road and Wood Lane, the planners left a broad east-west strip for a new electric railway across the estate.

Despite all this, the many residents obliged to travel London-wards to work were to suffer years of inadequate public transport. Although the local authorities had warned that new railway facilities were a prerequisite, and the Ministry of Transport had asked the LCC to consider this factor before making a start, the Ministry of Health, anxious to get as many houses as possible built under the 1919 Act, rode roughshod over all, pressing hard for work to begin. They had their way.

Some slight grounds existed for expecting improved railway services. When the Midland Railway had taken over the Southend line in 1912, they had accepted an obligation to prepare an electrification scheme, and in 1919, the Underground's Frank Pick had virtually promised a parliamentary committee that when the line was electrified, District Railway trains would use it beyond Barking. In the event, Becontree had to wait twelve years for its electric trains, and the LCC's hopes of linking the estate to the Ilford and Barking tramway systems were never realised, as we shall see when we return to the transport scene in a moment.

Construction of the estate started in September 1920 under the main contractors, C. J. Wills and Sons Ltd, work continuing almost without a break until 1938. Some houses in the first section, at the north-west corner of the site, were ready for occupation in the winter of 1921 and the whole of this portion was completed in 1925. After some initial troubles, a satisfactory output was reached, so that by 1927 a labour force of around 6,000 was erecting some hundred houses a week, with 12,130 completed by the end of that year. The late twenties were the peak period for activity, and in 1932, with the estate assuming final shape, there were 17,874 houses and flats occupied by about 83,000 people.

Towards the end of the thirties, a site of 32 acres in the Gale Street district was used for 800 houses of larger type intended for letting at remunerative rents to the highest-paid workers. As some of these were built by firms which had erected houses for sale in the London area (M. J. Gleeson, and Henry Boot and Sons), it is not surprising to find their elevations, with their curved bays and corner windows, almost indistinguishable from contemporary private construction.

Work at Becontree was aided by the geography of the site. The land acquired by the LCC ran gently down to the north bank of the

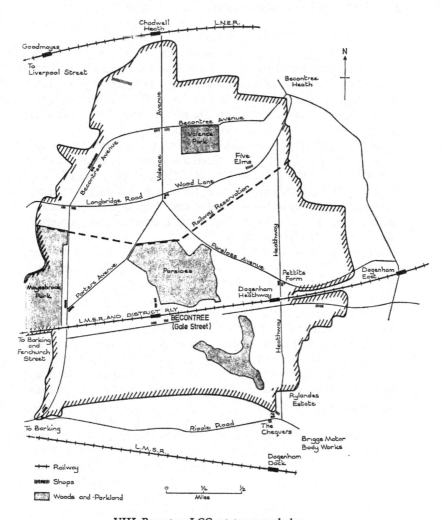

VIII Becontree LCC estate: general plan

Thames, where a 500-foot jetty equipped with four 5-ton steam cranes handled waterborne deliveries of building materials. From here, a standard gauge steam railway passed through the centre of the estate to a junction with the LNER at Chadwell Heath, enabling materials arriving by rail or water to be delivered direct to each zone of building activity. The estate railway also served block yards manufacturing concrete slabs and a well-equipped machine shop where cranes, locomotives and other construction plant were maintained. Some idea of the immensity of the Becontree project can be gained from the fact that by the end of 1927 38 miles of roads and 80 miles of sewers had been laid out.

With an almost complete lack of local employment opportunities, virtually all the original tenants faced a long journey to work. This was a fairly standard feature of the LCC cottage estates of the twenties, but particularly severe at Becontree, not only by reason of the estate's immense size, but because there was no significant amount of local employment available until about fifteen years after the arrival of the first residents.

The early houses were within reasonable walking or cycling distance of Chadwell Heath and Goodmayes stations, where some twenty-two trains were available inwards between 4 a.m. and 10 a.m., but these trains became increasingly crowded as private building expanded districts further out such as Gidea Park, Harold Wood and Romford. Conditions for the pioneer settlers at Becontree eased a little with the introduction in December 1922 of an eight-minute-interval bus service from Green Lane, Becontree to Ilford, whence there were additional trains to London as well as trams and buses to East and West Ham. Bus service was strengthened in 1924 and by that summer there was an alternative route into Ilford, giving a combined frequency of twenty buses an hour; there was also a seven-and-a-half minute service to Barking Broadway, where a change could be made to trams for East and West Ham or the District trains to the East End and the City.

Less fortunate were the first tenants of the central and southern zones of the estate, obliged to make their way over muddy roads and paths to Dagenham or Dagenham Dock stations where they found a somewhat sporadic service to Barking and Fenchurch Street. Some alleviation came in 1924 with a bus every fifteen minutes along Ripple Road into Barking. A further small mercy was the opening on 28 June 1926 of Gale Street Halt, sited on the estate just west of Dagenham station. Shortly after this, the LMSR made some improvements in the train service, but there was no road service to the Halt.

Until May 1927 there was no north–south bus through the estate. In that month a new route along Heathway brought all three LMSR stations within walking distance of public road transport. Two years later, this road was covered by an extension of LGOC route 148 running every ten minutes from Leytonstone to Dagenham (Chequers) via Wood Lane.

Although the LCC had offered to give all necessary land if the District Railway were extended from Barking into the estate, the cost of acquiring the remainder of the route and the equipment deterred the Underground Company from making a start on a line destined to carry little beyond twice-daily peak hour flows of workmen's trains. Equally there was no stampede by private enterprise to support a 1925 proposal for a Kearney Monorail tube between Becontree and London.

High-speed tramways on the estate were first mooted by the LCC in 1920, when it was suggested that Ilford might extend from its terminus at Chadwell Heath over the Dagenham boundary and southwards across Becontree, returning west along Ripple Road to join the Barking system at East Street. Neither Ilford nor Barking councils showed the slightest enthusiasm for this plan, but when it was revived in 1928 by the Metropolitan Tramways Council there was some mild support from Barking. Difficulties with Ilford (whose council always evinced a staunchly independent attitude towards matters metropolitan), coupled with the belated emergence of a firm plan to electrify the LMSR beyond Barking weakened any further interest in the tramway scheme. The electrification of the railway provided the London and Home Counties Traffic Advisory Committee, who had shown some interest in Becontree's needs, with an excuse to defer other ideas.

The construction of a second pair of tracks between Barking and Upminster for use by District electric trains, made possible by government assistance under the Development (Loan Guarantees and Grants) Act, 1929, gave the estate a fair measure of the transport facilities it so badly needed. Gale Street Halt was rebuilt as Becontree station, opening on 18 July 1932, and a new station, Heathway, between Becontree and Dagenham, was provided for the opening of the new service on 12 December. Dagenham station itself was enlarged and modernised.

On the evening before the electric service started, the booking office at Heathway was besieged by a large crowd, and by closing time, the clerks had sold over 2,000 workmen's tickets.[1] The District Line soon became the favoured route to East and West Ham as well as to London, leaving the buses to subsist on short-distance traffic. Charing Cross was brought within forty-one minutes of the estate compared with seventy-five before, and there were numerous trains (thirty-three inwards between 5.30 a.m. and 9.45 a.m. soon after the opening).

As most of the central and southern parts of Becontree were now within reasonable walking distance of a railway station, there was less to pay in fares. A workman could get to the City for 9½d return, only ½d more than his opposite numbers at Downham or Bellingham paid, and only a penny more than from Norbury or St Helier. Without surprise, we can note Lord Ashfield's complaint of 1934 about the difficulty of getting an adequate return on the capital for this extension; the Upminster line, he revealed, lifted 40 per cent of its daily traffic in a single peak hour, compared with a maximum of 26 per cent elsewhere on the Underground.[2]

Although the Sterling Engineering Works at Dagenham Dock took on a few Becontree men, and a steel-rope plant was opened there in June 1927, in general the area round the estate remained without industry for over ten years, so that 1931 found less than one third of the occupied residents working within five miles of their homes. It was in that year that a dramatic change took place in the industrial balance, although the immediate impact of the arrival of the Ford Motor Company at Dagenham Dock was minimal. This was because both Ford and the associated Brigg's Bodies and Kelsey Hayes Wheel companies brought most of their work force with them from Manchester and in any case had no requirement for large numbers of unskilled men. Lacking the necessary residential qualifications, the Mancunian immigrants were of course unable to get houses on the LCC estate, but Richard Costain and Sons helped out with their Rylandes Farm Estate (1931–4), opposite Brigg's new factory. This had three-bedroom houses in blocks or semis, the latter selling at £795 with garage.

The importance of the arrival of Ford was that it acted as a catalyst. Industrial development around Becontree was afterwards rapid and in 1937 an *Evening News* investigator found firms making drugs, refrigerators, accumulators, toys, hosiery and footwear with-

[1] Terence Young, *Becontree and Dagenham*, Pilgrim Trust, 1934.
[2] In a speech to students at the London School of Economics, 5 March 1934.

in a short distance of the estate, some of these no doubt using female labour from Becontree. But still the amount of travel to work remained high; of 22,505 tenants questioned by the LCC at the end of 1937, 61 per cent worked in central London, 25 per cent in the area of the estate, and 10 per cent between Becontree and London; 14,493 members of tenants' families were at work, 58 per cent in London, 36 per cent locally.[1]

During the first ten years or so, a typical Becontree household comprised husband and wife between thirty and forty years old, with three or four children, the adults originating from the East End of London, though not the most overcrowded areas. Almost all the inhabitants were from the upper strata of the working-class, employed in manufacturing or transport; among the latter were many busmen, whose relatively high wages and permanency of employment made them a particularly stable element, always prominent in the organisation of community activities.

Very much a one-class estate, Becontree had few problems of social friction, but because it was so extensive and diffuse, and unlike some other LCC 'out-county' estates, was not welded to unity by middle-class encirclement, a sense of community grew with difficulty. A tenants' association was formed in 1924, but its monthly magazine died in 1929 after only two years' life. Some sterling social work was done by outsiders at a centre established in 1929 at Pettits' Farm, Heathway. Later this became the focus for over thirty educational, cultural and social organisations.

As in all working-class communities, the public house played a major role in social life. Four country beer houses included in the land annexed by the LCC soon became overcrowded, so much so that drinkers were forced to mingle with the waiting children outside, exposing them to rowdiness, bad language and fighting, a state of affairs which soon brought complaints from the self-appointed guardians of morals and good behaviour. Although not noticeably enthusiastic in encouraging the development of community life on its inter-war estates, the council was obliged to take the drink question seriously. After due deliberation, it was announced that the four beer houses would be rebuilt and two new establishments would be added; they were to be neither 'public houses', 'inns' nor 'hotels' but 'licensed refreshment houses', conforming to strict requirements of design, management and use. Under the terms of lease these buildings were to be 'for the general

[1] RCGDIP, minutes 16 February 1938, 27.

entertainment and refreshment of the population' and no employees of the lessees were to have direct pecuniary interest in what the
LCC unappetisingly referred to as 'alcoholic liquor'. The Council
would retain the freeholds, charging a ground rent to the managers,
normally one of the major breweries. Instead of 'bars' there were to
be 'refreshment rooms' with plenty of seats, and spacious dining-
rooms, which would also serve for meetings and social gatherings.
The first of these houses at Becontree was the rebuilt Church Elm,
of 1927, with its light refreshment bar, dance hall and public
dining-room. As the estate neared completion in the late thirties
there were nine 'improved' or completely new refreshment houses
open.

But even on the higher than average Becontree incomes, heavy
drinking and the attendant betting could not be maintained through
the week without some recourse to 'uncle'. Young mentions that in
the twenties the 9.30 a.m. buses on Mondays from both the Church
Elm and the Five Elms stops were filled with women carrying
bundles to pawn at Barking. This journey was rendered unneces-
sary with the opening of a pawnshop in Dagenham in 1931.[1]

Despite its great size, Becontree had no hospital, but when the
Ilford Cottage Hospital was rebuilt as the King George General
Hospital in 1931, the LCC offered a £10,000 grant in recognition
of the demands that would be made upon it by the estate residents.
In that year, the King George opened an outpatients' clinic near
the Five Elms, on a site leased from the LCC at a peppercorn rent,
after the council had contributed £6,500 towards the cost of the
building and equipment. At the end of the thirties there were
fourteen doctors in residential practice on the estate, roughly one
to every 8,300 inhabitants.

The social centre mentioned earlier, 4 large cinemas, 27 places of
worship and a greyhound-racing track catered for other needs.
Shops were distributed fairly evenly over the estate area, eventually numbering about 400, sited in 15 different centres and supplemented by a large number of street traders, who followed their
customers to this and other LCC estates. Shops were usually built
by private enterprise; in 1928 J. G. Tilley had some advertised at
£1,600 (£400 deposit, seventeen years to pay), averring that a
hundred had been sold in the previous eighteen months.[2]

Education facilities were a major problem in the early years,
beyond the power of the LCC to remedy. There was nothing until

[1] Young, op. cit. [2] EN 13 June 1928.

September 1923, when Essex County Council opened a primary school in Chitty's Lane. Before then, with virtually no places available in existing schools, the children of the Becontree tenants ran wild all day, no doubt having a marvellous time on and around the building sites and estate railways. Serious overcrowding of primary schools persisted until 1930, whilst the secondary education provided by the Essex County Council was for many years considered by the LCC to be not only inadequate, but below its own very high standards. Eventually the completed estate was furnished with 30 schools.

Of the 2,770 acres retained for development, 505 were set aside for recreational open space. The principal areas were Parsloes Park (surrounding the farm of that name, and opened in July 1935), Mayesbrook Park (on the west side), and Valence House Park (in the north).

Concentration of LCC housing on the Becontree scale was not repeated elsewhere, nor were the problems it created ever forgotten at County Hall. But despite the best efforts of the County Council to move the responsible authorities, because the LCC could never obtain statutory powers to deal with such matters as transport and education on estates outside its boundaries, it was not always possible to avoid the same difficulties and deficiencies. A brief survey of the other 1919-39 cottage developments will complete the picture.

Bellingham: or starving stations succoured
The 250-acre Bellingham estate, located in the fork formed by the confluence of the Catford Loop and Mid-Kent railways, just south of Catford, was begun under the 1919 Act, work starting in October 1920. After three years, the contractors, Sir Robert McAlpine and Sons, had completed 7 miles of roads, 12 miles of sewers and 2,090 houses and flats.[1] Most of the material came by rail via sidings provided on the up side of the line at Bellingham and a steam-worked standard gauge estate railway over a mile long. Sand and gravel were taken from pits on the nearby Downham Estate.

McAlpine's houses were of stock red bricks and red tiles, with the occasional bay window to relieve the uniformity of the terraces. There were also 6 experimental houses by the Tibbenham Con-

[1] 403 five-room, 111 four-room parlour, 1,100 four-room non-parlour, 188 three-room, 156 three-room flats, and 132 two-room flats.

struction Company, with walls made by filling an oak frame-work with concrete. The average cost of construction of all the houses on the estate was very high (£1,125 including land).

Prices had fallen considerably when Blackwell and Meyer of Bexleyheath added 32 more houses in 1929. Similar in size to the majority of the earlier ones (four main rooms) they cost the LCC only £443. Meyer was accumulating valuable experience for his New Ideal Homesteads, which he was to launch one year later.

South of Southend Lane, the 50-acre golf links within the boundary were left undisturbed until 1936 when 546 more houses and flats were built there.[1] The estate then possessed 2,668 homes, housing a total of around 12,000 people.

At the east side of the site, in Randlesdown Road, the LCC leased plots for privately-built shops, adding 6 more of its own in 1932. Also in this road was the Fellowship Inn, built by Barclay Perkins and Co. to the approved 'licensed refreshment house' pattern. As the estate was within the County of London, the LCC could provide 2 large schools, one opened in 1923, with 1,076 places, the other ready two years later, with 1,124. Anglican and Congregational churches were built facing one another across Bellingham Green, the central open space.

Bellingham's layout, a neat drawing-board pattern, was designed to fit as much as possible into the triangular site, but some obeisance was made to garden suburb ideals by preserving trees in small greens at the major road intersections.

Public transport by both road and rail was adequate. There were railway stations at each end of the base of the triangular site (Lower Sydenham and Beckenham Hill), with a third (Bellingham) half-way down the east side. As the outward spread of London had stopped just north of the estate boundary in 1915 the last two stations had been among the quietest on the SECR suburban lines. Both railways serving the area were electrified in 1925, afterwards affording fast and frequent service to Blackfriars, Holborn Viaduct, London Bridge, Cannon Street and Charing Cross all at a 9d return workmen's fare. Tickets issued at Bellingham rose from 154,025 (2,727 seasons) in 1924 to 313,743 (4,832 seasons) in 1934. Road services available in the Bromley Road a quarter-mile east of the estate included a 6d workmen's return tramcar facility to Westminster and the City.

[1] Mostly four-room houses and three- and four-room flats.

Concrete Castelnau

Castelnau, at the tip of the Barnes loop of the Thames and just south of the West Middlesex Waterworks, was conceived as a 1919 Act development, but with the change in housing policy, it was not until 1925 that the LCC bought the 51¼ acres from the Lowther Trustees at a price of just over £600 an acre. From 1925 until 1928 Henry Boot and Sons (London) erected roads, sewers and 643 houses, all of them qualifying for subsidy under the 1924 Act.[1] Boots used a special method of their own, forming cavity walls of concrete piers and panels. As an experiment, 57 houses were provided with electric heating and cooking equipment.

The layout included a number of closes and a main artery (Barnes Avenue) carefully aligned to the proposed Thames bridges at Dorset Wharf and Chiswick Ferry.

There was no difficulty about providing a school as the LCC was on home ground. The population of some 3,000 were within walking distance of the important Hammersmith Broadway traffic centre and were also served by buses to Barnes station in the south.

Downham: the Tramway Estate

A winding road, built to carry an electric tramway, formed the main route through the centre of the 522-acre Downham Estate[2] developed under the 1919 Act. Here, just south of Corbett's Edwardian Catford, Holland, Hannen and Cubitts began work in March 1924, using a railway system connected to the SR up-through line between Hither Green and Grove Park stations. Construction was completed in the summer of 1930.

Most of the houses were of traditional design, in red or stock bricks, with red tiled roofs, some with red tile-hung bays. Altogether, 6,071 dwellings were provided,[3] in 1930 leased at rents ranging from 12s 1d to 14s for two-room flats to 17s 9d and 21s 5d for five-room houses, all inclusive of rates and water.

As much of the area was within the County of London, the LCC included 7 primary schools with a total of 6,104 places, an 800-place

---

[1] 193 three-room, 122 four-room non-parlour, 177 four-room parlour, 151 five-room.

[2] 'Settlement on the hill', commemorating Lord Downham (W. Hayes-Fisher, M.P.), President of the Local Government Board at the initiation of post-war housing policy in 1918, and chairman of the LCC 1919–20.

[3] 729 five-room parlour, 1,559 four-room parlour, 1,311 four-room non-parlour, 2,060 three-room non-parlour, sixty-four four-room flats, 128 three-room flats, and 216 two-room flats, all with kitchenette and bathroom.

Central School, and an open-air school for 130 children. On its territory, Bromley Council added a school for 1,040 pupils. Six sites were sold off for churches, chapels and a mission hall whilst 8 acres were allocated to privately-built shops. The licensed refreshment house, Downham Tavern, was opened in May 1930 on the central artery. Managed by Barclay Perkins and Co, this establishment had a ground-floor luncheon room, 43 ft by 40 ft, and a 53 ft. by 40 ft. public lounge, both with serving counters screened off and closed to public access. Also on the ground floor was a 61-square-foot recreation room, and above it, a dining and recreation hall of equal size. A roof-garden looked down over the surrounding gardens with their tennis courts and bowling green.

Open spaces were provided on a generous scale, occupying a third of the total acreage. All round the site many existing trees were kept, and new ones were planted.

The 74-foot-wide Downham Way, with its double-track tramway, linked the main London–Bromley road with Grove Park station. Opened in two stages, the tramway was completed on 15 November 1928. Although there were firm plans to extend it north-eastwards to Eltham, where it would join the lines to Woolwich, these never materialised. Curiously, despite the simultaneous construction of road and tramway on LCC-owned land, no attempt was made to segregate the tracks from motor traffic on a median strip or side reservation as was done in several large provincial housing schemes of the twenties and thirties. The trams ran to Victoria (also to Southwark Bridge at rush hours) for a workmen's return fare of 6d. From Grove Park station, residents of Downham could reach London Bridge by frequent electric trains at 8d workmen's return (9d to Charing Cross).

Contiguous with Downham to the north is the 78-acre White-foot Lane Estate, where 1,021 four-room cottages and three- and four-room flats were built by Higgs and Hill between 1936 and 1939. This development brought the combined population to over 30,000, making it the third largest LCC estate of the between-wars era.

Roehampton, or Vicissitudes Bring Variety

Last of the 1919 Act schemes was the Dover House or Roehampton Estate at Putney, between Richmond Road and Putney Heath in what had been a private park, once the property of the American financier, John P. Morgan. Of the 147 acres bought, only 94 were used, the remainder, at the south end, being sold later on building lease to William Willett at over £700 an acre.

Road and sewer work by H. Wood and Sons began in April 1920 and the house construction contracts were let at the end of the year to Leslie and Co. and F. G. Minter, As progress was slow and prices were sliding down, contracts were terminated with compensation after erection of 624 houses. Construction was resumed at the end of 1922 with a new contractor and much lower prices, but work was again stopped in 1923 after the failure of the firm. The 168 houses of the second contract were eventually finished in December 1924 by the Unit Construction Co. Unable to obtain offers at prices considered reasonable, the LCC entrusted completion of the estate to C. J. Wills and Sons as an extension of their value-cost contract for Becontree. Work was concluded in 1927, the last of it under the 1923 Act. Altogether there were 1,212 houses and flats[1] sheltering a population of 5,380 in 1938.

Some trouble was taken to preserve the cultivated natural beauty of the attractive site. The wooded character of Putney Park Lane was partially saved and at the side of Dover House Road a group of mature elms escaped the axe. The houses themselves presented a varied appearance, reflecting the changes in the building programme: multi-coloured and stock bricks; rough-cast; lime-whitened Flettons; and both tile and slate roofs.

Privately developed shops were included on a leased strip at the northern boundary, shielded from Upper Richmond Road by a shrubbery, and almost a mile from some parts of the estate. The LCC erected a 996-place primary school on the western side of the site.

Barnes station, on the electrified line to Waterloo, was between half and one mile's walk from the estate, but buses were available in the Upper Richmond Road and at Putney Heath. In 1924, shortly after an LCC proposal for a tramway up from Wandsworth High Street had been frustrated by the opposition of the borough council, the LGOC started a bus service through the centre of the estate.

Watling: the Underground Estate

After Becontree, the largest estate north of the Thames was that known as Watling, situated in the Hendon urban district, between

---

[1] 322 five-room, 348 four-room non-parlour, 186 four-room parlour, 262 three-room, 28 three-room flats and 66 two-room flats.

the Edgware Road and the main line out of St Pancras. Here 500 acres were purchased from the trustees of Sir George Blundell Maple and finance was governed by the 1923 and 1924 Housing Acts.

The LCC had long envisaged a large estate in north London; in his evidence to the Joint Committee on Electric and Cable Railways (Metropolis) in May 1892, the chairman of the council's public health and housing committee had suggested that the proposed Hampstead tube railway 'might be continued four or five miles out beyond Hampstead, so as to start a new town, some distance from the edge of the county'. When the extension of the tube railway towards Edgware at last became a firm possibility at the beginning of the twenties, the plans were inked in.

Although on heavy clay, the site was a pleasant one, well wooded and broken up by the Silk Stream, whose banks were reserved for a continuous 45-acre open space through the estate.

Work was entrusted to the well-tried Becontree contractors, C. J. Wills and Sons, who made a start in February 1926. As elsewhere, a network of railways was laid, connected to the LNER Edgware branch at Mill Hill, The Hale. The first houses were ready in April the following year and all 4,021 dwellings[1] had been finished by the spring of 1930. Methods of construction varied from the traditional bricks and mortar (1,974 houses) to concrete external walls (1,331), steel frames (252) and timber frames (464). The last three types were adopted to maintain the required rate of production at a time when skilled building labour was in very short supply; in view of the inadequacy of the fire brigade of still half-rural Hendon, the timber houses were at first equipped with 12 feet of rubber hose. In 1935–6, 14 larger houses for letting at higher rents were added, bringing the estate population at the end of the thirties to 19,110.

Main roads 50 feet in width afforded east-west links, also providing access to the Underground station (Burnt Oak) on the western boundary. Subsidiary roads 30 to 40 feet wide followed the contours, avoiding existing trees wherever possible.

As at Becontree, the local education authorities did not exactly hasten to provide schools. In the autumn of 1927 when there were 896 children of school age on the estate, 269 were without places.

---

[1] 668 five-room parlour, 858 four-room parlour, 927 four-room non-parlour, 1,215 three-room non-parlour, 100 four-room flats, 140 three-room flats, and 110 two-room flats, all with kitchenettes and bathrooms.

Although Hendon's schools had over 2,000 vacancies at the time, none was sited at convenient distance from Watling. A school was opened within the estate in the following year, but the LCC children lacked full provision until January 1930. By the end of 1931, when the 640-place Orange Hill Central School was opened, there were 5 schools at Watling, providing 6,000 places at a cost of around £200,000 to the Hendon ratepayers. Two more schools were added by 1939.

Surrounded by middle-class suburbia, the estate, known to some as 'Little Moscow', generated not a little antagonism in the early years. A major concern of the local press in the twenties was the effect of the influx on the majority of Hendon's Tory M.P. They were soon reassured. At the local level, Watling returned Labour councillors. Communists were few; in April 1932, for example, in a total poll of 2,523, the two CP candidates secured 85 and 83 votes.

In the early thirties the estate housed a fair number of junior civil servants and postal workers, also local authority employees and bus workers, and these played the predominant role in the social organisations. It is interesting to note that in 1936 there was a thriving eight-year-old Conservative Association with 150 members on its books. But although the newcomer had proved to be a fairly well-washed, orderly child, the social fears remained. At the opening of the Hendon Constitutional Club in February 1934, Sir Hugh Davison considered the possibility of a tube extension beyond Edgware: 'we cannot say what kind of people might settle down there, and if they were the same as those lower down, it might be difficult'.[1] At any rate, the Conservative wives of upper-middle-class Mill Hill were happy to find a whole new pool of domestic labour on their doorsteps: 'On many occasions it has been my pleasure to employ for household duties young ladies from the Watling Estate. In practically every case I have found them to be most diligent in their duties, kind to my children and exceptionally clean . . .'.[2]

The better to meet their common problems and the hostility without the walls, the early inhabitants, most of them from Islington and St Pancras, banded together in January 1928 to form what was to be one of the most successful tenants' associations of any LCC estate. Their initial capital of £5 was donated by a doctor who became vice president, and the president was a clergyman. In

[1] HTBG 23 February 1934.
[2] Letter in the *Watling Resident* March, 1935.

the following May there appeared the first issue of a lively paper, *The Watling Resident*, which reached a sale of 3,000 copies in August 1929. Dances, concerts and whist drives were organised, and in 1929 a building fund was started for a community centre, money raising including an annual carnival 'Watling Week' with baby shows and other outdoor activities. The centre was eventually completed with the help of a loan and a grant from the Pilgrim Trust. Designed by G. E. S. Streatfield ARIBA, the £3,650 building was opened on 18 January 1933 by Edward, Prince of Wales. By this time, the original tenants' association had evolved into the all-embracing Watling Association, with assistance from the National Council of Social Service. Working from the Community Centre, the WA co-ordinated the activities of the various social and recreational organisations operating inside the estate.

Towards the middle thirties, much of the early enthusiasm seemed to have dissipated; there were fewer battles to fight, and the ardent communal spirit of the pioneers had been somewhat overwhelmed by the growth of the estate population. In March 1936, the *Watling Resident* was selling just under a thousand copies, which meant that it was seen in less than a quarter of the households. Another symptom of the malaise was the dilution of the strength of the original organisations by factional secession. Even so, community activities at Watling were sustained in great variety, in contrast to their almost complete absence in most private enterprise estates.

Watling's Underground station at Burnt Oak opened on 27 October 1924, well before the main part of the estate was finished, and within a few weeks of the inauguration of the Edgware tube. Its frequent service of trains to the City and West End, accessible for a workmen's return fare of 7d, formed what the *Watling Resident* described as the 'connecting link with civilisation', and as might be expected, the bulk of the London-bound traffic was handled in the single hour before the last workmen's train each morning. The steam railway stations at Mill Hill (on the LMSR line to St Pancras) and Mill Hill (The Hale) (on the LNER line to Finsbury Park, Kings Cross and Moorgate) were separated from Watling by unmade roads across private housing estates. Even after the roads were made up in 1931, these two stations were little used by Watling tenants. More popular were the Edgware Road tramcars and buses, providing cheap access to the industrial district three miles to the south, around the North Circular Road.

The estate's main shopping area in Watling Avenue, between the Underground station and the Edgware Road, soon assumed the animated aspect of an inner London working-class shopping centre, complete with street traders, pavement displays of goods, and windows obscured with whitewashed details of the latest bargain offers. For the more affluent stall-holders, a covered market was opened in the main road during 1936.

Further shops were erected for the LCC in 1931 in Watling Avenue east of the railway as the original provision was judged insufficient. Along the main Edgware Road, the presence of the LCC estate and a large number of new private estates encouraged shop development in the late twenties and the thirties, attracting the main multiples and a large departmental store for the London Co-operative Society (1936).

Other amenities came only slowly. Until January 1930, Watling had no public telephones apart from one at the railway station. In that year, a maternity and child-welfare clinic was opened on the estate, at once doing great business, for Watling had more children to the acre than any other part of the extensive Hendon urban district. An LCC-type 'licensed refreshment house' was planned, but was vetoed by the Hendon licensing authorities who had a dislike of public houses combined with dance halls (there was of course no lack of drinking places in Edgware village, a short walk to the north). The site was used for the Community Centre.

A thousand-seat cinema designed by George Coles was opened on 25 February 1929 by Frank Cross. Situated on the Edgware Road, the Regent quickly built up a large clientele, not least for its 3d children's matinees on Saturdays. Ten months after opening, it was fitted for sound projection, and the stage turns which had been included between the silent films were abandoned. A 600-seat balcony, a new Compton organ, and a waiting- and tea-lounge were added in 1932, when the building was given a new frontage in cream mottled terra cotta set in dark purple brickwork together with a Levanto marble surround to the main entrance. At this time performance was continuous from 1.30 p.m. daily (1 p.m. on Saturdays).

St Alphage, at the southernmost tip of the estate, near the Edgware Road, was opened for Anglican worship in 1927. A Wesleyan Hall followed within two years. By the end of the thirties, Watling had two more churches and a Salvation Army Citadel.

Wormholt: on the Dust of the White City

In 1925, the LCC purchased for development 68 acres of a large area originally acquired and partly built over by the Hammersmith Council. The site adjoined the Old Oak Estate and the land used for the White City Exhibitions of 1908–14. Many of the houses were built either side of the inner section of a new arterial road called Western Avenue.

Wilson Lovatt and Sons, the contractors, started work in 1926, relying on road transport for the delivery of building materials to the construction sites. The main part of the estate, promoted under the 1924 Act, was completed by June 1928. In 1934, 12 flats built brought the total number of properties (mostly three- and four-room cottages) to 894, accommodating about 4,000 people. Further flats were added, on the White City site itself, between 1936 and 1939.

Within easy reach were the Central Line tube trains at East Acton station, whilst people living in the southern section were close to the frequent bus and tram services along Uxbridge Road. After 1929 buses on the new Western Avenue linked Wormholt with the industrial areas around Park Royal and beyond.

St Helier: the LCC Invades Suburban Surrey

Largest of all the LCC estates south of the Thames, second only in size to Becontree itself, was St Helier,[1] covering 825 acres between Morden and the river Wandle, south of Mitcham and astride the 1926 Sutton Bypass. This land, mostly in the urban districts of Merton and Morden, and Carshalton, with a smaller part in Sutton and Cheam, was purchased between 1926 and 1929, the greater portion being developed under the 1924 Housing Act.

As at Downham, open spaces were provided on a lavish scale, to a total of 120 acres. Within the estate, the Bypass was widened to 110 feet with footpaths and grass verges and a further 15 feet between the edges of the greens and the flanking houses. Roads parallel to the Bypass, 49 feet wide, had intercommunicating spurs which enabled tradesmen's vehicles to serve most of the houses on the main road frontage without entering the through traffic stream. At the south end of St Helier Avenue, at the intersection of six roads, a traffic roundabout was built. Here was the main shopping centre, the Market, a large cinema and the usual licensed re-

[1] After Lady St Helier, an LCC alderman and councillor 1910–27.

freshment house (The Rose). Although the Council built the shops themselves, George Cross astutely secured a site in nearby Wrythe Lane, letting 6 shops before building. Within five years there were 30 shops here and double that number by 1938.

The master contractors were the trusted C. J. Wills and Sons, who began work early in 1929. Some material came by road, but the bulk was delivered to sidings at Mitcham on the Wimbledon to Croydon railway, whence an extensive light-railway system on cinder-ballasted tracks took the main-line wagons direct to the building sites. The contractor's railway depot was about a mile south of Mitcham, and here, in 1933, a visitor found six spotless 0—6—0 saddle-tank locomotives, one dating from 1888. Some of these hard-worked machines had seen service at Becontree and Watling. This railway, the last of the LCC estate systems, had no signals, but the numerous crossings of public roads were protected by gates and warning boards.[1]

St Helier was very largely completed by the end of 1934. At the end of the thirties there were 9,068 houses and flats, principally three-room, four-room, and five-room cottages, housing almost 40,000.

Some 78 acres west of the Wimbledon and Sutton railway were transferred to private building firms. The Morden Council also received 10 acres here for an open space and another 25 acres were leased to the trustees of the Douglas Haig Memorial Homes and the Housing Association for Officers' Families, who erected flats for disabled ex-servicemen and service widows.

Although the LCC failed in its attempts to get powers for a tramway extension into the estate, the transport facilities were not unreasonable. For those who did not wish to cycle, the industrial zones at Mitcham and Croydon were readily accessible by bus and train, whilst there were frequent buses to the tube terminus at Morden, with its 6d return workmen's facility for the nine-mile run to the West End and City. On the western edge of the site, the new Wimbledon and Sutton Railway's station in Green Lane, named after the estate, stood on part of the 12 acres conveyed free of charge to the SR. This line offered an 8d workmen's return for the roundabout 13½-mile ride to Holborn Viaduct. Its service through the small hours encouraged newspaper, postal and market workers to live in the area.

Co-operation with the local education authorities was unusually

[1] *Railway Magazine*, April, 1933.

harmonious with the result that schools came fairly quickly into the estate. A large hospital was built in Rosehill Park, Wrythe Lane, in 1938.

Seeking further room for expansion of St Helier, the LCC applied in 1936 for a compulsory acquisition of the 150-acre Morden Park, but Morden Council managed to secure its preservation as an open space at a cost of £145,000 with the aid of the Surrey County Council. London Transport, currently struggling with heavy peak-hour overcrowding at Morden station, no doubt heaved a great sigh of relief.

A Second Wind

Before the outbreak of World War II the LCC had begun housebuilding on 5 more estates, some of which were not finished until the 1950s. Two more developments, Hainault (Chigwell) and Headstone Lane (Harrow) had been started, but no houses were ready until after the war.

Begun in 1934, the Mottingham estate was just north of Elmstead Wood, about a mile south of Mottingham station on the Dartford Loop line. After construction of roads and sewers by direct labour, the 145 acres were covered with 2,337 houses and flats (mostly three- and four-room cottages and two-room flats) erected by Wilson Lovatt and Sons. In 1938 the completed estate was housing just over 9,000 people.

Two sections of Marvels Wood, 25½ acres in all, were left as open space. To the west, the estate adjoined the smaller 1926 estate of the Lewisham Borough Council, whilst further west, beyond the railway was Downham, the whole forming a 2½-mile-long belt of local authority housing through what was predominantly a middle-class area.

Much smaller was Thornhill, south of Charlton, in the angle of Shooters Hill Road and Woolwich Common, where 45 acres were acquired in 1934, 36 of them to remain as open space. Road and sewer construction by direct labour started in November 1934, Henry Boot and Sons completing the development with 380 flats and cottages during 1936–7. A year later the estate housed 1,600.

In West Ealing, south of Perivale Park, between the Ealing–Greenford railway and some earlier private development, estate construction began in 1936 on the 140-acre site of the County Council's former Residential School. The Unit Construction Company erected 1,599 houses and flats and 18 shops and by 1938 the estate population was about 5,300. This Hanwell estate had three railway stations within a mile of its centre, one of them on the main line into Paddington. The factories around Western Avenue were easily reached by bus or cycle.

At Kenmore Park, Kenton, in 1935, the LCC took over a 58-acre estate which had been started by a private developer. On completion of the transfer, the firm was required to finish the half-built roads and sewers, after which the Unit Construction Company moved in to erect 579 cottages and 73 flats for the Council. Completed in 1938, this estate was housing 2,708 people later that year. The main Kenton Road, with its buses to Kenton station, was about half a mile from the centre of the site, whilst the Honeypot Lane factory areas were close to the eastern boundary.

Some mention has been made in Chapter 9 of the Friday Hill estate at Chingford. A total of 1,600 dwellings were planned on the 118 acres purchased here, and work started in 1938, but only a small part was ready by the beginning of the war.

Chapter 17

HITLER STOPS
THE SPRAWL

Security for £25

The rearmament programme announced in 1935 and started in the following year inevitably affected a fully extended building industry. Not only was there a rise in the cost of materials, but the competition for labour brought higher wages. House prices, which had already shown some signs of increasing after 1932, continued upwards in the following years, although in an atmosphere of fierce competition, many builders tried hard to keep their costs and margins as low as possible, delaying price increases as long as they could, and then trying to manage with as little as 5 per cent. In October 1938 Laing announced price reductions on some of their London estates 'as a token of gratitude for the continuance of peace', but this was more of an attempt to revive sales which had flagged badly during the war scare of the previous month.

Fears of the coming war and its effects on London reverberated in the building market at a surprisingly early stage. In July 1934, before Hitler had fully consolidated his position as ruler of Germany, and before the Home Office had issued the first of its air-raid precautions directives to the local authorities, a firm of builders in Middlesex (Sandell and Wren, of School Road, Ashford) were suggesting to *Evening News* readers that they might 'Live on an estate that will provide protection for your Dependants in the future. A Bomb and Gasproof Dugout now in the course of construction that will offer safety to every resident'. This shelter, designed to accommodate 200–300 people had airtight doors and electric light. It was 18 feet deep, 30 feet wide and 40 feet long, with concrete walls 3 feet thick and an 18-inch roof buried under 4 feet of soil and a 2-foot-thick concrete bursting platform. Although the original initiative appears to have been the builder's, the advice of the Home Office was readily obtained.

In 1937 and 1938, as international tensions grew, a number of

London builders started to advertise concrete shelters, supplied as an extra to the house, at around £25 (in one case 'another 6d a week'). Some houses were sold with gasproofed rooms. At Dormers Wells Lane, Southall, in 1937 the doors and windows of some new houses were supplied with seventeen hinges which could be tightened with wing nuts against rubber piping, converting the main bedrooms into a gasproof shelter for up to twelve hours. This little luxury, which like some of the official instructions oddly assumed that the enemy might drop gas bombs but not high explosives, cost a mere £5.[1] A year later, a firm trading under the name Dugouts Ltd erected seven-room 'A.R.P. Bungalows' at Hornchurch to advertise its air-raid shelters. For an inclusive price of £950, the owner enjoyed the use of an electrically lit shelter for eight or nine people, reached through a trapdoor in the floor of the smallest bedroom. Here, it was claimed, he would be safe against direct hits by bombs up to half a ton in weight, and against gas.[2] It was certainly worth the prospective purchasers' while to look for something of this kind as the official metal shelters ('Andersons') issued free of charge to householders from February 1939 were only distributed outside the LCC area to those earning less than £250, in a very limited number of districts.

This restriction was the consequence of declaring most of the Greater London area a 'neutral' zone, not regarded as in sufficient danger to justify the evacuation of schoolchildren. In their publicity, the builders made the most of this; although it was perhaps reasonable enough to imply that the Worth Park Estate at Three Bridges, '26 miles from the danger zone' was safe, claims in 1938–39 advertisements that such areas as Ashtead, Banstead and Sudbury were unlikely to be bombed were much less credible. Crouch hopefully suggested Raynes Park 'far enough for safety', despite its factories and important road and rail junctions. Fairway Homes of Potters Bar were a little more convincing with their announcement: 'the greatest possible protection against air attack with its attendant horrors is to hand on this estate, by virtue of its proximity to the open country. Fields and woods may be reached by walking only three minutes'.[3] Others scratched around for something to offer, hoping to keep sales moving. J. Montgomery, of Hinchley Wood, making sure that you didn't mistake his meaning, suggested that

[1] TEG 22 January 1938.
[2] TEG 17 December 1938, HF April 1939.
[3] HF May 1938.

the solid wood block floors of his houses would be 'helpful in the prevention of gas (A.R.P.)', whilst a little more convincingly, W. J. Drinkwater and Sons of Feltham claimed their flat concrete roofs offered some protection against incendiary bombs. It was all right as long as you had some forewarning of what type of bomb was to be dropped on your particular area.

On 26 August 1939, the *Evening News* carried what was to be the last advertisement feature of the great age of London suburban development. From 'the Pick of the Safety Zone', some anxious and hitherto hesitant readers no doubt made up their minds at last, after mulling over the relative merits and safety of Ewell, Sanderstead, Ashtead, Mitcham and half a dozen other sites. As the almost universal expectation was that devastating air raids on London would follow close upon declaration of war, the weeks at the end of August and the beginning of September 1939 saw many long-empty new houses occupied, so that when the air attack did begin in earnest a year later, there were few vacant houses within the outer suburban ring. Not that residence in the new suburbs offered the promised safety in any great measure, for many received a fair share of bombs, often dumped by air crews turning away from the better protected inner area. But their more open layout made the assault just that little less fearful.

As war preparations mounted, there was a quiet but steady response from the men of the suburbs. The results of appeals early in 1938 for air-raid wardens, first-aid workers and auxiliary firemen overwhelmed the facilities available for training, so that the Czech crisis of September found Hendon and similar areas well below strength in trained men. In that month, gas masks were assembled and distributed in the face of considerable difficulties and those requiring anything but average sizes were not all immediately supplied. During the period leading to the outbreak of war Hendon's establishment of 2,400 air-raid wardens was steadily recruited; by July 1939, 2,107 had enlisted. Enthusiasm was less marked on the Watling Estate, where of 350 required, only 88 had been secured at the beginning of March. There was also a subdued response in the borough generally to appeals for men for rescue and demolition parties and decontamination squads; of 669 men required for the former, only 140 had been obtained at the end of July. The Territorial Army had no difficulty in finding suburban recruits. At the opening of the Burnt Oak Drill Hall in April 1938 it was announced that the Anti-Aircraft battalion it was to house had 1,492 men, some 20 per cent above the establishment. In 1936, as war fears mounted, the Territorial Army establishment for Middlesex had been increased from 3,000 to 11,000; by March 1939, strength had reached 9,000.

Restraining London's Growth

In one respect Hitler's war brought London great benefit as it was indirectly responsible for the establishment of a wide and continuous Green Belt in place of the tentative and ineffective open space preservation measures of the thirties.

For over a century, ever since the suburbs had started to sprout in strength, the assumption had been that London would go on spreading outwards with constantly improved transport facilities acting as veins and capillaries to feed the new growth. As we have seen, the Underground and LPTB chiefs never tired of voicing their special interest in the expansion and redistribution of London's population.

But there were others who saw the folly and impracticability of unrestricted exogenous growth as they watched building swallowing more and more open land. Development at six, eight or ten houses to the acre was extremely greedy of space (yet not done in spacious fashion), and although the population of Greater London increased by about one tenth between 1921 and 1931, the occupied land virtually doubled. By the end of the twenties there was much anxiety about the amount of recreational open space accessible to the expanding population.

The concept of a green girdle or parkway strip around London to preserve amenities and recreational land was first mooted by Lord Meath, William Bull, George Pepler and others early in the century,[1] but it was not until the late twenties that serious consideration was given to adopting some such device as a remedy against the evils of galloping suburban growth.

In 1927 the Minister of Health (Neville Chamberlain) told the inaugural meeting of the Greater London Regional Planning Committee that one of the possibilities they should consider was an agricultural belt around Greater London which would separate the city from satellites or fresh growth further out. Sir Raymond Unwin, the Committee's technical adviser, somewhat modified this in the 1933 Report by proposing a girdle of recreational open space

[1] David Thomas, *London's Green Belt* (Faber & Faber, 1970).

up to six miles wide, beyond which new development would be planned in an open space environment instead of the traditional idea of retaining some open space within otherwise unlimited building land.

Meanwhile concern about the loss of open land in outer London had increased and when the Labour Party gained control in 1934, its leader, Herbert Morrison, ably assisted by Richard Coppock, his Parks Committee chairman, evolved a practical scheme, in the face of refusal of financial support from the Conservative Government. In January 1935, the LCC announced its willingness to assist neighbouring county and county borough councils by meeting up to half the cost of acquiring or controlling land they wished to recover 'to provide a reserve supply of public open spaces and of recreational areas, and to establish a green belt or girdle of open space lands, not necessarily continuous, but as readily accessible from the completely urbanised areas of London as practicable'. A sum of £2m. was set aside to meet grants until March 1938.

Encouraging progress was made with this scheme, but to remove doubt about the powers of councils to participate and to ensure that the selected areas were permanently preserved from building, the Green Belt (London and Home Counties) Act was passed in 1938. This allowed councils to acquire land by agreement or to declare land part of the Green Belt, and provided that no part of such land should be sold or built upon without the consent of the Minister of Health and the contributing authorities. Councils were also given power to acquire Green Belt land without the assistance of the LCC.

Morrison told the Barlow Commission in February 1938 that the LCC's objective was a continuous belt 1 to 5 miles wide; that over 44,000 acres had been designated in the six counties around London, including 16,053 in Buckinghamshire, 9,114 in Essex and 8,695 in Middlesex; but the allocated sum was almost exhausted.[1] Five years later, the total acreage stood at 72,000,[2] but there was still nothing like a continuous belt, only a scattering of green patches on the map, almost all within a 10- to 20-mile radius of Charing Cross.

Notable acquisitions included the 2,000 acres of Enfield Chase in Middlesex, Nonsuch Park, Ewell, and Shabden Park, Chipstead, both in Surrey, all these in 1936 and 1937. In most cases building

[1] RCGDIP, minutes, 27, 16 February 1938.
[2] Patrick Abercrombie, *The Greater London Plan*, 1944, para. 245.

development value was extracted by the landowners. When 115 acres of woodland and meadow between Epsom and Headley came into the market in 1938, local residents suggested it be bought as Green Belt, but Banstead UDC had already sanctioned the erection of 800 houses, so the landowner wanted to 'get his price'.[1] A typical transaction was the purchase by the Middlesex County Council in 1935 of the 306-acre Denham Court Estate. A building developer had already bought it for £38,000, but without knowing the identity of the other party, willingly sold it at an increment of £4,000.[2]

As the county councils were not planning authorities, there was virtually no control of development bordering areas designated as Green Belt. Thus land values appreciated and as time passed the councils were obliged to pay inflated prices when wishing to extend areas already bought. Those holding or developing land did not hesitate to use its proximity to protected areas as an asset when advertising it for sale – there was even a 'Green Belt Estate' at Yeading Lane in 1938-9. Another disappointment arose when it was found that access to Green Belt Land was often denied to those who wished to use it for recreation. G. R. Mitchell, secretary of the Ramblers' Association, was complaining in 1937 that what had been planned as a buffer between town and country 'becomes instead a magnet for new houses'.[3]

By the summer of 1939 London's sprawl was licking the fields and woodlands at points between 10 and 15 miles from the centre, the flood held back only here and there by the few Green Belt lands. Now, by accident of history, it was to be frozen, establishing a high-tide mark which would remain as the edge of continuously built-up London for years to come.

With the outbreak of war, building slowed down, coming to a complete halt by late spring 1940. When the fighting was done, before resources were available to enable building to begin again, the situation was completely changed by the Town and Country Planning Act, 1947. This enabled counties and county boroughs to refuse permission for further development in specified areas against compensation to be dispensed by central government, thus allowing at a stroke the formation of the continuous, all-purpose Green Belt which had been a principal component of Professor Abercrombie's advisory Greater London Plan of 1944. The new

[1] TEG 9 July 1938.
[2] TEG 9 November 1935.
[3] *News Chronicle* 25 November 1937.

belt, enshrined in the various development plans receiving ministerial approval between 1954 and 1959, was 5 to 15 miles wide.[1] Effectively sealing the London of 1939, the area now known as Greater London,[2] it included much land secured for building before 1947.[3] A hundred years of uninhibited growth had come to an end.[4]

[1] Not all of it was 'green'; the Belt covered existing residential and industrial use, which was unaffected, and the open parts were by no means all agricultural, timbered or recreational.

[2] Strictly not the present GLC area, but that area together with those outer districts which remained separate after the formation of the GLC in 1965.

[3] An example was an estate of 208 acres either side of the Kingston Bypass at Hinchley Wood, sold in May 1939 for £250,000 to H. Elliott, a Surbiton builder, who proposed to erect a 'garden city' of 1,600 houses priced between £1,000 and £1,500.

[4] Today the Green Belt established in the 1950s remains largely inviolate, but in recent years some building has been allowed in areas of negligible amenity value.

EPILOGUE: OR
PLANNING UNPLANNED

We have seen how, after steady growth in the first decade of the century, a halt for war and subsequent recovery, a most propitious climate encouraged speculative building around London to flourish at an unprecedented rate until the needs of all but the lowest income groups were met. And we have examined in some detail the physical results of this great surge of private building and the accompanying much more limited output of the local authorities. That the outer layer of London which emerged from all this activity was neither well balanced in its constituents or visually and psychologically satisfying is common ground. It happened largely because there was no positive planning on a regional scale, and was worse than it might have been because such planning powers as did exist were not properly used by most of the local authorities. Professor Robson summed it all up very lucidly and vividly in his evidence to the Barlow Commission in 1938.[1] After describing how London's pleasant countryside had been covered with thousands of houses of all descriptions, '... the devastating onrush of the speculative builder, aided and abetted in one notorious instance by a railway company turned landowner', which no local authority 'even pretended to regulate and guide for the common good', he went on to say that quiet and peace of rural surroundings so eagerly sought by the migrating householders was in many cases destroyed by the development that accommodated them. This was 'a consequence which only an intelligent legislator or far-sighted administrative authority contemplating the whole metropolitan region could have foreseen. And neither was to be found in the body politic of the nation'.

Just what went wrong?

[1] W. A. Robson, Ph.D., Ll.M., reader in administrative law and later Professor of Public Administration, University of London, evidence to RCGDIP, 15 June 1938.

Inspired by the success of the garden suburbs, and of Letch-worth, the first garden city, an idealistic Liberal government had introduced the first legislation in 1909. This was simply an enabling measure, concerned only with the planning of land in course of development or likely to be used for building. It allowed borough, urban and rural district councils to prepare schemes which could lay down conditions such as density of building, zoning of land use, and the width and direction of roads. Once compiled, the detailed plan required the approval of the central government department (the Local Government Board).

In London the pioneer user of this measure was the Ruislip-Northwood UDC. Electrification of the Metropolitan Railway had stirred interest in the area and both King's College Cambridge, who wished to develop 1,300 acres of their land as a garden city, and the UDC, concerned at the sale of 20 ft. by 100 ft. plots by an American syndicate, were anxious to see some sort of overall control in what was still mainly a rural area.[1] The scheme which finally emerged covered 5,750 acres and was approved by the Local Government Board in September 1914, when the population was still only about 7,000. It set out distances between building lines, laid down re-quirements for building design, outdoor advertising, and the loca-tion of shopping areas and industry; permitted densities varied from eight through six to four houses per acre. About 234 acres were zoned for industry, but well over two thirds of the controlled area was allocated to housing.

Post-war legislation did little to remedy the basic defects of the original Act. To prevent delays in the provision of houses, a 1919 Act allowed developers to proceed without waiting for approval of a complete town-planning scheme, and required all local authorities with population of 20,000 and over to present a completed scheme by 1923. This Act also allowed councils to purchase land compul-sorily for town-planning purposes. An attempt was made to miti-gate the disadvantages of the piecemeal, low-level approach by providing for joint committees to be set up to prepare schemes covering several local authority areas, but failing delegation of powers by the constituent councils (a highly improbable event), such committees had no executive functions. A third Act in 1925 extended the time for the preparation of schemes to 1929, con-solidated earlier legislation, and enabled county councils to partici-pate in the preparation of schemes. The final pre-war Act was that

[1] RCLG, evidence of E. R. Abbott, 17 May 1922.

19. Edgware: the first scars. The Underground railway and station under construction in 1923. The old Rectory and the Portsdown Estate can be seen opposite the station site; to the right of the station, construction of George Cross's first parade of shops is just starting. (Photo: Aerofilms Ltd.)

Edgware: some signs of progress. The area around the Underground station on 29 May 1926. Opposite the station Leslie Raymond's Mall shops can be seen, with the preparations for further extension of the Underground very prominent to the right. The George Cross shops to the right of the station are still incomplete. In the top right-hand corner, new houses can be seen along Edgwarebury Lane, in Edgwarebury Gardens and in The Drive. (Photo: Aerofilms Ltd.)

20. Edgware matured: Curton houses in Edgwarebury Lane, north of the Bypass in 1971. (Photo: Alan A. Jackson.)

Restrained Modernism in Edgware: John Laing 'Coronation' detached house of 1938, Edgwarebury Lane. This type, with three bedrooms, and cloakroom and w.c. in the hall, sold at £1,145 freehold. (Photo: Alan A. Jackson.)

21. Tudor superpub: Edgware's Railway Hotel of 1931. (Photo: Alan A. Jackson.)

Stoneleigh Park mellowed: chalets of 1933 in Clandon Close. (Photo: Alan A. Jackson, 1971.)

22. Becontree: plain-faced LCC cottages at Hunter Hall Road, 1929.
(Photo: Greater London Council.)

Becontree: median strip for electric tramway, Valence Avenue. (Photo:
Alan A. Jackson.)

of 1932, which conferred the force of law on town-planning regulations made by the Ministry of Health (the department which had replaced the Local Government Board in 1919), dropped the compulsion to prepare schemes and extended the planning provisions to all types of land.

The situation was further complicated by the Restriction of Ribbon Development Act, 1935, which gave county and county borough councils, as highways authorities under the Ministry of Transport, powers to control frontage development along all classified and certain other roads. The area affected included a building line up to 220 feet back from the centre of the roads concerned and the provisions enabled the number of new roads communicating with the main artery to be restricted to the absolute minimum required by the needs of the parallel development. Service roads of agreed width, parallel to the controlled road, were to be provided for any houses built on that road's frontage. It will be seen that these powers not only overlapped those of the borough, urban and rural district councils in regard to town planning, but brought on to the scene another set of authorities and a second government department.

It is not difficult to find reasons why all this legislation failed to bite effectively, producing such a dismal result. The principal central department, the Ministry of Health, preoccupied with other even more urgent social problems, exercised little positive direction, gave the minimum of guidance to the local authorities and brought no strong pressure upon them to prepare or co-ordinate their schemes. At the local level, there was a dearth of properly qualified planning advisers and experts. Much more important, the areas of the designated planning authorities were generally too small to allow the design of satisfactory schemes and (as always) the local councils were mutually jealous and suspicious, reluctant to delegate executive power to other bodies covering wider areas. Where a species of joint action was evolved, the councils usually lacked experience in co-operation of this type.

A major omission from the procedures was the provision of transport facilities. With the single exception of the LCC, there was no effective consultation between the planning and housing authorities and those responsible for new road and rail services. The parliamentary bill procedure under which new railways were usually authorised took no account of land planning requirements and was primarily designed to protect private property. In its report for

1937, the London and Home Counties Traffic Advisory Committee remarked that builders and landowners ought not to expect transport facilities to be laid on like gas, electricity and water: 'future big developments should be related to existing or contemplated road and rail facilities and we recommend that the Board and the four main-line railway companies should be brought into consultation before any important building schemes are decided upon'. But it was rather late in the day for such brave talk.

The careful protection of private interests embodied in railway procedures was also present in the town-planning legislation's stringent compensation provisions. These were such as frequently to inhibit impecunious local authorities from bringing to a halt building activity considered undesirable in the context of their scheme, or even from formalising a comprehensive area scheme. Above all, the town-planning provisions failed because they placed the primary responsibility on the local councils, who for this purpose were too inward-looking, too weak financially, and too numerous for effective co-operation. In the London Transport area there were no less than 133 different authorities exercising planning powers in 1938. It was, as Frank Pick so appositely said to the Barlow Commission, 'Town planning by sections, which amounts to no town planning at all in regard to London as a whole'.[1]

There were of course some attempts to remedy the matter. As a result of pressure upon the Minister of Health from a number of interested bodies who wanted a statutory town plan for Greater London, a creature with the impressive title of the Greater London Regional Planning Committee had been brought to life as early as 1927. This consisted of no less than 138 members, representatives of each of the local authorities, including the county councils, from an area up to 25 miles from Charing Cross. Although it had the inestimable benefit of Sir Raymond Unwin as its technical adviser and report writer, its powers were limited to giving advice, and it achieved nothing beyond a 1929 report making the fairly obvious recommendation that a Joint Regional Planning Authority should be set up with executive powers in the more important matters covering the whole region. During the 1931 government economy campaign, Unwin and his staff were dismissed to save £3,000 a year. Two years later, the Committee was reconstituted, still limited to giving advice. In desperation, the LCC withdrew financial support in 1936, retiring within County Hall to prepare its own

[1] RCGDIP 1938 Q.3357, 2 March 1938.

plan.[1] Shortly after this, on 30 September, the Committee expired. Its successor, set up in the following year, was the Standing Conference on London Regional Planning, again without teeth, manacled with a small income, and only able to consider those questions fed to it by the Ministry of Health or the local authorities. In one direction however there was some sign of progress: for the first time, there was positive recognition of the importance of public transport, with the co-option of representatives from the LPTB and the main-line railway companies at the inaugural meeting.

Thus at the time our period closes, territorial planning of Greater London was still non-existent outside the limited inner zone controlled by the LCC, although the Standing Conference had succeeded in persuading the Minister of Health to approve an investigation into the ways and means of drawing up a master plan for the London Region which would include an agricultural green belt around the built-up area. This move laid foundations for the work that was to be done in the stimulating climate of wartime reaching fruition in the renewed idealism of the immediate post-war years.

The sudden, wide-ranging onslaught of the private builders across outer London in the later twenties and through the thirties was little affected by the pitifully inadequate planning measures which have been described. Both the waste of opportunity and the resultant ugly monotony are appalling to contemplate, and the damage done will take generations to repair. But there was also very real achievement. Finding a new home within their financial reach, many thousands had their living standards transformed; in a few short years, the sum of human happiness was immeasurably increased. Any alternative would have taken very much longer.

Today, the influences and effects of this vast unplanned suburbia of private enterprise are still working their way through the psyche of the metropolitan community. The rejection of suburban values and way of life by a section of contemporary youth springs from deeper wells, though we can note in passing that a piece of youth culture, the Beatles' song *She's Leaving Home*, was illustrated with a

[1] The LCC, alone among county councils, had held powers as a primary planning authority since 1909, but as there was little or no undeveloped land in its area, it remained virtually impotent in planning matters until the 1932 Act (which it fostered) allowed planning of areas already built over.

drawing of a typical London 1930s semi.[1] More pertinent is a shallowness of local allegiance and a lack of community spirit found almost everywhere in the outer suburban belt, characteristics which very largely stem from the haphazard and often dormitory nature of the inter-war growth. During the thirties unsatisfactory *ad hoc* adjustments to local authority status and boundaries panted after the rapid spread of bricks and mortar. Throughout the period of this book, the LCC area remained static as an increasing proportion of London lay outside it, with no sense of belonging. When in 1965 an administrative concept called Greater London was at last breathed into life, the boundaries were to exclude not only the historic City core, but substantial portions of the continuously built-up area as, in response to political pressures, boundaries were deflected inwards from the outer limits carefully drawn by the Royal Commission.[2] Administrative functions were split between the Greater London Council, the new top-tier authority, and enlarged boroughs that were to find their size a discouragement in the development of loyalty and social cohesion. Although it is much too early to say that the 1965 changes were not bold enough the new Greater Londoners at first exhibited strong signs of apathy towards the new regime.[3]

For now, at any rate, the London of this book still seems semi-detached.

[1] *Beatles Illustrated Lyrics*, Macdonald Unit 78, 1969, p. 80.
[2] For example, Epsom and Ewell, entirely within continuously built-up Greater London, was left outside the GLC area.
[3] Interviews carried out by BBC Television on the occasion of the GLC elections in 1970 found passers-by in the streets of Greater London quite unable to state the political complexion of the GLC majority party or the names of their own councillors. Several could not even interpret the initials GLC.

Appendix 1

GREATER LONDON POPULATION 1901–39

Whole area*

1901	6,586,269
1911	7,225,946
1921	7,488,382
1931	8,215,673
1939 (mid-year estimate)	8,728,000

* Greater London area, being the Metropolitan Police District as defined by the Metropolitan Police Act, 1946 (Census 1951).

1901–11: Increases over 50 per cent

Figures from census returns, districts as existing in 1921.

	1901	*1911*	*comparable 1921 figure*
Chingford UDC	4,373	8,184	9,481
Ilford UDC	41,244	78,188	85,191
Wanstead UDC	9,179	13,830	15,297
Bushey UDC	4,564	6,978	8,091
Acton MB	37,744	57,497	61,314
Ealing MB	33,031	61,222	67,753
Finchley UDC	22,126	39,419	46,719
Hanwell UDC	10,438	19,129	20,485
Harrow on the Hill UDC	10,220	17,074	19,468
Hayes (Mx) UDC	2,594	4,261	6,304
Hendon UDC	22,450	38,806	56,014
Ruislip-Northwood UDC	3,566	6,217	9,113
Southall UDC	13,200	26,323	30,261
Southgate UDC	14,993	33,612	39,120
Wealdstone UDC	5,901	11,923	13,439
Wembley UDC	4,519	10,696	16,191
Hendon RDC	8,647	14,160	17,660
Barnes UDC	17,821	30,377	34,281
Beddington and Wallington UDC	8,403	14,322	16,308
Carshalton UDC	6,746	11,634	14,023
Coulsdon and Purley UDC	8,277	18,872	21,493
Epsom UDC	10,915	19,156*	18,803*
Maldens and Coombe UDC	6,233	12,137	14,503
Merton and Morden UDC	5,470	14,140	17,534
Mitcham UDC	15,015	29,606	35,118

Note

* Figures distorted by inclusion of LCC mental hospitals (opened 1902–7).

1921–31: Increases over 50 per cent

These figures are adjusted to conform with the areas as they existed in 1938–9 and are therefore comparable with those in the 1931–9 table below. (Source: *London Statistics* Vol. 41, LCC, 1939). The figures for Banstead, Coulsdon and Purley, and Epsom and Ewell relate only to those parishes in these areas situated inside the Metropolitan Police District (i.e. Banstead, Woodmansterne; Coulsdon, Farleigh, Sanderstead; Epsom, Ewell, Cuddington).

	1921	*1931*
Bexley MB	21,104	32,626
Harrow UDC	49,020	96,656
Hayes and Harlington UDC	9,842	22,969
Hendon MB	57,566	115,640
Heston and Isleworth MB	47,463	76,254
Potters Bar UDC	3,222	5,720
Ruislip-Northwood UDC	9,112	16,035
Uxbridge UDC	20,626	31,887
Wembley MB	18,239	65,799
Banstead UDC	8,615	13,089
Beddington and Wallington MB	16,451	26,328
Carshalton UDC	13,873	28,586
Coulsdon and Purley UDC	21,577	37,909
Epsom and Ewell MB	22,946	35,228
Malden and Coombe MB	14,495	23,350
Merton and Morden UDC	17,532	41,227
Mitcham MB	35,122	56,872
Sutton and Cheam MB	29,733	48,363
Chingford MB	9,506	22,076
Dagenham MB	9,127	89,362
		(879 per cent)
Ilford MB	85,194	131,061

1931–39: Increases over 50 per cent

The 1939 figures are mid-year, from the Registrar General's estimate as quoted in *Statistical Abstract for London 1937–46* (LCC). These figures are comparable with those for the same areas appearing in the table above.

	1931	*1939*
Bexley MB	32,626	80,110
Chislehurst and Sidcup UDC	27,182	63,140
Crayford UDC (MPD)	16,229	25,200
Orpington UDC (MPD)	18,271	49,510
East Barnet UDC	18,549	34,480
Feltham UDC	16,064	32,770
Harrow UDC	96,656	190,200
Hayes and Harlington UDC	22,969	50,040

	1931	1939
Ruislip-Northwood UDC	16,035	47,760
Wembley MB	65,799	121,600
Banstead UDC (MPD)	13,089	28,480
Carshalton UDC	28,586	59,510
Epsom and Ewell MB	35,228	62,960
Esher UDC (MPD)	22,197	44,150
Malden and Coombe MB	23,350	39,930
Merton and Morden UDC	41,227	72,150
Surbiton MB	30,178	49,450
Sutton and Cheam MB	48,363	76,510
Barking MB	51,270	77,500
Chigwell UDC	16,338	25,100
Chingford MB	22,076	39,460

Year by year growth in selected areas 1931–39

These areas are the same as those used in the 1921–31 and 1931–39 tables above. The figures are taken from *London Statistics* vols. 40 and 41 (LCC), and *Statistical Abstract for London* 1937–46 (LCC).

	1931	1934	1935	1936	1937	1938	1939 (mid)
Banstead	13,089	23,320	24,800	25,670	26,900	27,500	28,480
Bexley	32,626	51,930	59,970	69,000	74,380	77,020	80,110
Carshalton	28,586	38,110	51,000	57,000	58,030	58,730	59,510
Chingford	22,076	27,841	29,690	32,850	35,970	37,510	39,460
Coulsdon and Purley	37,909	46,340	48,570	51,460	53,920	55,070	56,400
Dagenham	89,362	98,710	100,300	102,000	105,500	107,400	109,300
Epsom and Ewell	35,228	43,200	46,320	51,850	56,830	59,930	62,960
Harrow	96,656	132,049	144,280	160,300	174,800	183,500	190,200
Hayes and Harlington	22,969	29,471	31,560	34,080	39,770	43,930	50,040
Hendon	115,640	131,070	134,160	140,650	143,800	145,100	146,200
Heston and Isleworth	76,254	87,797	90,970	95,000	99,420	100,500	102,000
Ilford	131,061	146,070	151,390	157,300	163,000	166,900	169,800
Malden and Coombe	23,350	30,720	32,280	34,480	37,270	38,820	39,930
Merton and Morden	41,227	55,550	57,440	61,000	65,530	68,980	72,150
Mitcham	56,872	60,560	62,070	64,411	65,620	66,020	66,370
Ruislip-Northwood	16,035	21,202	24,930	30,650	36,270	40,820	47,760
Sutton and Cheam	48,363	65,330	69,050	72,530	74,530	75,580	76,510
Uxbridge	31,887	35,458	38,140	39,700	41,950	42,800	45,150
Wembley	65,799	92,160	99,120	107,550	114,700	118,800	121,600

Major growth points outside Greater London area (Metropolitan Police District). Increases over 50 per cent 1921–38.

Source: Greater London Plan, 1944, Appendix 2.

	1921	1938
Dunstable MB	8,945	13,760
Slough MB	20,285	50,620
Billericay UDC	12,431	34,730
Hornchurch UDC	17,489	76,000
Romford MB	20,738	54,600
Baldock UDC	2,518	3,829
Chorleywood UDC	2,444	3,734
Hoddesdon UDC	7,461	11,950
Letchworth UDC	10,544	15,990
Rickmansworth UDC	8,634	18,700
Welwyn Garden City UDC	901	12,150
Hatfield RDC	8,516	16,500
St Albans RDC	12,568	21,030
Watford RDC	12,213	19,240
Welwyn RDC	2,499	3,997
Crayford UDC*	12,295	24,590
Orpington UDC*	18,628	46,320
Caterham and Warlingham UDC*	17,108	27,100
Coulsdon and Purley UDC	23,115	55,070
Leatherhead UDC	11,233	21,170

* whole area including that part in the Metropolitan Police District.

Appendix 2

SUBURBAN ELECTRIC TRAMWAY DEVELOPMENT
1901–32

4. 4.1901	Shepherds Bush–Acton Hill	LUT
4. 4.1901	Shepherds Bush–Kew Bridge	LUT
27. 6.1901	East Ham–Ilford	EHC
27. 6.1901	East Ham–Barking	EHC
6. 7.1901	Kew Bridge–Hounslow	LUT
10. 7.1901	Acton Hill–Southall	LUT
26. 9.1901	Norbury–Croydon–Purley	CC
4. 1.1902	Croydon–Addiscombe	CC
10. 1.1902	Thornton Heath branch	CC
24. 1.1902	West Croydon–Selhurst	CC
14. 3.1902	Selhurst–Norwood Junction	CC
27. 3.1902	Manor Park–Wanstead Park	EHC
13. 8.1902	Hounslow (The Bell)–Hounslow (The Hussar)	LUT
13. 8.1902	Isleworth–Twickenham	LUT
13. 9.1902	Twickenham–Richmond Bridge	LUT
14. 3.1903	Ilford–Chadwell Heath	IC
14. 3.1903	Ilford–Barkingside	IC
2. 4.1903	Twickenham–Teddington–Hampton Wick– Hampton Court	LUT
4. 4.1903	Twickenham–Hampton–Hampton Court	LUT
15. 5.1903	Westminster/Blackfriars–Tooting (Totterdown)	LCC
27. 5.1903	Ilford–Loxford Bridge (for Barking)	IC
3.10.1903	Plumstead–Welling–Bexleyheath– Northumberland Heath (for Erith)	BE
1. 6.1904	Southall–Uxbridge	LUT
19. 6.1904	Kennington–Brixton (Water Lane)– Streatham (Liby)	LCC
22. 7.1904	Finsbury Park–Wood Green	MET
20. 8.1904	Manor House–Tottenham (Seven Sisters)	MET
20. 8.1904	Wood Green–Tottenham (Bruce Grove)	MET
3.12.1904	Cricklewood–West Hendon–Edgware	MET
12. 4.1905	Stamford Hill–Tottenham–Edmonton (Silver St.)	MET
3. 6.1905	Tottenham (Ferry Lane)–Walthamstow– Woodford	WC

3. 6.1905	Walthamstow–Chingford Mount	WC
3. 6.1905	Walthamstow–Higham Hill	WC
3. 6.1905	Walthamstow (Forest Rd)–Leyton Boundary	WC
7. 6.1905	Highgate–Finchley–Whetstone	MET
7. 6.1905	Barking (centre)–Ilford (Loxford Bridge)	BC
19. 7.1905	Edmonton (Silver St.)–Edmonton (Town Hall)	MET
8. 8.1905	Tooting (Totterdown)–Tooting (Broadway)	LCC
24. 8.1905	Edmonton (Town Hall)–Lower Edmonton	MET
26. 8.1905	Abbey Wood–Erith–Northumberland Heath (Bexleyheath)	EC
6.12.1905	Wood Green–Hornsey–Alexandra Palace West	MET
14.12.1905	Norwood Junction–Penge Boundary (Selby Rd)	CC
30. 1.1906	New Cross–Lewisham	LCC
10. 2.1906	Penge Boundary (Selby Rd)–Penge	SMET
14. 2.1906	Bexleyheath–Crayford–Dartford–Horns Cross	DC
1. 3.1906	Hampton Wick–Kingston–Surbiton–The Dittons	LUT
1. 3.1906	Kingston–Kingston Hill	LUT
1. 3.1906	Surbiton–Tolworth	LUT
30. 3.1906	Cricklewood–Willesden Green	MET
11. 4.1906	Wood Green–Alexandra Palace East	MET
12. 4.1906	Anerley–Crystal Palace (CP High Level 28.5)	SMET
12. 4.1906	Penge–Crystal Palace (Thicket Rd)	SMET
26. 5.1906	West Croydon–Mitcham–Tooting Junction	SMET
26. 5.1906	Brentford–Hanwell	LUT
26. 5.1906	Kingston–Ham/Richmond Park Gates	LUT
26. 5.1906	Kingston–New Malden	LUT
10. 6.1906	Lewisham–Catford (Rushey Green)	LCC
4. 8.1906	Whetstone–New Barnet (Hertfordshire boundary)	MET
5. 8.1906	Tooting–Earlsfield–Wandsworth	LCC
17.10.1906	Harlesden–Stonebridge Park	MET
10.11.1906	West Croydon–Wallington–Carshalton	SMET
19.11.1906	Camberwell Green–Dulwich Library	LCC
27.11.1906	Stratford–Leyton–Leytonstone–Walthamstow	LC
28.11.1906	Wood Green–Bounds Green	MET
21.12.1906	Carshalton–Sutton	SMET
22.12.1906	Paddington (Lock Bridge)–Harlesden	MET
22.12.1906	Battersea–Wandsworth	LCC
28. 3.1907	New Barnet (Hertfordshire Boundary)–High Barnet	MET
27. 4.1907	New Malden–Raynes Park	LUT
2. 5.1907	Raynes Park–Wimbledon	LUT
4. 5.1907	Lewisham–Lee Green	LCC
11. 5.1907	Bounds Green–New Southgate	MET
7. 6.1907	Wood Green–Palmers Green	MET
27. 6.1907	Wimbledon–Merton (LCC Boundary)	LUT
27. 6.1907	Merton (Haydons Road)–Earlsfield (Summerstown)	LUT

13.10.1907	Tooting Broadway–Merton (LCC Boundary)	LCC
13.10.1907	Tooting Broadway–Tooting Junction	LCC
31.10.1907	Edgware–Stanmore (Canons Park)	MET
11.12.1907	Lower Edmonton–Freezywater (Hertfordshire Boundary)	MET
23.12.1907	Willesden Green–Harlesden (Craven Park)	MET
15. 4.1908	Stonebridge Park–Wembley	MET
17. 4.1908	Freezywater (Hertfordshire Boundary)– Waltham Cross	MET
17. 4.1908	Woolwich–Plumstead	LCC
30. 5.1908	Harlesden–Shepherds Bush–Hammersmith	LCC
3. 6.1908	Palmers Green–Winchmore Hill	MET
26. 7.1908	Plumstead–Abbey Wood	LCC
19.12.1908	Dulwich Library–Forest Hill	LCC
23. 1.1909	Hammersmith–Putney Bridge	LCC
8. 4.1909	New Southgate–North Finchley	MET
30. 5.1909	Loughborough Junction–Herne Hill–Tulse Hill–West Norwood	LCC
1. 7.1909	Winchmore Hill–Enfield	MET
31. 7.1909	Streatham (Library)–Norbury (Croydon Boundary)	LCC
7.10.1909	Harlesden–Acton	MET
16.12.1909	Clapham Junction–Wandsworth	LCC
17.12.1909	North Finchley–Golders Green	MET
22.12.1909	Hampstead (LCC Boundary)–Golders Green	MET
21. 2.1910	Golders Green–Cricklewood	MET
23. 7.1910	Woolwich–Eltham	LCC
5.11.1910	Streatham–Tooting	LCC
5.11.1910	Earlsfield (Summerstown)–Earlsfield (Garratt Lane)	LCC
14.12.1910	Wembley–Sudbury	MET
20. 2.1911	Enfield–Southbury–Ponders End	MET
25. 2.1911	Brockley–Forest Hill	LCC
30. 1.1912	Putney Bridge–Wandsworth	LCC
29. 5.1913	Forest Hill–Catford (Rushey Green)	LCC
5. 4.1914	Catford (Rushey Green)–Catford (Southend Village)	LCC
26.11.1920	Lee Green–Eltham (Eltham Church 27.3.1921)	LCC
28. 9.1926	Catford (Southend Village)–Downham Estate	LCC
15.11.1928	Downham Estate–Grove Park Station	LCC

30. 6.1932   Woolwich (Well Hall Road)–Eltham Green
                     (partly opened 1.10.1931)   LCC

Abbreviations

BC	Barking Council Tramways	LCC	London County Council Tramways
BE	Bexley Council Tramways		
CC	Croydon Corporation Tramways	LUT	London United Tramways
DC	Dartford Council Light Railways	MET	Metropolitan Electric Tramways
EC	Erith Council Tramways	SMET	South Metropolitan Electric Tramways & Lighting Co.
EHC	East Ham Corporation Tramways		
IC	Ilford Council Tramways	WHC	West Ham Corporation Tramways
LC	Leyton Council Tramways	WC	Walthamstow Council Light Railways.

Appendix 3

SUBURBAN MOTORBUS ROUTE DEVELOPMENT
1910–39

In *November 1910*, the London General Omnibus Company was operating daily motor bus services through the suburban area as follows:

CRICKLEWOOD–BRONDESBURY–Victoria
DOLLIS HILL–CRICKLEWOOD–Charing Cross–Tower Bridge Road
CHILDS HILL–Victoria
HARLESDEN–KENSAL GREEN–Waterloo
PUTNEY–Piccadilly–Kings Cross–Barnsbury
PUTNEY–Bank–WANSTEAD
PUTNEY COMMON–Bank–EAST HAM
KENSAL RISE–Bank–Shoreditch
WILLESDEN GREEN–Holborn–Bank–ILFORD–SEVEN KINGS
BARNES–MORTLAKE–Charing Cross–Liverpool Street
TURNHAM GREEN–Bank–London Bridge
EALING–ACTON–Bank–Plaistow
WEST NORWOOD–WEST DULWICH–Charing Cross–Hammersmith

(The services from Golders Green station to Hendon and Finchley, sponsored by the Underground Company are mentioned in chapter 4).

By *August 1914*, the network had been greatly extended and the services then operating between the suburbs and the central area were as follows:

GOLDERS GREEN–Victoria
CRYSTAL PALACE–Camden Town
PUTNEY STATION–Stroud Green
KENSAL RISE–South Hackney
WILLESDEN–Old Ford
BARNES–Liverpool Street
WOODFORD GREEN–WANSTEAD–Elephant and Castle
BUCKHURST HILL–SNARESBROOK–WANSTEAD–Elephant and Castle
DULWICH–Shepherds Bush
HENDON–London Bridge
GOLDERS GREEN–London Bridge
PUTNEY STATION–Hornsey Rise
PUTNEY–East Ham

EALING BROADWAY–London Bridge
WILLESDEN–London Bridge
TURNHAM GREEN–WEST NORWOOD
LEWISHAM–Crouch End
WOOD GREEN–SHOOTERS HILL
PUTNEY–Homerton
ACTON HIGH STREET–BARKING
ACTON GREEN–BARKING
SEVEN KINGS–ILFORD–Victoria
KENSAL RISE–Hackney Wick
TWICKENHAM–Highgate
PALMERS GREEN–WOOD GREEN–Victoria
SOUTHGATE–Victoria
HADLEY WOODS (COCKFOSTERS)–Victoria
PUTNEY–Highbury
EAST SHEEN–Liverpool Street
RICHMOND–Hammersmith
WEST NORWOOD–Liverpool Street
WALTHAMSTOW (CROOKED BILLET)–Elephant and Castle
HITHER GREEN–LEWISHAM–West Kilburn
HOUNSLOW–ISLEWORTH–Peckham
WALTHAMSTOW (WOOD STREET)–Camberwell
CATFORD–West Kilburn
TEDDINGTON–Herne Hill
EPPING FOREST–CHINGFORD–Victoria
GROVE PARK–West Kilburn
MUSWELL HILL–London Bridge
TURNHAM GREEN–Hammersmith–London Bridge
FARNBOROUGH (Kent)–BROMLEY–Shoreditch
STREATHAM COMMON–Shepherds Bush
CRYSTAL PALACE–Shepherds Bush
ACTON GREEN–Liverpool Street
WANSTEAD–Victoria
BARKING–West Kilburn
PLUMSTEAD COMMON–West Hampstead
PUTNEY–TOTTENHAM
SOUTH CROYDON–Shoreditch
WIMBLEDON PARK–SOUTHFIELDS–TOTTENHAM
WEST HENDON–Shoreditch
SOUTH CROYDON–Oxford Circus
WOOD GREEN–Herne Hill
CATFORD–Oxford Circus
PUTNEY–Stoke Newington
TOOTING–HARLESDEN
RAYNES PARK–MERTON–TOOTING–Liverpool Street
TOTTENHAM–Elephant and Castle
BARNES–Camden Town
EDMONTON–TOTTENHAM–Victoria
EARLSFIELD–Kings Cross

DULWICH–Shoreditch
MITCHAM–Oxford Circus
PLUMSTEAD–Kings Cross
PLUMSTEAD–OLD CHARLTON–Kings Cross
PUTNEY–Liverpool Street
CATERHAM–WHYTELEAFE–KENLEY–PURLEY–
    CROYDON–STREATHAM–Stockwell
HAMPTON COURT–KEW–Liverpool Street
REIGATE–MERSTHAM–COULSDON–PURLEY–
    CROYDON–Stockwell

In addition there were the following services running between suburbs
without entering the central area:

SIDCUP–GREENWICH PIER
MERTON PARK–PUTNEY BRIDGE
EALING BROADWAY–PETERSHAM–KINGSTON–
    SURBITON
EALING BROADWAY–TWICKENHAM–KINGSTON–
    SURBITON
SOUTH CROYDON–PENGE–SYDENHAM–CATFORD–
    LEWISHAM–BLACKHEATH–WOOLWICH
KINGSTON–ESHER
EALING BROADWAY–NORTHFIELDS (local service in
    Ealing)
HOUNSLOW–WINDSOR
GOLDERS GREEN–WEST HENDON
GOLDERS GREEN–FINCHLEY–BARNET–ST ALBANS
PUTNEY BRIDGE–ROEHAMPTON
PUTNEY BRIDGE–KINGSTON HILL
ILFORD BROADWAY–CRANBROOK PARK (local service in
    Ilford)
FRIERN BARNET–MUSWELL HILL–Highgate–Stamford
    Hill–Clapton
SHOOTERS HILL–KIDBROOKE–LEWISHAM
ROMFORD–SEVEN KINGS–ILFORD–STRATFORD
BROMLEY–WESTERHAM HILL
WANSTEAD–North Woolwich
WALTHAMSTOW (HOE ST)–Cubitt Town
EALING BROADWAY–BRENTFORD–KINGSTON–
    SURBITON
BLACKHEATH–WESTCOMBE PARK–Bow Road
SLOUGH–MAIDENHEAD
BROMLEY–BECKENHAM–PENGE
BECKENHAM JUNCTION–PARK LANGLEY (local service in
    Beckenham)
HOUNSLOW (Underground)–BEDFONT–STAINES–EGHAM
WATFORD–BUSHEY–STANMORE–EDGWARE–WEST
    HENDON–CRICKLEWOOD–Kilburn

North West London bus route development 1910–39

Owing to the multiplicity of new services, service variations and complications, space does not permit even an outline review of bus route development in the whole London suburban area after 1919. One of the most important sectors for suburban growth after 1919 was the north-west; the following survey shows the development of *daily* LGOC and LPTB services from 1910 onwards.

1910

By November 1910, the LGOC had established radial routes along the main roads from central London as far as Childs Hill, Cricklewood (Dollis Hill), Willesden Green, Kensal Rise, Harlesden, Wormwood Scrubs and Ealing. As mentioned in chapter 4, services were also operated for the Underground from Golders Green Station to Hendon and to Finchley.

1911

Routes were extended: from Childs Hill to Hendon via Golders Green; from Willesden Green to Willesden (Neasden Lane); from Ealing to South Ealing.

1912

Link between Hendon and West Hendon (Welsh Harp); extension from Dollis Hill to Welsh Harp; link Harlesden–Willesden (Neasden Lane); extension Wormwood Scrubs to Harlesden; local service in Ealing (Ealing Broadway circuitously to Northfields station). Golders Green to Finchley, Barnet and St Albans.

1913

Extension from West Hendon to Edgware, Stanmore and Watford; link Cricklewood–Willesden Green; link South Ealing–Kew Bridge; link from Ealing Broadway to Surbiton via Brentford and Kingston.

1914

Nil.

1915–17

Link Turnham Green–Chiswick–Tooting–Wimbledon.

1920

High Wycombe–Beaconsfield–Uxbridge; Ealing–Surbiton route extended to Hook; Watford–Bushey Heath–Stanmore Common–Harrow Weald–Wealdstone–Harrow–South Harrow; Croxley Green–Watford–St Albans; Bushey–Watford–Kings Langley–Berkamsted; Hemel Hempstead–Watford–Bushey.

1921

Golders Green–St Albans extended to Harpenden; Hounslow–Cranford–Harlington–West Drayton–Yiewsley–Uxbridge; extension from High

Wycombe to West Wycombe; Ealing–Hook route extended to Leather-head via Chessington; Hitchin–St Albans; Watford–Chesham; Wheat-hampstead–St Albans–Radlett; St Albans–Hertford.

1922

Northfields–Ealing–London Bridge; Golders Green–Highgate–Stroud Green–Finsbury Park; Watford–Bushey–Elstree–High Barnet; Watford–Leavesden Green–Abbots Langley; Watford–Rickmansworth–Northwood –Pinner–Harrow; Watford–Croxley Green–Rickmansworth–Uxbridge; Golders Green–Mill Hill–Edgware–Stanmore–Wealdstone–Harrow–South Harrow; extension Ealing to Hanwell (service to London Bridge).

1923

Brentford to London Bridge; extension from Hanwell to Southall (service to London Bridge); Ealing–Northfields–Brentford; St Albans–Watford–Rickmansworth; Bushey–Northchurch; St Albans–Welwyn Garden City; Watford–Enfield–Waltham Cross.

1924

Golders Green–Hendon–North Circular Road–Neasden–Wembley–Sud-bury Town; Sudbury Town–Harlesden–Putney–Balham; Hayes–Bot-well–Harlington–Hounslow link; Willesden Green–Kingsbury link.

1925

Colindale (Edgware Rd)–Colindale station extension; Sudbury Town–Harrow link.

1926

Sudbury Town–Alperton–Ealing Broadway link; extension from Brent-ford to Lampton via Great West Road; Southall–Norwood Green–Houns-low link.

1927

West Hendon–Kingsbury Green–Kenton–Harrow link; Harrow Weald–Bushey Heath link; Edgware–Brockley Hill–Elstree–Boreham Wood. Routes in Hendon diverted to serve Hendon Central station.

1928

Greenford–Sudbury Hill station link; Greenford–Ealing link; Stonebridge Park–Brent–Finchley via North Circular Road.

1929

Uxbridge–Cowley–Iver–Richings Park estate; Uxbridge–Windsor; Hayes–Uxbridge link; Sudbury Hill station–Sudbury link; Mill Hill–Hendon Central–Brent via Watford Bypass; Pinner–Eastcote–Ruislip–Ickenham–Uxbridge (Messrs. Loumax until 1930).

1930

South Harrow–Northolt link; North Harrow–Headstone Lane–Hatch End–Pinner; Preston Road station–Wembley link.

1931
Golders Green local service to Laing Estate (Pennine Drive).

1932
Hayes–Yeading (West End); Southall–Greenford link; Greenford–Western Avenue–East Acton–Putney Bridge; Burnt Oak–Stag Lane–Kingsbury link.

1933
North Harrow–Wealdstone link; Kenton–Wealdstone link; Burnt Oak–Mill Hill link; Mill Hill–Totteridge–Whetstone link. Golders Green local service (Laing Estate) extended to Cricklewood Broadway.

1934
South Harrow–Rayners Lane link; West Ruislip–Uxbridge via Swakeleys Road link.

1935
Ealing–Park Royal–Stonebridge Park via North Circular Road link.

1936
Burnt Oak–Queensbury–Kenton link; Sudbury–North Wembley–Dollis Hill link.

1937
Nil.

1938
Hayes End–Hillingdon link; extension Boreham Wood to Barnet Bypass (Laing estate); Preston Road–Kenton link; North Harrow–Rayners Lane link; West Drayton–Yiewsley–Uxbridge link.

1939
South Harrow–South Ruislip–Ruislip Manor–Ruislip; extension Ruislip–Ruislip Lido.

(*source*: LGOC and LPTB route maps 1910–39).

Supplementing the General services before 1933 were those of independent operators, mostly starting in the early twenties. The following were
taken over by the LGOC in 1926:

Cambrian Coaching and Goods Transport Ltd
Southall–Liverpool Street
Hounslow (Hussar)–Liverpool Street
Uxbridge–Liverpool Street
Western Omnibus Co. Ltd (Randalls)
Greenford–Kings Cross

The following independent services survived to be taken over by the
LPTB in 1933–34:

E. Brickwood Ltd (Red Line)
Sudbury–Kings Cross
Ryan
Sudbury–Kings Cross
Birch Brothers
Hendon–Mill Hill
City Motor Omnibus Co. Ltd
Hounslow Heath–Peckham
Bucks Express (Watford) Ltd
Watford–Oxford Circus
Fikins & Ainsworth Ltd (started 1922)
Harefield–Rickmansworth
Harefield–Denham
Harefield–Uxbridge
Harefield–Northwood
E. Prentice (Chiltern)
Aylesbury–Watford Junction station
Premier Line Ltd
Colindale–Old Ford
Loumax
South Harrow–Eastcote
Mrs V. A. Sayers (Royal Highlander)
Eastcote–Uxbridge
Eastcote–South Harrow
Greenford–Ealing
F. Steer (Colne)
St Albans–Shenley
St Albans–London Colney

Appendix 4

NEW SUBURBAN RAILWAY FACILITIES 1901–40

Note: For stations still open, the name currently in use is shown.
E = Electric service from the opening of the new line.
Q = Widening, usually to four tracks from two.

New station	New lines	Electrifications
1901		
West Ham	Q. Seven Kings–	
Goodmayes	Goodmayes	
1902		
Cranley Gardens	Q. Goodmayes–Romford	
1903		
Newbury Park	Ilford–Woodford loop	
Barkingside		
Fairlop		
Hainault (1)		
Grange Hill		
Chigwell		
North Ealing	E. Acton Town–South	
	Harrow	
Park Royal (2)		
Alperton		
Sudbury Town		
Sudbury Hill		
South Harrow		
Park Royal	Old Oak–Hanwell/West	
GWR (3)	Ealing via Park Royal	
	Q. Hampton Ct Junc.–	
	Woking	
1904		
Smitham		
Elmstead Woods	Q. Elmstead Woods–	
	Orpington	
Ruislip	Harrow–Uxbridge	
Uxbridge (Met.)		
Greenford	Park Royal–Greenford	
North Acton		
Perivale (GWR)		

New station	New lines	Electrifications
Cowley		
Castle Bar Park		
Trumpers Crossing Halt (4)		

1905

Drayton Green	Q. St Johns–Elmstead Woods	
Letchworth		Baker St–Harrow– Uxbridge
Napsbury		
Ickenham		Acton Town–Hounslow West
Hounslow West		
South Acton		Ealing Bdy.–Victoria– East Ham
		Wimbledon–Putney Br.– High St. Kensington
		Richmond–Turnham Green

1906

Wembley Hill	Neasden–Northolt Junc.	
Sudbury & Harrow Rd.		
Sudbury Hill (5)		
West Ruislip	Greenford–High Wycombe	
Denham		
Gerrards Cross		
Beaconsfield		
Old Oak Lane Halt		
Rayners Lane		
Eastcote		
Mill Hill The Hale		
Bandon Halt (6)		
Beeches Halt (7)		
Bingham Rd (8)		
Spencer Rd (9)		

1907

Uxbridge High Street (10)	E. Charing Cross– Golders Green	
Golders Green		
Northolt Halt (GWR)		

1908

| Northfields | Q. East Ham–Barking | East Ham–Barking |
| Wood Lane | | |

New station	*New lines*	*Electrifications*
Preston Road		
Brondesbury Park		
Eltham Park		
South Ruislip		
1909		
Hounslow East		
Dollis Hill		
Emerson Park		
1910		
Grange Park	Grange Park–Cuffley	
Gordon Hill	(Enfield station	
Crews Hill	resited)	
Cuffley		
Moor Park		
Gidea Park		
1911		
Reedham	Q. Hammersmith–	Victoria–Streatham Hill–
Brentham	Turnham Green	Crystal Palace.
1912		
Stamford Brook		
Watford West	Watford–Croxley Green	
Croxley Green		
Harrow & Weald-	Willesden Junc.–Harrow	
stone (Subn)	(LNWR Suburban	
Kenton	Line)	
North Wembley		Peckham Rye–Tulse
Wembley (Subn)		Hill–Streatham Hill–
Stonebridge Park		West Norwood
Harlesden		(London Br.–Crystal
Willesden Junc.		Palace LL).
(Subn)		
Ruislip Manor		
Denham Golf Club		
1913		
Headstone Lane	Harrow–Watford Junc.	
Bushey (Subn)	(LNWR Suburban	
Pinner and Hatch	Line)	
End (Subn)		
West Harrow		
	Q. Finchley Rd–West	
	Hampstead	
1914		
Carpenders Park	Q. Willesden Green–	Willesden Junc.–
	Wembley Park	Earls Court

New station	*New lines*	*Electrifications*
Shepherds Bush (H&C)		
Goldhawk Road		
Seer Green & Jordans		

1915
Maida Vale
Kilburn Park
Queens Park
North Harrow

E. Paddington–Willesden Junc.
Q. West Hampstead–Willesden Green

Waterloo–East Putney–Wimbledon

1916
Barnes Bridge
Kensal Green

Kingston–East Putney (Point Pleasant Junc.)
Kingston–Wimbledon
Kingston–Shepperton
Barnes–Hounslow–Twickenham
Malden–Hampton Court
Malden–Claygate (11)
Broad Street–Richmond–Kew Bridge

1917

Willesden Junc.–Watford

1920
Welwyn Garden City
East Acton
Ealing Broadway (CLR)

E. Ealing Broadway–Wood Lane

1922

Full service: Broad St.–Watford
Euston–Watford–Croxley Green branch

1923
Northwick Park
North Acton (CLR)
West Acton
Brent
Hendon Central
Hillingdon

E. Golders Green–Hendon Central

New station	New lines	Electrifications
1924		
Bayford	Cuffley–Langley Junc-	
Hertford North	tion (for Stevenage)	
Stapleford		
Watton at Stone		
Colindale	E. Hendon Central–	
Edgware	Edgware	
Burnt Oak		
Iver		
1925		
Motspur Park	E. Rickmansworth–	Harrow–Rickmansworth
Croxley	Watford (Met.)	Elmers End–Hayes
Watford (Met.)		Balham–Coulsdon North
		Selhurst–West Croydon–
		Sutton
		Raynes Park–Epsom–
		Dorking North
		Leatherhead–Guildford
		Surbiton–Effingham
		Junction
		Victoria/Holborn Via-
		duct–Herne Hill–
		Orpington
		Holborn Viaduct–
		Orpington via Catford
		Loop
1926		
Gale Street Halt (12)		Charing X/Cannon St.–
Northolt Park (13)		Bromley North
Brookmans Park		Charing X/Cannon St.–
Tooting Bec	E. Clapham Common–	Orpington
Tooting Broadway	Morden	Charing X/Cannon St.–
Colliers Wood		Beckenham Junction
South Wimbledon		Charing X/Cannon St.–
Morden		Addiscombe
South Greenford		Charing X/Cannon St.–
		Dartford via North
		Kent, via Dartford
		Loop and via
		Bexleyheath
1927		
Riddlesdown		Watford–Rickmansworth
Byfleet and New		(LMSR)
Haw		
Sunnymeads		

New station	*New lines*	*Electrifications*
1928		
Petts Wood		London Bridge–Streat-
		ham–Coulsdon North
		Sutton–Epsom Downs
		Norwood Junc.–Selhurst
		–Streatham–Tulse Hill
		London Br.–Norwood
		Junc.–East Croydon–
		Purley–Caterham
		Purley–Tattenham
		Corner.
1929		
Wimbledon Chase	E. Wimbledon–South	Epsom–Sutton
South Merton	Merton	Streatham–Sutton
		Holborn Viaduct–Tulse
		Hill–Wimbledon
		Crystal Palace LL–
		Beckenham Junction
1930		
Morden South	E. South Merton–	Hounslow/Feltham
St Helier	Sutton	Junc.–Windsor
Sutton Common		Wimbledon–West
Sutton West		Croydon
Birkbeck		Dartford–Gravesend
Hainault (reopened)		Central
North Sheen		
Whitton		
Waddon Marsh Halt		
Hinchley Wood		
1931		
Syon Lane	Q. Gidea Park–Romford	
1932		
Park Royal West		Purley–Reigate/Three
Stoneleigh		Bridges
Woodmansterne		
Upney	Q. Barking–Upminster	Barking–Upminster
Heathway		
Manor House	E. Finsbury Park–	
Turnpike Lane	Arnos Grove	
Wood Green		
Bounds Green		
Arnos Grove		
Kingsbury	E. Wembley Park–	
Canons Park	Stanmore	
Stanmore (Met)		
Belmont Halt		
(LMSR)		

New station	*New lines*	*Electrifications*
	Q. Wembley Park–Harrow	
	Q. Acton Town–Northfields	
1933		
Southgate	E. Arnos Grove–Cockfosters	
Oakwood		
Cockfosters		
West Finchley		
South Kenton		
Berrylands		
Northwood Hills		
1934		
Osterley (resited)	Q. Gidea Park–Shenfield	Bickley Junc.–St Mary Cray
Ruislip Gardens		
Queensbury		
Upminster Bridge		
1935		
Elm Park		St Mary Cray–Sevenoaks
Albany Park		Nunhead–Lewisham loop
Bingham Road (reopened)	E. Woodside–Sanderstead (reopened)	Orpington–Sevenoaks
Coombe Road (reopened)		
Selsdon (reopened)		
1936		
Falconwood		
Roding Valley		
Hersham		
1937		
		Surbiton–Woking–Guildford
		Weybridge–Chertsey–Staines
		Woking–Farnham–Alton
1938		
Malden Manor	E. Motspur Park–Tolworth	Dorking North–Horsham
Tolworth		
1939		
Chessington North	E. Tolworth–Chessington South	Virginia Water–Reading
Chessington South	E. Highgate–East Finchley	Ascot–Ash Vale
		Aldershot–Guildford

New station	New lines	Electrifications
		Gravesend–Gillingham
		Swanley Junc.–Gillingham

1940

East Finchley–High Barnet

Planned or in construction in 1940; stopped by the war:

Brockley Hill	E. Edgware–Bushey Heath	Finsbury Pk.–East Finchley
Elstree South		Highgate–Alexandra Palace
Bushey Heath	E. Chessington South–Leatherhead	Finchley Central–Edgware (17)
Rushett	E. Liverpool St.–Leyton (14)	North Acton–Denham (16)
Leatherhead North	E. Leytonstone–Newbury Park (15)	Leytonstone–Epping (18)
	E. Drayton Park–Finsbury Park	Newbury Park–Woodford (19)
	Q. North Acton–Denham (16)	Liverpool St.–Shenfield (20)

References
(1) Closed 1908, re-opened 1930
(2) Moved to new site on Western Avenue 1932
(3) Closed 1937
(4) Closed 1926
(5) Opened as 'South Harrow and Roxeth'
(6) Closed 1914
(7) Rebuilt as Carshalton Beeches station 1925
(8) Closed 1915, re-opened 1935
(9) Closed 1915
(10) Closed 1939
(11) Electric trains Surbiton to Claygate withdrawn 1919, restored 1925
(12) Rebuilt as Becontree station 1932
(13) Opened as 'South Harrow', the original South Harrow on the same line then renamed 'Sudbury Hill'
(14) Completed 1946–7
(15) Completed 1947
(16) Completed as far as West Ruislip only 1947–8
(17) Completed to Mill Hill East only 1941
(18) Completed 1947–9
(19) Completed 1948
(20) Completed 1949

Appendix 5

CO-PARTNERSHIP HOUSING ESTATES

The idea of co-partnership housing societies which would establish a truly co-operative system of house and estate ownership was originated in the 1880s by Benjamin Jones of the Co-operative Union. Edward Vantissart Neale and others formed the pioneer association, Tenant Co-operators Ltd, in 1888. The movement received a considerable boost in the early years of the present century, largely owing to the efforts of Henry Vivian M.P., who assumed chairmanship of the 1905 Co-partnership Tenants' Housing Council and its ally Co-partnership Tenants Ltd, formed two years later. The first body was propagandist, the second gave practical advice to new schemes and assisted them to obtain capital.

With the object of securing his personal interest in the prosperity of the development as a whole, each tenant of a co-partnership estate was required to take a minimum share in the company's capital. To safeguard the estate from deterioration and speculation, it was vested in the single-co-operative ownership of the tenants in perpetuity. It was a case of *these houses are ours* rather than the more usual *this house is mine.*

Starting capital for co-partnership schemes was sought from private individuals, who needed to possess some idealistic interest, as the rate of return was low. Further assistance was available after the passing of the Housing & Town Planning Act of 1909, which enabled the Public Works Loan Commissioners to grant loans to co-partnership schemes for working class houses built to certain standards. These loans went up to two-thirds the valuation of the houses and land, and were only made if the company's dividends were limited to 5 per cent.

Three important London schemes may be noticed: *Ealing Co-partnership Tenants Ltd* was formed in 1901 by Henry Vivian and Thomas Blandford to develop 32½ acres at Ealing between the river Brent and Castlebar Hill. This was to become known as Brentham, or the West London Garden Village. About 140 houses had been completed at a density of eight and twelve to the acre when John Burns opened the estate's recreation ground in June 1908. Rents ranged from 6s 6d to £1 a week, according to the number of rooms (four to eight). Each tenant was obliged to take out at least five £10 shares in the company. The development included a social club and institute, with boys' club, ladies' sewing circle and tennis and cricket clubs. In 1914, the estate, substantially complete, contained 510 houses, served by its own halt on the GWR Paddington–High Wycombe line.

Hampstead Tenants Ltd About 72 acres of the Hampstead Garden Suburb was developed on co-operative lines by this company, formed in 1907. The first houses, ready in that year, were let at rents from 6s to 15s a week. A club house (at Willifield Green) and homes for the elderly were included in the development.

Great Western (London) Garden Village Society This society developed estates at Hayes, Middlesex (east of Coldharbour Lane) and at West Acton (east of the railway line), the latter including shops. Between 1924 and 1931, 762 houses were erected on both estates. The society was fully co-operative and each tenant was required to take out a £50 share. Land was purchased by the railway company, who also paid for the roads and sewers, leaving the remainder of the development to the society, which was charged ground rents yielding a 4 per cent return on the outlay. The GWR also lent the society up to 90 per cent of the building costs, repayable over fifty years at 4 per cent, the balance to be found from loan stock and the shares of the tenants and investors. Further assistance was provided by the state subsidies available under the 1923 and 1924 Housing Acts. All the tenants were railwaymen, paying rents from 8s to 13s 9d a week according to the size of house. Rates could be paid weekly as an addition to rent. Both estates, with their houses, were designed by the architect T. Alwyn Lloyd.

Appendix 6

SPECIFICATIONS AND PLANS OF LONDON SUBURBAN HOUSES

New Ideal Homesteads Ltd,
Type 'K'. In blocks of four,
Mossford Park, North Ilford, 1934,
and other sites. £595 (Plan 3).

Hall and staircase: 5 ft. 6 in. by 10 ft. Front door with tiled canopy. Arctic glass window at side of door. Meter cupboard under stairs. Two-way light switches hall and landing. Chair rail around hall and up staircase, lincrusta paper from this rail to skirting.

Drawing-room: 13 ft. by 10 ft. 4½ in. Large four-section semi-circular bay window. Well-type fireplace with tiled surrounds and solid mahogany mantel (mottled or plain tiles to colour choice). Gas and electric power points by fireplace.

Dining-room: 13 ft. 9 in. by 10 ft. 4½ in. Brown tiled surround to fireplace. Back boiler in fireplace to provide hot water supply. Oak mantel surround. French casement doors to garden. Gas and electric power points at fireplace.

Kitchenette: 10 ft. by 5 ft. 6 in. Tiled to dado height with white glazed tiles, black and white ornamental strip and black capping. White porcelain deep sink with detachable draining board. Two gas points (cooker and copper). Larder, kitchenette cabinet with glazed doors. Outside door glazed in upper panel.

Bedroom 1: 10 ft. by 13 ft. 6 in. Bay window as drawing-room. Tiled fireplace for coal or gas (gas point).

Bedroom 2: 13 ft. 9 in. by 10 ft. Four-light window. Heated linen cupboard and wardrobe cupboard between fireplace and window.

Bedroom 3: 7 ft. 9 in. by 6 ft. Gas and electric power points.

Bathroom: 7 ft. by 6 ft. All walls tiled to dado height with white glazed tiles, ornamental black and white strip tiling and capping. Lavatory basin attached to wall, waste and water pipes exposed outside tiles. Panelled bath. W.C.

New Ideal Homesteads Ltd
Type 'A2' chalet (semi-detached)
Mossford Park, North Ilford, 1934,
and other sites. £745 (plan 4).

Drawing-room: 16 ft. 3 in. by 11 ft. 9 in. Well-type fireplace with tiled surround and mahogany mantel. Gas and electric power points. Five-light semi-circular bay window.

Dining-room: 13 ft. 9 in. by 12 ft. 3 in. French casement doors to garden. Well-type fireplace with tiled surround and oak mantel. Gas and electric power points. Built-in cupboard.

Kitchen: 10 ft. 6 in. by 8 ft. Black and white tiled floor. Walls tiled to dado height with white glazed tiles, ornamental strip tiling and capping. Dresser 7 ft. long by 2 ft. wide along window length. Electric point for iron. Larder with two shelves and tiled slab. Slow combustion boiler for hot water supply. Deep white porcelain sink, large draining board, nickel taps. Gas points for cooker and copper. Coal store accessible from inside and out. 8 ft.-wide cement paving outside kitchen round to dining-room casement doors.

Bedroom 1: 16 ft. 3 in. by 11 ft. 10½ in. Bay window as drawing-room. Electric wall-fire, gas and electric power points. Lighting points over bed and over window.

Bedroom 2: 11 ft. 10 in. by 10 ft. 4 in. Electric wall-fire. Lighting points over bed and over window.

Bedroom 3 or Study: (on ground floor) 10 ft. 5 in. by 7 ft. 10½ in. Oriel bay window with seat. 2 kW. electric fire in tiled surround.

Boxrooms combined floorspace 200 sq. ft. under eaves, reached by doors from bedrooms 1 and 2.

Bathroom: 6 ft. 9 in. by 7 ft. 4½ in. (ground floor). White glazed tiles to dado height, ornamental black and white strip course and black capping. White porcelain enamelled square-ended bath enclosed with marbled panels. Lavatory basin bracketed out from wall. Heated linen cupboard. Heated chromium-plated towel rail.

Separate W.C. (£20 reduction if combined with bathroom).

Hall: 8 ft. by 7 ft. 4 in. (at side of house). Lighting points controlled from hall and landing.

New Ideal Homesteads Ltd,
Type 'D.B.1.' Detached
bungalow, Mossford Park, North Ilford, 1934,
and other sites. £795 (plan 5).

Sun Loggia at front with 6 ft. by 6 ft. quarry-tiled floor.

Entrance Hall: French windows either side of front door.

Dining-lounge: 16 ft. by 14 ft. Tiled fireplace set in oak mantel. Gas and electric power points. French doors to sun loggia.

Kitchen: 12 ft. by 9 ft. Deep white porcelain sink, nickel taps, draining board. Gas copper and cooker points. Electric point for iron. Fitted dresser-cupboard under window with table top. Boiler for hot water supply. Floor and walls tiled.

Bathroom: 9 ft. by 7 ft. White glazed tiles to dado height, black and white strip and black capping. Square-ended porcelain enamelled bath enclosed in marbled panels. Lavatory basin bracketed from wall, nickel taps. W.C.

Bedroom 1: 12 ft. by 10 ft. Electric wall-fire.

Bedroom 2: 12 ft. by 9 ft. Electric wall-fire.

Spare Bedroom: 9 ft. 1½ in. by 8 ft. 9 in. Electric wall-fire.

General specification applying to all New Ideal Homesteads houses, 1934:
Exterior walls: on concrete foundation, minimum 9 in. thick. Ground
concrete under all ground floors eight parts aggregate to one part cement.
Sleeper walls of 4½ in. brickwork supporting ground-floor joists. External
walls of 9 in. solid brickwork rendered with two coats of cement mortar
and finished with clean shingle except where shown as facing brickwork.
Interior partition walls, brick built, 3 in. thick.
Damp-proof course: double slate, embedded in cement.
Roofs: English hand-made sand-faced roofing tiles laid to a 4 in. gauge on
1 in. by ¾ in. battens nailed to 4 in. by 2 in. rafters. Every fifth course of
tiles nailed with 2 in. stout nails.
Ceilings: Plaster ceiling board. 8 ft. minimum height floor to ceiling.
Windows: Wooden casements with transoms and opening fanlights.
Internal doors: Four panelled.
Front door: Glazed in arctic glass in upper panel; Yale-type latch with
three keys and barrel bolt.
Moulded skirtings and architraves to all rooms.
Ceilings panelled and papered to match friezes; walls papered to choice;
internal paintwork to choice.
Copper tubing to water system.
Flush-type electric light wall switches in bakelite finish; ceiling roses,
flexes and lampholders supplied; power points with plug holders and
switches.
Dwarf brick wall with posts and chains in front; entrance gate.
Rear boundary close boarded fence 6 ft. high, posts set in concrete.
Side division fences in chestnut paling strongly fixed criss-cross fashion.
Length of 6 ft. close-boarded fencing at immediate back.
Car drive made up with gravel for semi-detached houses.

> E. & L. Berg Ltd,
> 'Type 88', semi-detached,
> Ashtead Woods Estate 1939,
> and other sites. £1,020 (plan 6).

Entrance Hall: 9 ft. 5 in. by 5 ft. 6 in. at narrowest point. Concealed staircase with walk-in cloak cupboard under. Quarry tiled, roofed porch.
Drawing-room: 12 ft. by 15 ft. 1 in. Six-light bay window. Well-type
fireplace with ornamental tiled surround. Gas and electric power points.
Dining-room: 12 ft. by 13 ft. 9 in. Double French casement doors
with pebble glass and lead lights from hall. Double French casement doors
to garden. Well-type fireplace with ornamental tiled surround. Electric
power and gas point.
Kitchen: 12 ft. 6 in. by 7 ft. 11 in. Fitted cabinet with flap table. Slow
combustion boiler for hot water supply. Gas points for cooker and boiler.
Electric power point. Deep white butler sink with teak draining board.
Tiled to shoulder height. colours to choice, Quarry tiling to floor around
boiler and cooker.
Fuel store: (brick built) outside back door, for 5 cwt coke, 8 cwt coal.

23. Downham: LCC austerity and trams—Downham Way from Old Bromley Road, 19 April 1928. (Photo: Greater London Council.)

Downham: by LCC tram to your LCC front door. Temporary tram terminus at Southover, Downham Way, 16 March 1928. (Photo: G. N. Southerden, courtesy V. E. Burrows.)

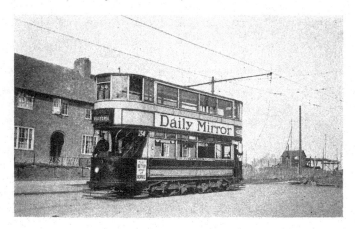

24. Watling: Montrose Avenue under construction, 1926. The light railway in the foreground has a siding into the materials dump. (Photo: Greater London Council.)

St Helier Estate, LCC, in 1934. Austerity relieved with bays and gables borrowed from the styles of the speculative builder. (Photo: Greater London Council.)

Integral garage: 14 ft. 8 in. by 8 ft. Double doors at front, door to garden.
Side entrance, with close-boarded gate.
Bedroom 1: 12 ft. 3 in. by 15 ft. 8 in. Panel electric fire in tiled surround.
Six-light bay window. Electric power point.
Bedroom 2: 12 ft. 6 in. by 14 ft. 2 in. Six-light bay window. Panel electric
fire in tiled surround. Electric power point.
Bedroom 3: 9 ft. 7 in. by 8 ft. 2 in.
Bathroom: Tiled to shoulder height to choice of colour. Square-ended
porcelain bath with tiled panelling and cupboard under. Chromium-
plated taps and shower fitting with mixer. Pedestal lavatory basin with
chromium plated taps. Chromium-plated heated towel rail.
Separate W.C.
Heated linen cupboards off landing with slatted shelving.
Boxroom: 14 ft. 6 in. by 8 ft. under sloping roof. Reached from Bedroom 1.
General specification (applicable to all Berg houses of this period):
Roof: English hand-made sand-faced tiles over closeboarding and felt.
Principal rafters 4 in. by 2 in. at 14 in. centres. Purlins 5 in. by 3 in. with
4 in. by 2 in. struts.
Windows: Crittal steel frames, leaded lights. Special hinges to allow easy
cleaning.
Curtain boxes to conceal runners. Curtain rails.
Arctic or coloured glass to choice in hall, front door, bathroom, lavatory,
back door and side kitchen windows.
Doors: Front doors in oak or pine to choice, internal doors British Colum-
bian pine with five horizontal panels, lever type handles, all fitted with
mortice locks.
Hot water system: Copper piping throughout. 22½-gallon copper hot water
cylinder. All pipes in loft wrapped. Loft tank 30 gallons, galvanised
rivetted iron, cased.
Walls: Double slate or lead core bitumen damp course on cement plinth.
External walls all facing bricks or stucco to choice, cavity 11 in. walls to
ground floor, 9 in. rendered walls elsewhere. 9 in. forecourt walls and oak
gates.
External and internal paintwork and finish: to choice.
Ceilings: 8 ft., plasterboard, coved.
Floors: Narrow strip British Columbian Pine.
Fences: 6 ft. close-boarded cedarwood at immediate rear. Boundary fences
in close-boarded cedarwood with cedarwood lattice tops.

A. W. Curton Ltd,
Type '3A' semi-detached £1,140
  ,, ,, detached   £1,200
Edgwarebury Lane Estate, Edgware, 1935 (Plan 8)

Hall and staircase: Staircase with movable panel, solid oak handrail and
newel posts with pedestal lamp.
Drawing-room: 12 ft. 3 in. by 17 ft. 3 in. (into bay). Doors in side of bay,
leading to garden. Tiled fireplace, polished hardwood mantel to choice,

non-dust-collecting cornice, picture rail, moulded skirting. Wireless aerial installed.

Dining-room: 13 ft. 6 in. by 14 ft. 9 in. (into bay). Oak panelled walls, plaque rail, moulded skirting, oak mantel, tiled fireplace (or all-brick fireplace).

Kitchen: 9 ft. 3 in. by 10 ft. 6 in. (into door recess). Black and white tiled floor and white tiled dado. Dresser with glazed cupboards and enamelled table top. Gas washing-machine. Deep white glazed sink with detachable draining board. Power point for iron etc. Shelved larder.

Brick-built coal store at back of house

Bedroom 1: 12 ft. by 14 ft. 9 in. Picture rail, recessed cupboard (under front gable). Tiled fireplace and hearth with wooden mantel (or all-tiled).

Bedroom 2: 12 ft. by 14 ft. 9 in. Picture rail, tiled fireplace and hearth.

Bedroom 3: 7ft. 6 in. by 9 ft. 3 in. Corner window.

Bathroom: 7 ft. 6 in. by 6 ft. Marble or coloured tiled dado to choice. Porcelain enamelled square enclosed bath. Chromium-plated shower and mixing valve. Pedestal lavatory basin with chromium-plated corner-placed taps.

Airing-cupboard: With slatted shelves.

Separate lavatory: With 'low-down' suite.

General specification applying to all A. W. Curton houses (1935):

Foundations: Taken down to solid bottom; composed of ballast Portland cement concrete 2 in. thicker than required by local authority, and reinforced with steel rods. Rapid hardening cement used in winter months.

Drains: Each house separately connected to main drainage.

Damp course: Double slate.

Walls: 9 in. brickwork with rustic facings to front, side and back elevations up to tiled oversailing courses.

Rough Casting. All external walls above oversailing course rough cast with two-coat work, cement and sand impregnated with damp-proofing solution, final coat Crystal Spar or clean shingle.

Beams and half-timbering: Solid English Oak, properly framed together.

Roofs: Boarded and covered with antique sand-faced tiles with swept tiled valleys.

Carcassing timbers: Well-seasoned yellow deal of generous size, properly framed together.

Plastering: Ceilings lathed with lathing reinforced with galvanized wires. Finished with white superfine Hydro-Keen's cement.

Doors: Single panelled; choice of door furniture.

Windows: Wooden casements glazed with British 24 oz. drawn glass and leaded lights.

Staircases: Panelled, or balusters, to choice.

Floors: Pine in most houses, suitable for polishing. Oak parquetry extra: Hall £8, Lounge-hall £15, Reception rooms £15 each.

Water Heating: Enamelled Ideal coke boiler or gas circulator, heating airing-cupboard, kitchen sink, bath and lavatory basin.

Electricity: Power points on each floor, and in kitchen. Flush switches, fuse boxes and pendants fitted.

Gas: Points at all fireplaces. Gas washing-machine installed.

Wireless: Indoor aerial fitted.

Bathroom: All walls covered to dado height with coloured tiled or marble to client's choice of colour. Hot and cold mixer hand spray fitting to bath. Chromium-plated hot towel rails in all four-, five- and six-bedroom houses.

Oak Panelling: Fitted to Dining-room or Lounge-hall in all houses.

Decorations: To choice. Exterior paintwork in white lead, internal work in enamel or grained and varnished as desired.

Gardens: Good size, enclosed with close-boarded wooden fences with oak posts. Front gardens turved; crazy patterned concrete path to house.

(£1,650 four-bedroom detached house on 39 ft.-wide plot, £1,705 and £1,730 four-bedroom detached houses on 42 ft. 6 in.-wide plots).

Plan 1

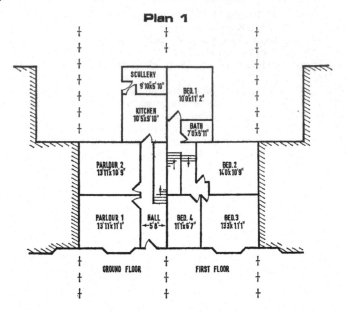

Corbett Class A House. Downshall Estate, Ilford, 1903. £256 10s. Leasehold. Ground Rent £5 1s

Plan 2

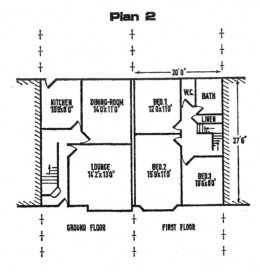

Terrace house. Cannon Hill Estate, Raynes Park, 1925. £695

Plan 3

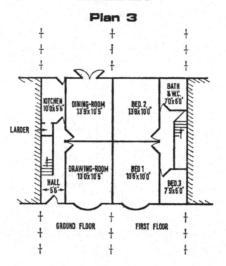

New Ideal Homesteads terrace house. Mossford Park Estate, Ilford, 1934. £595

Plan 4

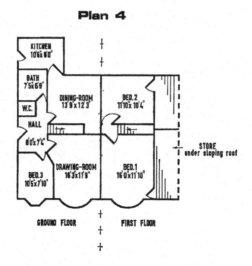

New Ideal Homesteads A2 chalet (semi-detached). Mossford Park Estate, Ilford, 1934. £745

Plan 5

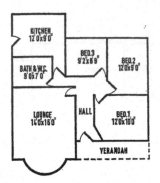

New Ideal Homesteads DB1 bungalow. Mossford Park Estate, Ilford, 1934. £795

Plan 6

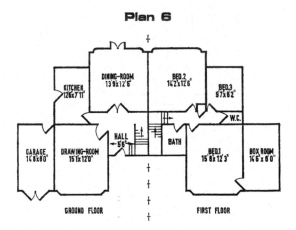

E. & L. Berg semi-detached house. Ashtead Woods Estate, 1939. £1,020

Plan 7

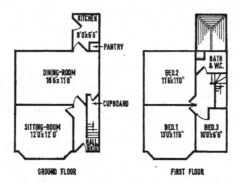

T. F. Nash detached house, Marshalswick Farm Estate, St Albans, 1939. £710

Plan 8

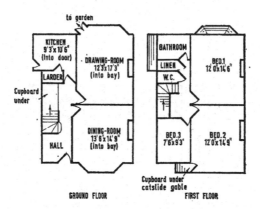

A. W. Curton Ltd Type 3A house. Edgwarebury Lane Estate, Edgware, 1935. Semi-detached £1,140, detached £1,200, garage £65 extra

Plan 9

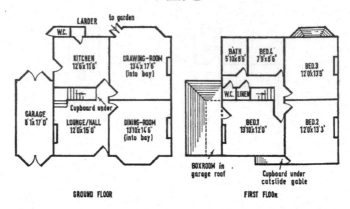

A. W. Curton Ltd Type 4C house. Edgwarebury Lane Estate, Edgware, 1935. Semi-detached £1,550, detached £1,650

Plan 10

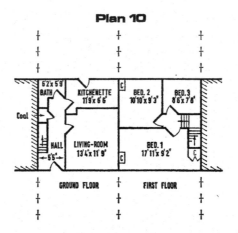

LCC four-room cottage Type S3, 1927

SELECT BIBLIOGRAPHY

(1) *General Economic and Social Background*

Aldcroft, Derek H.,   *The Interwar Economy: Britain 1919–39* (Batsford, 1970)

Branson, Noreen and
 Heinemann, Margot, *Britain in the Nineteen Thirties* (Weidenfeld and Nicolson, 1971)

Briggs, Milton and Jordan
 Percy,   *Economic History of England* (University Tutorial Press, 1967)

Cecil, Robert,   *Life in Edwardian England* (Batsford, 1969)

Clapham, Sir John,   *An Economic History of Modern Britain, Vol. 3, 1887–1929* (Cambridge U.P., 1951)

Cole, G. D. H. and
 Postgate, Raymond, *The Common People, 1746–1946* (Methuen, 1949)

Cross, Colin,   *The Liberals in Power, 1905–14* (Barrie and Rockcliff, 1963)

Gregg, Pauline,   *A Social and Economic History of Britain, 1760–1966* (Harrap, 1966)

Hill, C. P.,   *British Economic and Social History 1700–1939* (E. Arnold, 1961)

Lewis, J. Parry,   *Building Cycles and Britain's Growth* (Macmillan, 1965)

Marcus, Geoffrey,   *Before the Lamps went out* (Allen & Unwin, 1965)

Marriott, Sir J. A. R., *Modern England, 1885–1945* (Oxford U.P., 1948)

Marwick, Arthur,   *The Deluge* (Bodley Head, 1964)

Marwick, Arthur,   *Britain in the Century of Total War* (Bodley Head, 1968)

Montgomery, John   *The Twenties* (Allen & Unwin, 1970)

Mowat, Charles Loch, *Britain between the Wars, 1918–40* (Methuen, 1968)

Nowell-Smith, Simon (ed.), *Edwardian England, 1901–14* (Oxford U.P., 1964)

Pollard, Sidney,   *The Development of the British Economy, 1914–67* (E. Arnold, 1969)

Priestley, J. B.,   *The Edwardians* (Heinemann, 1970)

Richardson, H. W.,   *Economic Recovery in Britain, 1932–39*
         (Weidenfeld and Nicolson, 1967)
Taylor, A. J. P.,   *English History, 1914–45* (Oxford U.P.
         1965)

(2) *Urban Growth, Planning and Design*
Aldridge, Henry, R.,   *The Case for Town Planning* (National
         Housing and Town Planning Council,
         1915)
Creese, Walter L.,   *The Search for Environment: The Garden
         City Before and After* (Yale U.P., 1966)
Hall, Peter,   *World Cities* (Weidenfeld and Nicolson,
         1966)
Juian, Julian,   *An Introduction to Town Planning* (1914)
Mumford, Lewis,   *The City in History* (Secker and Warburg,
         1961)
—   *The Green Belts* (H.M.S.O., 1962)

(3) *Housing Policy and Construction; general*
Aldridge, Henry, R.,   *National Housing Manual* (National
         Housing and Town Planning Council,
         1923)
Ashworth, Herbert,   *Housing in Great Britain* (Skinner, 1957)
Bauer, Catherine,   *Modern Housing* (Allen & Unwin, 1935)
Becker, Arthur, Peter, *Housing in England & Wales During the
         Business Depression of the 1930s*
         (Economic History Review, vol. 3, no. 3)
Betham, Ernest, (ed.) *House Building 1934–36* (Federated
         Employers' Press, 1934)
Bowley, Marian,   *Housing and the State, 1919–44* (Allen &
         Unwin, 1945)
Clarke, J. J.,   *The Housing Problem, its growth,
         legislation and Procedure* (Pitman, 1921)
Cornes, James,   *Modern Housing in Town and Country*
         (1905)
Davey, Norman,   *Building in Britain* (Evans Bros, 1964)
Dewsnap, Ernest, Ritson, *The Housing Problem in England, its
         Statistics, Legislation and Policy*
         (Manchester U.P., 1907)
Elsas, M. J.,   *Housing Before the War and After*
         (Staples, 1945)
Howkins, F.,   *An Introduction to the Development of
         Private Building Estates and Town
         Planning* (Estates Gazette, 1926)
Jenkins, Alan,   *On Site, 1921–71* (Heinemann, 1971)
Myles Wright, H.,   *Small Houses* (Architectural Press, 1937)

Nettlefold, J. S.,   *Practical Housing* (Fisher Unwin and
                                   Garden City Press, 1910)
Richardson, Henry W. and
  Aldcroft, Derek, H.,   *Building in the British Economy Between
                                   The Wars* (Allen & Unwin, 1968)
Thompson, W.,   *The Housing Handbook* (National Housing
                                   Reform Council, 1903)
Thompson, W.,   *Housing Up to Date* (1907)
Townroe, B. S.,   *A Handbook of Housing* (Methuen, 1924)

(4) *Building Societies*
Cleary, E. J.,   *The Building Society Movement* (Elek,
                                   1965)
Hobson, Oscar, R.,   *A Hundred Years of the Halifax: The
                                   History of the Halifax Building Society,
                                   1853–1953* (Batsford, 1953)
Price, Seymour, J.,   *Building Societies, Their Origin and
                                   History* (Franey, 1958)

(5) *Transport: general*
Aldcroft, Derek H., and
  Dyos, H. J.,   *British Transport* (Leicester U.P., 1969)
Buchanan, C. D.,   *Mixed Blessing, The Motor Car in
                                   Britain* (Leonard Hill, 1958)
Burtt, Philip,   *Railway Electrification and Traffic
                                   Problems* (Pitman, 1929)
Klapper, C. E.,   *The Golden Age of Tramways* (Routledge,
                                   1961)

(6) *Cinemas: general*
Shand, P. Morton,   *Modern Theatres and Cinemas* (Batsford,
                                   1930)
Sharp, Dennis,   *The Picture Palace and other Buildings for
                                   The Movies* (Evelyn, 1969)
Sully, H. B.,   *A Short History of the Cinema in
                                   Middlesex, 1910–65* (Middlesex Local
                                   History Council, Bulletin 18, 1964)
Tonkin, W. G. S.,   *Show Time in Walthamstow* (Walthamstow
                                   Antiquarian Society, 1967)

(7) *London Suburban Geography, Administration, Growth and Life*
Abercrombie, Patrick,   *Greater London Plan, 1944* (HMSO,
                                   1945)
Clayton, R., (ed.)   *Geography of Greater London* (G. Philip
                                   and Son, 1964)
Clunn, Harold P.,   *The Face of London* (Spring Books, 1950)

Coppock, J. T., and Prince,
H. C., (eds.)   *Greater London* (Faber, 1964)
Davies, A. Emil,   *The Story of the London County Council*
(Labour Publishing Co., 1925)

Davies, A. Emil, and
Gower, E. E.,   *Tramway Trips and Rambles* (R. E.
Taylor, 1907)
Duff, Charles,   *Anthropological Report on a London
Suburb* (Grayson and Grayson, 1935)

Forshaw, J. H. and
Abercrombie, Patrick,   *County of London Plan* (Macmillan, 1943)
Gibbon, Sir L. G. and
Bell, R. W.,   *The History of the London County Council,
1899–1939* (Macmillan, 1939)
Hall, P. G.,   *The Industries of London since 1861*
(Hutchinson, 1962)
Harris, Percy,   *London and Its Government* (Dent, 1931)
Harrison, Michael,   *London Growing* (Hutchinson, 1965)
Haward, Sir Harry,   *The London County Council from Within*
(Chapman and Hall, 1932)
Lipman, Vivian D.,   *The Rise of Jewish Suburbia* (Jewish
Historical Society of England, vol. XXI,
1968)
Pearson, S. Vere,   *London's Overgrowth and the Causes of
Swollen Towns* (Daniel, 1939)
Peel, Mrs C. S.,   *How We Lived Then, 1914–18* (Bodley
Head, 1929) Chapter 1 and Appendices.
Rasmussen, Steen Eiler,   *London, The Unique City* (Cape, 1937)
Richards, J. M.,   *The Castles on The Ground* (Architectural
Press, 1946)
Robson, W. A.,   *The Government and Misgovernment of
London* (Allen & Unwin, 1948)
Smith, D. H.,   *The Industries of Greater London* (King,
1933)
Thomas, David,   *London's Green Belt* (Faber, 1970)
Trent, C.,   *Greater London, Its Growth and
Development Through the Ages* (Phoenix,
1965)
—   *London, Aspects of Change* (McGibbon
and Kee, 1964)
—   *Reports on the Location of Industry*
(PEP, 1939)
—   *Royal Commission on London Government,
1921–3* (HMSO, 1923)
—   *Royal Commission on the Geographical
Distribution of the Industrial Population,
1938–40* (HMSO, 1940)
—   *Report on Greater London Drainage*
(HMSO, 1935)

(8) *London Suburban Rail and Road Transport*

Atkinson, F. G. B. and
Adams, B. W.,   *London's North Western Electric* (Electric Railway Society, 1962)

Bennett, E. A. and Borley,
H. V.,   *London Transport Railways, A List of . . . Dates . . .* (David and Charles, 1963)

Course, E. A.,   *London Railways* (Batsford, 1962)

Course, E. A.,   *The Bexleyheath Railway* (Woolwich and District Antiquarian Society, Vol. XXX, 1954)

Day, J. R.,   *The Story of London's Underground* (London Transport, 1966)

Gibbs, T. A.,   *The Metropolitan Electric Tramways, A Short History* (Tramway and Light Railway Society, 1962)

Jackson, Alan A., and
Croome, D. F.,   *Rails Through the Clay, A History of London's Tube Railways* (Allen & Unwin, 1964)

'Kennington'   *The London County Council Tramways Handbook* (Tramway and Light Railway Society, 1970)

Kidner, R. W.,   *The Dartford Loop Line, 1866–1966* (Oakwood Press, 1966)

Kidner, R. W.,   *The Oxted Line* (Oakwood Press, 1972)

'Line 112 Group'   *The Railway to Walthamstow and Chingford* (Walthamstow Antiquarian Society, 1970)

Moody, G. T.,   *Southern Electric* (Ian Allan, 1968)

Morris, O. J., (ed.)   *Fares Please, The Story of London's Road Transport* (Ian Allan, 1953)

Peacock, Thomas B.,   *Great Western London Suburban Services* (Oakwood Press, 1970)

'Rodinglea'   *The Tramways of East London* (Light Railway Transport League, 1967)

Sommerfield, Vernon,   *London's Buses* (The Underground Co., 1933)

'Southeastern'   *The Tramways of Woolwich and South East London* (Light Railway Transport League, 1963)

'Southmet'   *The Tramways of Croydon* (Light Railway Transport League, 1960)

Spence, Jeoffry,   *The Caterham Railway* (Oakwood Press, 1952)

Thomas, J. P.,   *Handling London's Underground Traffic* (The Underground Co. 1928)

Thomson, L. A.,   *By Bus, Tram and Coach in Walthamstow* (Walthamstow Antiquarian Society, 1971)

Travis, A. S. and Egan, H.,	*The Early History of the Metropolitan District and Metropolitan Railways in Wembley* (Wembley Transport Society, 1963)
Wagstaff, J. S.,	*The London Country Bus* (Oakwood Press, 1968)
White, H. P.,	*A Regional History of the Railways of Great Britain, vol. 3: Greater London* (David and Charles, 1970)
Wilmot, G. F. A.,	*The Railway in Finchley, a Study in Suburban Development* (Finchley Public Libraries, 1962)
Wilson, Geoffrey,	*London United Tramways, A History, 1894–1933* (Allen & Unwin, 1971)
—	*London General, the Story of the London Bus, 1856–1956* (London Transport, 1956)
—	*Suburban Timetables* (Southern Railway, various dates, 1931–9).
—	*Improving London's Transport* (Railway Gazette, 1946)
—	*Reports of the London and Home Counties Traffic Advisory Committee* (various dates from 1925 to 1939) (HMSO)
—	*Reports of the London Traffic Branch of The Board of Trade* (annual, 1908 to 1915, HMSO)
—	*Reports of The Road Board* (annual, 1920–1 to 1938–9, HMSO)
—	*Royal Commission on London Traffic, 1905* (HMSO, 1905)

n.b. The files of *The Railway Magazine* contain many studies of London suburban railways. Since 1950 these are in the main soundly based on original research; earlier articles are somewhat less reliable, especially as to dates.

(9) *Local studies*

Caunt, George,	*Ilford's Yesterdays* (Caunt, 1963)
Clark, Nancy,	*Hadley Wood, Its Background and Development* (Ward Lock, 1968)
Cross, George,	*Suffolk Punch* (Faber, 1939) Chapter 17: Edgware.
Dunlop, Sir John,	*The Pleasant Town of Sevenoaks* (Dunlop, 1964)
Durant, Ruth,	*Watling, A Social Survey* (King, 1939)
Gent, John, B., (ed.)	*Croydon, The Story of a Hundred Years* (Croydon Natural History and Scientific Society, 1970)

Green, Frank, and Wolff,
Dr Sidney, *London and Suburbs, Old and New*
(Souvenir Magazines, 1933)

Howarth, E. G. and
Wilson, M., *West Ham, A Study in Industrial and
Social Problems* (Dent, 1907)

Howkins, F., *The Story of Golders Green and Its
Remarkable Development* (Ernest Owers,
1923)

Jefferson, E. F. E., *The Woolwich Story 1890–1965*
(Woolwich and District Antiquarian
Society, 1970)

Jowett, E. M., *An Illustrated History of Merton and
Morden* (1951)

Kemp, W. A. G., *The Story of Northwood and Northwood
Hills, Middlesex* (Kemp, 1955)

Law, A. D., *Our Town, 100 years of Local Government
in Walthamstow* (Walthamstow
Antiquarian Society, 1966)

Marshall, G. J., *History of Cheam and Sutton* (1936)

Nunns, B. N., *Brief Notes on Longlands* (unpublished
manuscript, 1965)

Radcliffe, Sir Clifford, *Middlesex* (Evans Bros, 1954)

Reid, D. A. R., *The Development of the Borough of
Wimbledon and the Urban District of
Merton and Morden as a dormitory
suburb of London* (unpublished thesis,
1950)

Robbins, Michael, *Middlesex* (Collins, 1953)

Stokes, Alfred, *East Ham* (Stokes, 1920)

Tasker, George E., *Ilford Past and Present* (Hayden, 1901)

Young, Terence, *Becontree and Dagenham* (Pilgrim Trust,
1934)

— *Know Your Finchley* (Finchley Borough
Council, 1958)

— *Harrow Before Your Time* (Pinner and
Hatch End W.E.A. Local History Group,
1972)

— *Annual Reports of The Medical Officer of
Health* (for the various local government
districts, 1900–39). In the preparation of
this book those for Hendon UDC,
1906–31, and for Epsom RDC, Epsom
UDC, and Epsom & Ewell Borough
Council, 1927–39 were specifically consulted.

Guides and Directories: Too numerous to mention separately are the 'Official Guides' to individual districts, published by Ed. J. Burrow & Co. and
others (usually annually) with the blessing of the local authority. Although

these provide a good deal of basic data, the advertisements offer the best value for the researcher; the maps, year by year, can be used to appreciate the pace of suburban expansion. Other guides were issued by the Homeland Association, who also produced *Where to Live Round London* in two volumes, *Northern Side* and *Southern Side*, in a number of editions between 1906 and 1913. The various suburban guides sponsored by the railway companies (see Chapter 12) give details of train services and fares, local rates and living expenses, property available, and schools; again the advertisements yield much of interest about the state of suburban development. The well-produced volumes issued by the Southern Railway are notable for large numbers of photographs which give an excellent impression of the appearance of the new suburbs of the twenties and thirties as they were growing. *Kelly's Directory*, issued periodically for all London suburban districts, gives the local history student lists of every householder and tradesman, street by street, as well as basic data on the area.

(10) *Housing in Greater London*

— *Housing of the Working Classes in London, 1885–1912* (LCC, 1913)
— *London County Council Housing 1927* (LCC, 1928)
— *London County Council Housing, 1928–30* (LCC, 1931)
— *London Housing* (LCC, 1937)
— *London Statistics 1936–8*, vol. 41 (LCC, 1939)
— *London Housing Statistics, 1946–8* (LCC, 1948)
— *London Housing Statistics, 1957–8* (LCC, 1958)
— *Housing Service Handbook* (LCC, 1964)

(see also 11 below)

(11) *Primary Sources, Newspapers, Periodicals and Ephemera*
Much of the material for this book was found in the advertisements and reporting of the London *Evening News* over the years 1900–39; various other daily papers read less thoroughly included the *Daily Express* and the *Daily Mail* both of which featured estate advertising. Local newspapers heavily used, over the periods shown, were: the *Hendon and Finchley Times* (later the *Hendon Times and Borough Guardian*) (1900–39); the *Ilford Guardian* (1891–1906); the *South Essex Recorder* (later the *Ilford Recorder*) (1898–1906); the *Golders Green Gazette* (1923–30); the *Edgware Gazette* (1927–39); the *Ewell Times* (1937–9); the *Cheam Times* (1930–3); the *Sutton Times and Cheam Mail* (1931–4); the *Epsom Courier and Ewell Times* (1933–7) and the *Stoneleigh Times* (1933–9).

Of periodicals consulted, much the most rewarding are the *Estates Gazette* (period 1930–9) and the *Homefinder and Small Property Guide*

(1931–9); the latter's comprehensive advertisement coverage for the whole Greater London area and beyond is invaluable. Specialist information on two important aspects of suburban development is available in the *Railway Magazine* (1900–39 consulted), the *Railway Gazette* (1905–39 consulted) and *Cinema Construction* (later *Cinema and Theatre Construction*) (1929–39 consulted).

Builders' and developers' sales brochures and booklets studied included those issued by: Atkinson and Marler; E. and L. Berg; G. T. Crouch; A. W. Curton; Davis Estates; J. C. Derby; John Laing and Son; New Ideal Homesteads; Noel Rees; and Hugh F. Thoburn. The contemporary consumer's viewpoint is to be found in the magazines issued by the residents' associations; use was made of the *Resident* (Stoneleigh R.A.) and the *Watling Resident*. Some suburban public libraries have collections of estate agents' catalogues and auction sales notices; those at Hendon and Epsom provided a number of indicators for the local studies in this book.

There is an abundant supply of primary source material on transport, particularly railways, readily accessible at the offices of British Transport Historical Records (now part of the Public Record Office). Research for this book concentrated on the board and committee minutes and reports of two of the main London suburban railways, the Southern and the Metropolitan.

The feel and appearance of the developing twentieth century suburbs is encapsulated in thousands of postcard views published from 1901 onwards; between 1901 and 1914 almost every street and road then existing was recorded in this way. These cards are now collectors' pieces; some public libraries have small selections, but the finest and most comprehensive accumulations remain in private hands.

Index